Daniel Frescó (1960) worked for five years alongside Sergio Kun Agüero in the research, writing and production of this book.

He has been in journalism since the 1980s. He has vast experience in print media, radio and television in Argentina. After an initial stint in Radio Continental, Radio Mitre and the Clarín newspaper, he dedicated himself to sports journalism. He was correspondent for TyC Sports in Italy for 14 years, covering national and international events. He moved onto directing for various networks and was also the head of news programming for Televisión Pública, the national broadcaster.

In 2004, he published his first book, Secuestros S.A., an investigative piece on the surge of kidnapping in Argentina. His next book was Manu: El Cielo con las Manos, the first biography of Emanuel Ginobili, four-time NBA champion with San Antonio Spurs and the greatest basketball player in the history of Argentina. Currently, he heads his own social media, radio and TV consultancy firm.

@DanielFresco

AGÜERO

Born to Rise

MY STORY

AGÜERO

Born to Rise

MY STORY

Prologue by
LIONEL MESSI

Written by
Daniel Frescó

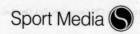

Sport Media

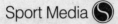

Sport Media

Published by Trinity Mirror Sport Media
Publishing Director: Steve Hanrahan
Executive Editor: Paul Dove   Executive Art Editor: Rick Cooke
Senior Sub Editor: Roy Gilfoyle
Senior Marketing Executive: Claire Brown
Sales and Marketing Manager: Elizabeth Morgan

Translated by
Robert Hunt
for Premier Language Solutions

Proof reading and football consultancy:
Philip Dickinson

Translation approval:
Adam Nasimoff

Additional interviews with Sergio:
David Clayton

Front and back cover images: Tony Woolliscroft

Jacket design: Rick Cooke

Paperback Edition
Published in Great Britain in 2015.
Published and produced by: Trinity Mirror Sport Media,
PO Box 48, Old Hall Street, Liverpool L69 3EB.

Agüero-[...] r City FC.

To my parents Leo and Adriana

To my brothers and sisters Jessica, Gaby, Mayra,
Daiana, Mauricio and Gastón

To my godfather Dario

To Emiliano Molina (in memoriam)

To my mentors and coaches

To my friends, who are always there for me

To my girlfriend Karina

To my representative Hernán Reguera, and to all the people at the
company Eleven GT, for our journey together

To all my fellow professional footballers

To all my team-mates throughout my career,
both at youth and professional level

To all who love football

To Argentina, my country

And especially to my son Benjamín, the light of my life

Contents

Foreword

I can very clearly remember the first day that I saw Kun. Of course, back then I didn't know who he was or even what he was called, let alone that I would later meet him in person or that, from then on, we would become great friends.

I was in Rosario when I saw him on that first occasion, enjoying some time back in my home city with my family because it was July – and at Barcelona, where I was already living, we had a break for the holidays. A few days before, I had turned 16 with the same hopes and dreams as ever: that one day I would be able to play in the first team. I knew that it was just a matter of time, but that didn't make me want it any less.

It goes without saying that football already took up every hour of my waking day. And that Saturday in July was no exception. Including on that evening, when I took the opportunity to watch the match that was being shown on television: Independiente vs. San Lorenzo, in the last round of fixtures in the domestic league.

I remember little or nothing of the match itself. But I do recall the moment that they showed a boy in the Independiente squad who, I thought, must be about the same age as me, and who was about to make his debut. I then heard the commentators say that he had recently turned 15 and that he was going to become the youngest player ever to play in the Primera División. That moment has remained etched on my memory ever since. Not so much for his face nor, as I say, his name, which I struggled to recall. But because at such a young age he had taken a major step forwards in football, the same as I had imagined for myself on so many occasions.

A year-and-a-half later, by which time I had already started to play in the Barcelona first team, I saw him again. It was a very funny, chance encounter at the Argentinian Football Association's training complex at Ezeiza. I know that the story is recounted later in this book, so I won't give many more details. Except to say that he didn't know who I was back then, and nor did I initially make the connection with that 15-year-old boy who I'd seen making his first team debut on television in Rosario.

But a few months later, in June 2005, we were to come across each other again, this time as part of the Argentinian Under-20 squad that was going to compete in the World Cup for that age group over in Holland. We went straight from that casual chat to seeing each other out on a football pitch, in the last training session before travelling to the World Cup. And we clicked right away. We were the youngest players in the squad, which meant that we spent more time together. Kun was only just 17, and I was about to celebrate my 18th birthday.

What can I say about Sergio back then…? That he was a real character, a really sound guy, capable of listening and then saying exactly the right thing to let you know he was there for you or, with perfect delivery, to make you burst out laughing. And on the field, he was talented, a winner, a born competitor who never knew when he was beaten. These were qualities that we shared, and that helped us form a bond that would be strengthened over the years when we met up with the national teams. Most of those occasions have been with the senior Argentina squad, where both our individual and shared dreams have encountered so many highs and lows. And I'm sure that there will be many more to come, hopefully more of the former than the latter.

I got to know Kun's story from hearing it and, in large part, because I was able to live through it alongside him. I know all about the respect he has for his roots and for his family. And about all the energy and effort that has gone into him accomplishing so much. So I'm delighted that he wanted to share this book with us, his story, which I have the pleasure of being a part of. Because his story has a little bit of many of us in it, and it shows us as we are: people who, beyond the extremely professional world that we inhabit, still have the same desire, the same amateur spirit and the same love for football as when we were kids. And also because it shows, in much detail, the path taken by all of us who at some point dreamed about being someone in football. And because, more importantly, it can serve to show all those who share those same dreams today, that nothing is easy, but that it is worth giving it a shot.

LEO MESSI

Prologue

I doubt the events of May 13, 2012 will ever be far from my mind. All the season's hard work came down to one game, and we were just 90 minutes from securing the ultimate prize and winning Manchester City Football Club's first title for 44 years.

We knew this was a special moment for us and our supporters because we had to win the match to claim the Premier League title, but we still had a job to do and couldn't lose our focus.

We were at a hotel in Manchester city centre and we were trying to be as relaxed as we could be. Me and some of the lads were playing cards, but throughout the game we would glance at one another, perhaps thinking about the game the next day.

It had been such a long wait for our supporters and so much depended on us winning the game. Despite us going about our normal routine, there was something in the air that evening, maybe a sense of destiny – either that or just nervous tension. I slept soundly, as I always do, but the following day I felt anxious because I wanted the game to begin, for us to win and for it to be over.

It was a crazy situation because we knew the scenario required to win the title but I felt I'd die if we didn't win or that I'd kill myself if we blew our chance!

Okay, maybe that's a little dramatic, but it felt like there would be nothing to look forward to again if we failed to win. This was our moment; our time and we had to take it. It was a strange feeling and not one I'd had before or want to have again. It just hit me like a truck.

Roberto Mancini's team talk was actually shorter than it usually was. He read the team out as normal but that was basically it. There were no words needed, we just had to get out there and do the business and we knew exactly what was needed. It was all about winning the game – nothing more, nothing less – and Mancini knew there was little he could say that would alter the situation at that stage.

We went through our normal routine and tried to keep ourselves busy, while gradually moving into our own individual zone.

We were nervous, full of adrenaline and excited, but we were also ready to take our place in the history of the club. There could be no half-measures, no relying on luck and no regrets. Walking down the tunnel and out on the pitch was a little different than normal.

Of course, there was a fantastic, deafening welcome, but the fans who had been behind us helping us all season were edgy as well, which added to the tension.

It was a beautiful sunny day and I had sensed during the warm-up that the crowd was up for it, as you'd expect, but you could also feel the expectancy and hope that can only come as a result of so many years without winning the championship as well.

The feeling in the stadium was very emotional and nervous and I felt it, too. If you don't guard against it, such weight on your shoulders can drain you both mentally and physically before you've even really begun so we had to let as much as possible bounce off us.

At last, the wait was over and the game began, but to my own personal disgust, I couldn't escape the fact that I was playing like a dog and nothing was going for me. In fact, everything I tried failed. Of all the games to play as though I had two left feet!

I wanted to play my part to the full and help the team but I was beginning to feel as though I was actually a hindrance, so when Pablo Zabaleta scored the opening goal before half-time, there was an out-pouring of relief from everyone. I was very happy for Pablo because he has been a close friend of mine for so many years and he deserved it, even though he only gets one or two goals every 100 games! At least his goals mean something when he finally does find the net.

So we went in at the break feeling in good shape and everything seemingly on track — surely all we had to do was play our game, keep things tight and fulfil our destiny. QPR had defended well and made things difficult, as we expected they would, but they had offered virtually nothing offensively. However, we began the second half and, in truth, we weren't prepared for what was to come.

QPR changed their tactics and began to come at us a bit more and free themselves from the defensive shackles they'd been in throughout the first half. They needed to find a way back into the game so when they scored out of virtually nothing, the doubts began to creep in.

Djibril Cisse chased onto a long pass from Shaun Wright-Phillips, Joleon Lescott couldn't get his head to the ball and instead glanced it backwards and Cisse capitalised with a low shot from just inside the box. Suddenly, the anxiety was back – we had to find another goal.

Then, a few minutes later, the make-up of the game changed again. I saw Carlos Tevez on the floor and went over to see what had happened. It seemed everything had suddenly gone a little crazy. When he started to get up he was insulting Joey Barton in Spanish calling him something that translates closest to 'bad milk' – an expression you might aim at someone who is overly aggressive. You can draw your own conclusions from that!

I didn't know what had happened but could see Barton was getting more and more heated so I went to stop Carlos from reacting and maybe getting himself sent off so I told Barton to calm down and that he was crazy. He thought I was confronting him, but I was attempting to defuse the situation and he must have thought I was swearing at him in Spanish or something.

When the referee came to him and showed him a red card, he kneed me in the side as he walked off the pitch. I have no idea why he did that and, to this day, I would love to know the answer because my intentions had been nothing other than taking the heat out of the situation.

Ah, well! So they are now at a disadvantage, the score is 1-1 and there are 35 minutes remaining. We have an extra man but they could have had nine men and it would not have made any difference because we were playing so badly. We couldn't find any space or a way through and it just felt as though the stars weren't aligned in our favour. Even more so when we conceded a second QPR goal through a Jamie Mackie header 10 minutes later.

We'd switched off. The sending off had actually worked

against us because it seemed inevitable that we would go on and win without actually stepping things up. Our dream was becoming a nightmare and there seemed no way out.

The clock continued to tick down and Mancini brought Edin Dzeko and Mario Balotelli on with Carlos one of those who made way. I was relieved I still had the chance to be able to make a difference. We had three recognised strikers on the pitch but, in truth, we were all trying to find the goal that would spark us back to life, but it just wouldn't come.

Our supporters, bemused and stunned, seemed resigned to us blowing our opportunity because in the past, there had been so many occasions when City had failed their audition when it mattered the most – 'typical City' is the phrase, I believe – but we were here to change all that and we couldn't allow failure so long as there was still time to make a difference.

The assistant referee held up the board to tell us there were five added minutes to be played and I thought it was all over. How could we find two goals in the time that remained? It was impossible, done and dusted and I felt I wanted to cry, get off the pitch and be as far away from the stadium as possible.

The only way I could see us scoring was by a set-piece because our probing through the middle was just being suffocated by a wall of defenders. Then, at last, a lifeline. Two minutes into injury time, Edin Dzeko heads home from a David Silva corner to make it 2-2 and I thought, maybe we still have a chance. Maybe…

The goal gave us a lift and urgency, but we still had to find another goal and now with just seconds remaining. I just wanted one opportunity, one chance to find the net and win the game and fulfil the sense of destiny we'd all felt for those final few weeks of the season. When all had seemed lost after we'd been beaten by Arsenal and fallen eight points behind Manchester United with only six games remaining and we kept believing to the point that we got inside the heads of the United players who began to drop points. To get this close and then throw it all away would have been devastating, but we weren't going to allow that to happen.

When Mario had come on, I spoke with him briefly as he walked past me, telling him to stay close because they were defending so deep and there was no space at all. I said that we could either play a one-two or maybe he could hold the ball up and lay it off for me to shoot maybe from the edge of the box if the opportunity arose.

There were almost 95 minutes on the clock and time was up so it was now or never. We had a throw-in and the ball was steadily coming back up the field – the urge was to hit it long and hope for the best, but that wasn't our style. We had to remain true to the principles that had served us so well. I dropped deep to pick the ball up from Nigel de Jong and pushed the ball forward, closing in on Mario. I played the ball to him with the outside of my foot, but he was falling over under a challenge and as he fell, he managed to nudge the ball back to me. There was no room to shoot but I saw a chance to burst into the box instead.

As I pushed the ball past Taye Taiwo, I felt contact on my right foot and in a microsecond, I had to decide whether I carried on or went down looking for a penalty – the contact was only slight so I continued on. This was it, the one chance I'd hoped would come and I had to make it count, so I hit the ball as hard as I could and hoped for the best.

I remember seeing the ball hitting the back of the net, hearing a deafening roar and things are hazy after that! I pulled off my shirt and wheeled away swirling it above my head as I went a little crazy. I knew that the time was up and that goal was going to win us the title but the shock didn't set in until my teammates dragged me down on to the ground and started telling me they loved me. Mario grabbed me and said, "You f***ing idiot! I love you big b****cks!"

I can barely recall lining up to kick off again and the next thing I knew, I could see people celebrating and was aware of people running onto the pitch but I was still a little dazed and was thinking 'what's going on?' City fans were coming up and hugging me and telling me they loved me and thanking me but I was still in shock with it all. I suppose I felt a little crazy and looking back, I think, what an idiot! I could have just celebrated the day and the events after the goal in a normal way but the truth was I was too far gone. We had done it, but in the most dramatic way imaginable and I don't think any of us had anything left at that point.

I was so exhausted in the dressing room by the emotion of it all, I just wanted to sit down and gather my thoughts, but of course the celebrations were just kicking in and we were throwing beer and champagne over each other, having our picture taken with the trophy and the party was just beginning.

After I'd showered and got changed, I turned on my phone and there were hundreds of texts pinging through including one from each member of the Argentina national team, from the keeper through to the bench. I'd have been three days answering all the texts so I waited until I joined up with them again on international duty and thanked them personally.

I saw my parents later and obviously everybody was very

happy but I was still confused as to what all the fuss was about because I was still in a daze. We had a team dinner later with our families and my mother had a shot of something or other. She was happy until the next day on that one small drink, as she never normally drank, and she was chatting away happily all night. She was having a great time, and so was my dad.

On the way home, everyone was singing in the minibus and enjoying themselves but I felt pretty detached for some reason and it was starting to get on my nerves a bit. I was starting to wonder what was wrong with them all.

That night, before I went to bed, I got the Internet up on my laptop and watched the goal again before I went to sleep. I don't recall much else until the following day. When I woke up, I had breakfast and watched the highlights of the game and then started to become aware of some of the commentaries from around the world and I started to realise what a mad, crazy goal it had been and just what it meant. I particularly liked the Martin Tyler 'Aguerrrroooooo!' commentary!

Seeing the City fans celebrate on TV brought everything home, too. It was incredible to think that the goal would go down in the club's history because it had been so long since we'd won the league.

By the day of the victory parade around Manchester city centre the next day, the magnitude of what we'd done and the goal I'd scored had finally begun to sink in. It was different again on the bus and we were jumping up and down singing 'Championi!' and could see the fans close up and they were really going for it which was great to see. I felt like a Hollywood superstar for a few hours, but I'm more experienced now and I promised myself the next time we won the title I'll celebrate in a normal way and enjoy the moment properly! Thankfully, I didn't have to wait long to find out. It was an unbelievable day, one I will never forget and cherish as long as I live. The problem is, how can I ever top that…?

****

I always knew that I had been born to play football. Even when I was very little. And I never thought for a moment about trying to understand why. For me it was very simple: I just wanted to play, wherever I could, with whoever I could, against whoever happened to be there. All the time. It was all about joining in whatever kickabout was going. And then, it was just a matter of having fun. On the neighbourhood *potreros*, be it the earth pitches or the concrete ones…

Everything that happened afterwards came naturally and, you could say, perhaps too quickly. So quickly that it was hard to claim to be aware of everything that was happening to me. Like when I made my debut in Argentina's Primera División at the age of only 15. The truth is that I understood little or nothing about what it all meant… but how I enjoyed every second! And even though I gained in experience, that same enjoyment would remain over the years to come.

My eternal bond with Independiente, my first steps in Europe with Atletico, and then joining Manchester City and achieving so much in such a short space of time. I've enjoyed everything, not to mention all I've been lucky enough to experience at various levels with the Argentinian national teams.

It then occurred to me that it might be important to put down everything that I've been through over these years in a book.

Now I've finished it, I have to admit that the original idea took off in a way that I hadn't appreciated at the time. The thing is, going page by page through a book that was to tell my own story taught me that my personal journey had been shaped by so many connected events, so that if one of them had not taken place, none of it would have been the same. The effort and sacrifice of my parents, the guidance of many coaches and mentors, the support of so many good people, all of it was crucial in leaving me to worry about nothing more than letting my love for football run free.

Having reconstructed in such fine detail what took place over those years helps me to understand that it was worth all the effort, that nothing came about by chance and that everything, in its own way, has an explanation. That's why I'm so glad that I insisted that 'My Story' should start right back at the very beginning. Not just because it's the least well-known part, but also because it's important to know where we came from. Because it demonstrates that the paths we all take, and which define our identities, are not always lined with gold. And because knowing who we are, and not forgetting that, is what makes us stronger and better people.

For this reason, over the following pages you will find not just the story of what happened from my birth onwards – a birth which, you will see, is a unique story in itself – but also what took place before, from my parents' lives in the province of Tucumán onwards, which goes to explain in no small part everything that came later on.

What did come next – a childhood and adolescence shaped by so much football – is told in great detail, so much so that I was able to reconstruct those images of the past with an accuracy that I never imagined when, together with my family and my representatives, we started to develop the idea of putting a book together to tell my story.

It was an idea that started to take shape in 2009 when we invited the experienced journalist Daniel Frescó to help us construct it. Over five years of extensive conversations in Madrid, Buenos Aires and Manchester, during which we meticulously went through each stage of my life, little by little the backbone of the book came together, which was then fleshed out firstly by interviews with all of the people who, in one way or another, influenced my personal and sporting development, and secondly by the detailed research that gave 'My Story' the strongest of foundations.

My thanks go to Daniel for his professionalism, and for having been able to faithfully reproduce my ideas and thoughts. I also value the mutual trust which has characterised our work together, and which has ensured that we have ended up with the best possible end product.

Having had the opportunity to closely follow this project has also allowed me to recognise that the text contains a public acknowledgement, a personal tribute that I needed to pay, to all those people who did so much for me at various stages in my life, and who willingly and good-humouredly gave their recollections and recounted their memories in order to assist with the research. Members of my family, friends, team-mates, coaches, agents. There are many of them and they will crop up time and again, named accordingly, on every page – they have my complete gratitude for having lent their time to this project.

When we started, we didn't know up until exactly which point the book would cover, nor when it would be published. But we didn't need to know. The unfolding events took the decision out of our hands. For the Spanish edition, which was published a year before this one, we decided to finish with the goal in the dying seconds against QPR, because it marked the end of an era, securing the Premier League title for Manchester City in 2012 after a 44-year wait, and meant so much to me and to so many others. It seemed to us at the time that it was, quite naturally, the best conclusion to this first experience of committing my memories to print.

However, when it came to publishing the book in English, I decided that it was necessary to extend it to include accounts of my experiences during my second and third seasons at City. Not only because the on-field results fortunately warranted their inclusion, but mainly because it was during this period that I was able to confirm the accuracy of my first impressions in Manchester: that I had found the ideal place to achieve the target that I had set for myself of growing both as a person and as a player.

When I decided to come and play in English football, I was convinced that I was coming to one of the best leagues in the world. It had appealed to me from a young age, and I followed it closely. So much so that when I played video games, I even played as English teams. Which ones? You'll find out later on in the book...

Coming to England when I was 23 and being able to join the squad at Manchester City was a great decision. Because it was important to raise the level of competition around me. This is something I needed deep down. And here I found a very professional league that set me those challenges I needed, and a club that took me in from the very first day and who offered me all that was required for my football to develop further.

And what can I say about the fans? Whatever words I find, they will never be enough. From day one, I have felt their wonderful support, which has given me no choice – in the best sense – but to try and return this affection on the field of play. Fortunately, my team-mates and I have been able to do so. To have won two league titles, a Community Shield and a Capital One Cup in three years has exceeded all my wildest expectations.

Therefore, the stories of my experiences with City are as important for me as the accounts of what I went through at other stages of my life. And to write it all down in my biography is like a personal way of showing my gratitude to the club.

Many people tell me that I'm part of Manchester City's great history. Of course, it's something that fills me with pride. But what I'd like to point out in return is that there is something else which is just as significant and strong, and that is that you are already part of my story. This gives me a real sense of fulfilment, one that will stay with me forever as another source of great pride.

I'll give you an example. These past years, when I'd arrive at the Etihad and see the gigantic photo showing the goal against QPR, I didn't just see myself, but all of us. Because that photo encapsulates us all. The people at the club and my team-mates who fought so hard to win that title. And, of course, all of the fans whose endless support made it possible.

In those faces that I saw and that I still remember, from so many games of football and from the unforgettable pitch invasions in celebration of those long-awaited titles, I can see true passion as well as a unique emotion that stirs in us to this day.

That emotion reflects something that I learned when I was

little and, here at City, I found the perfect place to confirm it once and for all: that giving all you have, and fighting to the very end, will always have its reward; and the enjoyment we get from that – despite the moments of great anxiety and tension along the way – gives more sense to our lives. 'We'll fight to the end' is not just one of City's mottos and chants. It's also symbolic of a club that never gives up, that never knows when it is beaten, even in the most trying circumstances, and that gives the word 'believe' a much stronger, wider, greater meaning. More than anything, it is the capacity to believe that anything is possible that defines us all.

I do not want to end this prologue without expressing my gratitude to football itself, which has given, and continues to give, sense to my life. I'm sure you'll agree that there is nothing more beautiful than football, for what it awakens in us, how it moves us, and the passion that it generates in us. With the passing of time, I have become a professional player, but my love for the game remains the same as when I was a boy. This motivates me more than anything else.

Lastly, I want to especially dedicate this book to my son Benjamín, the light of my life. When I look into his eyes I see the same boy that I was, and everything that is still to come. I hope that he finds inspiration over the course of these pages. The same inspiration that I found in my parents, which allowed me to grow and my passion to develop, without interference and with a sense of freedom to follow my goals.

SERGIO KUN AGÜERO
Manchester-Buenos Aires,
July–August 2014

Under A Lucky Star

It was in November 1987, three months after arriving in Buenos Aires, that Leonel Del Castillo, Adriana Agüero and their little daughter Jessica could finally settle into a home that they could call their own. They had moved to the city from the northern province of Tucumán, leaving behind many unfulfilled dreams and a bitter family farewell, and heading towards a new life together that seemed to contain so much promise.

In reality, their new home was nothing more than a small room with bare walls, only just big enough for the three of them. They would soon become four, as it was here that their first son was born. He was nicknamed 'Kun', an epithet that the boy would retain in later years as fate led him to dazzle the crowds that fill football stadiums around the world every week.

The poor neighbourhood that was to become their home had been christened La cueva de las víboras, or '*the cave of the vipers*'. Although understandably apprehensive, the young couple knew that it was the only place that they could settle with their scant possessions. In truth they had very little, lacking even the barest of necessities. They were short of almost everything, in fact, aside from a sense of humour and a huge appetite for life. Adriana had just turned 17, and Leo was only 19 years old.

The house was located to the west of the Greater Buenos Aires area. The local neighbourhood, González Catán, forms part of La Matanza, the most populated of the districts surrounding the capital with 1.2 million inhabitants across its 305 square kilometres. By contrast, the limited space set aside for the young family consisted of nothing more than a small strip of land at Leo's step-brother's house. They were surrounded in the immediate vicinity by dirt roads, dusty in the summer and muddy in the winter, while the nearest tarmac was to be found 400 metres away.

The threatening stream called Las Víboras, from which the neighbourhood took its nickname, passed by only 50 metres from their door. When the rains came it could become dangerous, something to which they would soon be able to attest. It took a lot of effort, the little money they had and the help of a friend to build the four walls that they would come to call home. In fact, money was so tight that they couldn't even afford enough bricks to finish the job. All they could think of was to turn the bricks through 90 degrees onto their thinner edges and stack them up on their ends. They joked about their 'inverted' house, but at least the walls were now high enough to finish the job by adding a sheet metal roof on top. They were unable to plaster the walls, but did install a cement floor. Inside there was only enough space for one double bed for Leo and Adriana, a smaller one for Jessica, and a makeshift wardrobe made out of bricks and wood. They had also bought a second-hand liquid gas cooker but only two of the rings worked, leaving the oven to be used as storage for some glasses and plates. The sum total of their belongings was completed by one of those picnic tables that come with garden chairs and can all be folded up into one carrying case. Outside, they dug a partially covered cesspit that served as their toilet.

Their neighbourhood was peripheral and increasingly unsafe, but one of its few positives was that it was close to the local *potrero*[1]. It was there that Leo, Kun's father, would head every weekend to play football, the sport which had always been his main passion. Out on the rough pitches, in the games that sprouted up every Sunday, he could display his attacking skills and turn out for whichever of the local teams wanted him to strengthen their numbers. Given that there was always money riding on these matches and tournaments, there was also the chance that he could earn a bit of extra cash in exchange for his ability and goals. This was nothing new to him, as he had done the same back in Tucumán.

Even though he would never become the professional footballer of his childhood dreams, through his talent for the sport he could at least earn a few more pesos to go alongside the meagre salary that he was bringing in from his day job at a

---

[1] *Potreros* are areas of open ground in urban Argentina that are often used as local football pitches for impromptu games. They will vary in standard but are usually earth pitches with very little grass.

bakery in Bernal, in the southern part of the district.

Meanwhile, Adriana set about her domestic chores, which helped in some way to distract her from the mixed feelings she had about their troubled exit from Tucumán and the impact of their arrival in Buenos Aires. She could not stop thinking about the sight of her father on the train carriage, pleading with her not to go. And, worse still, what she saw through the train window as they set off: there was her father on his knees, crying on the platform… She had got the impression that, right at that very moment, something inside of her had died. For a long time she could still feel the tears that had run down her face throughout the 18 hours of that initial journey.

The shock of suddenly seeing the vast, unfathomable urban maze of Buenos Aires and its surrounding districts was no easier to bear. The sight of this sprawling metropolis, the third most populated in Latin America after Mexico City and Sao Paolo, was simply overwhelming for someone who had never left her hometown. Yet she had made the decision to start afresh alongside Leo and Jessica, a new and difficult life but one which would unquestionably be their own. And even in moments of adversity, she was comforted by the thought that the decision she had made was the correct one.

She had certainly got off on the wrong foot in Buenos Aires but, over time, Adriana would look back on the early days with good humour. On first arriving at the Retiro train station, she cut the figure of an innocent country girl: while trying to use an escalator she tripped and broke the heel of one of her shoes, and had to hobble the rest of the way as if she were lame. But, thanks to her unshakeable determination to keep pressing ahead, she was able to patiently withstand all the challenges that lay ahead at their chosen destination. The main one was that there was no running water. They had no choice but to load up two 20-litre containers, one in each hand, and walk the 100 metres to a neighbour's house to fill them up using her water pump. Of course, the real hassle came with the return journey, but Adriana was less concerned by the weight of the containers than by poor little Jessica who would stumble alongside her, still only 15 months old.

Although she did not yet know it, there was another reason for Adriana to avoid physical exertions like these: without realising, she had been pregnant for two months. Her period was a bit irregular but, as this was nothing out of the ordinary for her, she thought that everything was in order. But by the end of November she had started to suspect that she may be pregnant, so she headed off for tests at the González Catán hospital. A week later it was confirmed that she was indeed expecting her second child. On hearing the news, Leo remained level-headed and told Adriana not to worry about the future and that they would cope with each other's support. They were not to be intimidated, regardless of the lack of space at home or the absence of money in the bank.

"I was reassured by how calmly Leo greeted the news. If it was fine by him, then it was fine by me too," asserts Adriana.

At this stage she was certain of two things, although she was only to be proved correct on one account. Just as she had known that Jessica would be a girl, on this occasion she knew that the new baby would be a boy. This did indeed turn out to be the case. But her second hunch was not so accurate. She thought that there would be no complications throughout her second pregnancy, just like the first time. But it was not to be. Instead, over the coming months they would be put to the test by a series of harsh setbacks that would ultimately help to shape the personalities of this as yet young and naïve couple. Through these experiences, they would come to appreciate the true value of effort and sacrifice. And, in the future, this was something that they would be sure to pass on to their son.

*Sunday, September 11th, 2005. **The home of El Rojo in Avellaneda, Greater Buenos Aires. Independiente vs. Racing. 38 minutes gone in the second half.***

It was on this day that 17-year-old Kun Agüero, led by the hand of Ricardo Bochini and with Arsenio Erico and Vicente de la Mata looking down upon him from above, took his first step on the road to greatness. He collected Martín Pautasso's pass in midfield where, still in his own half and tight to the left touchline, he left Martín Vitali trailing in his wake. Lifting his gaze, like a predator fixed on his prey, he set off majestically, decisively towards Racing's goal. Now closing in on the opposition penalty area, he squared up to his backpedalling marker, Diego Crosa. Agüero halted suddenly to put him off balance, before feinting past him on the outside. He then cut back into the area, once more evading the defender's attempted tackle. Next he rolled his right boot over the ball, shrugging Crosa off entirely to leave himself one-on-one with goalkeeper Gustavo Campagnuolo. Finally came the exquisite finish with his unfavoured left foot to make it 4-0, sending the home supporters into ecstacy and paying a fitting homage to his friend and team-mate Emiliano Molina, who had died tragically two months previously. It had taken him 13 seconds to cover the 52 metres between receiving the ball and scoring.

It never rains, but it pours

The year of 1988, into which Adriana's second child was born, had not got off to the best of starts in Argentina. Cracks were starting to show in the so-called Austral Plan, put in place by Raúl Alfonsín's government to halt inflation and get the country's economy under control. The austral itself, the new currency that had replaced the peso and was initially worth 80 US cents, had already started to devalue. In February, the rate was six australs to one dollar. In the middle of the same month an Argentinian idol, former middleweight boxing champion of the world Carlos Monzón, was arrested on suspicion of murdering his wife Alicia Muñiz in the city of Mar del Plata. In the same city on March 5th the tragic death of actor Alberto Olmedo, who had fallen from the 11th floor of the Maral 39 building, was the cause of deep and widespread mourning. And in a strange way even the weather seemed to reflect the turbulent times ahead, as two heavy storms bore down over Buenos Aires in March, breaking all previous rainfall records and leaving death and devastation in their wake.

Although this water affected everyone, the less well-off and the residents of low-lying areas suffered the worst. One such area was González Catán, the district of 170,000 residents where Leo and Adriana had built their house. Their circumstances were made all the more precarious by their proximity to the Las Víboras stream, reported by non-governmental organisations to be one of the most polluted in the district. The first warning came on Friday, March 11th, when 115 millimetres of rain fell in a matter of hours. Thousands of people were forced to evacuate the Greater Buenos Aires area. On this occasion, the water fortunately drained away as quickly as it had fallen.

"We were knee-deep in water," remembers Leo. "We had got hold of some trestles and were able to store our furniture up high and out of harm's way. But just imagine the scene, with Adriana already six months pregnant. We got through it this time, much to our relief. But the next downpour was much worse, and there was no way of pulling through it."

As the old saying goes, "it never rains, but it pours". A fortnight later, the residents of Buenos Aires would be forgiven for thinking that they had been hit by the Great Flood. On Friday, March 25th, between the early hours of the morning and the start of the afternoon, 100.9 millimetres of rain fell over an area made up of the capital city, its surrounding metropolitan area and much of the province of Buenos Aires.

The deluge caused rivers and streams to overflow and nothing could stop the floods. Provisional figures reported five deaths and the forced evacuation of over 20,000 people. Two thousand of the evacuees were based in La Matanza, where authorities declared a state of emergency and called for the help of the army to assist in rescuing those who had been left isolated by the rising waters, but had refused to abandon their homes for fear of falling victim to looters. Leo and Adriana were among them.

"We thought that it would be like the previous flood, and that in a few hours the water would start to go down. So we stored everything on the trestles again, including Adriana and Jessica this time," says Leo.

"The water was rising faster and faster, and it wouldn't drain away," adds Adriana. "There I was, with my pregnant belly and my daughter, on a bed which we'd balanced on trestles. Leo was down below, preparing milk for our little girl. We wanted to cope, but it was impossible."

Impossible was the right word for it. The following day, Saturday, March 26th, the intense weather continued with another 100 millimetres of rain falling. A disastrous situation was further exacerbated. Thirteen had now died as a result, and the number of those evacuated had reached 42,000. By Sunday – with a total of 330 millimetres of rain having fallen since the start of the deluge – those figures had reached 24 dead and 57,000 evacuations, almost all of them in different areas throughout Greater Buenos Aires. La Matanza was particularly badly affected, with 60 percent of its surface under water. It did not help that 70 percent of its roads were dirt tracks. Leo, Adriana and Jessica were three of the 5,000 evacuees from this district.

"When the water reached a metre high, there was nothing else for it and we decided to leave," remembers Adriana. "In my state, we had no choice. We just had to somehow forget about the fear of being robbed, and Leo helped Jessica and I to evacuate our house."

Media coverage on television and in the newspapers showed evacuation operations involving firemen with inflatable rafts and lifeboats, making their way through the affected areas to provide assistance to those in need. It also showed other people who chose instead to make their own way out in improvised vehicles packed with all the belongings they could carry. Wall-to-wall images of desperate and anguished faces were relayed. Roads were blocked off, 30,000 homes were left without electricity, 100,000 telephone lines broke down, and 200,000 people were directly affected. Yet the true public face of the catastrophe was to be found in the evacuation centres that sprung up in the worst affected areas. In particular, public schools came to the fore. Less well-off families with hardly any belongings crammed into these schools, in order to receive government aid and the food and mattresses that people were sending out of solidarity for the victims. Leo and Adriana arrived at one such establishment, but were almost immediately transferred to a religious school nearby.

All the accumulated water continued to cause the levels of local rivers to rise, particularly the Reconquista and the Matanza, whose streams and run-offs covered huge expanses of the metropolitan area. This in turn meant that the flood did not end with the rainfall, but instead continued for several days after.

"Although it stopped raining on the third day, it took a long time for the water levels to fall back down. We had to spend a fortnight at the school in the end. We slept on mattresses alongside other families. Nobody could imagine when we might be able to return home," say Adriana and Leo. They would never forget this month of March, or indeed the months that followed which held more moments of anguish and uncertainty in store for them. Above all, they will always remember the dangers to which their soon-to-be-born son was unwittingly subjected.

An enforced rest

Their relief at finally returning home only lasted a few hours. Shortly after arriving, as they started to assess the damage done to their belongings by the flood, Adriana began to feel contractions and her waters broke. Six-and-a-half months pregnant, and scared at the thought that she could lose her baby, she travelled to the González Catán hospital where she was told, following a full check-up, that there was a 50 per cent chance that her baby would be born prematurely. They also explained that the hospital was not equipped to deal with such an eventuality so they transferred her to the Piñero hospital, located in the Flores district in the city of Buenos Aires. This was not uncommon, as many of the patients in the city's public hospitals were from the surrounding metropolitan area, where public health services were often inadequate.

If transferring hospitals was nothing out of the ordinary, the news from the doctors at the Piñero – which they reached after an exhausting three-hour journey involving two buses and a train – was less expected.

Not only did they confirm the risk of a premature birth, but that Adriana would also have to remain at the hospital resting until further notice.

The specialists explained to them that the best thing for both mother and baby would be for the pregnancy to be prolonged for as long as possible, in order to minimise the risk of a premature birth and the negative consequences that this could potentially bring.

Leo and Adriana had no real time to take in the impact of this troubling diagnosis. Instead, shaken by the news, they had to quickly think about how they would organise themselves. Their families were too far away to help, and they had next to no friends in the area. They would have to manage on their own, as best they could.

Their main issue was Jessica, who could not stay at the hospital with her mother. They arranged that sometimes their little girl would be left in the care of a neighbour, and that at other times Leo would take her to work at the bakery. In the end they would have to make do with this set-up, that they had only envisaged lasting a few days, for much longer than expected.

Adriana stayed in one of the three simple but clean inpatient rooms in the neonatal department on the first floor of the Profesor Dr. Victorio Monteverde maternity ward at the Piñero hospital. The room had yellow tiling on the lower half of the walls, with yellow paint from the middle up to the ceiling. There were six yellow beds occupied by women waiting to give birth or those that had already done so. Alone in this room, Adriana felt an overwhelming sense of solitude.

"I wanted to do everything they told me because I wanted my baby to be okay. This was my one great desire. But they didn't even let me go to the toilet. I was alone, and still so young. I was 17 years old and I didn't know anybody. All I had was Leo. It was so hard," remembers Adriana, who also recalls that from this moment her only contact with the outside world was through one of the room's three windows looking onto the hospital's interior courtyard.

The Piñero, which had been opened in 1917, showed the grim side of old public hospitals in Buenos Aires. Although having undergone some modifications and remodelling, the layout was practically the same as it ever had been: the main area at the front overlooking the Avenida Varela where the administrative headquarters were found, behind which stood the emergency rooms overlooking a rectangular courtyard, 70 metres by 40 metres, around which the rest of the wards stood. To the right and left were the admissions clinic and psychopathology ward. And right at the end, facing the main ward and separated by the narrow square, was the maternity ward. Throughout the first weeks, the image of this square – with its traditional cement benches, trees starting the transition from summer to autumn, and cats liberally scuttling around – was all that Adriana could access of the outside world. In truth, it was often a sombre image that in no way helped to raise her spirits.

For almost the whole time she stayed in bed – under the watchful care of the nurses who dictated her routine and brought her food, and the doctors who checked up on her from time to time – her only company was to be found within the four walls of this indoor world.

"I was the only permanent inpatient. The other mothers came and went with their newborn children. I spent much of every day crying. On top of that, I was worried about Jessica. At night it was even worse, at least until I could get to sleep," she recalls.

The prescription of total rest was alleviated little by little, but not too much. They allowed her to walk around what little space there was in her room, as well as letting her spend a few minutes down at the square where Leo would arrive like clockwork to visit her between 4pm and 5pm.

"I would be lying if I said that he missed a day. From the very start, I would spend the afternoon looking through the window until I saw him arrive. He came every day. But because they wouldn't let him into the room, I would slowly walk down the stairs from the first floor to the ground floor and meet him outside in the little park area where we could chat. Leo, and the child that I was carrying, were my only real company during this time," says Adriana with an expression on her face that, even today, reflects her pride and recognition of her husband's efforts.

"I was working at the bakery in Bernal, and I would go to the hospital after finishing for the day before heading to González Catán to collect Jessica. But I'd often pass by the house first to pick up our girl and take her with me, so that the two of them could spend some time together," confirms Leo.

At the time, as now, he considered his sacrifice to be entirely natural and not worth making a fuss over.

"It was what I wanted to do and what I had to do. So I just did it," he says.

"I have always been very close to my parents. From as far back as I can remember, my old man was always alongside me. He came with me to all the pitches where I played. I never told him, but he gave me a sense of protection. I was very small and, although he could get wound up when things weren't right, he didn't put any pressure on me and knew to teach me instead that there were problems that I had to learn to set straight on my own. And he gave me plenty of tips on how to sort things out on the football pitch. He is a true football man, someone who knows what makes those who love the sport tick. And he'd often help me out with a knowing wink so that I could escape punishment from my mum, who wouldn't let me play football with my friends when I got into trouble. My mum is the best in the world, and knows me as well as anyone. She just has to look at me to know what's going on. I know the sacrifices they made for me and my family. And I'll never forget that."

SERGIO AGÜERO

An Argentinian Miracle

The down time afforded to Adriana at the hospital allowed her to learn much more about teenage pregnancies, as well as the issues involved in childbirth and premature deliveries. This was not simply through observing the other situations around her in the room but because, in addition to speaking with those on the verge of giving or just having given birth, she read the books and magazines available on this subject in the maternity library. She dedicated much of her time to reading, observing and asking questions. And so everything from the different types of childbirth, emergencies, advice about breastfeeding to suggestions about looking after the baby, all was absorbed by this worried and curious teenager who had just turned, on May 11th, 18 years old. Naturally she never imagined that all of this new knowledge would influence her judgement when the time came to take important decisions during her own delivery.

"In the three months that I was there, I saw countless cases. From young mothers who didn't even have a partner coming to visit them, to others who spoke about having had an episiotomy or a caesarean section. All of this really helped me," says Adriana.

She is right about everything, except the amount of time that she stayed at the hospital. It was actually just under two months, rather than three. The sheer intensity of what she went through was so great that it feels like, at a distance, the enforced period of rest was longer than it actually was. Her convalescence effectively lasted from around the start of April until the last days of May, when she was finally discharged exactly 15 days before her due date. Adriana, who by now knew everything concerning labour and maternity like the back of her hand, was excited by the news.

Not only had she managed to prolong her pregnancy to its natural length, but she would now also be able to return home. So it was no hardship for her to leave the hospital. Her eight-and-a-half month pregnant belly was no weight for her to bear, and it seemed lighter still when she arrived back to find that Leo had repaired the house, plastered the interior walls and installed damp proofing.

"It was such a relief to return to normality. After what I'd been through… you just don't know how happy I was to look after Jessica again, to wash clothes, to prepare meals and to fill up the water containers," smiles Adriana on remembering those days, with the same dimples in her cheeks that her son would later inherit.

At three o'clock in the morning on June 2nd, Adriana started to feel increasingly regular contractions and by six o'clock they were even more painful and intense. She managed to warn Leo, who was already leaving for work. He chose to stay at home, given the likelihood of Adriana imminently going into labour. Yet despite the unequivocal signs, Adriana preferred to carry on with her everyday chores. Not even the intense chill – the thermometer showed 3.4 degrees at 08:20, the coldest time of the day – could stop her from handwashing the clothes as normal.

It was not until 10 o'clock in the morning that she realised that she was entering labour. She couldn't waste any more time and had to leave for the Piñero hospital. Leo, who had scooped Jessica up under one arm and had a small bag under the other, knew the way thanks to his regular visits to see Adriana at the same hospital. So all he would have to do was repeat the same old journey, although admittedly under very different circumstances. In her condition Adriana was unable to walk normally and so, despite his natural anxiety, Leo had to slow down for her. They walked the four blocks to the main road and, after the usual wait, took the number 96 bus. After 10 minutes, they got off at the González Catán railway station to take the Belgrano Sur line towards the city. They took the train for 45 minutes as far as Villa Soldati, a stop already within the city of Buenos Aires.

"Taking a taxi wasn't an option. We didn't have that kind of money. But despite the contractions, I was calm. I even remember spending the whole journey eating *churros*[2]," says Adriana. But the 10 stations between González Catán and Soldati seemed like many more on this occasion for Leo, who was starting to look worried. He was too restless even to glance over the newspaper being read by one of the passengers nearby. If he had done so, he would have seen the headlines about the Reagan-Gorbachev summit; about the Argentinian government's proposal to Great Britain to reopen a bilateral dialogue, six years on from the conflict in the South Atlantic; and that one dollar was already worth 9.40 australs. And he would also have seen the photo of the last-minute goal that had earnt a draw for Racing de Avellaneda in their match against River Plate, giving them the chance to face off for the Supercopa against Brazilian side Cruzeiro. His mind was not on the news, however, it was on getting to the hospital as quickly as possible.

From Soldati station they took the number 76 bus to the Flores

---

[2] A *churro*, sometimes referred to as a Spanish doughnut, is a fried-dough pastry-based snack.

cemetery, which was near the hospital. The whole journey had taken almost three hours.

All that remained was the short walk to Piñero itself. They walked round the Flores cemetery, passed in front of its main gate, crossed Calle Balbastro and undertook the last 200-metre stretch on Avenida Varela. Being straight uphill, this final walk can be a nuisance for anyone, let alone for a young woman in labour. By this point, Adriana's initial calmness had given way to evident exhaustion. Leo was in such a rush that he had not realised that, even with Jessica in his arms, he was striding well ahead of Adriana. His pregnant wife was really struggling by now and gasping for air. Every so often, she would call for him not to leave her too far behind. Leo would then have to retrace his steps and try to keep the same painfully slow pace as his tired wife.

They walked past the courtyard of a complex of buildings that bordered the hospital, then skirted the fence that separated the walkway from the hospital. Out of anxiety, Leo marched off ahead again and, without looking back, he reached the large hospital gate by himself. The security guard, noting Leo's flustered appearance, stopped him at the entrance and asked where he was going. "It's my wife," said an anxious Leo. "She's about to have a baby." All that the guard could offer in return was a look of surprise. There was no woman to be seen, let alone one going into labour.

"He was walking so quickly that he had left me about 100 metres behind. Suddenly I could see someone gesturing at me from the hospital gate. It was Leo, standing alongside a security guard, trying to get me to hurry up," tells Adriana. Leo stood waiting and, once she had arrived, once more sped off to the emergency ward. Adriana knew the hospital and where she was going, however, so she walked past the emergency ward, crossed the courtyard, walked along the edge of the Cooperative Association section and headed straight for the other end where the maternity ward stood and where she would be treated in the paediatrics wing. In his haste, Leo had gone the wrong way.

Just before three o'clock in the afternoon, Adriana started off up the stairs that she had climbed so many times before. The 27 steps up to the first floor seemed to go on forever, even with the support of the familiar black handrail. On reaching the top, she turned left straight through the door to the labour room to be seen by one of the doctors on duty. When Leo belatedly arrived, he was made to sit in the waiting room. By this stage Adriana was already in a bed in the labour room, and had been put on a drip to hasten the already imminent birth. She felt calm, despite the pain of her contractions.

Although somewhat dazed, she knew that it was now just a matter of minutes. However, she then heard the voice of the doctor informing her that the baby was stuck and that in its current position she would be unable to give birth. The doctor suggested that forceps be used to straighten its position. "No, not with forceps," replied Adriana, with huge self-assurance. Despite her current situation, the long journey on two buses and a train, not to mention her tender age, she had the clarity of thought to request them not to use forceps.

"The thing is, while I was a patient at the hospital I had watched and listened to everything, both the mothers and the nurses. And I had seen babies born using forceps that were almost crushed... I didn't like it... I'd also read about it in books. Although in certain cases it worked absolutely fine, there was no way that I would accept my baby being born in that way," she recalls now, with the same conviction that she had at the time.

The obstetrician explained that, if she did not want forceps to be used, they would have to fracture the baby's collar bone and even perform an episiotomy with three or four incisions. "If the baby's collar bone will easily heal, then go ahead, that's fine. As for me, make as many incisions as you need. But no forceps," she insisted. The doctor reassured her that the collar bone would heal in a few days, and would have no adverse consequences for the child. Adriana gave her consent and, a few minutes later, the baby slipped out into the hands of the midwife. The time was 15:23.

"You have a beautiful, healthy boy," she told her enthusiastically. It was all Adriana could do to lift herself to see this baby, for whom she had fought so hard while he was growing within her. On seeing that it was indeed a little boy, it confirmed what she had predicted throughout the whole pregnancy. She was so sure, in fact, that what little clothing she had already bought for the baby was in light blue.

The doctor's voice snapped her out of her daydream. "This child was born *con un pan debajo del brazo*," he asserted, using an old expression meaning that the boy would bring fortune to his parents. Adriana assumed that this doctor, whose name she would never know, had said this after learning of her medical history, of the time she had spent previously at the hospital and of her traumatic pregnancy. However, in the few minutes that had passed since her arrival, the doctor had not had the time to read up on her case. Now sat up, she had a moment to get to know her new son and hold him tight against her chest.

She trembled at this first contact. The doctor, after completing his initial checks, said goodbye with a kiss and wished her the best of luck. Adriana, who was now being cared for by the nurses, could not help thinking about the obstetrician's premonition.

In a few seconds, she ran through everything in her mind: the day that she had met Leo in the province of Tucumán four years previously, the hard times that they had shared before deciding to leave for Buenos Aires, the flooded house and the evacuation, the period of enforced rest and the times that they had feared for the wellbeing of the baby she was carrying. At this moment, on seeing their son – who they would later name Sergio Leonel – the worst fears started to melt away. And she thought that the doctor was right, that her son had indeed been born under a lucky star.

After so many setbacks, it was almost a miracle that he had been born at all. She thought to herself that it was God's own will for this baby to have come into the world. He was a handsome boy. Healthy, strong and tough, without a hair on his head. He was 59 centimetres tall and weighed 9lb 11oz. Reassured by his healthy appearance, Adriana wanted Leo – who was still sitting anxiously in the waiting room – to come and meet his son as soon as possible. She thought once more about the doctor's words and she smiled: "*Un pan debajo del brazo*".

These were words that for many years would ring hollow. No more so than on his fourth birthday, when they could for the first time put on a small party for their beloved child. But the words would later prove much more prescient, as the doctor's assertion came to represent a prophecy fulfilled. This miraculous birth would not only bring much fortune to the family but would produce another miracle, in the form of a rare, unique talent, a gem in its purest form, so difficult to find in the empassioned and sprawling world of football.

*Sunday, May 13th, 2012. **Manchester. Etihad Stadium. The final weekend of the Premier League season. Manchester City vs. QPR. 93 minutes and 20 seconds.***

At this precise time, on an afternoon when sounds and pictures would be broadcast around the world of an epic finale that saw Manchester City become champions of England for the first time in 44 years, Sergio 'Kun' Agüero momentarily personified what it takes to become a footballing legend. City's dream of that title, which seemed to be within their grasp after making up an eight-point deficit in the run-in, was one minute and 47 seconds from slipping through their fingers in the worst imaginable circumstances: a draw in this last match would hand the title to Manchester United, their eternal rivals. City had gone one up thanks to a Pablo Zabaleta goal but QPR, who were fighting to avoid relegation, had turned the game around with only 10 men. Disappointment and anguish were etched onto faces everywhere around the packed Etihad Stadium. But on 91 minutes and 13 seconds, with the first of five additional minutes indicated by the referee Mike Dean having already lapsed, Bosnian striker Edin Dzeko headed in a corner taken by the Spaniard David Silva to make it 2-2, and a chink of light suddenly appeared for City. This one last glimmer of hope soon became a reality. Guided by his instinct, his outstanding natural talent and all that he had learnt from his mentors, Kun pulled out of the opposition's heavily guarded penalty area. In seven seconds he was able to conjure up the miracle required to unleash so much pent-up emotion and to transform it into pure euphoria. After 93 minutes and 13 seconds he received possession from De Jong, feinted away from his defender and, with the outside of his boot, delicately caressed the ball to Balotelli in search of a one-two. With his back to goal, the Italian held off his marker and, with one final effort as he fell to the floor, dragged the ball on with his right foot to feed Sergio, who burst into the area, went past Taiwo with a touch oozing in class and then beat goalkeeper Paddy Kenny's outstretched hand with a fierce right-footed shot. A goal to seal the win and the title, as well as a place in both the history books and the hearts of so many. He was soon to turn 24 and it was his first season in the Premier League, his sixth in Europe after five years at Atletico Madrid. With the cry that greeted this goal, screamed by thousands around the world, everything came together: his love for football, the passion of the people, his past, his present and his future.

The Garden Of
The Republic

The rain is the ultimate source of Tucumán's rich flora and vegetation, the reason for which the smallest province in Argentina is known as the 'Garden of the Republic'. In the autumn of 1984, that same rain would cause a chance encounter, sewing a seed that would later blossom into life and ultimately amaze the world.

The autumn was rumbling on uneventfully like any other for Adriana Agüero. At the tender age of 14 years, having celebrated her birthday on May 11th, she knew what was expected of her and her twin sister Analía: to look after their younger brothers Rodolfo (9 years old), René (5) and the younger twins

Daniel and Walter (4). Their father Rodolfo and mother Ana were obliged to spend much of their time away from the house at their respective workplaces. He was a handyman at the provincial Government House and she was a domestic worker.

While her parents worked, Adriana kept the house in order and cooked for her younger brothers. It was hard work but she never complained. She had learnt to cook by watching her mother and a neighbour, quickly becoming an expert at making their everyday stews. The reward came every Sunday, when her mother would be at the house to make escalopes and home-made pasta, much to the delight of the Agüero children.

Caring for her brothers was character-building work. Adriana had needed to develop an air of authority, to ensure that none of them broke the rules that their parents had set to keep order while they were away. If they ever gave her trouble, then a quick telling off from their older sister was usually enough to stop things getting out of hand. In addition to generally keeping order and cleaning, she also made sure not to neglect the little things such as making sure that there was a fireguard in front of the heater on cold days, in order to stop the little ones from burning themselves.

On one day, just like any other, she went to the back of the house to hang up some clothes that she had just hand-washed. She had lived in that small house her whole life, on Calle Olleros in the crowded 11 de Marzo neighbourhood in the town of San Miguel de Tucumán. It backed onto another house from which it was separated only by a wire fence that, although low, was enough to divide the two properties. She headed towards the clothes lines to hang up a load of washing, which was heavier than usual because it was still damp. Hurrying along quickly as always, she did not pay sufficient attention to the boggy conditions under foot that had resulted from the recent rainfall. Her first few steps were sure enough but, just as she was getting to the washing lines, the damp clothes and a bit of bad luck came together and conspired against her. One false step later and she lost balance, slipping and falling heavily down onto the mud.

In truth, it did not overly bother her that she was now wet and muddy, or even that those clothes that she had slaved over cleaning were now filthy once more. But what did annoy her was the sound of roaring laughter coming from behind the fence that separated the house from their neighbours. As she tried to sit up, she could make out a boy on the other side of the fence who, overtly but without any malice, was laughing at her misfortune.

He was a little older than her, but she did not recognise him as being from the neighbourhood. She knew that the couple who had recently moved into the house had daughters, but had not heard of any sons. Her pride dented, she did not look back at him. Instead she stood up and, hiding her anger, started to hang up the clothes as if nothing had happened. She told herself not to let the incident spoil her day. But on the inside her anger grew, as did the volley of unspoken insults aimed at the stranger who had laughed at her. And this internalised anger would rise up every time that she came across him in the neighbourhood. It was not long before she became aware that the boy's name was Leonel Del Castillo and that he was the eldest son of the couple who had recently moved into the neighbouring house.

From this point on, that first incident would cast a shadow over their occasional meetings. She could not forget the sound of that roaring laughter. The boy, meanwhile, wanted to get to know his neighbour better. But he knew that he would have to turn on the charm this time.

Later on in life, it would dawn on the two of them that the unfortunate incident caused by the rains of Tucumán had marked the start of a relationship that would lead from teenage romance to a lifetime alongside one another. There would be more little slips along the way, but no great falls. And the reward for all the sacrifices, generosity and devotion would come in the shape of their second of seven children who, like a blessing, would inherit all of those qualities and would rise up on to a stage where he could demonstrate them for the whole world to see.

Saturday, July 20th, 2002. **The city of Rosario, in the province of Santa Fe. Rosario Central's reserve team pitch. 12:18 in the afternoon.**

It was on this lunchtime that Kun Agüero, offering a taster of what he would later bring to the top table of international football, made his first significant statement for one of Independiente's youth teams in a major Argentinian football tournament. El Rojo were taking on the home team and the game was petering out to a 1-1 draw. Independiente's ninth team, the 1988 categoría[1], simply had to win to be crowned champions. The second half's regulation 30 minutes had elapsed, and there were barely 30 seconds remaining of the three minutes added on by the referee. Independiente were pressing forward when, all of a sudden, three

---

[1] In Argentinian football, the term *categoría* refers to a team made up of players who were all born in a certain year. The 1988 *categoría* was therefore a team of players all born in the year 1988.

Rosario Central attackers broke downfield. They bore down on Bruno Mora, the one last, solitary line of defence protecting goalkeeper Emiliano Molina. Mora reacted perfectly to dispossess the opposition striker, halting the counter-attack and quickly releasing the ball to his number five, Orellana. The ball was instantly transferred to Sergio Agüero. He received possession just ahead of the opposition midfield and, after carrying the ball forwards a few metres and leaving an opponent in his path, touched it on to the number 16 who was running up alongside him. José 'Pepe' Sosa was making a run down the right wing and called for the pass. He received the ball, burst forward into the area and, after feinting back inside to beat a defender, crossed with his left foot. Kun had been tracking the attack in the centre of the pitch and, stealing a march on the goalkeeper and a defender, met the ball first and dispatched it into the back of the net. That made the score 2-1 with virtually the last kick of the game. The final whistle sparked mass celebrations. Independiente's little gem was starting to live up to his promise. It was the first youth team championship that he had competed in, and his first title. Kun was starting to make waves. He had only just turned 14, and that afternoon in Rosario had given him a taste for glory that he would savour time and again in the years to come.

The Fulbipibes

There was no way that Adriana Agüero could have known that her neighbours had a son because, since they had moved to the neighbourhood, she had neither seen nor heard anything about him. The fact is that Leo, as Leonel was known, spent more time out of the house than he did in it. Adriana was more likely to see his father Juan Carlos, a well-respected solderer who worked at an agricultural machinery factory, or his mother Blanca, a devoted housewife, or even his younger sisters Iris and Claudia. But it would be rare to catch sight of Leo, who as a teenager dedicated most of his daylight hours to his true passion: playing football on whichever pitch happened to be to hand. If there was a game being played, he simply had to go and join in.

He had honed his football skills from childhood in the 9 de Julio neighbourhood of San Miguel de Tucumán where his family had moved to, having lived for a time in Buenos Aires, the city where he was born on August 7th, 1968. When he turned five, the family decided to return to their home province. The 1,311 kilometres that separate Buenos Aires and Tucumán proved to be no distance at all for little Leo: he quickly settled into the way of life back at his parents' homeland, even developing a Tucumán accent and adopting the local way of pronouncing the rolled 'R' sound.

Throughout these years, Argentina was still feeling the effects of the significant political and institutional crisis that had shaken the country in the 1970s.

The everyday lives of normal people still bore the scars of successive military dictatorships, as well as the rise of the guerrilla revolutionaries – who had occupied hillside areas in Tucumán and were later forcefully removed during the so-called Operation Independence. There was also the return of General Juan Domingo Perón from exile in Spain, his presidency and his death; the military coup d'état of 1976 and subsequent ferocious military dictatorship that saw so many deaths and *desapa-*

recidos[2]. Tucumán, whose population density of 50.7 people per square kilometre was second only to the province of Buenos Aires, would also suffer economically with the closure of more than 70 sugar mills. At the time, the sugar industry was the province's main economic activity and these closures saw many people facing unemployment and the possibility of having to leave the area.

Still young and detached from such concerns, Leo Del Castillo simply carried on wreaking havoc with his raw pace and cheeky dribbling skills on the local *potreros* near his house. On one of these, at the age of eight, he came across one of San Miguel de Tucumán's most enigmatic characters. Known simply as 'Don Cuquino', he was the manager of the youth teams in his home district of Villa Urquiza. His teams were known for their calmness in possession, for their outstanding results in local tournaments and for the spirit that he managed to instil in the youngsters: play to entertain yourselves, and to entertain others. Imprinted with this philosophy, his teams' victories took care of themselves. Don Cuquino did not think twice about inviting Leo to join the 1968 *categoría* that he was putting together. The boy could not have been any luckier. Joining this team would give him the chance to be a part of one of the best football schools around and to meet, among the organisers, some mentors whose teachings would serve him well in all

---

[2] Argentinians use this term to refer to the thousands of people who were victims of forced disappearances during the years of military dictatorship. People who were seen to be an ideological or political threat to the military junta were regularly abducted and illegally detained. Although many never returned, the government of the time denied any knowledge of or involvement in their disappearance.

walks of life. In addition to Cuquino, one of his main mentors was Antonio Escobar, who was known for sniffing out the most gifted players. But his defining character trait was his passion for assisting in the physical, moral and educational development of 'his' boys.

For no other reason than to feel useful, Escobar took time out from work at his tyre repair shop at home on the corner of Calle Ayacucho and General Urquiza, a few blocks from the famous Plaza Independencia square, to organise the teams. Escobar took a particular interest in the 1968 *categoría* as it included one of his sons, Tony, who was a useful goalkeeper. Being better off than most of the other boys' fathers, he would take it upon himself to pick them up in his car from their houses, many of which were located in the area's poorer neighbourhoods. He did so happily enough, even if from time to time he would have to deal with distrusting parents who were reluctant to let their sons go.

"They were all good boys, very humble and big-hearted," says Antonio, 32 years down the line. "But they were the sons of working-class parents who had neither the time nor the money to ferry them around every weekend so that they could play football." Leonel was one such boy who, consequently, found the perfect companions to stand in for his father, who was constantly consumed by his work.

Antonio was never one for favouritism when it came to 'his players', but he felt a special admiration towards Leo. "He was a high quality footballer," he declares without hesitation. "A natural, elusive and daring goalscorer among the best that I've ever seen. And I've seen a few, you understand?"

When talking about Leo, his son Tony unhesitatingly uses the nickname *El Loco* – the madman – in reference to his unbridled joy when playing. "*El Loco* was one of a kind. He would nutmeg you, then feint and shimmy past you on this side and that. He would leave opponents for dead. And when he scored a goal, he would kill himself laughing." Tony recalls that Leo was a touch thin at this stage, but still strong enough to hold off opposition players. "He struck the ball well with both feet and was a great finisher."

Villa Urquiza's 1968 *categoría*, a team without a home ground and not belonging to a club, played under various names at different times. These names could refer to the sponsors that had covered the cost of the boys' kit, or to a club which they had been asked to represent. However, the name by which they were most commonly known – and under which they entered most competitions – was Fulbipibes. They were named after a brand of football boots, *Fulvencito*, whose adverts and accompanying comic strip were all the rage in the 1970s. The adverts claimed that the boots were "for smart *pibes*[3]".

In these days, all that mattered to the boys was making sure that they were prepared and ready to play their weekly matches. But at 10 years of age, a rival focus of attention suddenly emerged to challenge these football-dominated weekends: the 1978 World Cup, which was held in Argentina and would see the home side emerge victorious. Although none of the matches were played in Tucumán, Leo and his friends followed it all on television and made sure not to miss a beat. César Luis Menotti's team lifted everyone's spirits in spite of

---

[3] *Pibes* is often how Argentinians refer to 'kids' or in this case, young footballers.

the absence of Argentinian football's great young hope, Diego Armando Maradona, who was still just 17 years of age at the time. Wins against Hungary and France and defeat to Italy in the first phase, followed by the win against Poland, the draw with Brazil and finally the much commented-on 6-0 thrashing of Peru, all saw spirits raised further still. Then came the mass celebrations after a 3-1 victory over Holland in the final. Leo watched enthralled as Daniel Alberto Passarella lifted the cup and the team performed their lap of honour, and he began to dream of one day being a part of such an event. Little did he know that those distant names, Menotti and Maradona, would in one way or another become entwined with his own life in years to come.

"I believe that my dad's childhood experiences really helped him to better understand my own feelings towards football. I wanted to play all the time and in any game that I could. And occasionally I'd have to sleep over at a coach's or team-mate's house, just so that I could play the next day. He understood this perfectly. He also didn't want me to miss out on playing in the top flight, like he had. So when he realised that I was good enough, he decided to do all he could to help me get there. When he was 27, he stopped playing in the Saturday and Sunday leagues that he was involved in, just so that I could carry on playing. He took me everywhere, from one pitch to another. It always seemed perfectly normal to me, having him forever by my side. But now that I'm older, I recognise that not all fathers wanted or were able to do what he did. When I was back in Tucumán a while ago, one of my old man's friends told me that I had enjoyed the luck that he'd never had.

In other words, I had a Leo alongside me. He was spot on."
SERGIO AGÜERO

Those with a good memory in Tucumán have not forgotten the impression made by the Fulbipibes in the local youth tournaments, where each title that they won served as another example of their prodigious talent. Evidence of the team's winning streak appeared in *Nuestro Club*, a magazine published by San Martín de Tucumán – one of the two most popular football clubs in the province – in October 1979, a month in advance of the institution's 70th birthday. Under the title of "Forward thinking football's finest triumph", the magazine reported on a youth football tournament organised by the club as part of UNESCO's International Year of the Child, a tournament won by Fulbipibes. A photo of the winning team, showing Leo Del Castillo at the tender age of 11 and sporting a striking fringe, is included alongside the report itself. The latter makes reference to the tournament's top goalscorers chart, headed up by none other than Leo Del Castillo himself, with 24 goals.

The boys could only take their next step to becoming professional footballers when they were old enough to be registered for the youth teams at San Martín de Tucumán. Those who were selected, following a demanding trial, would register at the Tucumán football league's headquarters. The first to do so was Tony Escobar, on June 7th, 1983. Next came Leo Del Castillo on August 2nd, 1983, only five days before his 15th birthday. He registered as number 32,843 on page 224 of book 12. Shortly after, the majority of the Fulbipibes team followed suit. Reunited at San Martín, and playing with the same spirit as they had in their junior league days, they were crowned champions in two successive seasons of the competitive Tucumán league, which was made up of 50 clubs, 30 of which were classified as Division 'A' sides. The matches were always tough contests but, buoyed by their successes, Leo and his team-mates dreamed of future glories.

However, due to varying circumstances, the members of this initial group would end up each going their own way. Leo, who had got as far as training with San Martín's reserve team, left after a series of setbacks and misunderstandings with the coach. He would try his luck elsewhere, but this continued to elude him as he found himself hampered by his own inexperience and by difficulties in re-registering with another team. Tony Escobar was left disillusioned and hung up his gloves. He never wanted to keep goal again, not even back in the local tournaments. Everyone went their own way and only a few stayed in touch with each other.

Many years later in 2001, when Tony Escobar was already 33 years old, one of his childhood friends paid him a visit: it was *El Loco* himself, Leo Del Castillo, who was back in Tucumán for a few days from his new home in Buenos Aires. During this reunion of old friends, he told Tony that one of his sons was playing in the youth teams at Independiente de Avellaneda, one of the biggest clubs in Argentina's *Primera División*[4].

Tony took in the news, and would henceforth keep on the lookout for any new youngsters appearing in the first division. A few years down the line, he found himself watching an eye-

---

[4] The Primera División is the top flight of professional football in Argentina, akin to the Premier League in England or La Liga in Spain.

catching youngster who had broken into Independiente's team. The kid was very young indeed, with a very familiar running style. He noticed that this new player had a very particular way of beating a man, managing to leave the opposing defenders for dead. He enjoyed watching him confidently dribble the ball and apply exquisite finishes. All of it was so reminiscent of how *El Loco* Leo used to play, way back in his childhood and teenage years. The youngster perhaps worked more on his physique and was a little stockier, but the two certainly looked alike. He therefore supposed that it had to be his friend's son. The kid had a strange nickname. They called him Kun. Stranger still, his surname was not Del Castillo but Agüero. He remained none the wiser until a little later, when any element of doubt was removed.

The youngster was, indeed, the son of his friend Leo. Kun Agüero, who at 16 years of age had already started to make his mark in Independiente's first team, was confusingly – and for reasons that would be explained at a later date – known by his mother's surname rather than by that of his father. This confirmation that Leo's son had made it at the highest level filled Tony with pride and joy. Out of pure talent and class, one of their sons had realised the dream of playing in the top flight of Argentinian football. Leo had clearly passed on his best qualities to this boy, including the adventurous and streetwise spirit of the old Fulbipibes.

Tony also knew without a shadow of a doubt that the road that had led the boy to this point had been lined with the same experiences that so many of them, and Leo in particular, had been through when they were young. The hard times that would melt away, immediately cured by the pure tonic of football every time they came across some open ground to set up a pitch. The times when they slept round at neighbouring houses, when others opened their doors and their hearts to look after them as best they could. The times when games went on well into the evenings, and when leagues were contested for nothing but glory. These were the days of long journeys, hard sacrifices and high hopes. Days spent dreaming about the first division and packed stadiums. What Tony did not know, however, was that this was just the start of it. And that over time Kun would reach the very highest level and bestow upon the football world a unique feeling for the game, inherited from his friend Leo and born out on the *potreros* of the "Garden of the Republic".

Friday, November 26th, 2004. **Buenos Aires. The Libertadores de América stadium. Independiente vs. Estudiantes de La Plata. 22 minutes into the first half.**
This night would offer Kun Agüero the opportunity to recreate the magic that he had demonstrated in the reserve leagues and, in doing so, live up to his reputation as a future crack[5] that had been spreading since when — in 2003 and at the tender age of 15 years, 1 month and 3 days — he had become the youngest ever debutant in the history of Argentinian professional football. Younger than Maradona or Carlos Tevez. Younger, on an international level, than Pele, Ronaldo, Raul or Messi. It was only the second time that he had started a first division match. His team was trailing by two goals to nil when he received the ball close to

---

[5] In much of Latin America and Spain, a team's star players are referred to as their *cracks*.

the 'D' of the opposition penalty area. Then, in an instant, with a strike of the ball reminiscent of both the class of José Omar Pastoriza and the power of Daniel Bertoni, he unleashed a shot that fizzed past goalkeeper Herrera and buried itself in the top left-hand corner of his net. It was his first goal in the top division. He was 16 years old, wearing the number 20 shirt. It would not be long before he would inherit another shirt that destiny seemed to have set aside for him: the emblematic number 10 once worn by Bochini, whose true and rightful successor Kun Agüero would in time prove to be.

Time to leave

Just a few months after registering with San Martín de Tucumán, Leo moved with his family to the 11 de Marzo neighbourhood. At 15 years of age, the opportunities presented to him by football seemed to point towards a bright future. Around this time, that opportune slip and chance encounter with the neighbour that he would later learn to be called Adriana Agüero took place. Her name had been passed on to him by Ricardo Juárez, nicknamed 'Luque' due to his resemblance to Leopoldo Jacinto Luque, who wore number nine for the Argentinian national side and had starred at World Cup 1978. 'Luque' was two years older than Leo and, although a less gifted footballer, he was no less passionate about the sport. The two hit it off as soon as young Leo had arrived in the neighbourhood. They became inseparable and formed a friendship that, barring a couple of short interruptions, has lasted to this day.

'Luque' played an essential role in bringing Leo and Adriana together, because he lived only two houses away from the Agüero residence and knew the family well. In truth, there were very few places or occasions on which Leo could attempt to charm Adriana. On the one hand, her father Rodolfo was really quite strict, and controlled, or attempted to control, his daughter's every move. This was not insurmountable, as Adriana's life was slow and predictable enough to find little moments to see each other. But at the same time, she had still not forgotten about the slipping incident and paid Leo next to no attention.

Her time was still largely spent taking care of her brothers. During the small amount of free time that she had, Adriana took the opportunity to practise her new hobby, one that was suddenly all the rage among girls in San Miguel: women's football. Her team's coach was none other than 'Luque' himself.

"She used to play on the right wing," he says, "although I must admit that Analía, her twin sister who played as our number 10, was the better player."

The matches took place on a piece of land right in front of Leo's house, on the same makeshift pitch where the boys would play, on the rare occasions that it was not being used for their games. This particular characteristic of Leo's house – that it was located right alongside a *potrero* – just happened to repeat itself in each of the many houses that the Agüero-Del Castillo couple would inhabit over the coming years. Almost a year after the slipping incident, a chance encounter in the city centre lit the fuse between the two teenagers. From this moment on, Adriana's initial desire "never to see him again" gave way to an attraction that would grow and grow. The first stolen kiss, in the surroundings of the 9 de Julio park, was the start of a courtship that would have its fair share of ups and downs.

Suspecting that something was going on, Adriana's father started to monitor his daughter's life even more closely. However, faced with his domineering presence, the young couple found in 'Luque' the ideal alibi for their secret meetings. And these meetings were becoming more and more frequent. Adriana became pregnant six months later although, inexperienced in such matters, she did not realise it. This was towards the end of 1985 and she was still only 15 years old.

"It was my mother who noticed, and took me to see the doctor. That was when we found out about it, on December 7th, 1985. And the next day, my mum told Leo's parents. I was over the moon, even if my mum and dad weren't so happy. But I wanted the baby," says Adriana today.

She has an unhurried and simple way of speaking, and a flawless memory. These traits are reflected in her iron resolve, which came to the fore as she made up her mind to celebrate this creation of new life and have her baby. The news, however, hit the two families like a ton of bricks and forced them together to discuss how to deal with the situation. As was only natural, the meeting took place in neutral territory, which is to say where the two houses met at the back of their yards. Separated only by the wire fencing that divided the two properties, the Del Castillos and the Agüeros came face to face with each other. Only Leo, Adriana and the two sets of parents were present. The strength of Adriana's convictions left no real room for discussion: she made it quite clear that she wanted to have her baby.

"We remained in silence throughout practically the whole conversation. It was our parents who spoke. They gave their opinions without asking us what we wanted. Then I spoke up and told them what I thought. And that was that," says Adriana.

The resistance coming from both families had no bearing on Adriana and Leo's decision, and from this moment on they would live together in one house or the other. The young couple's physical proximity to the two families stood in stark contrast to how emotionally distanced they became from their disapproving mother and fathers.

The main cause for concern was how young Leo and Adriana were – 17 years and 15 years respectively – as well as uncertainty over the couple's future together. As a result, their relations with their elders became increasingly strained. However, Adriana enjoyed her pregnancy, despite the subtle disapproving glances from some of her neighbours. Leo was similarly content, and closely followed her routine check-ups.

At this time, he was perhaps not even aware that his dreams of making it as a footballer had started to slip out of his reach. He had risen to the level of San Martín de Tucumán's reserve team, but his differences with the coach saw him become estranged from the club. He had trials at other clubs like Almirante Brown de Lules and Argentino del Norte in the provincial league, both of whom accepted him. But he remained a registered player with San Martín and, with the club refusing to release him from these commitments, he was unable to make headway elsewhere.

Furthermore, he had to think seriously about how he was going to provide for their as yet unborn baby. It was for this reason that he started spending more time at the Mercado del Norte, the local market, where he would earn some money doing any odd jobs that came his way. He would give help to whoever needed it and also sold turrón, a sweet nougat snack, to the tradesmen.

Of course, he would also bring in some cash playing football. Known to be an excellent player, he was a much-coveted resource for those teams in his neighbourhood or at the market who required his services. In return they would pay him a little amount that, to a 17-year-old, nevertheless felt like a small fortune.

With the reverberations of World Cup 1986 in Mexico still being felt, a tournament which again saw Argentina crowned champions and Diego Armando Maradona crowned the best player in the world – after scoring the greatest goal in the tournament's history – Adriana was admitted to the San Miguel maternity ward on Calle Mate de Luna. And after an arduous labour lasting three-and-a-quarter hours on August 7th, 1986, the very same day as Leo turned 18, their first daughter was born. They named her Jessica.

A year later they would leave for Buenos Aires, determined to make their own way in life. Leo indefinitely put his dreams of becoming a professional footballer on hold, but was intent on marching ahead into the future with his young family. Adriana, meanwhile, was convinced that she needed to leave her father's household in order to start the next stage of her life.

Together, despite their own personal doubts and those expressed by others, they wanted to find their way in a world that would prove to be particularly inhospitable for them. But they knew that many hurdles would be placed in their path. They would settle down in the vast urban area of Buenos Aires, where a passion for football is able to unite a disparate range of people inhabiting contrasting districts, from the most prosperous to the most peripheral. From one such area, named Los Eucaliptus de Quilmes, and above all on its *potreros*, the figure of Leo and Adriana's second child would emerge. This would be where his gifts would first come to light, where he would first realise that football coursed through his veins like a raging torrent. And that it would be something he breathed, consumed and lived for.

His Name Is Sergio

After giving birth, Adriana remained in hospital for another two weeks. Although she was personally given the all-clear after three days, the baby boy would have to remain under observation: x-rays were to be taken every other day to closely trace the progress of his fractured collar bone.

Having spent two gruelling months in the same hospital during the pregnancy, staying a little longer in that same room with her son – who was feeding regularly and showing a healthy appetite for his mother's milk – felt more like a reward than a punishment for Adriana.

But due to the baby's delicate shoulder, she naturally took particular care when lifting and changing him or handling him during feeding, even when the doctors and nurses explained to her that there was nothing to fear and that he could be held and lifted up as normal.

Around this time, a baby had been stolen from a public hospital in the area. This had sent shock waves throughout the maternity wards of Buenos Aires, resulting in a state of collective paranoia. For this reason, Adriana would not leave her baby's side during their time in hospital, even for an instant. She would wake up two or three times a night to check up on him and, despite the nurses' advice to the contrary, regularly had him sleep in the bed alongside her.

After two additional weeks at the Piñero, the specialists informed Leo and Adriana that the collar bone had safely healed. This delay had allowed the two of them to think about what they would name their son, a matter to which they had given next to no thought up until this point. There was no time for a great debate, however.

Leo had always liked the name Sergio, on account of two close childhood friends who shared it. With the name evoking such fond memories, Leo suggested that they take it for their son. Adriana was in agreement although she also wanted the baby to be called Leo. Although he was not so keen on this, a happy medium did seem to present itself: they would name their first son Sergio Leonel. In actual fact, Adriana preferred to spell the name as Lionel, with an 'i'. Leo's mother had also wanted to name her son in this way, but had been refused permission at the civil registry. Those days of restrictions on the very freedom of parents to choose a child's name in Argentina had not been consigned to the past.

In spite of the years that had gone by since Leo's birth, history was to repeat itself when Adriana tried to register her son's name as Sergio Lionel. The second name could not be found on the authorised list and, as a result, she resigned herself to naming the boy Leonel with an 'e'.

Interestingly, in other parts of the country these rules were not so strictly enforced. For example, just a year before Sergio's birth and 306 kilometres away from the capital in the city of Rosario, the civil registry had indeed granted a baby boy the name Lionel. This was in June 1987, and the boy's parents were none other than Jorge and Celia Messi. More curiously still, the two of them had originally chosen the name Leonel for their son, spelt with an 'e'. It was only because of some confusion when Jorge Messi registered the name that it ended up as Lionel with an 'i'.

Looking back now, it is a strange quirk of fate that the boy who should have been named Leonel became Lionel, and the one whose name should have been Lionel ended up as Leonel. Coincidences aside, Lionel Messi and Sergio Leonel Agüero would years later find themselves united by a much stronger bond. This bond would be written in a shared language – one of talent and inspiration, rather than letters and spelling – in which the two of them would compose pages for the history books out on the football pitch.

*Tuesday, August 19th, 2008. **Beijing, China.** **Argentina vs. Brazil. The semi-final of the men's football tournament at the Olympic Games. Seven minutes into the second half.***
On this day, the wide world of football first sat up and took notice of a partnership that, both on and off the field of play, would bear spectacular fruit in the years ahead. It was the day that Kun

Agüero broke the old curse against Argentina's fiercest rival and, together with Lionel Messi, stood out as the architect of a victory that took their country to the final of an Olympic Games tournament that they were to go on and win. Fernando Gago collected the ball in midfield and touched it on to Messi. The Barcelona man played a perfect pass into Kun who, on the edge of Brazil's penalty box, laid the ball off with his first touch to Gago and went for the return pass in the area. But the ex-Boca Juniors midfielder had spotted Ángel Di María cutting in from the left wing and played the ball his way. Di María struck a cross-come-shot that Kun, tightly marked and on the run, deflected into the back of the net with his chest. That made it 1-0 to Argentina. A scream of emotion rose out of Kun, who then put his thumb in his mouth to announce to the world that he was to become a father. He was 20 years old and the triumphant embrace he shared with Messi simply mirrored the other successes that they had enjoyed together three years earlier, at the Under-20 World Cup in the Netherlands. It was also a forerunner to the many future goal celebrations they would share together in the light blue and white of the Argentinian national team.

Not being able to give the boy their chosen second name was of minor concern to Leo and Adriana, compared with what happened as they left hospital.

The two of them were still considered to be minors – Leo being 19 years of age and Adriana having recently turned 18 – and they were not legally married. Argentinian legislation did not allow a child to take the paternal surname if the father in question was a minor. As such, the medical certificate with the proof of their son's birth, handed to the couple in the hospital, only indicated the boy's maternal surname, Agüero.

This certificate was written up with the details from the only personal identity document that Adriana had to hand: a copy of her own birth certificate that she had brought with her from Tucumán. The proof of birth, signed by the obstetrician Liliana Rivara and the 'participating witness' Graciela L. Mercado, makes reference to the birth of a baby boy called Sergio Leonel Agüero, on June 2nd, 1988 at 15:23 at Varela 1301, the address of the Piñero hospital. It goes on to indicate that the baby's mother is Adriana del Valle Agüero, an 18-year-old Argentinian who, as the certificate explains, disposed of 'no documents'. The fields reserved for the first name and surname of the father, normally indicated on birth certificates at the time, remained empty.

Four years later, by which time they were no longer legally considered to be minors, they were once more prevented from rectifying this omission.

For them both to be fully recognised as Sergio's parents, they needed to provide their respective national identity documents in perfect condition.

"From then on, we kept on having issues with our documentation. Our national identity documents had been lost in the flood," says Adriana, who admits that they had never paid much attention to keeping them in order beforehand. "So Leo could not be formally recognised as the father, nor could his name appear on the birth certificate. They wouldn't let us. I still only had my birth certificate, but to do anything – legally speaking – we would both need to have our papers in order."

Just like at the hospital, they were given a birth certificate at the civil registry with the following information: "Piñero area,

Volume 2A, number 1144, year 1988". It details, just as the hospital certificate had done previously, the name of Sergio Leonel Agüero. The fields reserved for the first name and surname of the father are, once more, left blank.

It worried Leo that Sergio's surname in the official documents was Agüero rather than Del Castillo. He would have liked the boy to have taken his family name.

The pride that he felt towards his son, however, far outweighed this inconvenience, and the prominence of the Del Castillo genes became perfectly clear in all that Sergio was to go on and accomplish.

"It always felt to me like I was born to play football, as if this had always been my destiny. And I also knew that it would fulfil one of my father's dreams. His friends are always telling me what an amazing player he was as a kid; they even tell me that he was better than I am. And well, I obviously inherited it, didn't I? I've managed to do what he never quite managed. And so much of this is down to him. My mum, on the other hand, knows nothing about football. Unbelievable though it might seem, the first time she came to see me play was on the day that I made my debut in the Primera División. But she still knew everything that was going on in my life. On more than one occasion when she felt like she needed to, without me knowing, she came down to a training session to put some of the other pushy mothers back in their place. She would always defend her children to the hilt. I believe that I inherited her guts, her dedication, her fighting spirit, her generosity. She has always been an example to me."

SERGIO AGÜERO

Goat's milk

Leo and Adriana's status as minors also worked against them when they tried to get the all-clear for Sergio to return home. The only way that they could all leave hospital was to have Leo's step-brother sign a document serving as proof that he would take responsibility for them.

On the day that Sergio was discharged, a sporting event just so happened to be attracting coverage from all sorts of media outlets. On June 18th, 1988 Racing Club drew with Cruzeiro in Brazil and in doing so won the Supercopa. It was the first piece of silverware that the other club from Avellaneda had claimed in 22 years. Coached by Alfio 'Coco' Basile and featuring the talents of 'Pato' Fillol, the Uruguayan Rubén Paz, Néstor Fabbri and Ramón Ismael Medina Bello, the team's triumph sent its fans into delirium as they celebrated the end of such a long trophy drought. The preferred target of their gloating was their fierce local rival, Independiente, whose fans would have to withstand a barrage of often cruel jokes at their expense.

The coincidence of the two events, however, later came to seem like a divine signal. It would become clear that fate was reserving more than one opportunity, in the years to come, for the baby leaving hospital to allow fans of *El Rojo*[1] to take revenge on their lifelong enemy. And on such occasions, the barrage of jokes would be sent back in the opposite direction.

Sergio was always Adriana's most demanding child, particularly when he was hungry. Although he was breastfed until

---

[1] *El Rojo* is the nickname of Independiente.

eight months – "every three hours, at least," says his mother – this was not enough on its own. The first solution they found to satisfy his appetite was to supplement his diet with milk bought from a man with a cart who passed by their door. He did not sell cow's milk, but rather goat's milk. "It was all we could afford," Adriana smiles. "Cheaper but, very definitely, milk nonetheless. And not too bad for him at all." However, from the age of three months she also started to feed him solids.

"Sergio was a very quiet baby. But he had an incredible appetite. I already knew that, from his fourth or fifth month onwards, we would have to start giving him other food. But he was already demanding more at two months of age. So I started to feed him soup, pumpkin, anything…" says Adriana who, from this moment, would spend a large part of every day cleaning Jessica and Sergio's nappies.

"We bought fabric," she says, "then trimmed it down and made it into *chiripás*[2]. We could never have given them disposable nappies, they were far too expensive."

Leo and Adriana's financial circumstances were indeed rather precarious. But, as it went, they would not have been able to buy one-use nappies even if they had wanted to. This was because in February 1989 – with Sergio turning eight months, coinciding with another pregnancy for Adriana – the so-called Primavera Plan came into effect.

Devised by Raúl Alfonsín's government in order to curb the soaring levels of inflation, the plan caused a sharp currency devaluation that led to unprecedented hyperinflation in the

---

[2] Amerindian trousers made with a cloth tucked in at the front.

country. Argentinians were unable to pay for their shopping at supermarket tills, as the prices of products that had been taken from the display racks only minutes earlier had already gone up. This phenomenon was accompanied by sudden shortages of certain products, disposable nappies among them. The rate of inflation, which had stood at 9.6% in February 1989, reached 78.4% in May. This exacerbation of the economic slump was then followed by a social and political breakdown.

In the middle of widespread supermarket lootings, early elections were called and power was handed to the victor, the *peronist*[3] Carlos Menem. The rate of poverty had grown from around 25% in February to a record 47.3% in October. Every layer of society was affected but, as was the case during the floods, the poorest people bore the main brunt.

For the Agüero-Del Castillo household, things took a real downturn when the bakery where Leo worked fell victim to the crisis and shut down. Mass bankruptcies, spreading to countless companies and businesses across Argentina, caused a significant rise in the rate of unemployment.

Jobless, without a regular wage and in the absence of any new employment opportunities, Leo sought the only refuge available to him: football. The shopkeepers at González Catán's bigger shops and butchers had their own teams which competed in various tournaments, and they always kept his name on file. This playmaker, with the number 10 shirt on his back, stood out above everyone. He was therefore in high demand. For a long time, getting paid for playing football at weekends was the

---

[3] Peronism is a political movement based on the legacy of former President of Argentina Juan Domingo Perón and his second wife, Eva Perón.

only way for Leo to earn some money, aside from odd jobs that would come his way only rarely.

"Tournaments were played for money in various neighbour-hoods, so I would try to play in as many matches as possible," says Leo, recalling those difficult times with a smile. "On Sundays, I would play up to five games in one day. If the team that had invited me to play were eliminated, another would always come knocking. I always got by because they saw that I knew what I was doing on the pitch."

Furthermore, at night he would enter penalty competitions where 10 teams of two would each pay 10 pesos to enter. It was a straight knock-out tournament, with the winners taking home the pot. Between the football tournaments and the penalty competitions – where he would invariably reach the final – Leo managed to scrape together enough money to at least feed his family. That family had welcomed a new addition on July 12th, 1989, with the birth of Gabriela, the third member of the young Del Castillo-Agüero clan.

The Chetti family

Sergio, who by this time was already crawling everywhere, had stopped sleeping in his parents' bed and was now sleeping side-by-side in Jessica's bed. Meanwhile, it was little Gabriela's turn to sleep in with their parents. In this way, this young family of five managed to all inhabit a house that seemed increasingly small for them. Yet despite the arrival of his little sister, it was still Sergio who demanded the most attention. As soon as he was awake, he would follow Adriana wherever she went.

"He was very much a mummy's boy," says Adriana. "Wherever I went, he followed behind. But always crawling – he was a bit too lazy to start walking." This lethargy over taking his first steps lasted until the end of 1989, by which time he was already 18 months old.

"One day I turned around and there he was, stood perfectly still on the edge of our bed and smiling from ear to ear. He just started walking, and from that point on he never looked back. That's not to say that he didn't carry on following me everywhere. And if I went out, he would cry so much that his face turned purple," remembers Adriana.

In February 1990, after returning briefly to Tucumán in search of employment, they resolved to move back to Buenos Aires and start afresh. But they would not be able to carry on where they had left off at their house in González Catán. In their absence, what few possessions they had left behind were stolen, and they had to look for another place to live.

They managed to rent a modest property at 1090 Calle Pedro Morán, in Florencio Varela, south of Buenos Aires. It was a small house constructed from a typical mixture of lime and sand, without any external rendering. There was only one bedroom but at least, unlike their previous home, the house had a kitchen and toilet.

Their time in this neighbourhood – a hard-up, working class area with dirt roads – was short-lived, but significant nonetheless. As it was here they got to know a family, one of whose members would have the privilege of bestowing a nickname upon Leo and Adriana's son that he would carry long into the future and that would, in time, be the trademark by which that child would become internationally famous.

*Sunday, September 23rd, 2007. **The Vicente Calderón stadium. Atletico Madrid vs. Racing Santander. 69 minutes on the clock.***

On this day Sergio Agüero put his name forward as the true and rightful heir to Fernando 'El Niño' Torres — who had recently departed for Liverpool — and thereby assumed the mantle previously held by Kiko, Paulo Futre and the Argentinians Rubén Cano and 'Ratón' Ayala. In great form after taking home all the honours from the Under-20 World Cup in Canada, Sergio started his second season in Spain playing the sort of football that justified the millions that Atletico had spent on acquiring his services. He was on target with a header from José Antonio Reyes' right-wing cross that left goalkeeper Toño with no chance, registering his side's second goal on the day and taking his personal tally to three goals in four games. By this time he had already started the move that led to Raúl García's opening goal, and he would go on to set up Diego Forlán with a searching through-ball for the third. When he departed on 85 minutes, to be replaced by Mista, a roar sounded out around the Calderón stadium. The fans had coined a new anthem: "Kun, Kun, Kun, Kun…" It was part-battle cry, part-football chant, and entirely in honour of the new man leading the chorus out on the field of play.

As fate would have it, once again there was a football pitch right in front of the house that the Agüero-Del Castillo family had found in Florencio Varela. This *potrero*, known as 'La Quinta', was nothing more than a dirt pitch complete with metal goalposts without nets, but it was here that the spicy local derbies between rival neighbourhoods would take place. It was the first pitch that little Sergio would begin to go to, now that he had just turned two, although initially it was just to go along there with his father.

Leo was 22 years old by this stage and his football ability remained undiminished, allowing him once more to earn some extra pesos by taking part in the local tournaments on that nearby pitch. He may have been a total newcomer and unknown in the neighbourhood, but his ability was such that a team called Fantasma invited him to join them as soon as they saw him play. Thirty-team tournaments were played on Sundays, with matches starting at 08:30 in the morning and being played until dusk. Each match lasted 15 minutes. Everyone put in some money, and the winning team kept the pot. It was through the games played on that bit of open ground, the true spirit of football, that the Agüero-Del Castillo family started getting to know the people who lived in the area. They grew particularly close to the Chetti family who lived in the same block but on a different street, named Calle Argentina.

The Chettis, although twice their age, became Leo and Adriana's first friends in Buenos Aires. Jorge Chetti, then 45 years of age, was a metalworker who still enjoyed the recognition of being the star centre-forward for both his factory and his trade union's football teams. He and his wife Elsa had six children.

One of their sons, called Sergio but known to all by the nickname 'Cuevita', had inherited his father's football ability and he starred in the games he regularly played for a team named Juventud Unida at 'La Quinta'. Through their shared love of football, a friendship naturally blossomed between him and Leo. In one small step, this friendship evolved and the two families became a part of each other's daily routines. And so that is how it became a regular sight to see Cuevita taking little

Sergio's hand and leading him to the *potrero*, and then seeing the boy return covered head to toe in mud after spending his time rolling around on the floor alongside the pitches while the matches were being played. Cuevita's sister, Susy, was left in charge of the little ones when the two sets of parents were at work and so would often also accompany the two of them to the pitches.

In those days Leo was taking any odd jobs that came his way, which were often on construction sites, even if he was not really cut out for this type of work. At least, in this way, he scraped together enough money to feed his children. With his modest income he could also afford to buy his family their first luxury item, a 14-inch screen colour television set, their first ever, purchased at one of the shops on Calle Boedo in the capital city. Given that paying for a cable television service was out of the question, they had to make do with picking up channels via the set's built-in aerial. This did not guarantee them the best picture quality and also meant that they could only receive the free to air channels. It was only after much juggling, and thanks to a flimsy homemade aerial fashioned out of a potato and two knitting needles, that they were occasionally able to clear the fuzzy snow that would interfere with the picture whenever they tried to watch a programme. It was on this small set that they watched and suffered during World Cup Italia '90, as Germany won the title against an Argentinian side – marshalled by an embattled Diego Armando Maradona – that had reached the final against all the odds.

Completely detached from such matters, and unconcerned by the interference to the television picture, at exactly four o'clock every afternoon little Sergio would perch on the edge of his parents' bed, his eyes glued to the screen as he watched a Japanese cartoon that simply captivated him.

Only 26 episodes had been made of the cartoon, which dates back to 1975. But they had been translated and broadcast around the world, and enjoyed some success in territories as diverse as Great Britain, Canada, Australia, Mexico, Russia and Italy.

The original name of the series was 'Wanpaku Amukashi Kum Kum', although in English it was simply called 'Kum Kum'. The cartoon was set in the Stone Age and followed the adventures of a mischievous boy who lived with his family and friends in a tribe at the foot of a mountain, and who spent his days running around the countryside and dexterously jumping over crags with a club in his hand.

Kum Kum's adventures were intended to teach young viewers that the path to adulthood could be a bumpy one. But the skilled work of the series' creators, who combined humour with a dose of realism, captured a huge audience of fans from all over the world. In Argentina, the cartoon's name translated as 'Kum Kum, the little caveman' and it was broadcast on the ATC channel. Not only was this the only television channel that had remained under state ownership following the privatisation of the rest of the capital's broadcasters under Carlos Menem's *peronist* government, but it was one of only two channels whose signal could be picked up on the television that Leo had bought. The public channel's scarce funds obliged it to repeat outdated programming, including the young Sergio Agüero's favourite series.

This programme was actually one of the few things that would calm the boy down when his mother had to leave him and go to work. Adriana was still working by the hour as a domestic cleaner, often alongside her new friend Elsa, Jorge Chetti's wife. The country's economic situation was going from bad to worse, and many factories continued to lay off staff. Jorge was one of the many Argentinians who increasingly found themselves at home during the day, meaning that he was forever in the company of the Agüero-Del Castillo children, who were spending more and more time at his house.

Kun

Nobody remembers exactly when it happened. But soon enough, people started calling Sergio by the name of the character in the Japanese cartoon that fascinated him so much. Some point towards his physical resemblance to the cartoon character, who wore a similar fringe. Others say it had more to do with their shared penchant for mischief, and cite the little toy cars that Sergio would smash against walls. Or maybe the nickname was chosen because he used to imitate the way the cartoon character ran.

Nineteen years later and at the age of 63 years, Jorge Chetti nevertheless still claims responsibility for the nickname and, with barely disguised pride, recalls another reason why it stuck. Perhaps down to the sheer number of times he had watched Kum Kum on the television, Jorge points out that the few monosyllabic noises that used to come out of Sergio's mouth all sounded like "koo" or "koom" (as Argentinians pronounce 'kum'). These were the sounds that he would make when trying to say something, or make a request.

"He was so small that he could barely pronounce any words. Everything he tried to say came out sounding like "koo" or "koom". This was his response to everything. There I was trying to teach him the names of different things, but going mad as he just repeated the same noises. From then on, I started to say "Kun, come over here" or "Kun, go over there"... This is when we all started to call him Kun. And that nickname, from such innocuous beginnings, stuck forever."

What is absolutely certain is that the first complete words that Sergio learned to say were "Mamá" and "Papá". As well as these words, and the expressions that Jorge Chetti was teaching him, Kun started adding others and quickly widened his vocabulary. "He would repeat everything he heard. He developed a really wide and varied repertoire from walking back from the football pitch with his dad and Cuevita. And you can quite imagine what sort of words they were...," counters Adriana. It is not hard to imagine. This repertoire, as Adriana calls it, was made up of the sort of insults that are inevitably heard on football pitches the world over.

Jorge Chetti – sat in the same house where he first called the boy Kun, and where Kun would grow to call him "grandpa" – recalls that he lived with a ball at his feet.

"Absolutely, ever since he was tiny. He would kick it up in the air, really powerfully. To think, he was only three years old... I called him a frog, because he had a puffed out chest like a frog. He already looked like a footballer, even back then... but we never thought he would go so far," he explains while proudly showing off his collection of Sergio's shirts from various teams, complete with personal dedications (one of which reads: 'to my grandpa Jorge Chetti').

His wife Elsa adds: "I'll never forget the sight of him arriving home, my son's boots tied around his neck and a ball under his arm."

It was the difficult times that really brought the Chetti and Agüero-Del Castillo households closer together.

"When Adriana had something to eat, she would bring it round to ours to share with us. On many other occasions, we would bring the food. Just imagine, we had six children and they had three. So we shared what we could get our hands on, even eating the frogs that Jorge caught around here. The men would also go fishing, with Leo and Kun."

On June 11th, 1991, the three children mentioned by Elsa would become four, following the birth of Kun's third sister Mayra. It was none other than Cuevita who took Adriana to the maternity ward where she gave birth. Many years later, Kun would reserve a particular fondness for Cuevita, who was always warm company at the times when Kun's successes in football had led to him living far away from his country and family.

Six weeks after Mayra had been born, the Agüero-Del Castillo family was on the move once more. The owner of the house on Calle Pedro Morán where they were living had decided to sell up and demanded that, should they want to buy it from him, they could only do so in exchange for all of their possessions inside. Having put so much effort into gathering together a respectable collection of furniture for their family, Leo and Adriana simply could not accept the offer and would therefore have to look elsewhere.

It was for this reason that, on August 30th, 1991, the Agüero-Del Castillo family moved from Florencio Varela to Quilmes.

Or to the humble neighbourhood of Los Eucaliptus, to be exact, also in the south of the extended metropolis of Buenos Aires. Leo and Adriana, aged 23 years and 21 years respectively, together with their four children Jessica (5), Sergio (3), Gabriela (2) and the barely six-week-old Mayra, would begin a new stage in their lives during which their hardships would in time be left behind and replaced by new dreams. A stage during which the boy of the family would start his gradual transformation, from little Sergio to 'Kun Agüero' himself.

Los Eucaliptus

The district of Quilmes is one of the oldest in the Greater Buenos Aires area, located 20 kilometres to the south of the capital city. It owes its name to the Quilmes people, an indigenous tribe who, just like the Agüero-Del Castillo family, were natives of the territory where the province of Tucumán now lies.

The stern resistance shown by the Quilmes people in the face of their Spanish invaders, who only overcame the tribe after 130 years of fighting, typifies their sense of pride and fighting spirit. When they were finally defeated, they were driven out of their fortress homeland in the Calchaquíes Valleys and, in a form of ethnic cleansing, were led by the Spanish to the south of Buenos Aires on the banks of the La Plata river.

In the year 1666, following a journey of over 1,300 kilometres during which hundreds lost their lives, 200 families were forcibly settled in a reservation. The area that they inhabited would later be named after that original, indomitable people. And 300 years down the line, Quilmes was to become one of the most thriving suburbs in the metropolitan area of Buenos Aires, made up of nine towns spread over an area of 125 square kilometres, and boasting a socially diverse population of over 500,000 residents.

In the 1960s, particularly at weekends, the area's plentiful green spaces became the venue for impassioned games of football played out between local friends and families. Residents of the towns of Quilmes Este and Bernal Este flocked, in particular, to a piece of land positioned where the two met, at the crossing of Avenida de La Plata and Avenida Lamadrid, the latter still a dirt road at the time. In this vast park, stretching 200 metres in each direction up the two roads, football asserted its dominance over all other sports.

The park was notable not just for its football pitches, but also for the tall eucalyptus trees that surrounded them and continued to grow for another 200 metres beyond the park's boundaries. The biggest pitch was also the best maintained, with nets on each of its goals, and was therefore reserved for adult matches and local league games. The other two, smaller pitches were used by school children, who would race to start their games as soon as classes were over.

All those who frequented the park knew to take extra special care on windy and rainy days, as the trees had weak branches and they were afraid of being hit if one of them came crashing down. Today, residents with long memories can still recall the park keeper's little hut, whose walls were painted in vertical stripes of black, red and white. The park was known as La Soledad, supposedly after an old billiards bar located on the other side of the same corner of Lamadrid and La Plata, facing the park.

On the other corner, just by the start of a row of eucalyptus trees marking the entrance to the pitches, one of the locals would generally be found selling the typical street food known as *choripán*, a traditional Argentinian sausage sandwich. A stop-off at this typical, improvised stall was an absolute must for those who, having finished playing, wanted to kick off their own form of 'extra time' where food would be eaten and debates would rage about the game that had just been played.

The La Soledad park was a world of its own, an open air meeting point for all the men of the surrounding neighbourhoods, which largely consisted of low houses inhabited by middle-class families who were keen to climb the social ladder. But this mini-society that revolved around the park was to suffer a heavy blow at the end of the 1960s. Around this time, the de facto government of Juan Carlos Onganía implemented a controversial plan to wipe out the *villas de emergencia*. The *villas* were precarious, densely populated settlements that generally appeared in lowland areas, offering polluted groundwater but not equipped with drinking water or sewers. From 1940 onwards, such settlements expanded significantly throughout the metropolitan area of Buenos Aires.

Thousands of countryside residents, who had been suffering from a stagnant rural economy, were attracted to the capital throughout the decade due to a high demand for labour, triggered by the process of industrialisation. However, the country's constant political and economic crises, which led to the closure of numerous companies and an increase in unemployment, saw an increasing number of citizens marginalised from industrial production. As a consequence, both the number of precarious settlements and the size of their populations inevitably increased. The Onganía dictatorship now pompously pledged to relocate the residents of these *villas* to large purpose-built housing developments. Until the construction of the latter was complete, those who were being uprooted would be forcibly, but supposedly temporarily, moved to areas known as the *Núcleos Habitacionales Transitorios* (Transitory Housing Hubs), where each family would reside in a pre-constructed hut measuring 13.3 square metres.

One of the locations chosen for this stage of transition – which would eventually prove to be anything but temporary, as construction works remained incomplete and people were left to fend for themselves – was none other than the La Soledad park. For the residents of Quilmes Este and Bernal Este, the arrival en masse of these groups of marginalised people resulted in the loss of not only their land, but also of parts of their identity, their personal history and their everyday leisure activities that they so enjoyed. This new marginalised community settled down and quickly started spreading directly over their much-loved football pitches. And so it was that the days of meeting up and playing football at La Soledad were confined to their favourite childhood memories.

What they were not to know at this stage was that the magic sprinkled over those pitches by so many years of football was to remain imbued in the earth, like some sort of spirit from a golden age, and that it would then be mysteriously transferred to a future resident of the area. And that 20 years down the line, fate would have it that from this particular precarious settlement – which would go on to take its name from the very eucalyptus trees that lined the park – the figure of Kun Agüero would emerge to turn the dreams of the children of La Soledad into reality.

Spirits of La Soledad

The first vivid memories that Kun has of his childhood are from his days in the *villa* of Los Eucaliptus in Quilmes. He arrived with his family in 1991 at only three years of age, and would leave in 1999, by which time he was eleven and his footballing ability was already starting to pay dividends on and off the field of play. This ability was nurtured for the eight years during which he lit up the *potreros* of that very neighbourhood.

Even though Los Eucaliptus was small in comparison to the other *villas* of Greater Buenos Aires, it proudly boasted no less than three football pitches. Two of them were used mainly for women's and children's football, while the playing surface on the third one was larger in size but similarly made of bare earth. This final pitch was the only one still standing from what had at one point been the La Soledad park, and it was here that footballers, young and old, would contest their hard-fought local leagues or challenge teams from other neighbourhoods nearby. The chalk that marked out the touchlines, penalty areas, halfway line and centre circle regularly disappeared, and had to be marked out again when possible.

The lines were not just rubbed out because of the many

games played there, but also because the pitch was immediately surrounded by many of the *villa*'s flimsy houses. This meant that people were continually crossing from one side of the pitch to the other, scuffing their feet on the lines as they went about their daily routines. But this space did have one obvious benefit: it was one of the few areas in the settlement where no remains were to be found of the trees, the majority being eucalypti, that lined the ground on which the *villa* was built. The closest trees stood either behind the little houses, or at least well back from the touchlines. The games could therefore be played on an unobstructed surface, free from roots or anything else that might impede the players.

The same could not be said, on the other hand, about the two smaller pitches. This was especially true of the one beside Avenida Lamadrid, which also served as one of the entrances to the *villa*. There, a tight row of seven sturdy eucalyptus trees divided Avenida Lamadrid from the neighbourhood and one of its football pitches. This particular *potrero* was located in an especially poor area within the community, where some of the original trees were still standing.

One such tree was right behind an improvised wooden structure that served as a goal. As a result, eucalyptus fruit was strewn all over the pitch, getting in the way of the players and pricking their feet. Therefore, out of necessity, those who played there became blessed with a unique sense of control, as the ball seemed to have a mind of its own.

The pitch was 40 metres wide and on its far side stood the first houses, packed in tightly next to one another, that marked the starting point of the *villa*. The neighbourhood then stretched into the distance by way of a series of intricate, narrow alleyways. Inevitably enough, and remaining faithful to their tradition when moving house, the Agüero-Del Castillo family were to move into that first row of dwellings, directly facing the football pitch. In fact, the front door was barely half a metre from the makeshift spot from which the team playing left-to-right would take their corners. Football had always been in the background of family life and, with a pitch now quite literally on their doorstep, it took on an even more prominent status. Kun was to grow up in this unique environment, and it was only natural that the sounds, smells and colours of football would gradually seep into his pores.

Years down the line, when he was already a celebrated footballer looking back at photographs of this strange set-up, Kun showed some friends in Madrid that little gap between the old house and his beloved pitch.

"Look there, right where the corner is, that's where I would sit and watch the games when I was little. And that door to one side, that was the entrance to my house," he told them excitedly.

What Sergio did not know was that the *villa* of Los Eucaliptus, and the house in which he resided, had been constructed on top of the football pitches of La Soledad. The very pitches whose legendary spirit would seize his body and soul and, via a supernatural process of transferral, would bestow upon Kun the collective footballing virtues of all those who used to patrol the *potreros*. Or at the very least, that is what those who reside here – in this corner of suburbia made from dirt and dreams – would have you believe.

*Thursday, July 12th, 2007. **National Soccer Stadium, Toronto. The Round of 16 at the***

Under-20 World Cup in Canada. Argentina vs. Poland. A minute into the second half.

On this day, Kun Agüero confirmed that he should always trust the instincts that he had first nurtured on the football pitches of Los Eucaliptus. Poland's Dawid Janczyk had opened the scoring, before Ángel Di María temporarily brought the scores level. The second half was barely underway when Kun received Emiliano Insúa's pass from the left in the penalty area with his back to goal. Marked by Adrian Marek, he deftly controlled the ball with his right foot and allowed it to bounce, before imperiously flicking it over the defender and dispatching a left-footed volley into the far corner past goalkeeper Bartossz Bialkowsky. That gave Argentina a 2-1 lead. And four minutes from the end of normal time, he served up another finish oozing with audacious cheek, a majestic dummy leaving the Polish goalkeeper on the seat of his pants and allowing Kun's right foot to do the rest. That sealed the 3-1 win and a place in the quarter-finals. He was 19 years of age, and his talent seemed to be the product of a convergence between his own gifts and the spirit of those football lovers who used to meet at the potreros of La Soledad.

Two birthdays in one

At the time that the Agüero-Del Castillo family settled into Los Eucaliptus, it was calculated that over 500,000 people were crammed into the 385 such *villas* found in the Greater Buenos Aires area. However, despite a comparable social make-up, Los Eucaliptus was different to others such as Itatí, also part of Quilmes and one of the country's largest *villas* with 50,000 inhabitants spread over 100 acres. It was much smaller, with approximately 1,000 families occupying an area of 30 acres that extended 200 metres beyond the old stretch of park that had once been known as La Soledad. The property that Leo managed to buy – paying 500 pesos, money that he says he "scraped together by playing lots of football matches" – was part of the first row of houses and was a simple house made from a lime and sand material, with a large living area, a narrow bedroom and a toilet, lying alongside others of very similar construction.

Although they arrived in high spirits, life at the new house did not get off to the best of starts. Indeed, they moved in on August 30th, 1991, which is Santa Rosa's day in the calendar of the saints. On that very evening, Santa Rosa lived up to the popular myth that the arrival of her day is always marked by stormy weather.

"The roof was full of holes. I spent the night making sure that no water got in, to avoid another flood. But it was no use…" remembers Adriana who, angered by this turn of events, made sure that they spent the next day carrying out the necessary works to ensure that it would be the last time they went through this trauma.

"We put new metal sheets on the roof, we plastered the outer walls, we split the bedroom so that the children slept in one half on bunk beds and we slept in the other half. We tiled the floor and also had a bit of space for a dining area and kitchen," says Leo.

Adapting to life in this new *villa* was not all plain sailing for the Agüero-Del Castillo family, although they also admit that they never had serious problems. "We didn't know anyone. And more than once we had to keep certain people at arm's length, the sort that you always get who want to take advantage of you. Life in a *villa* is never easy, but they steered clear of us," says Adriana.

However, to prevent anything untoward happening, Leo and Adriana made sure that one of the two of them was always back at the house with the children. Susy, Jorge Chetti's daughter, was there to help out when neither of them could do so. The absence of trustworthy neighbours lasted until December 31st, 1991, when they made their first true friends in Los Eucaliptus. A couple of the same age, who lived in the adjacent house, passed by to say hello and from this moment a bond was formed that remains to this day.

Gustavo, whose surname just so happened to be Castillo, and his wife Ana became good neighbours and the best of friends. At this time Leo, whose efforts to pay the bills took him from one job to another, was driving a taxi and Adriana was still getting paid by the hour as a domestic cleaner.

Thanks to the money coming in from these jobs, in addition to a small amount of savings and out of a lot of love, they were finally able to host a birthday party for Sergio in June of 1992. It would be his first party, although the celebrations were not only for him.

Taking advantage of the proximity of Kun and Mayra's birthdays, on June 2nd and 11th respectively, the family would simultaneously celebrate their son turning four and the first birthday of their youngest. And so it was that Sergio – surrounded by balloons and dressed in jeans and a red jumper with a blue collar, complete with a charming embroidered dog on its chest – finally had the chance to blow out the candles of his own birthday cake.

The cake had been made by Jorge Ariza, a pastry chef who worked with their neighbour Gustavo Castillo in a nearby bakery. Jorge was known simply as 'The Baker', and he would be one of the first local amateur football scouts to take Kun under his wing. But Jorge was not alone in helping to shape the young boy's character. As the years went by, many others involved in football would do likewise. All of them would first have to gain the approval and permission of a discerning Leo who, drawing on his own childhood experiences, intuitively knew to leave part of his son's personal and footballing development in the safe hands of others.

Without Sergio's exceptional ability and his father's shrewd guidance, none of what he later achieved would have been possible. Yet the additional supervision of good people, who cared only for Kun's natural development and not for the economic interests that would later emerge as the extent of the boy's talent became apparent, was the last piece of a jigsaw that would nurture his growth and put him on the path to greatness.

"I know what it means to trudge through the mud, to sleep without a roof over your head, and to have to scrape together enough money just to feed your children. It was a constant struggle for me and Leo. That's why we feel so proud. You have to remember where you come from and make sure you never change, no matter how much money you have. Of course, money can buy you material possessions. And we've been able to buy things that we never previously had, all thanks to Sergio. But money is no guarantee of anything. If you have

last-minute complications in childbirth, money can't help you.
Some people think that money can buy love. Absolute nonsense.
I always say to Sergio and the others that if you are not bitter
or hateful towards others, you are a better person. You have to
stay faithful to strong values and be generous. To help others,
regardless of what anybody has or doesn't have. Even at the
worst of times, we never refused to give a helping hand or a
plate of food to anyone. And ultimately, if you do this without
any self-interest, life will reward you."

ADRIANA AGÜERO

'Gracias Kun!'

In 1993, a few months before his fifth birthday, Sergio started attending a nursery school located close to Los Eucaliptus on Avenida Dardo Rocha. It took him longer to settle in at preschool than Adriana had expected. For the first few months, in fact, she had to wait outside the school each day in case there was some sort of incident, which there was more often than not. Sergio was averse to being kept away from his mother in a classroom and, if he was unable to draw anyone's attention, would get up to all kinds of mischief.

"He started crying every time I left. He would make a mess, turn on taps, run all over the place… The teachers couldn't control him," Adriana recalls.

Despite his initial troubles, Sergio did take part in the celebrations to commemorate the May Revolution, dressed in a patriotic outfit – complete with a top hat that Adriana had hired – and dancing with a little girl who was dressed as an old lady.

However, Sergio's problems continued and the school recommended that he see a psychologist.

"I took him to the children's hospital and, after four interviews to assess him, they told me that there was nothing to worry about and that their tests had shown him to be a very intelligent boy. They explained to me that Sergio was used to having more freedom, and that he found it hard to spend so much time in an enclosed space. They asked me how I would like to be shut in one place for eight hours," says Adriana.

The diagnosis made by the specialists only served to reiterate what had become clear: Sergio had no trouble socialising, but he just preferred to have more freedom. The psychologists were unaware, however, that the moments he most cherished were actually those that he spent playing football, the sport which had already become one of his favourite pastimes. Nothing captivated him like playing with a football, and this attraction to the beautiful game was only getting stronger and stronger.

In 1994, Sergio swapped the light blue check overalls of nursery school for the white uniform of primary school, as he started first grade, at school number 36 in Quilmes, seven blocks from Los Eucaliptus. He started his first day full of enthusiasm, proudly showing off his new backpack, but over the subsequent days that initial excitement gradually dwindled away. He did not have the same troubles as he experienced at nursery school and, in actual fact, he even received praise for his drawing ability.

However, it was already very clear in his mind that those four hours of school per day, from eight o'clock in the morning until midday, could not pass by quickly enough. He would literally drag Leo or Adriana all the way back to their house, and of course the football pitches, after school finished, forever anxious to be back on the *potreros* of Los Eucaliptus with his friends, to start the next in their endless round of games.

In the evenings, a local derby would be played between those who lived towards the front of the *villa* and those whose houses were nearer to the back. Given the location of his house, Sergio started off playing for the former. But due to the influence of Cristian Formiga, a boy of his age from the other side of the *villa* with whom he struck up a strong friendship, he ended up changing teams.

"With Kun on your team it was always harder to lose. Or, more to the point, it was easier to win," Cristian asserts 15 years later, at the same *potreros* and with the same easy smile.

Cristian knew Kun as well as anyone back in those days and, in his straightforward and modest way, made a good case for why his friend should swap and play for his team. He says that Kun's only argument against it was that the Dragon Ball Z cartoons started at the same time on television, and he did not want to miss them. However, what ultimately tipped the balance for Kun was the prize on offer for the winners. For even though the majority of those taking part were only five or six years old, they all managed to scrape together a few cents to give the winning team a pot to keep. It totalled no less than one whole peso, impressive takings for boys of their age.

"And with this money – a fortune for us – we would buy these little juices. They amounted to not much more than frozen fla- voured water, not quite an ice cream, and were really cheap, maybe ten cents each. They weren't the tastiest but it was a luxury for us, they were the cheapest ones there and the only ones we could afford," says Cristian.

For his part, Kun remembers a particular detail that set these games apart and stoked the fervour with which they were played even more.

"We played the first to eight goals. And the games were very tight. Sometimes we would start at three in the afternoon, and only finish three or four hours later. The problem was that nobody could score the winning goal, and every time someone equalised we'd have to keep adding more time. Eventually we had to bring in a time limit to stop the matches going on forever."

In those days in Los Eucaliptus, Sergio and Cristian formed a partnership that offered an unrivalled goal threat, one that was soon recruited by other teams who recognised the value of having this deadly duo in attack. Cristian's memories come flooding back as he chuckles about the two words that he used to repeat over and again in the games that he played alongside his partner in crime: "Gracias Kun!" Cristian was always their teams' top goal scorer thanks to Kun's precise passes, meaning that this cry of gratitude soon became a ritual that was repeated game after game.

The first club

It seemed perfectly natural to Leo and Adriana that Kun would like football, even if they did not envisage a great future for him in the sport at this stage. Adriana, in particular, was more concerned with other issues such as his schooling and his personal hygiene. Leo, on the other hand, was more concerned by his own form in the games of football he played. He had started to turn out in the competitive Liga de Bernal league, wearing the number 10 shirt with great distinction for Dardo Rocha, a team made up of local university students and young professionals.

It was there that he met Eduardo 'Motoneta' González, a journalist who hosted a radio programme all about Independiente de Avellaneda. González was one of those to give the Agüero-Del Castillo family a helping hand around this time, and would later provide them with crucial connections who helped Kun in his development.

"I played with that team on Sundays, and I'd take Sergio along to the matches with me. While the game was being played, he'd be behind one of the goals, being looked after by friends from the neighbourhood who had come to watch me play. I had my own fans," says a proud Leo, who recalls that he would soon start to look upon his son in a different light. "I went there to play my match, but at half-time, while we were having a rest, we would watch our sons playing two-on-two games. Sergio was the smallest and the shortest. And we used to kill ourselves laughing as he would lead the bigger, taller boys a merry dance. This was how, to my surprise and joy, I started to realise that Sergio's football ability was something really quite out of the ordinary."

As well as joining the Dardo Rocha team, Leo was also playing for a team in Los Eucaliptus called 'El túnel del tiempo' (The Time Tunnel). By then, Kun was a regular companion for his dad on match days. "There was a time I went to play a tournament at a club called Open, in Avellaneda. Sergio hung around, as he always did, off the pitch with the other kids. The guy that had organised the tournament, who was the manager of another team called Club Social y Deportivo Belgrano, came up to me after my game had finished and asked me how old my son was. He told me that he'd seen him play with the other boys and that he wanted him to join his team. Because Sergio would just get the ball and run rings round everyone. He really caught the eye. I didn't need long to think about it, I just gave him my blessing. That was the first club he played for," Leo confirms.

But he was not to stay there for long. He only managed to play in some preliminary matches for Belgrano in the Argentinian Children's Sports Federation (FADI) *baby fútbol*[1] league in Avellaneda, in which over 100 clubs compete. The FADI is the most competitive league in this area of southern Greater Buenos Aires, boasting around 320,000 residents and bordering the capital city itself. But the distance between their house in Los Eucaliptus and the club, located at number 3200 on Calle Belgrano, was too much of a hassle for Leo, who ended up deciding that it was not worth taking him all that way.

Sergio Neyra, the future manager of Belgrano who was 13 years old at the time and playing his last year in the FADI league, has vivid recollections of Kun's fleeting but eye-catching spell at his club.

"I remember he came with a friend called Cristian and that, as soon as he started to play, they came looking for me and said 'come to the pitch, this kid's impressive'. I could see it after only a few minutes. He just left the others strewn out on the floor. A complete natural..." he says in a notably measured way.

---

[1] As the name suggests, *baby fútbol* is a sport derived from association football. It is played on small pitches, with teams allowed only five players on the field of play at any time. It is particularly popular among children of between 5 and 13 years of age in Argentina, Chile, Uruguay and Colombia.

Belgrano is just one of the many local clubs scattered through-out Avellaneda, each separated by only a few blocks from the next. These clubs are a true social phenomenon and one that holds the key to the amazing structure of children's football, which feeds into the dependable pool of players who go on to star in the top leagues. Seven thousand children take part in the FADI leagues in Avellaneda alone, with 350 matches being played on 50 different pitches on any given Saturday. The leagues take place on an annual basis across five divisions: A, B, C, D and E. Teams are also divided into seven different age groups, starting with the six and seven-year-olds who just play friendlies designed to encourage their interest in the sport. The other five age groups, where games are played for points and teams can be promoted and relegated, are made up of children of 8 years and upwards. Seven separate games are played on each football pitch per day, starting at 2:30 in the afternoon and continuing until the evening with just a 10-minute break between them.

A vast organisational structure is required to maintain this continuous flow of games. Referees, supervisors and disciplin-ary panels are appointed, and particular arrangements are put in place to cater for all the parents, relatives and friends who meet up to watch the games. This phenomenon is not unique to Avellaneda, but something that takes place in all the districts of the metropolitan area, in all the towns of the Buenos Aires province, in the capital city itself and in all of Argentina's 22 provinces. In all of these places, different local tournaments akin to the FADI league are held, either in the *baby fútbol* or '*tierra*' formats, the latter, ('*earth*') being thus named in reference to the bare pitches on which its games are played.

Across the country, hundreds of thousands of youngsters demonstrate their passion and desire to be crowned champions of their age group, all the while fuelling their dreams of one day reaching the highest levels of senior football. In this way, every weekend Argentina becomes a vast breeding ground for young footballers, one that is renewed every year and that plays the role of a natural fountain, watering the young shoots of talent that spring up spontaneously across the country.

All the players are united by endless passion and a profound love of the game. But only certain chosen ones ever get to see their dreams become a reality. One of them was Sergio 'Kun' Agüero, whose natural talent – a gift that first shone through in his performances for teams in different leagues throughout the city and metropolitan area of Buenos Aires, such as Primero de Mayo, Loma Alegre, Los Primos, 20 de Junio, Pellerano Rojo, Crucesita Este and Bristol – would significantly and precociously develop, resulting in him becoming the youngest player ever to make his debut in the top flight of Argentinian football.

*Tuesday, September 16th, 2008. **Philips Stadium.** **Eindhoven, the Netherlands. Champions League.** **PSV vs. Atletico Madrid. Thirty-six minutes into** **the first half.***

On this night Kun Agüero led the way for his team, ensuring that Atletico's return to the Champions League, after an eleven-year absence, went as smoothly as possible. He had already opened the scoring in the first minute of the match, stealing a march on an opposing defender to convert Luis García's cross. Thirty-five minutes later, he would make it two. Frenchman Sinama Pongolle surged up the left flank and cut the ball back into the centre, where

Kun controlled it with his left foot on the edge of the six-yard box before sending a ferocious shot with the same foot past goalkeeper Andreas Isaksson. The two goals set Atletico on their way to a winning return, confirmed with a third from Maniche in the second half. They also served as notice that hunger to win is insatiable, and that there is no greater motivation than a passion for football fuelled by years of competitions where all that was at stake was glory itself.

Everything
Has A Start

Kun's brief spell at Belgrano proved to be just the start of what would become, over the following years, meat and drink for this tireless boy: a diet of non-stop, uninterrupted football. His journey as a footballer started in 1993, before he had even turned five years of age, and his first stops would be at Primero de Mayo in Bernal and Loma Alegre in Quilmes.

Not for one minute did Kun ever consider this footballing journey to be a chore, but he instead delighted in giving full rein to his permanent desire to play football, to enjoy himself and, in doing so, to perfect his virtuoso talent with the ball at his feet.

More specifically, the transition from playing on the pitches of Los Eucaliptus to competing in district leagues against much stronger opposition allowed Sergio, from an early age, to understand the camaraderie of his team-mates, the intimacy of a dressing room and the meaning of competition. This step up to a more demanding level of football nevertheless proved to be no trouble for Kun. Quite the contrary, in fact, as his natural gifts found a more befitting environment in which to develop. His young age was no barrier and he displayed a striking maturity on the pitch, there for all to see, both in terms of what he achieved and how natural it all appeared to him.

One of Kun's first opportunities to prove his precocious talent came about almost by chance. Jorge 'The Baker' Ariza, who had made the cake for Kun's fourth birthday, gladly accepted an invitation from his colleague Gustavo Castillo, the Agüero family's neighbour, to watch an impromptu tournament in which he would be playing for his local team. Although only personally involved in youth football, Jorge also enjoyed watching the occasional adult game too. His job as a baker aside, the 34-year-old spent all his free time looking for the right boys to form the best possible teams at Primero de Mayo, a community youth centre located on the intersection of Calle Pilcomayo and Calle Lafuente in Bernal Oeste that played in the FADI leagues.

Driving around in his ancient Siam Di Tella car, 'The Baker' would scour the *potreros* of the modest local neighbourhoods, where thousands of young footballers would be out kicking a ball around on any given day. Thanks to his keen eye for talent, combined with a personable nature that persuaded parents that his was the right team for their sons, Jorge was able to put together competitive teams whose loyalty, commitment and ability saw them competing for titles against the strongest teams.

This was not at the forefront of his mind, however, when he accepted Gustavo's invitation that afternoon. It was simply a good opportunity to head out with his friend and enjoy a game of football. However, on that day he saw the first signs of a path opening up for him, leading towards a dream that he had long since imagined – that of discovering a boy who could reach football's highest levels – and that would ultimately be made reality years later. For it just so happened that on his friend Gustavo's team, made up entirely of residents of Los Eucaliptus, there was one player – named Leo – who really caught his attention. Jorge appreciated the signs of a true footballer in Leo, someone who showed vision and class every time he touched the ball.

However, even more eye-catching, there seemed to be a smaller version of that talented player beside the pitch, later described by Jorge as a "short, stocky five or six-year-old boy with a good physique". "Run here", "play it there", he heard the boy shout with a voice that, although clearly that of a child, seemed unusually shrewd. When the match was over, he wasted no time in asking his friend Gustavo who the kid was.

"If he knew how to give those instructions," Jorge says today, "it's because he had the intelligence to read the game. I thought to myself that he had to be a good player. But I must admit that when I saw him play properly, he exceeded all my expectations."

The boy in question was none other than the son of the talented footballer that he had been watching moments earlier on the field of play or, to be more exact, Gustavo's neighbour back in Los Eucaliptus. His name was Leonel del Castillo, and his son had an odd nickname: Kun. He later discovered that the cakes that he had once made for Gustavo were in fact for the boy's fourth birthday party. He did not give it a second thought and, wasting no time, put together an offer for Sergio to join the team he was building at Primero de Mayo. Leo, who always tended to raise the stakes, responded with a challenge: "If your team of boys can beat mine, I'll let you have Kun."

The challenge match – between Jorge's *pibes* and a team of local boys from Los Eucaliptus put together by Leo – took place on the cement football pitch at Primero de Mayo, and was won by the home team. "Even though we were up against Kun, we managed to win. The thing is, they were used to playing on earth pitches. Controlling the ball on cement is different," assures Jorge. As good as his word, Leo honoured his promise, and Kun joined Jorge's charges.

What Leo saw in Jorge – his friendly nature, the way he treated his boys and the spirit he imparted to them – brought to mind those people who had mentored him when he was little. And just as Antonio Escobar had done in Tucumán, it was Jorge who would pop by to pick his son up and take him to training or to matches in Buenos Aires. It was a scene that Leo knew all too well: an old car, packed with hopeful boys being looked after by a generous man who provided them with both food and moral guidance. That Jorge showed such generosity was not because he was especially well-off, but rather because this scouting and mentoring of the 'little *pibes*' – as he likes to refer to them – was, and remains to this day, one of his true passions in life.

"Now that I had Leo's consent, and with permission from Adriana, I would pass by the *villa* to collect Kun," says Jorge. "When I arrived, he used to ask me to hold on a few minutes.

You see, he was always playing games or penalty shoot-outs with bigger boys, 12 or 13-year-olds. He never wanted to go without having finished. He would play them for loose change and would always win. Then with the money, he would buy these little juices they sold in the *villa*. The same image invariably pops into my head: Sergio running after the car with that 'prize' in his hand, ready to carry on playing."

Collecting the boys – the majority of them from less well-off families living in the nearby neighbourhoods, including many from Los Eucaliptus itself – was one of the parts of Jorge's routine that he took most seriously. "I gave them all the same level of attention. I tried to make sure that they were honest and respectful. And, bar a couple of exceptions, we managed to do so."

Of course, when speaking of Kun's natural ability, Jorge can eulogise endlessly about what made him stand out from the rest.

"Already, at only five years of age, he had that something extra that sets the chosen ones apart. He was touched by a magic wand. It wasn't just talent. It was intelligence, the shrewdness to analyse what was happening on the field of play. He saw things one step ahead of the others, and that made the difference. And when you sometimes thought that he had faded out from a game, he would pop up all of a sudden and win it by himself. He would drop deep and demand the ball on the floor from the goalkeeper, then jink his way past everyone. And they'd be kicking lumps out of him...! But he would carry on without complaining and would end up teeing up a free team-mate for a goal, or just score by himself. They couldn't stop him. It was a complete riot."

Jorge's scouting work all came together at the Primero de

Mayo club itself where he, and others like him who shared his passion, completed their work with the boys. The institution survived thanks to the contributions of its members, all of them residents of the one-storey houses and dirt roads nearby, who were granted access to the facilities in return for a modest sum that often went unpaid. Unsuspecting visitors to Primero de Mayo would be struck by the grills that were placed only a metre back from the right touchline of the cement pitch, near to the wooden benches where the substitutes sat and closer still to the entrance gate. It was this unique feature that really epitomised the club's homely atmosphere, however, as people would ritually flock there week on week for the unmissable barbecues held before or after the games.

At this time, works had just started on the construction of new dressing rooms and another pitch, complete with a roof. The building materials for these works were piled up behind one of the metal goals and these, as well as the comings and goings of the builders, became the habitual backdrop to the boys' training sessions and matches.

Kun joined both the 1988 and the 1987 *categorías*, as FADI regulations allowed players who were up to a year younger to be included in squads. Although Kun gave away a year of age to the other players – at a time in a child's life when this is no small advantage, particularly with respect to physical development – he more than made up for it with his contribution on the pitch, where his ability made light of that age difference. It was, in any case, an advantage that he would go on to cede to opponents during the early stages of his professional career.

The teams that Sergio joined at Primero de Mayo, all managed by Carlos Alberto 'El Correntino' Ramírez, delighted the club's followers, who happily paid an entrance fee of four pesos to watch their matches. The fame that they were acquiring was such that many other spectators, who were neither fans nor members of the club, started coming to watch them play. And for good reason. During Kun's spell at Primero de Mayo, this humble club from Bernal Oeste put their heavyweight opponents into the shade, the 1987 boys rising all the way from Division C to Division A, winning an unprecedented and historic hat-trick of FADI championships.

Those glory years are today remembered with nostalgia, as well as a sense of pride that goes almost beyond the edge of reason.

"It was a great team, with Kun as its talisman. As well as pure ability, he struck the ball so powerfully. A free-kick was almost as good as a goal. For his age, you could already see he was different. He went everywhere with Cristian Formiga, with whom he dovetailed so well out on the field of play, whether they were playing on concrete or earth pitches. They had a telepathic understanding. Cristian was the goalscorer, but it was Kun who really stood out. He was the playmaker on concrete surfaces, and more of a finisher on earth pitches."

These are the words of none other than 'El Correntino' Ramírez. He can speak with authority about what made Kun stand out, given that he coached him at both Primero de Mayo and in the class of 1988 at Loma Alegre, a club that took part in the now defunct Liga Quilmeña league, played on earth pitches. At the same time as he started at Primero de Mayo, Sergio had also joined the teams at Loma Alegre, who played at a piece of land located 15 blocks from Los Eucaliptus consisting of two well maintained football pitches and who boasted, in addition to their neat grass playing surfaces, a group of coaches who took good care of the boys as they developed as footballers.

Saturday, December 3rd, 2011. Manchester. Etihad Stadium. Manchester City vs Norwich. Gameweek 14 of the Premier League. 32 minutes into the first half.

Kun and his team-mates were determined to do everything possible to maintain their devastating start to the league campaign and to hold on to their position at the top of the table. Yet the team's patient play kept breaking down as it encountered Norwich's defensive wall. That was until a searching pass by the Frenchman Samir Nasri found the marauding Micah Richards who, on reaching the by-line, quickly sent a low cut-back into the centre. The ball's path was slightly behind Sergio who, arriving at pace on the edge of the six-yard box, could not take it in his stride. He managed to control it with his right foot and, on the half-turn, feigned to take a shot at the Norwich goal, well protected by goal-keeper John Ruddy and five other defenders. Kun beat one of them as he cut the ball back with his left foot, while the others now leaned to follow him as he threatened to head right. In a split second, and glimpsing the smallest chink of light shining between the defenders from the right-hand corner of Ruddy's goal, he subtly toe-poked the ball through a forest of legs and across the line. The goal, his eleventh in the Premier League, made it 1-0 on the night and sent his team on their way to a 5-1 victory. The Citizens would thus move to a total of 38 points from 14 games with 48 goals scored, a record that had the club dreaming of silverware on the horizon. Kun was 23

*years old at the time and had arrived at City only three months
previously. With this display of talent and audacity, qualities as much down to his own intuition as to the hours he had
spent playing on potreros, he proved himself to be a player
capable of knocking down walls and finding light at the end
of the darkest tunnels.*

Loma Alegre

Wearing the white and blue – and, later, orange – of Loma
Alegre, Kun competed in the Liga Quilmeña which, throughout
the 1990s and up until its dissolution a few years later, brought
together the cream of the crop of the area's young footballers.
Just like the majority of other leagues, teams competed for titles
on an annual basis, and the rules relating to player ages and
categorías were also similar.

On the other hand, one of the differences was that, as the
matches were played on bigger pitches than *baby fútbol*, teams
were made up of seven players including the goalkeeper.
Moreover, these leagues had one unique feature: if a team
scored the first seven goals or opened up a seven-goal lead, the
game was brought to an end even if the regulation 40 minutes
– divided into two halves of 20 minutes – had not yet elapsed.
The application of this rule, unnecessary in most matches,
started to become more and more commonplace after Kun
joined Loma Alegre.

On a number of occasions, both the 1987 and 1988 boys
scored the requisite number of goals to see their games end
early due to the rule automatically kicking in.

"There were times," recalls Leo, "when they didn't even reach the end of the first half. After 10 or 15 minutes, the match would have to be declared over. They only had to break sweat against two or three of the other teams. It was some team."

One of the first photographs of Sergio posing with a football team dates back to these early days. It is from 1993, and he is to be seen standing on the smart, green pitch alongside his team-mates from Loma Alegre's 1987 group. Everyone in the picture – five standing up, Kun among them, and another four kneeling down – is wearing their full football strip: blue shorts, white socks with blue trim at the top, white shirts with blue collar and cuffs, and a circle of stars on the sleeves. Although so small in stature, the impression that the photo gives of Kun is already one of a fully-fledged footballer.

"You saw this little *pibe* and you knew right away that you were looking at a footballer. The calves, the knees… you watched him play and you realised that he couldn't be anything other than a footballer. He just had this incredible look of a foot-baller…," says Rubén Amarilla, a friend of Adriana's, neigh-bour and friend of the Agüero–Del Castillo family in Los Euc-aliptus, and whose son Darío – Toto, as he was known – was one of Kun's team-mates in the class of 1988 at Loma Alegre.

Another photo from the same period stands out as it serves as proof of the one, fleeting occasion that Leo was manager of his son's team. "It was right at the start, at Loma Alegre. But it wasn't a good experience. Any of the other dads could get suspicious of the fact that my son was in the team, or could complain because so-and-so wasn't starting. I realised it was better just to carry on as a dad, not as a manager," says Leo.

In the photo, he can be seen alongside his charges, who were at that time all wearing the same shirt with 'Carnicería Carlitos' (Carlitos' Butchers) emblazoned across their chests, promoting the sole and privileged sponsor of the team.

The photographer on both occasions – and to thank for having kept these pictures – was Ángel 'Machi' Almada, father of Maxi, another of Kun's team-mates, and also a Loma Alegre official.

"The 1987 and 1988 *categorías* were special. Almost all the same boys that started playing carried on together, year after year, without any changes in personnel. The 1987 team won youth tournaments in 1992 and 1993. And in 1994, they became champions of their age group. And Kun? He was smarter than the rest. He would control the ball, flick it up and hit it on the volley. It wasn't because he practised. It all came naturally, it was intuitive. It's difficult to teach anything to a player like that…," Almada adds.

In that very same year, 1994, when Sergio was six years old, the World Cup was played in the USA where the Argentinian team, managed by Alfio Basile, was eliminated in the quarter-finals by Romania after Diego Maradona's controversial positive drug test that inspired the number 10's famous quote: "They've cut my legs off".

That year's champions were Carlos Alberto Parreira's Brazil and their star player was Romario, with whom the boy from Los Eucaliptus would one day be compared.

It was with Loma Alegre that Sergio lifted his first trophy, although at this stage nobody could have thought that he would go on to lift more and more trophies until it became his trademark. In any case, this particular event lives on in the Agüero–Del Castillo household by way of a photograph taken of that very first time: Sergio dressed in white t-shirt, red shirt and blue jeans with his flies unzipped…

The team manager for Loma Alegre's 1987 group was Jorge Coria who, many years after coaching Kun, can still effortlessly describe what he was like at the time.

"The boy had an unbelievable love of football. This is what stood out the most: his love for the game."

Coria assures that "you didn't have to talk too much to Kun. Just give him some pointers. He liked to be the playmaker, but it was when he was up front that he really made the difference. What was obvious to me was that you couldn't impose restrictions on a player like that, or smother his feel for the game. And, moreover, that the team had to play for him."

Sergio himself backs up Coria's recollections. "At Loma Alegre, I floated around everywhere up front. I liked to drop deep to look for the ball. I would stop in midfield and call for the ball from the goalkeeper – if possible, I'd control it and set off from there."

Norberto Livoy, fellow Loma Alegre graduate and another of those who remained with the team throughout that whole period, remembers the first time that he saw Kun cry.

"It was a knock-out tournament with short games, all played in one day. Sergio entered it with the 1988 *categoría*. They had got to the final unbeaten and, if they'd won the last match, they would have been champions. But you know what football's like, don't you? They were leading the other team a merry dance, but then their opponents scored a goal and set about defending the lead. Kun was playing brilliantly, but the ball wouldn't go in for him. He even set up Formiga a few times, but he couldn't put it away either. And if that wasn't enough, Kun missed a penalty. Unbelievably, they lost. That's when I saw him cry. It was the first time. And we couldn't stop him…"

And Coria tells another anecdote that describes Kun to a tee: "He was already playing in Independiente's youth teams. And we had a friendly against Viejo Bueno, the local rivals. We thought that he wouldn't be able to make it because he had training. However, he turned up after 15 minutes of the game. It took an enormous effort just to put his shirt on, because he had already developed an impressive physique. He had always been quite stocky, but by this stage he had really filled out. He played for 15 minutes and scored the winning goal."

"I remember being taken for the first time to play on a cement pitch. I was used to playing on earth pitches at the villa, but this was different. It was a lot smaller. And it was also played at a much faster pace. To begin with, I didn't understand how to play there. But then I got used to it. Because I just wanted to play football. The only thing I wanted was to play, on whatever kind of pitch. I didn't even watch football on the TV. I used to get back from school, throw down my backpack and start running to the pitch, at the same time as I took off my school overalls. I do remember hearing match commentaries coming from radios as I made my way through the alleyways around the villa. And the only time that I would stop was if I'd heard that there was a free-kick to River Plate. Because Enzo Francescoli used to take them. And he would almost always score. It really impressed me how well the Uruguayan struck a dead ball. Afterwards, of course, I would carry on to the pitch as quickly as possible."

SERGIO AGÜERO

Mario Portinari, Lanús and Independiente

During these early years Kun played about four games per weekend outside of the *villa*: two for Primero de Mayo and two for Loma Alegre, in both the 1987 and 1988 tiers. However, this rate would soon increase because he started to join other teams, meaning that he would spend his Saturdays and Sundays constantly shuttling between different pitches in the Greater Buenos Aires area. Leo could see that this routine would become unsustainable were he not to commit fully to supporting his son's passion. It was at this point that he made a decision, and then informed Adriana.

"I'm not going to play football any more," he announced to his wife who, to begin with, did not believe him.

"It's true that at first I didn't believe him. But he was as good as his word. He played every now and again in our neighbourhood, but stopped playing for other teams at weekends. Those days were set aside for his son. It was in 1995," says Adriana, drawing from her excellent memory, "when Leo was 27 years old and Sergio was seven."

It was around this time that another character, who would go on to have a special influence over Kun during his formative years, became part of everyday life at the Agüero-Del Castillo household: Mario Portinari, a mechanic whose workshop stood just five blocks from Los Eucaliptus. Leo had met him when he took an old Peugeot 504 that he used for mini-cab work to be repaired. From this moment, the special affinity that the two of them shared would form a bond that spread to their families.

It can be said without any misgivings that it was in Mario's capable hands, in that old workshop on the corner of Avenida de La Plata in Quilmes, that little Sergio started to develop a strong attachment to what would later become another of his passions: cars. The noise of the tools hitting the cement floor, the spare parts almost strategically spread out in different places, the sound of engines purring… It all became music to his ears, in the same way as the sight of them being repaired became a visual spectacle for him. Many years down the line, Sergio himself would learn to drive in an old Ford Galaxy. But at this time Sergio had a particular fondness for another car: a Volkswagen Beetle owned by Mario that had come from Brazil.

The four mudguards were missing, the lights did not work, the passenger seat was conspicuous by its absence and the bodywork was painted with no more than an anti-rust primer. But maybe it was these little peculiarities that made 'el topolino' – as they christened it, named after the nickname for a Fiat 500 – so dear to Kun. And he got so much enjoyment out of the car, and all the more so when Mario took him to training in it.

Sergio missed the car greatly when the mechanic had to sell it to cope with the latest in a cycle of economic crises that hit Argentina and its people. Years later, with Sergio already a fully-fledged professional footballer, he suggested that Mario rescue this 'little gem' that had been so cherished. With money in hand, Portinari headed off to look for its buyer. And despite the time that had elapsed since the sale, he was fortunate enough to find him. However, when Mario relayed to him the unique story behind the Beetle, he received an answer that left him almost lost for words: "I wouldn't sell it to you for all the money in the world," he heard him say.

It so happened that the person who had bought it was a fanatical supporter of Independiente, and particularly Kun. When he found out that Sergio had used the car when he was little, he wanted it even more. From this moment on, he would boast about being the owner of the car for which young Agüero had a soft spot. But even if he could not get 'el topolino' back, Mario is still the proud owner of some other treasures: he possesses each and every one of the shirts that Sergio has worn in the different teams that he has played for, and in the different levels of the Argentinian national team. Even the training tops. All of them gifted to him by a grateful Kun. An enviable and quite unmatchable collection.

Football was another axis around which Mario's friendship with the Agüero-Del Castillo family strengthened, in that Portinari became the manager of one of the local teams that Kun played for. His strength of personality meant that he was always on the front line in the arguments out on the *potreros*, showing a firm hand when necessary and defending his friends. Furthermore, through his passion for *el Rojo de Avellaneda* and Kun's own links to this team, an unbreakable bond ended up forming between the two of them. A bond that was first strengthened in that workshop, a sort of refuge for Kun, in which he enjoyed not just the adventure of spending hours and hours there but also the special attention afforded to him by Mario who, in between cups of hot *mate*[1] and idle chat, taught him many secrets about cars and life itself.

The Agüero-Del Castillo family would later help Mario to prolong his own life when, in 2010, he suffered from serious health problems. They were on hand with everything required

---

[1] *Mate* is a caffeine drink infused with dried herbal leaves, popular in South America.

– both materially and spiritually – to make sure that their friend, who had previously protected and helped them so much, did not want for anything and could be seen to as God intended.

But a long time before that, during those first tough years in Los Eucaliptus, on Mario's prompting Leo had started working as the driver of a van taking music groups to their concerts out in the countryside. This new job allowed him to bring in a bit more money, although never enough, to support a family that had expanded again with the arrival of Daiana in December 1994 and of Mauricio in March 1996. Kun remembers the day that his first brother was born like it was yesterday.

"My old man had told me not to leave the house because, at any moment, they would be back with my mum and the newborn baby. But I went out to play on the pitch alongside our house all the same. And just at that moment, they arrived. I remember looking at the baby, then straight away asking for permission to carry on playing."

It was not the first time that Sergio ignored a 'suggestion' not to leave the house. These orders generally came from Mum, Adriana, who would ground Kun by way of punishment for some prank or other. However, he would always find a way to break the rules that were set. When it came to getting around the groundings, his neighbour Gustavo Castillo was one of his accomplices who would help him to climb over the wall that separated one house from the other so that he could get out. The proximity of the *potrero* acted as an insurance mechanism for Adriana's return. When they saw her arrive, a quick warning was enough to send Kun scuttling immediately back to his house, to once more scale the wall and then act as if nothing had happened.

The year 1996 also saw Kun attend a stadium for the first time to watch a game of top level football. It was a few days after his eighth birthday. To be precise, it was Wednesday, June 26th and the occasion was the final of the Copa Libertadores de América between River Plate and América de Cali from Colombia. Although Leo's heart was still with San Martín in Tucumán, he also followed River – the team from the Núñez neighbourhood of Buenos Aires – and did not think twice about taking his son along.

The party heading off from Quilmes to the capital city in the Renault 12 owned by 'El Correntino' Ramírez, Kun's manager at Primero de Mayo and Loma Alegre, also included Sergio's friend Cristian Formiga and his dad Daniel, both staunch fans of the team known as the *millonarios*.

The decision to go to the match was, in itself, quite risky. Not just because of the intense cold – on that day the thermometer had reached five degrees below zero – but also because they did not have enough money to buy their tickets which, in any case at that time of the evening, had already been practically sold out. In this way, unsure if they were even going to be able to get in, they set off to the Monumental stadium, which had been full for some time ahead of the match. River had lost the first leg in Colombia by one goal to nil, and therefore needed to win by more than a goal to become champions.

Although Sergio would argue that, given the choice, he would always opt to play rather than watch a match, the chance to see Enzo Francescoli and Ariel 'Burrito' Ortega, two of his favourite players, excited him. The night air left Kun dazzled by the floodlights that could be made out shining in the distance from River's stadium. It just remained to be seen whether they would be able to get in. With a bit of local nous and cheek, as well as a touch of luck, they were finally able to get into the stadium.

"Lots of people were left outside," recalls Cristian. "Including us. All of a sudden we saw that, at one of the gates, there were policemen letting some people in. We saw that people were giving them 10 pesos each, and managing to get through. We joined them and, the next thing you know, we were sitting snugly in the lower tier."

They went in at the exact moment that Hernán Crespo – the future Chelsea man, in his last game for River before being transferred to Parma in Italy – scored the opening goal for the *millonarios*, six minutes into the first half.

Kun was lucky enough to see Ortega at his best, and the Uruguayan Francescoli orchestrating play. But on that night all the plaudits went to Crespo who, 14 minutes into the second half, scored the second goal that would give Ramón Díaz's team victory and the second Copa Libertadores de América title in their history.

"What struck me most when we finally got in was the pitch, which, under the floodlights, seemed even greener. I think it was this, the colours, that grabbed my attention more than anything. In the stands, among the crowd, in the smoke… That's what I remember most from my first time," says Sergio.

As already mentioned, Kun and Cristian Formiga were thick as thieves throughout these years. They went to a football match for the first time together; they played together at Loma Alegre, at Primero de Mayo and on the local *potreros*; and, in their free time from school, they played on the video games console that Cristian had at home.

Together, they would also have their first opportunities to

attend trials at a Primera División club. Leo Del Castillo and Daniel Formiga took them to a club called Lanús, which was trying players out for its youth teams. The trial consisted of a game between one team made up of those hoping to join the team and another of those already on the books at the club, based in the south of Greater Buenos Aires.

"Sergio was eight years old, about to turn nine, and they made him play against a team from the 1986 *categoría*, full of boys who were two years older than him. To top it all, and despite having told the coach that he played up front, he put him at full-back. And obviously, he didn't complete a single tackle," says Leo.

Cristian adds that "it was the first time that we'd played on a full-size pitch. As well as giving Kun the number 4 shirt, they gave me the number 8. There was no point in playing. No sooner had we arrived than we had to leave."

Sergio remembers little of that trial, although he does recall a second opportunity at Lanús in that same year. "We went with someone my dad knew. This time they took us on but it was all for nothing in the end, because they warned him that I would have to become a member of the club to carry on playing there."

Leo corroborates his son's words. "I thought that they would at least give us an allowance to put towards the travel costs to get him to training. But the opposite turned out to be true. At the secretary's office, they informed me that I had to register him and pay for his membership, in addition to buying his shirts and other equipment. And for us, that was out of the question. We simply didn't have the money…"

Lanús was not to be the only club to let Kun slip by. The same was true of Quilmes, another of the big clubs in the south of

Greater Buenos Aires. Just like the second time round at Lanús, both Sergio and Cristian were accepted at the trial, but they were unable to stay on as the issue of money proved to be an insurmountable obstacle. "After two weeks of training, they told us that they wanted to sign us up. But that, in order to do so, we had to become members of the club. The subs were 15 pesos per month, which wasn't easy for me."

Paying this amount was simply a luxury that Leo could not afford. Supporting his family was becoming increasingly difficult, particularly with the arrival of their seventh child and third son, Gastón, in June 1997.

The possibility of Kun joining a big club became stronger when Leo took him to play at Independiente de Avellaneda. He could have had the same luck as at Lanús and Quilmes given that, in order to take part in the football school for boys of his age, he would also have to be a member of the club. However, the *rojos* — in addition to their youth teams that played in the Argentinian Football Association leagues — also had teams based at Villa Domínico, where the youngest players cut their teeth in competitions against the local neighbourhood teams. An opportunity presented itself for Kun here, as he did not need to be a member to take part.

"I knew that they were trying out players and I took him along," says Leo. "The first person to see him was Agustín 'Mencho' Balbuena, who asked me to bring him back the next week to start training."

Balbuena, who was in charge of training and developing the boys, was an ex-right winger who had shone for the *rojos* in the 1970s, a golden age for the club from Avellaneda during which its team earned the nickname 'King of Cups'.

It was Balbuena himself who, taking part in the final of the Intercontinental Cup for Independiente against Atletico Madrid in 1974, scored the only goal of the game played in Buenos Aires. The return match, played at the stadium on the banks of the River Manzanares in Madrid, was won by Atletico Madrid two-nil, a goal four minutes from the end by the Argentine Rubén Ayala enough to crown the Spanish team managed by Luis Aragonés champions.

Needless to say, Balbuena was a long way from imagining that the kid who had shone in that day's trial would go on to form a strong bond with the very same team from Madrid that he had faced 23 years previously

*Sunday, September 17th, 2006. **Bilbao. The San Mamés stadium. Atletico Madrid playing away to Athletic in the third game of the Spanish league season. 18 minutes into the second half.***

On this night, taking on the invisible mantle of other Argentinian goalscorers to have shone for the Colchoneros such as José Eulogio Garate, Rubén Cano and Rubén 'Ratón' Ayala, Kun started to more than justify his transfer fee and prove that those reports that Atletico had unearthed a real one-off talent were not so far-fetched after all. During the first half, goals from the Argentine Maxi 'La Fiera' Rodriguez and the Bulgarian Petrov had made it 2-0 to the visitors. And with 18 minutes played in the second half Sergio, on the run and wearing number 10 on his back, picked up Frenchman Luccin's pass into space in the centre-forward position. After evading Sarriegi with a touch from the outside of his right boot, and just as he was about to be cut off by another defender who was trying to close him down, he hit a right-footed shot from the edge of the area towards Aranzubia's left-hand post. The goal-keeper attempted to palm the ball away, but was helpless to stop it crossing the line. He was 18 years old, and had arrived on Spanish shores only three months earlier. It was his first goal for Atletico Madrid – although it would by no means be his last – in his first start for the club.

In these first months Kun played some friendlies in an Independiente shirt, even if his involvement was only sporadic due to his commitments at other clubs. This was not because he was not selected, but simply because he had started to play for Los Primos, a team from Berazategui who played in that district's local league.

At weekends he therefore shuttled constantly around. From one pitch to another, from one tip of southern Greater Buenos Aires to the other, Kun was in his element. Nothing could be better for him than to go on these pilgrimages to different fields of play, be they cement or earth, and to leave his mark at each one as he went; to play up to six games per weekend, his notoriety as a relentless goalscorer growing all the while.

Although he was a boy of few words, whose personality could often seem to be on the shy side, he was blessed with a special charisma that would slowly develop, until it became one of his most unique personal features. And what he did not say in words was expressed, in an impromptu manner, by his mere presence.

This was not because he had a domineering physique or because he demanded particular respect; in comparison, he was shorter and more reserved than many of his team-mates. But his natural and charming smile, dimples that appeared when he laughed, were like a magnet that drew everyone's attention.

And nobody could stop looking at him. What singled him out was that he managed to be the centre of attention without having any pretensions to this whatsoever. At the same time, he could appear somewhat distracted, as though what was happening around him was not really sinking in.

Until he suddenly made a comment – when he spoke, it was because he had something to say – and it was easy to see that he could indeed listen, that he had seen everything, that he had taken note of everything. And he did so with perfect timing and with the cheek of a boy who had grown up in a *villa*, but in a way that caused no offence to anyone present.

Kun did not have a malicious bone in his body. He went through life without drama or complications. He had a natural air of authority. Nothing was forced, there was no shouting or gesturing. Everything came about through his presence, his personal magnetism, that innate gift that pervaded everything.

These features of Sergio's personality were reflected, as if by a mirror, whenever he set foot on a football pitch: no drama, no complications. And there he would end up as the centre of it all, without having had any pretensions to being so. And nobody could take their eyes off him. He seemed absent or distracted but he took everything in. And what he had to say, he did so at the opportune moments, with the ball at his feet. He let his talent do the talking, and left his rivals lost for words.

He would appear with perfect timing, with a piece of magic that elevated him above the other players.

In this way, people were moved when they watched Kun on a football pitch. And this was no small thing in areas where scarcity, be it material or otherwise, was the run of the mill.

These characteristics became more and more pronounced, both on and off the field of play. Above all from 1998 onwards, when he turned 10 years old and the emotions that he inspired would start to be felt by more and more people.

Number Ten
Turns Ten

The end of 1997 saw Sergio, on his mother Adriana's insistence, making a great effort to finish fourth grade at school and preparing to receive First Communion. More out of duty than desire, he had been attending, on-and-off, the sessions run by a lady named Marita, who trained children at the little chapel in Los Eucaliptus.

The community's religious figures worked tirelessly to prevent local youngsters from social marginalisation – a fate that was increasingly common, not just in this neighbourhood but all throughout the poorest areas of Greater Buenos Aires.

Adriana's tenacity proved to be enough and, at her request,

Sergio attended a seminary at a religious school in Buenos Aires to complete his training. "I convinced him in the end. I knew at this point that it was now or never. Indeed, he made the most of it and came back with a little trophy from a tournament that they played there," confirms Adriana, underlining what her son's main concern had actually been.

The date set for the ceremony was Sunday, December 7th. That final decision on the date had only been taken a few days previously, which did not give the Agüero-Del Castillo family time to prepare as they would have wished.

"As we didn't know if he was going to be able to take communion, we hadn't even got him the clothes he needed," Adriana admits. "And we didn't have enough money to buy them. But a miracle took place. On the Friday night, Leo had the idea of going to the bingo hall at Lanús with my friend Rubén Amarilla. And God held us out a helping hand. They won the first game."

With this money, Adriana was able to head out on Saturday and buy a white shirt, a black tie, a black waistcoat embroidered with gold trim, and a pair of shoes. After that, they just had to convince Sergio to put on the clothes, brush his fringe and get him ready for the ceremony. Yet Kun's outfit – very uncomfortable for someone who was used to wearing sports clothing – was not all that was unique about the event. Due to the huge amount of children taking part, the hall in the little chapel proved too small, and a new location had to be found. As was only fitting, the chosen venue turned out to be… the little football pitch in front of their house.

"All of the parents agreed and so, the day before, we cleaned it, and cleared away the stones and rubbish. Then, at seven in the morning on Sunday, we started to lay out the chairs. Luckily it was a beautiful day for it and everything went perfectly," says Adriana.

The party was held afterwards on the patio of the house belonging to their neighbours Gustavo and Any, which sported decorative white and yellow balloons. The guests sat around a big table on plastic chairs. The cake – all three tiers of it – was provided by Jorge 'The Baker'. In any case, Sergio did not waste too much time in doing what he had planned along. As soon as he was able, he stripped off the uncomfortable clothing and, almost without being seen, headed out to run around at the exact same spot where he had taken communion moments earlier. For as soon as the ceremony was over, the improvised altar had immediately become a *potrero* once more.

The first front cover

As the year of 1998 dawned, Kun was presented with his first opportunity to compete in a tournament held at some distance from his home. This chance arrived after Loma Alegre's 1987 *categoría* were invited to take part in the eighth provincial tournament in the city of Luján, organised by the Western Association of Youth Clubs (ACIFO) and affiliated with the Buenos Aires Youth Football Federation (FEFIBA). For this humble club from Quilmes, it was a huge effort just to accept the invitation.

Gathering together the money needed for the trip was not a simple matter. However, the relative proximity of the tournament – Luján is only 90 kilometres away from Quilmes – and reassurances that the boys would be put up in family houses, made it easier for them to say yes. Jorge Coria, as team manager, and Leonel del Castillo and Ángel 'Machi' Almada, as team officials, were in charge of the party. During the tournament, they would have to compete against teams from different cities across the province of Buenos Aires. It would really put their potential to the test, which gave the team – made up of Kun and nine other players including Ángel and Hernán, Coria and Almada's sons – all the motivation they needed.

The tournament, divided into four groups of four teams, was to be played from Friday, January 2nd to Saturday, January 10th. Loma Alegre managed to knock out five teams in succession, and in doing so reached the final against San Lorenzo, the local favourites. A tough final loomed in front of a large crowd.

To calm their nerves, Coria, Leo and Machi took the boys on a trip to visit the stunning Luján Basilica, one of the Argentinian Catholic community's major landmarks. The cherished photos taken of the team from Quilmes posing in front of the temple would provide a lasting souvenir of their day out.

On Saturday, January 10th, 1998, the day of the final, the sports pages in the national newspapers were speculating over which players would make the Argentinian national squad for the World Cup in France, which was only six months away. National team manager Daniel Passarella publicly revealed his concerns at Ariel Ortega's lack of game time at Valencia in Spain, where he was being overlooked by his coach Claudio Ranieri, and singled out Juan Sebastián Verón, Marcelo Gallardo and Roberto Sensini as his on-field leaders.

The media were also discussing the international world of football, setting aside special coverage for the latest Madrid derby between Real and Atletico. But a long way from Spain, in the town of Luján, a publication by the name of *El Civismo*, which appeared twice-weekly on Wednesdays and Saturdays, dedicated the front page of its sports supplement to the final of the youth tournament that was to be played that evening.

Under the headline 'Final to be played tonight', it explained that: "Today the eighth Ciudad de Luján Provincial Youth Football Tournament will come to a close. In the 1987 *categoría*, Loma Alegre of Quilmes and local boys San Lorenzo will contest the final at 20:10."

In the sizable, caption-free photograph that accompanies the headline, a small but robust nine-year-old Sergio Agüero can be seen getting the better of an opponent in the semi-final. Without knowing it, that newspaper in Luján would therefore go on to have the privilege of being the first media publication to have run with a front cover photo of someone who would later appear time and again on the front pages of the biggest media outlets around the world.

On the inside pages of the sports section, the relevant details on the two finalists are accompanied by black and white photos. In Loma Alegre's team picture, Kun is to be found crouching down in the front row with the ball in his hand, and a young Jorge Coria, the team manager, is seen standing alongside his players.

The final between Loma Alegre and San Lorenzo kicked off right on time, in front of a significant crowd. More than 4,000 people were present to witness at close hand the climax of a tournament contested largely by 11-year-old boys. Those present recall an incredibly tight match. Loma Alegre struggled to a 1-0 win, thanks to a goal by Antonio Díaz.

"I'll never forget that finish," says the boss, Jorge Coria. "Kun broke down the right and sent over a perfect cross that Antonio

Díaz latched onto and stuck in the back of the net." The photos that were then published on the front page of *El Civismo* show the teams on a joint lap of honour, with all the players having swapped shirts, apart from Kun who was wearing an Independiente training top. And a photo on the inside pages showed all of Loma Alegre's players holding their individual winners medals and the tournament trophy itself, joined by manager Jorge Coria and a smiling Leonel del Castillo.

*Thursday, October 25th, 2007. **Moscow. The Lokomotiv Stadium. UEFA Cup. The hosts take on Atletico Madrid. The 40th minute of the second half.***

On this night, Kun Agüero took his place alongside football's finest artists. In the Russian capital, Atleti's defensive weaknesses had once again been exposed. Despite having led in the early stages through a goal from Kun, with only five minutes left Lokomotiv had turned things around and were winning 3-2. Then the Portuguese Maniche threaded a pass between two defenders that found Agüero on the edge of the box with his back to goal. Tightly marked, he spun and bore down on the goal defended by Pelizzoli. Closed down by the desperately onrushing goalkeeper and with almost no room for manoeuvre, he dinked the ball with his right foot just powerfully enough to chip him and score a subtle but, equally, spectacular goal. Agüero's performance in the match – which would finish 3-3 – led Lokomotiv manager Anatoli Byshovets to claim afterwards that "watching Agüero is like visiting the Prado Museum". A few days later, the Spanish sports newspaper Marca dedicated its front page to a picture of Kun at the Prado Museum, as well as four pages inside to a

feature on the player. At only 19 years of age, he had already been
granted a privileged position in the world's biggest media outlets.

Thanks to their unforgettable experience in Luján, a month later Loma Alegre would set off on another journey. In February, it was 1988 *categoría*'s turn to be given a taste of tournament football. This time it would be in the Amistad Youth Football Championship for this age group, held in the city of Chascomús, 115 kilometres away from Quilmes.

Loyal to his promise to always remain at his son's side, Leonel del Castillo again made the journey, although this time with his friend Rubén Amarilla whose son 'Toto' was on the team – and with 'El Correntino' Ramírez as manager. The party left in a school bus hired for the event – which took place during the school holidays – and, after two and a half hours on the road, arrived at Chascomús where the boys were divided up to stay with local families, as they had been in Luján.

"The best part of it was the experience itself," says Carlos 'El Correntino' Ramírez. "The majority of the *pibes*' families were not well-off, and it was the first time that they had been away from home. But they didn't cause any trouble at all. The families that they stayed with were so impressed with their behaviour."

And Rubén Amarilla recalls that the first match, which took place on Sunday, February 15th, pitted Loma Alegre up against the very boys whose families were putting them up.

"We didn't know which way to look. The thing is, we beat them 7-1, with five goals from Kun and two from Cristian Formiga. After how well they'd treated the boys… Afterwards, they supported us all the way to the final."

And no wonder. After such an auspicious start, all of those

taking part started to talk about "the little boys from Quilmes".

"Nobody gave us a hope," remembers Amarilla. "The boys seemed so small. But once they set foot on the pitch, they would then wipe the floor with them…"

And this is exactly how it panned out. The Loma Alegre boys won the following four games and in the final, played on Sunday, February 22nd, they defeated Sol de América from Florencio Varela. Loma Alegre were crowned champions having scored 28 goals – 16 of them by Kun – and conceded five.

'Loma Alegre wins Torneo Amistad 88' was the headline in the sports section of the *El Argentino* newspaper on Tuesday, February 24th. The report was accompanied by a photo of the winning squad.

'The light blues from Quilmes,' reports the newspaper, 'defeated Sol de América from Florencio Varela by two goals to nil in the deciding match, with goals from Sergio Agüero and Cristian Formiga. The boys from Loma Alegre, undoubtedly the tournament's stand-out team, deservedly lifted the trophy and received the biggest ovation of the night.'

The proud team manager, 'El Correntino' Ramírez, harbours no doubts whatsoever. "Out of all of them, Kun was the best. And as captain, he got to lift the cup."

Cacho Barreiro

The victories in Luján and Chascomús were to form the ideal platform for a year that would prove to be a turning point for Sergio Agüero, a year that would confirm what he had felt deep inside for a long time: that he had been born to play football.

It was something he felt even more keenly with each game, each goal, and each embrace he shared with his team-mates. With Primero de Mayo and Loma Alegre, he had played against teams from southern Greater Buenos Aires and other teams from far-off cities elsewhere in Argentina. And on each of these occasions, his game had benefited and his level of ability increased.

His name started to resonate throughout the world of youth football, where he was considered as a rising star. And various clubs were interested in taking him on their books. The most renowned clubs all looked to do whatever it took to reinforce their teams with the best players. They scoured around for those who really stood out among the youth set-ups at other clubs, in order to bring them on board. And the parents of the most coveted boys often found the temptations that were offered their way too good to refuse. Even more so, given that the majority of these boys came from disadvantaged backgrounds.

In Kun's case, it was his dad Leo who received the requests. At FADI or Liga Quilmeña games, he was regularly approached by representatives offering his *pibe* the opportunity to play at their clubs. These requests – which came attached to offers that were difficult to refuse – were becoming increasingly insistent. However, Leo knew that they must weigh the offers up before making a decision, one that would be informed as always by what was best for his son.

From these early years – Kun was still only about to turn 10 – he had the presence of mind to always opt for what he considered to be best for his son's development and to disregard, even for himself, the 'siren calls' that promised quick financial rewards. In this way, the final choice over where his son would play was always based on natural instinct, reinforced by the experience of his own childhood in Tucumán.

The bottom line was that he had to find somewhere with good, well-meaning people who could help Kun to keep on developing. This did not, however, mean that he was being innocent or naive in this regard. He was the father of a family, with seven mouths to feed. And his and Adriana's jobs were not enough to completely provide for such a large group all of the time. Sergio's extraordinary gift would from then on help to cover, if only in part, for when his parents' income fell short.

Leo's instinct to choose prudently was proved to be the right call when representatives from the Los Primos club in Berazategui – who, like Loma Alegre, played in the Liga Quilmeña – contacted him with a view to bringing Sergio in to play for their team. Los Primos was one of the leading clubs in the district and took excellent care of each of the 180 boys who played in the various age groups, surrounding them with everything they needed for their development.

On-field success came hand-in-hand with such dedication. One of the key reasons behind these successes was Cacho Barreiro, the manager of the 1988 *categoría* where Kun would end up.

"In the league, a lot was being spoken at the time about this *pibe* who was a real phenomenon," says Cacho, while taking a break from his work coordinating a construction site in the Barracas neighbourhood of the capital city. "And then I found out for myself when it was our turn to play against him. The club's owner, Ángel Giménez, told me to go after him. I put out a few feelers, we went to meet the family and Sergio started playing for us soon afterwards."

Cacho was an affable type who nevertheless acted more strictly with the boys for their own good. As well as incorporating Sergio into a squad that oozed class in every game and whose quality always stood out, Cacho took it upon himself to offer an almost personal attention to Sergio, both on and off the field.

"He was a rough diamond, in need of polishing. And that was my great challenge. Although I treated all the boys the same, I knew that here I was dealing with someone a bit special. And that much of what I could show him could help him to grow as a person and as a player."

The conditions offered by Los Primos in return for Kun joining their teams included something that the club's owner often did to help out the boys' families: he offered Leo the chance to use one of his cars to work as a private taxi driver, an offer Leo accepted with relish. Time would prove Leo to have been right all along about Los Primos. Sergio's spell there not only saw him collect numerous titles, even more importantly, he was able to identify with the club, gain more experience and make the most of Cacho Barreiro's guidance, which would remain with him forevermore.

"He was one of the ones who taught me the most," he recognises. "Particularly about not relaxing or switching off when we were winning. He always stressed this to me. And although he didn't shout at me, he didn't hold back from pointing out to me anything he considered to be a mistake. 'That's what you get for showing off', he once said to me halfway through a match that we were comfortably winning, when I missed a load of chances and had four great shots saved by the goalkeeper. He thought that I had given their goalkeeper the chance to grow in confidence, and that this would spread through their team. And that's exactly what happened, and soon enough they went ahead. Luckily I eventually managed to score the equalising goal.

"But even today, in games when I miss chances, it's as if I can hear Cacho's voice telling me 'come on Sergio, come on Sergio… put it away… put it away…,'" Sergio recounts while lifting his hands to cup his mouth, without raising his voice but almost perfectly imitating Barreiro.

"You see, I was never there just to keep flattering him," says Cacho. "While I always kept in mind that it was only a kid I was speaking to, I still tried to teach him that a sportsman had to take his development seriously. Even more so for somebody like him, who had such immense potential. I always asked him to look after himself, not to play too many games, not to burn himself out. And to take care over who he was hanging around with. He listened to me because he knew that I was giving him my all. But he also knew that he had to step up to fulfil what was demanded of him."

Kun's association with Cacho Barreiro grew successfully at Los Primos, where they won titles in the Liga Quilmeña and at the Evita de Berazategui Games. Even half-a-year before Sergio made his debut in Independiente's first team, he and Cacho won the Buenos Aires youth championship title for his age group.

"Once, in a match for Primero de Mayo against San Miguel in Ezpeleta, the half-time whistle had gone and I went to buy some choripan sandwiches from the club's food stall. And suddenly I hear all this cheering. I hadn't even realised that

the second half was underway. Later they told me what had happened. The second half had barely started, and Sergio's team-mate Cristian took possession in midfield and passed him the ball. As soon as he received it he flicked it up with one foot, and with a leap he arched his body and hit an overhead kick right into the top corner. I missed the goal, but everyone told me it was spectacular. Do you know what it's like to score a goal like that, on a pitch with small goals? At the end, I had to hide away. Because everybody was coming up to me to talk about Sergio. Even a few who wanted to take him to other clubs. For the sake of the other boys, I didn't like that to happen. But Sergio was impressive. Just to think, that was one of his best goals and I didn't even get to see it…"

LEONEL DEL CASTILLO

'Luigi'

If there was a certain chemistry between Kun and Cacho Borreiro, the same could also be said of his relationship with José Luis Servián – widely known as 'Luigi' – whose nickname was taken from the name of his factory which provided, and still does to this day, football shirts for the huge number of clubs in the metropolitan area of Buenos Aires. 'Luigi' therefore had an extensive knowledge of the world of youth football, and specialised in more than just the colours of the shirts that he himself designed. He was also the manager of 20 de Junio, a club that competed in the Lanús Youth Sports Association (ADILA). The ADILA comprised of more than 90 teams, and the set-up was similar to that of the FADI. 'Luigi' had first seen

Kun play when he was starting out at Belgrano.

"He was only a small kid with a fringe blown about by the wind, but he was so destructive with the ball at his feet. I later saw him again in a final for Primero de Mayo, a club where people like Jorge 'The Baker' and 'El Correntino' Ramírez were based, guys who always remained under the radar but who trained the youngsters really well. They beat a club called Monte, with Kun scoring the winning goal. I met Leo there, and we became close friends. When I suggested that Sergio play for 20 de Junio, he didn't hesitate. The thing is, he'd just had a disagreement with some of the directors at Primero de Mayo, and this finally convinced him," he explains very precisely.

Jorge 'The Baker' was one of those who most keenly felt Kun's departure, although nothing could rob him of the pride he felt at having been there from the start and having contributed to the boy's development. He stayed in touch with the Agüero-Del Castillo family, and the affection that characterises their friendship remains to this day.

Jorge would go on to follow Kun's future career closely and, despite being a fan of Racing Club, would celebrate his successes at their eternal rivals Independiente de Avellaneda as readily as anyone. Coincidentally, this passion for Racing was something that Jorge and 'Luigi' had in common.

They also shared the habit of approaching everything that they did with a sense of responsibility and passion. In the case of 'Luigi', this latter trait was so strong that he would never give anything less than 100 per cent in everything that he had committed to.

The process of taking care of the orders for football shirts at his factory was something that regularly had him working until the early hours. And, even if it meant depriving himself of sleep, he approached his role as manager of 20 de Junio with the same dedication. Yet owing to his determination to honour all of his commitments, 'Luigi' ended up being the butt of the boys' jokes at the club.

The players, Kun included, had got into the habit of running to the substitutes' bench in order to celebrate the goals they scored. This was not purely out of exuberance, but rather to stir their manager up and give him a fright, as 'Luigi' was often sat fast asleep on the bench while his team were playing their matches.

His genial nature guaranteed that 'Luigi' never stayed angry for long, and also endeared him to everyone. This included Leo and Adriana, with whom he enjoyed an increasingly trusting relationship, illustrated when they were named as his daughter's godparents.

"On many occasions I went to pick Sergio up from Los Eucaliptus on Fridays so that he could sleep at my house before I took him to play for the 1987 and 1988 *categorías* on the Saturday. And if not, Leo would bring him round. The boy had real charisma... Everywhere we played, people adored him. I had never seen them applaud a boy from another team before. You'd find all sorts in that kind of environment, and some of them weren't the friendliest, yet he would win around the opposing fans.

"I remember a game against Quintana. He scored 13 goals. It was in the 1988 *categoría* that he really stood out," explains 'Luigi', who nevertheless also stresses the importance of mother Adriana's role: "She had him on a short leash. If he gave her any nonsense, she wouldn't let him out. And I had to go and find her and try to persuade her. Thank God he has a mother like that... and, what's more, one who was raising so many children."

'Luigi' explains that Sergio's football ability surprised him on a daily basis and that, in the process of coaching the boy, he himself learned much in return. "I would always tell him not to insist on finishing off certain moves with a bicycle kick because, given the pitches were made from cement, he could injure himself when falling. And if he carried on doing it after my warning, on many occasions I would have to bring him off. Not because I wanted to hold him back, but in order to look after him and to prevent him coming to any harm. He was my responsibility, and I couldn't just let him do whatever he liked. But in this regard, I must acknowledge that he was a rebel with a cause. The thing is, scoring goals like that came so naturally to him that he did it instinctively. And it was hard for him to gauge the level of risk involved. You can't set limits for footballing instinct. This is something that I ended up learning from him."

The friendship between the two families went from strength to strength over the years, to the point that 'Luigi' became a permanent feature alongside Leo, accompanying him to each and every one of Kun's matches, tours and tournaments for Independiente's youth teams.

'Luigi' would bring a video camera on these occasions, and would try to record the steps taken by the young Sergio on those pitches. 'Try' being the operative word. Indeed, his best intentions to record the matches – during which the camera would be left running throughout – were scuppered by his own passion and excitement every time Kun pulled off one of his most spectacular bits of skill. At these moments, without realising it, the camera remained in his hand but pointed in another direction, while all of his senses, especially his sight, meant 'Luigi' was entirely focused on those epic pieces of action. And it is for this reason that in the majority of the videos – that would have otherwise provided recorded evidence of Sergio's goals for posterity – all that has been captured are images of the sky, of nearby trees, of the stands or the playing surface, all to the soundtrack of Leo and 'Luigi' screaming distinctively as they greeted goal after goal.

Saturday, December 6th, 2008. **Gijón, Spain.** **The El Molinón stadium. Sporting vs. Atletico Madrid. Four minutes into the first half.**
On this night, Kun Agüero remained faithful to his natural instinct to do whatever it takes to score a goal, while simultaneously proving that aesthetic beauty and football can indeed go hand in hand. Atletico had got off to the worst possible start in the match, and went a goal down after only three minutes to Bilic's header from a corner. From the next attack the Portuguese, Simao, crossed from left to right, where Maxi Rodríguez headed the ball back towards the penalty spot. The Greek, Seitaridis, failed to get his head to the ball but his leap distracted the defenders, who were left out of position. The ball bounced up right in front of Kun, who was just in front of the six-yard line with his back to goal. As the ball fell, he rose, arched his body backwards and struck the ball with a magnificent right-footed bicycle kick that left Cuellar rooted to the spot. It made the score 1-1, and opened the floodgates for Atletico to ultimately go on and win handsomely by five goals to two. The goal was chosen as the best strike in the

Spanish league that weekend. For Kun it was a goal that paid homage to all of those mentors who, during his upbringing, were careful never to restrict his talent, but who at the same time established the boundaries that he needed to go on and reach world football's highest levels.

Justice and rewards

On June 2nd, 1998, Sergio turned 10 years old in a burst of activity. Luckily for him, both the winter holidays and the football World Cup in France were just around the corner.

Like so many other Argentinians, he held high hopes for the squad managed by Daniel Passarella and featuring, among others, Ariel Ortega, Juan Sebastián Verón, Gabriel Batistuta, Claudio López, Diego Simeone and Marcelo Gallardo. He enjoyed the wins over Japan, Jamaica and Croatia during the group stages, and then rather endured the team's 2-2 draw with England.

"It was the match when Beckham was sent off after the incident with 'El Cholo' Simeone, which led to all sorts of controversy. During the penalty shoot-out that got us through to the quarter-finals, when Roa kept out the last penalty, we all celebrated by jumping on top of a table," says Sergio, who confirms that this is the first World Cup that he vividly remembers. His celebrations were not to last long, however, as on July 4th, Argentina were eliminated by the Netherlands, who won 2-1 thanks to Bergkamp's strike with only a minute left on the clock, shortly after Batistuta had shaken the woodwork with a fearsome shot and Ariel Ortega had been dismissed.

Kun had a good reason to forget about the World Cup when it was confirmed that Loma Alegre were soon to take part in another provincial tournament. They had already competed in – and won – tournaments in the south and west of the province of Buenos Aires, and here was the opportunity to measure themselves up against other teams from the northern area. The event itself was the XIV Provincial Tournament, held in the city of San Nicolás, organised by the Liga Nicoleña *baby fútbol* league and overseen by FEFIBA, which would take place between Monday, July 20th and Sunday, July 26th, 1998.

Before setting off, the rules that had been put in place stipulated that the boys had to present a medical certificate attesting to their good health. Kun's check-up was recorded on a sheet of card with the 'Quilmes School Youth Football League' letterhead, under the name of Sergio Agüero, of Argentinian nationality, 10 years of age. It was carried out by Dr. Luisa Farfián on July 15th, 1998, in other words one month and 13 days after his 10th birthday.

Under the heading 'Sensory Organs' the doctor noted 's/p', standing for 'sin problemas' or 'no problems', in relation to sight, ears and the backs of his eyes. The same abbreviation appears under the heading 'Joints' for the points relating to 'reflexes and coordination', and under 'Nervous System' relating to 'gait' and 'balance'. With respect to the 'Circulatory System', 'a resting pulse of 72 x 1' and 'a resting blood pressure of maximum 90 and minimum 60' are specified. The abbreviation 's/p' is once again noted under the heading 'Auscultation'.

But most striking of all, particularly as this was the first time that they had been measured since his birth, are the recordings of his weight and height: 32 kilograms (five stones) and 1.32

metres (four feet and four inches), respectively.

At last, with all the bureaucratic formalities completed, the delegation for the 1987 *categoría* – including team manager Jorge Coria and team official Leo Del Castillo – set off from Loma Alegre's home ground on a number 582 service bus that had been especially hired for the event.

Sergio travelled the 265 kilometres to San Nicolás with high hopes, absolutely certain that the strength of his team would be proved once more. However, the experience awaiting him would in fact go on to teach him – perhaps too early in his life – that certain non-footballing circumstances can conspire to get in the way of a deserved sporting success.

Once more the 16-team tournament was divided into four groups, and once more Loma Alegre reached the semi-final with an immaculate record: unbeaten and boasting the tournament's top goalscorer, Sergio Agüero, with seven strikes to his name.

On this occasion they would have to face a representative side from the city of Salto. A tight game played on Friday, July 24th, 1998 ended 1-1 (Loma Alegre's goal having been scored by Cristian Formiga) and would have to be decided by penalties.

"It was a tremendous match," recalls Machi Almada, who arrived right at the end as he had been to pick up Ángel de la Cruz, one of the boys who had needed to return home to Quilmes urgently because his mother had undergone an operation and who had arrived back in time to play the last 10 minutes of this game. "I even had to calm Leo down at one stage, because he had been wound up by certain refereeing decisions and wanted to withdraw Sergio from the field of play. Eventually, after a lot of effort, I managed to convince him and Kun stayed out there. It was a good job too, as the penalty shoot-out was so tough. It reached 7-7. Kun took the last penalty, just like he was playing around in his back yard at home, and that was the goal that took us through to the final," says Almada.

For the deciding match, which was scheduled for Sunday, July 26th, the boys' family and friends – encouraged by the team's recent victories – made the trip to San Nicolás in four mini-buses. They did not want to miss out on the final, to be played against the team representing the city of Las Flores. Kick-off had been arranged for four o'clock in the afternoon but, an hour before the start, the Loma Alegre delegation learned of an odd development.

The night before, officials from the Salto team had lodged a complaint with respect to De la Cruz's allegedly unauthor-ised inclusion in the semi-final. The Liga Nicoleña upheld the complaint, citing the rules of the Youth Football Federation of the Province of Buenos Aires, which prohibit any player from leaving the city and not staying at the house of his respective local family once the tournament is underway.

On this basis, they removed Loma Alegre from the final. The boys' anguish and disappointment was palpable. Their chance to win the tournament, earned fair and square, had been snatched from their grasp. According to the *El Norte* newspaper in San Nicolás, 'it did not count for anything that Loma Alegre, through their representative Leonel Del Castillo, had relayed the circumstances of the boy who had left and returned to officials at Club Libertad, the institution that was hosting the Loma Alegre boys.'

The same newspaper, in the 'Semillero' supplement on

Thursday, July 30th and under the title 'Así no!' (Not like this!), let it be known that the tournament 'did not deserve a final like the one it got', that the complaint 'resulted in a team that had legitimately won its right to play in the final being deprived of its place', and that beyond the pure rules and regulations which 'surely relate to the care of the boy who is staying at a private house, it fails to protect what is right in a sporting sense and, what's more, the situation did not amount to a serious infringement by playing an over-age player.'

For the record, the team from Salto beat Las Flores 2-1 and became champions while, out of protest, Loma Alegre did not turn up to play their third place play-off match against Lanús.

The return to Quilmes was not the triumphant one that everyone from Loma Alegre had been expecting. And the same obviously went for Kun, who swallowed his anger all the way home.

It was a tough blow to take, one that taught him that injustice exists in life, but there are also rewards. Just like the one that life had in store for him and his family in the very near future.

Independiente
De Avellaneda

To further pack an already intense footballing schedule – consisting of his commitments with Los Primos, 20 de Junio and the trips away with Loma Alegre – the year 1998 would see the start of Kun's involvement with Independiente de Avellaneda.

A large group of boys would gather at the club's 'Wilde' training complex and be divided into different teams, to play in what was known as the Liga Metropolitana, a sort of district championship where the youngsters cut their teeth against battle-hardened neighbourhood teams. The stand-out players would then have the opportunity to move up to *El Rojo's* teams which, from 11 years of age onwards, competed in the Argentinian Football Association's youth leagues.

"He had to train twice a week. Bochini was in charge of that group, and the coaches included Osvaldo Carrica," says Leo.

Ricardo Enrique Bochini, that great Independiente idol, would therefore be one of the first people to take note of Sergio's quality on a football pitch.

"At only nine years of age, his technique and power stood out. Very few others at that age could finish like he could, and he struck corners so powerfully that they reached the near post. They would also kick lumps out of him. But the kid would just get up, shout for the ball and carry on playing. He really stood out, he was different and had enormous potential," he states.

The fact that Bochini became Kun's first point of reference at Independiente is richly symbolic. 'El Bocha', as he is known to one and all, is widely considered to be the greatest player in the Avellaneda club's history. Not just because he wore the red of *El Rojo* throughout his entire 19-year professional career – and the number 10 shirt, no less – but because of the quality of his play and all the silverware he collected along the way.

Between his debut in 1972 and his retirement in 1991, he made 638 appearances, scoring 97 goals and winning the Primera División title four times, the Copa Libertadores de América four times, the Interamericana Cup three times and the Intercontinental Cup twice. Furthermore, he was part of the Argentina squad that won the 1986 World Cup in Mexico, coming off the bench to play a few minutes against Belgium in the semi-final. None other than Diego Armando Maradona himself implored Bochini to "paint, maestro" when he came on, in homage to a player who had been his childhood idol.

Agüero was only three years old when Bochini retired from the game so he never saw him play. Nevertheless he inherited a certain feeling for football from 'El Bocha', shaped by the history of a club like Independiente. Many years down the line, and from the hands of Bochini himself, Kun would also inherit the number 10 shirt. He would do that shirt proud by performing in unforgettable matches that inspired standing ovations from *El Rojo's* fans, the likes of which had not been heard since the 'maestro' himself was playing.

With Kun's star on the rise, and despite his tender years, people continued to approach Leo with offers from other clubs. At this stage, Eduardo González, the journalist who had his own programme dedicated to Independiente and who Leo had met at Dardo Rocha, suggested that he introduce the Agüero-Del Castillo family to someone who he believed could help to guarantee the best for Kun's continuing development.

'Motoneta' – as they used to call González – "explained to us that he lived off what he earned, and so the help that he sometimes gave us when things were a bit tight had its limits, and that we really needed to find some more substantial support in order to keep Sergio going in the right direction. Eduardo helped us purely out of his friendship with Leo. There was no other agenda. He then told us that he could introduce us to a friend that he'd spoken with about Sergio," explains Adriana.

The man in question was José María Astarloa, a lawyer who – as well as being a member and fan of Independiente, and president of the Peña Roja del Tigre supporters club – worked for a businessman named Samuel Liberman at one of the country's main cable television operators, where he was in charge of their legal affairs. Indeed, on one of the channels broadcast by

Video Cable Comunicación (VCC), and at Astarloa's request, González had started to produce and anchor a programme dedicated entirely to Independiente de Avellaneda.

"González told me about a 10-year-old boy who, from what he said, was a phenomenon and had been tipped for stardom by Bochini himself. And he asked me if I could help him. He spoke very well of his parents, told me that he was one of seven children and that he lived in one of the *villas* of Greater Buenos Aires. I must admit," concedes Astarloa, "that right at that moment I was quite apprehensive about the boy's age."

The lawyer's reservations were not held over what could have been considered somewhat of a gamble, but rather over his desire not to see such a young boy come to any harm or be unduly pressured. Before pressing ahead, Astarloa chose to consult Liberman. Although the entrepreneur's business interests were not linked to football, he had had some involvement in the signings of some players by River Plate, the club he supported. And, on more than one occasion, he had mentioned to Astarloa that he was interested in further exploring this line of business.

The first opportunity had arrived when some of his contacts offered him a stake in one of Independiente's young prospects. It turned out to be the Uruguayan Diego Forlán, who was taking his first steps in the Avellaneda club's reserve team and whose father owned 40 percent of his economic rights. Astarloa went to see him play but, before making his decision, he sought a more informed opinion. Going through González, he heard the views of Ricardo Bochini, who unflinchingly asserted that the Uruguayan had a big future ahead of him.

Despite it being a gamble for the future, Astarloa no longer harboured any doubts and, consequently, finalised the acquisition of the percentage held by the player's father. Years later Forlán would be sold for millions to Manchester United.

The second opportunity, following the precedent set by Forlán, emerged during that conversation with González. Of course, this time it was not a 17-year-old, but rather a boy of only 10 years of age. After having spoken with Liberman, who gave Astarloa his approval to move things forward, he accepted the invitation to meet the boy nicknamed Kun.

"One weekday afternoon, I went to the Villa Domínico training centre where Bochini introduced him to me. He was so small… First he did a few keepie-uppies, and then he started playing in a game. And Kun nailed it. It was him against the rest. He was picking the ball up on the halfway line and dribbling it all the way to the opposition goal. And he could play long passes too… He reminded me of 'El Bocha'. He had the same ability to see the wider picture while on the field of play. He took free-kicks and could place the ball exactly where he wanted. His corner kicks didn't just reach the 18-yard box, he would send them to the penalty spot. I was very excited by him. I said to them that, if we could, we were going to help him," recalls Astarloa.

He consulted his boss again, and together they resolved to start taking firm steps towards ensuring that this support came to fruition. "We said to ourselves that, regardless of the boy's progress, we would be helping out a family in need."

The Agüero-Del Castillo family finally met Astarloa at a clerk's office on the corner of Calle Maipú and Calle Corrientes. It was Tuesday, November 24th, 1998. The manner in which the meeting unfolded was indicative of the respect and care with which both parties treated the issue at hand: what really mattered was the boy's wellbeing.

José María Astarloa, Eduardo González, Leo and Adriana sat face-to-face around the rectangular table in the office. The lawyer explained that the proposal consisted of paying the family a set monthly amount, in addition to imminently purchasing them a new home so that they could leave the *villa*. In return, the family would transfer to them 100 percent of Kun's economic rights as well as the right to represent him over the following 10 years.

"The reservations that I had about dealing with a boy of that age," says Astarloa, "were left to one side, and I was reassured, when I vowed to them that if I saw that the boy was forced into playing football to honour the arrangement, the agreement would be terminated. And that it would only continue so long as the boy wanted to play football, and that this remained his vocation.

"Adriana, with tears in her eyes, said to me 'look, for Sergio there is nothing more beautiful than playing football and when he fights with his brothers and sisters I punish him, I don't let him play and he spends the whole day crying'. That's when I appreciated the calibre of people that I was dealing with. A great mum, whose only concern was for the happiness of her son," says José María.

This impression was further underlined when Adriana voiced her own fears over Sergio belonging to them forever, over being tied into obligations that they would not subsequently be able to fulfil, and over what would happen if in the future Sergio decided not to carry on playing football.

"He told us," remembers Adriana, "that they were going to

help Kun because they saw great potential in him; that they didn't want to use us, or be our son's owners; and that if this gamble paid off in the future, everything would be fine. But they said that if Sergio didn't make it, we wouldn't owe them anything.

"He seemed sincere, and this reassured me. But I still had my doubts. Unlike Leo, who was very sure not only about our son's potential, but that it would be in our best interests to reach a deal."

All parties present at the meeting recognised that they were in the company of good people, and all went home satisfied with the arrangement that had been established. An arrangement that ensured that in the future they would not be surrounded by unscrupulous representatives trying to force through deals at any cost, nor for parents looking to be 'rescued' economically without gauging the consequences.

Over the coming years, different circumstances would put them to the test. And on each of these occasions, correct decisions would be made by honourable people who proved to be as good as their word. Furthermore, Leo and Adriana would look back with satisfaction at having once more chosen what was best for their son.

José María Astarloa, for his part, was equally happy to have helped his cherished Independiente keep hold of a new favourite son, one who would bring the club success on the field and huge financial benefits off it.

And on a personal level, he would have the satisfaction of being involved with two footballers – Agüero and Forlán – who would go on to form one of the most outstanding attacking partnerships in the world.

The number 10

Only a few days after reaching the agreement with Astarloa, and with the end of the year fast approaching, Independiente started the selection process for the players who were aspiring to make up their 1988 *categoría* and represent the Avellaneda club in the youngest division of the AFA leagues during the 1999 season.

One man with a perfect memory of this occasion is Cristian Formiga, who was at Kun's side on the day that Agustín 'Mencho' Balbuena made his choices. "More than 200 *pibes* were there. They had us playing 10-minute games in teams of 11 players. Some in red bibs, and others in yellow. Kun and I sat together right at the back, so they would put us on the same team. But when the time came, he went on first. They played him as a number 10 and he stole the show.

"I was chosen for the next game and I didn't have a kick until someone sent over a cross and I headed it in. A few days later, they told Kun and I that we should report for a trip to Balcarce, where Independiente were playing a tournament."

Formiga's memory is a vivid one, but Adriana Agüero is even more precise in confirming that it was on December 10th, 1998 that they were informed of their selection.

The tournament, in which he would represent Independiente for the first time, was to take place between January 9th and 17th, 1999 in Balcarce, the birthplace of multiple Formula One world champion Juan Manuel Fangio, located 400 kilometres to the south of Buenos Aires. The tournament had already become a summer favourite in Argentinian youth football and was accorded extra prestige due to the quality of the 20 clubs and 700 players that came from all over the country to compete.

The biggest clubs, such as Boca Juniors, Racing Club, Independiente, Newell's Old Boys and Vélez Sarsfield, all came up against local favourites like Racing and Ferroviarios from Balcarce, or Aldosivi, San Lorenzo, Alvarado, Independiente, Kimberley and River from Mar del Plata.

For this reason, scouts turned out in force from all four corners of the country and abroad, all trying to get a glimpse of the potential future stars of Argentinian football.

In this very same Balcarce City Tournament one year previously, in 1998, Newell's Old Boys from Rosario were crowned champions having defeated Racing Club from Balcarce by six goals to one in the final. Three of those goals were scored by a boy who was yet to turn 10 years of age, and who was chosen as the player of the tournament: Lionel Messi. There could not have been a better opportunity for Sergio to compare his ability than to compete in a tournament featuring the very best players around.

The group from Independiente, headed up by Agustín Balbuena, arrived at Balcarce on Friday, January 8th, a day before the start of the tournament. Leo Del Castillo, yet again honouring his promise to remain at his son's side, was another member of the party. Hosting Kun on this occasion was the Aguayo family, whose house – whether by coincidence or not – was right next to a piece of land with a little football pitch.

José – the father of the family, who assembled silos for a job – was struck by Kun's power when he saw him play football with his son Martín but, when he then saw him playing in a competitive match, he knew that he was watching a boy with remarkable potential.

"When I saw him play, I realised that he was different. He had such strength and power off the mark, something you don't often see in boys of his age. He was his team's best player. And that's why he was the captain."

José is proud to have said to many of his friends, especially those who were Independiente fans, 'remember the name Agüero... he's going to be a phenomenon'."

Halfway through the tournament, Aguayo had to pass on his hosting duties to a friend of his, Raúl Ferreira, a massive fan of Independiente who put Kun up at his house, albeit for just a few days. Such was Ferreira's devotion that he even made up Kun's bed with an Independiente quilt cover.

The team from Avellaneda performed consistently throughout the tournament, although they were not to win the title. During the first phase, they successively defeated Mar del Plata 6-0, Gimnasia y Esgrima from Tandil 10-0, and Racing from Balcarce 3-0.

They saw off Adelia María from Córdoba in the quarterfinals, setting up a semi-final against a Newell's Old Boys team who were shaping up as real contenders for the title, and who featured at the time a real stand-out performer: Leandro Depetris.

"Back then people were talking about the Newell's number 9, a little blond-haired boy who scored loads of goals," says Sergio. The team from Rosario won by two goals to nil and subsequently became champions for the second year running. Meanwhile, *El Rojo* had to make do with fighting for third place, a position they secured by beating Racing from Avellaneda by the same scoreline.

The story of Depetris, voted player of the tournament,

became somewhat representative of the times. After that final in 1999, and at only 11 years of age, he was purchased by AC Milan in Italy, where he would play at youth level. After two years in Italy he returned to play for River Plate, then for Brescia in Italy and finally, in 2008 and by now 20 years old, he had a brief spell at Independiente de Avellaneda.

However, his progress as a footballer did not live up to initial expectations, and his story instead became a ready-made argument for those questioning the results of transactions that take minors abroad and away from their homes before they have first completed their formative training, a phenomenon that would become more and more commonplace as the years went by.

Balbuena was more than happy with Kun's performances in the tournament and, in addition to giving him the number 10 shirt and playing him on the left-hand side of central midfield, he started to realise that his new charge was attracting interest from several other clubs.

"At that tournament, there were already people from Boca who wanted to take him," he recalls. Furthermore, their third place was considered to be a commendable result, given that the squad was still a work in progress.

"I had nearly finished putting the 1988 *categoría* side together, but they still needed to play together to see how they gelled. I decided to include Kun, to bring him on board due to the level of play that he had demonstrated. And he didn't let me down. His arrival improved the team. At Balcarce, he was the player who really stood out," says 'El Mencho', to which Sergio himself adds that "I always liked to get forward. And I always ran at people down the left. Most of the defenders were big and

I was small, but I was quick. When I knocked it ahead, I would beat them for speed."

For Sergio, despite not having won the tournament, this first experience on tour with Independiente did him the world of good. In addition to the six goals he scored, his all-round play was a key component of the team and everyone was pleased with his performances. And in particular Balbuena who, on his return, immediately underlined to Néstor Rambert, the head of *El Rojo's* youth teams, that they had an excellent prospect on their hands. Rambert, one of the club's most experienced youth coaches who had been there for 14 years, knew Kun from having seen him play at Los Primos, where his nephew Sebastián – who had enjoyed a noteworthy spell playing for Independiente's first team – ran a little football school. 'Chanana', as he was known, did not need a second invitation to think about it, and on March 20th, 1999 he signed Kun for Independiente.

"No matter what kind of pitch I was playing on, I always learned things. The potrero at Los Eucaliptus demanded better ball control, I had to learn to gauge the best way to make a pass because the ball was harder to control. On the baby fútbol pitches I had to be more alive to playing one-touch football, and to shoot as soon as I got a glimpse of goal. On the earth pitches, on the other hand, I learned to become quicker, to run, to know how to use my body, to dribble and, when the ball came over the top, to spin and get in behind the defence and through on goal. Therefore, when you get to a grass pitch, everything seems easier. The Independiente youth teams played on better pitches. But sometimes they took us to train where the first team usually had their sessions. On those days, I would put my boots on with an even greater sense of

*anticipation. To step onto that grass, that green grass, it really hit
you. It just didn't compare to what I was used to. And as I was
so young, I didn't know if I would one day be able to play on a
pitch like that for real. Back then I never imagined that I would
go on to play in the first team. So the days when they took us to
play there were glorious…"*

SERGIO AGÜERO

Saying goodbye to the *villa*

On July 16th, 1999, 12 years after having arrived in Buenos
Aires and after eight years living at Los Eucaliptus, the Agüero-
Del Castillo family left the *villa* behind to move to a new home,
illustrating how much the 11-year-old Sergio promised as a
footballer.

The purchase of the house on Calle Carlos Pellegrini, a side
street off Quilmes Oeste where it reaches house number 3000,
was the result of the family's agreement with the lawyer José
María Astarloa, who registered the house under the names of
Leo, Adriana and their seven children.

"This reassured us a lot because I was scared of leaving our
house," says Adriana. "It was on quite a large bit of land, and
had two bedrooms, a living room, a kitchen and a bathroom.
It was a big thing for us, although it was also difficult for us to
leave our friends behind."

Even though their new home was only 10 minutes from Los
Eucaliptus, relocating meant distancing themselves – albeit
slightly – from their neighbours Gustavo and Any, from Rubén
Amarilla and his family, and from other friends that they had

made in the area where they had lived for so long. However, those initial fears melted away as time went by.

Although they saw each other less frequently, the distance that separated the family from their friends never affected the mutual warmth that was always shown when they met at various future family events, where they all got on as though they had never been apart.

Leo and Adriana were always able to look after themselves and their family. But they certainly knew that leaving the *villa* would mean leading their family away from an environment where they may be exposed to the wrong kind of influences, and enabling their children to grow up in better surroundings.

Furthermore, and for the first time, they would be able to reside in a family home boasting all the minimum material comforts. The timing of the move could not have been better.

A couple of years later, in 2001, living conditions across the whole of Argentina, and particularly in the less well-off areas, took a sharp turn for the worse after a sudden economic crash, the confiscation of people's savings held in banks as part of the so-called *corralito*[1] measures, a default on foreign debt payments, an unprecedented political crisis and a consequent social downturn that saw the poverty rate reach 50 per cent.

Against this backdrop, a substance made from cocaine-based paste known as 'paco' and also referred to as 'the drug of the poor', started to wreak havoc among the young people drawn into the margins of the *villas*. Los Eucaliptus was not exempt

---

[1] *Corralito* was the informal name given to the measures taken by the government to stop a bank run in Argentina during the financial crisis of 2001.

from this phenomenon, with serious ramifications felt in the population's already deteriorating quality of life. This general decline in living conditions was also famously reflected by a growth in the number of *villas* and other marginal settlements, which by 2011 numbered 864 across the metropolitan area of Buenos Aires, inhabited by over half-a-million families, as revealed by the non-governmental organisation Un techo para mi país (A Roof for my Country).

Another consequence of the move was that a short time previously, on March 16th, 1999, Kun had changed primary schools to start the sixth grade at the 'Alto Sol' school, a private establishment paid for by Astarloa.

"José María also helped us get food and clothes for the children. He always told me that, whatever we needed, we should let him know," recalls Adriana, who at this time was working between five o'clock and nine o'clock each morning for a company that cleaned offices. "The money that he gave us was for Sergio. So even if we were a bit short, we didn't touch it. We were very clear that it was his," she confirms.

If the year had lacked a certain element of excitement up until then, that was all to change in the month of October. Independiente had assembled a team of club legends, led by Ricardo Bochini himself and also featuring Jorge Burruchaga, Ricardo Giusti, Enzo Trossero and Daniel Bertoni.

A boy from the youth teams was undergoing expensive leukaemia treatment, so in an effort to raise money for him, national TV star, Marcelo Tinelli, and his entourage were to play a benefit match against *El Rojo's* all-star team.

Twenty thousand people made the journey to Independiente's Doble Visera stadium on October 11th, 1999 in support of this noble cause. Many people from Los Eucaliptus were in attendance, because the 1988 *categoría* were to play a warm-up match against Racing Club, their eternal rivals. And Kun and Cristian Formiga were going to take part.

"That day was the first time that I'd ever played at Independiente's home ground. And my luck could not have been better," says Kun. "We won 1-0, and I scored the goal from a penalty."

Cristian – who will never forget that day either – can remember the goal very precisely, Sergio's first at *El Rojo's* home ground.

"He danced past three opposition players and, when he got into the box, they brought him down for a penalty. Imagine how we felt. What with the stands so full of people. For us, it was so crazy. It was the first time that we'd played there. And Kun steps up and takes the penalty as if it was nothing, as if he was still in Los Eucaliptus. We couldn't believe it…" confirms Cristian who, shortly afterwards, stopped playing for Independiente but remained friends with Sergio.

To this day, he still lives at Los Eucaliptus and he speaks of Kun more as an idol than a friend… as if a huge chasm has opened up separating him from the days, a few years ago, when that same kid used to sleep at his house and they would go everywhere together.

Out of the admiration he feels for Kun, the colour of his heart – once the red and white of his beloved River Plate – faded away, before being repainted in different shades. Firstly, the red of Independiente; then the red and white of Atletico Madrid; finally, the light blue of Manchester City.

"These days, I support Kun," he says, defining his new football identity.

He enthusiastically collects newspaper cuttings of his old

mate, showing them to the new friends he makes who refuse to believe that he was Sergio's right-hand man as a child. And he laughs when he realises that – as fate would have it – the surname of one of Kun's closest partners during his professional career, Diego Forlán, starts with the same three letters as his own.

*Sunday, March 1st, 2009. **Madrid. The Vicente Calderón stadium. Atletico Madrid vs. Barcelona. The 86th minute.***

The dream night to dedicate to Benjamín, his newly-born son who was in the crowd, had got off to an inauspicious start. After 30 minutes of the first half, his team were already 2-0 down after goals from Thierry Henry and his friend Lionel Messi. However, Atletico had managed to recover. Firstly thanks to a great strike by Diego Forlán from outside the penalty area, and then with a strong diagonal burst into the box by Kun himself, who beat Valdés with a low shot into the corner of the net. But Henry once again gave Barca the advantage. Despite being 3-2 down, and defending in a way that always gave the opposition a chance, the momentum remained with the team from Madrid. And in attack, with such a feared strikeforce, they still had plenty to offer. Forlán made it 3-3 with a penalty, powerfully despatched to the Barcelona goalkeeper's right. And four minutes from time, Kun left his mark once more. He looked for the ball on the left wing and, squaring up to Dani Alves, played it inside to Maniche and headed into the penalty area for the return ball, which the Portuguese duly provided with a neat first-time pass. Puyol closed him down in the area and got a touch to the ball but could not remove it from Kun's path who, this time with his left foot, finished with a shot across goal that crept just inside Víctor Valdés' left-hand post. The 4-3 victory sealed an historic double comeback, confirmed the potency of an attacking duo among the best in Europe, and represented the best possible tribute to Benjamín, Kun's son, whose first visit to a stadium had given his new, proud father all the motivation that he had needed.

Kun's year on the move culminated in December 1999 when he travelled with *El Rojo* to take part in the 13th edition of a tournament in the city of Mar del Plata in the Buenos Aires province, organised by a local team also called Independiente. Sergio holds one special memory from this tournament, in which he again performed with distinction.

"I think that I scored one of my most beautiful goals there. Unless I'm mistaken, it was against Alvarado. I started off from halfway up the pitch, on the right. I dribbled past the whole of the opposing team, even the goalkeeper, and put it in. The final was against Ferrocarril Oeste. And we won it on penalties."

The penalties ended 4-3, and the team were crowned champions before setting off on a lap of honour. 'Luigi' had travelled with Leo to the 'Happy City', as Mar del Plata is known, and he recorded the final on his video camera. However, as has been mentioned elsewhere, a selection of highlights from the recording only features nearby trees, the fencing separating the spectators from the pitch and other random incidents from the match itself.

But he did record a penalty incident which – in terms of the type of move, the players involved and the final result – displays a sequence of events that would be repeated many times in the coming years: a foul on Kun in the opposition penalty area, a penalty being awarded, and a goal being scored from 12 yards by the Independiente goalkeeper Emiliano Molina.

In the case of that penalty in Mar del Plata, Emiliano struck it into the Ferrocarril goalkeeper's left-hand corner, while the latter threw himself to his right.

The subsequent celebration showed another team image that would go on to be repeated again and again. A tight group of boys in an endless congratulatory huddle, with one figure standing out above them all like a giraffe, that being the lanky frame of Emiliano who, given his stature, looked more like the father of the other boys.

Despite being of the same age as his team-mates, he was at least three or four heads taller than them all. It is enough to say that, at 11 years of age, he was easily 1.80 metres tall. At 14 years of age, when the majority of the boys were just starting to develop physically, Emiliano had already grown to 1.89 metres. This difference was even more noticeable with Kun than with other players, as Rambert himself would call him 'Shorty' or 'Little Guy' due to his small stature.

However, never can such an obvious physical contrast have gone hand-in-hand with such a special footballing bond. The assurance that Emiliano provided in goal, his height and his strength, as well as his understanding with Kun, would pay handsome dividends for the 1988 *categoría* at Independiente.

"Emiliano, who could kick the ball a long way, knew that I would always position myself halfway upfield, waiting to break away on the counter-attack. What's more, if he collected the ball quickly after a corner kick, he knew that I would be waiting for it and he would send it my way. This was a typical move of ours. We had a telepathic understanding. We scored loads of goals like that," Sergio points out.

Goals like that became even more frequent after Emiliano became the designated penalty taker, many of which were awarded for fouls on Kun. It came as no surprise when, in 2002, this team of youngsters, which had by now become Independiente's *ninth team*[2], were crowned champions of the Argentinian Football Association (AFA) league for their age group and boasted two outstanding goalscorers: Sergio Agüero and Emiliano Molina.

Alongside each other, they would also play in other *baby fútbol* teams around the province of Buenos Aires and the capital city itself, and would together begin their journey towards their first call-ups to the AFA's national youth teams.

"We became very good friends and I often went round to his house. I remember that the first time I went around, he said to me 'I'm inviting you, so don't do what you do in training when you come up to me and take it around me on one side or the other'," Sergio recalls of his friend today, with a smile.

"And I used to tell him all the time that I dreamed of scoring a beautiful goal against Racing Club in the Primera, one of those that would never be forgotten. And he would always reply

---

[2] From the age of 13 years, youth teams at the top clubs in Argentina stop being referred to as *categorías* and are instead denominated in direct relation to the first team. The sequence of teams is therefore the pre-ninth (*pre-novena* generally for 12-year-olds), ninth (*novena*, 13-year-olds), eighth (*octava*, 14-year-olds), seventh (*septima*, 15-year-olds), sixth (*sexta*, 16-year-olds), fifth (*quinta*, 17-year-olds), fourth (*cuarta*, 18-year-olds) and finally the third team (*tercera*, 19-year-olds, also known as the 'reserves'). The second team does not exist, although some teams may have a 'selección' team made up of the best players from the previous three teams.

'you're going to make it, and you're going to do it. And we'll celebrate it together'. That's what he always used to say to me…',"
Sergio remembers today, clearly affected by the memory of a friend who he inevitably associates with one of the toughest blows that life has dealt him.

This goal finally became a reality years later, with a piece of play just like he had imagined. But it was not accompanied by the celebration his friend had dreamt about. Two months before that goal, Emiliano Molina – who had suffered a serious road accident – passed away due to the injuries that he had sustained.

Kun, however, in a tribute for all to see, made sure that the goal was celebrated in the only way possible: in a personal communion when, having scored the goal and against a backdrop of general euphoria among *El Rojo's* fans, he lifted his gaze upwards and, pointing towards the sky, revealed a t-shirt that he was wearing under his Independiente shirt, upon which was printed "For you Emiliano".

I am a *Rojo*

The years 2000 and 2001 would prove to be the perfect rehearsal for what football, and life in general, held in store for Sergio over the years to come.

His routine of intense sporting activity did not let up for an instant, and instead demanded even more from him, demands that he fulfilled out of a desire to miss not even one of the matches that his teams were involved in.

At the start of 2000, in the month of February, he travelled with Independiente – on this occasion managed by former player Guillermo 'Luli' Ríos – to the province of Córdoba to take part in the Fifth 'Adelia María' National Youth Football Tournament, named after the town in which it was held. Boca Juniors had been champions on each of the previous three editions, and arrived with the tag of favourites for the tournament.

However, Independiente knocked them out in the semi-finals, in a match still remembered not just for its intense and hard-fought nature, but also for the strong winds that made it almost impossible for either team to pass the ball in the usual way. The match ended 3-1 to *El Rojo* and featured a goal scored by Sergio, one that still lingers fresh in the memory for 'Luigi', again present on this occasion and by now a loyal companion for Leo, video camera and all.

"They were one goal down. Emiliano Molina cleared the ball from his area, but it was blown back due to the strength of the wind. So, because the ball wouldn't reach him, Sergio went deep to look for it close to his own goal. He must have beaten at least seven players then reached the opposition penalty area and finished it off, a wonder strike. I must admit," says 'Luigi', "that on that occasion I was filming the ground again. But the goal has always been engrained in my memory."

The final – inconceivable though it may have seemed for the organisers – was against Lanús. The tie, played on February 12th, was real end-to-end stuff, finishing in a 2-2 draw after which, thanks to a penalty shoot-out, Lanús took home the trophy.

The local media in Adelia María picked out Sergio Agüero and Lautaro 'Laucha' Acosta as the players of the tournament,

the latter a Lanús striker who put in an outstanding performance on the night of the final.

Acosta would later score a dramatic goal in the second minute
of injury time against Uruguay for the Argentinian under-20
national team in the South American championship held in
Paraguay. That goal was to prove particularly significant for
Agüero's future. For with this victory, Argentina secured second
place in the continental tournament, thus qualifying the team
for the Under-20 World Cup in Canada that same year and
the 2008 Olympic Games in Beijing. Argentina – with Sergio
Agüero as a key figure and Acosta also in their squad – would
go on to win both tournaments. Kun and Laucha would cross
paths again as opponents, but this time in Spain's La Liga, while
playing for Atletico Madrid and Sevilla respectively.

The year 2000 would also see Kun playing for a club in the
capital city for the first time. The club concerned was Bristol,
from the Parque Patricios area, one of the stand-out clubs in
the so-called FAFI *baby fútbol* league (standing for the Friendship
Federation of Youth Football) which is made up of 141 clubs
throughout the city of Buenos Aires.

The intensity of the FAFI league is highlighted by the sheer
number of players involved each weekend: 9,000 boys of
between 7 and 13 years of age, spread over seven separate *categorías*.

Each *categoría* is made up of 18 teams, who all play 38 games
between April and November. Playing on a *parquet* or mosaic
floor surface, as stipulated by the rules of the league, was
nothing new for Kun. Just as he played for Bristol on Saturdays,
he had previously done so for 20 de Junio and, before that, for
Primero de Mayo. The pitches were 25 metres in length and no

less than 14 metres wide, and the goals measured two metres in height by three metres in width.

The 92 goals that he scored that year, for which he won the award for the league's top goalscorer, are testament to his mastery and ability to unsettle opponents on those surfaces.

This contribution helped Bristol secure the championship with 63 points and a phenomenal record: 29 games won, five drawn and only four lost. In doing so, Kun left his mark on the FAFI, a football breeding ground from which boys such as Fernando Redondo, Carlos Tévez and Javier Saviola had all emerged before becoming stars.

The progress of Saviola, or 'El Pibito', as the manager of River Plate, Ramón Díaz, christened him, perfectly mirrored that of Kun. Saviola had made his debut, with a goal, at 16 years of age in October 1998.

"As he had made his debut at such a young age, I said that I wanted the same for me. And when I played, I was always Saviola. I remember saying to my old man that I wanted to have boots like the ones he wore, which were entirely black," says Sergio who, although having dreamt of being like the River player, was certain as to the team he supported.

"Many people around me wanted me to be a River fan. But I was sure that I was Independiente through and through. And nothing was going to change my mind."

Indeed, if it were his heart's desire to play in the Primera División, it was always going to be with *El Rojo de Avellaneda*. However, this desire could easily have led him in a different direction, as a combination of different circumstances could have knocked him off this course.

The neglect shown to youth development at many of Argentina's top flight football clubs is one such circumstance.

There are only too many examples of clubs paying fortunes to bring in players from other teams, without investing a minimal proportion of this in their youth set-ups. This indifference towards their young players does not just harm their finances. It highlights a lack of due protection shown to those prospects in their youth teams who, in many cases and increasingly over the last few years, have been tempted to move to bigger clubs around the country or abroad.

In Kun's case, all of the circumstances were in place. The Agüero-Del Castillo family's financial situation was far from ideal, various clubs had started to make all sorts of approaches to try to take him to their teams, and Independiente's senior management at the time did next to nothing to hold on to a player who was already showing such high potential.

"We went through difficult moments with 'Shorty'," says Rambert. "It's just that there was an intelligence and clarity to his play, so wherever we went they wanted to steal him from me. Boca, River… they were putting pressure on Leo from all sides. His dad wanted to keep him at the club, but sometimes he didn't even have enough money to take the bus."

A tentative effort was made when Independiente offered Leo the chance to work as part of the youth teams' boot room staff. Evidence of this time is recorded in the April 21st, 2000 edition of the sports newspaper *Olé* where, in an article entitled 'They want to keep him for themselves, whatever it costs', the national press made a direct reference to Kun for the first time.

The article describes the offer, made by Independiente and accepted by Leo, to work as a kit man in order for his son to remain at the club.

A full-colour photograph of Sergio laid out on a table in the boot room with Leo standing at his side – with the caption 'the little star has to be looked after' – accompanies the report, penned by journalist Federico Del Río. It is worth highlighting some parts of this article dedicated to Kun, who is described as 'crafty' out on the pitch but 'quiet and softly spoken' off the field of play.

'The way he plays draws the attention of all the parents on the touchline. 'Look, that's little Agüero. You won't believe how good he is. Watch him, watch him' they comment as they mingle pitchside. The *pibe* is only 11 years of age, but his dribbling and goals catch the eye of even the least attentive spectators. To leave no doubt as to his quality, the Independiente youth team striker scored three goals in the first match of the league season against Yupanqui, followed by another six against Excursionistas in the second game', begins the report that also features Kun's first ever printed quotes: "Rambert lets me play where I want, from the midfield forwards. I like to get out wide. I'm right-footed, but I can strike the ball with both feet. Sometimes I score goals, up to five and six at a time. And if I see that I've got two defenders up against me, I take them on. I like to dribble around them."

Leo worked in Independiente's boot room for six months. He then left, due to differences with some of the management. "At this time the club functioned thanks to the work of Rambert and 'Luli' Ríos, who were killing themselves for the boys. But if it had been down to the management, not one of them would have stayed. It was as if, instead of helping them, they would sooner discard them," says Leo.

Rambert himself recounts an anecdote in which he was cited

by the Board of Directors for a complaint put forward by other parents, who said that he selected a player who sometimes missed training sessions.

"I explained to them that this boy would guarantee Independiente's future. And I asked them who they believed more, me or the parents who were complaining. Then I suggested: 'maybe you could give him the money so he can come to training and get around, so he can buy decent boots…?' I won the battle at this meeting, and they told me to carry on in the same way as before."

Out of his own humility Rambert does not say as much, but he reserves within himself the pride of having helped Sergio to stay at *El Rojo*, even if he prefers to give the credit to Leo and his family. "I always appreciated their principles in keeping Kun at Independiente, despite all the problems and difficult moments that we went through."

Kun's path through 2001 also included a stop-off at Crucesita Este, who took part in the FADI league and to whom he was introduced by his friend and goalkeeper Emiliano Molina, who also played at this club. Despite winning 35 games, drawing two and losing just one, they ended the season as runners-up. Indeed, the only team who managed to beat them, Villa Ideal, became champions.

At the same time, Sergio returned his friend Emiliano's favour and took him to play in goal at Bristol.

"On Saturdays," remembers Kun, "I would play three or four games. It would start at two o'clock in the afternoon in the FADI Avellaneda league with Crucesita, then off we'd fly afterwards with Emiliano to play at half three in the FAFI league for Bristol. If I arrived on time, I would then play for Pellerano Rojo, a team in Lanús. And at seven or eight o'clock in the evening I'd do the same for 'Luigi' at 20 de Junio. Sundays were spent with Independiente in the morning and with Cacho at Los Primos in the afternoon. Did I ever get tired? No... I wanted to play in all of them!"

*Wednesday, August 27th, 2008. **Madrid. The Vicente Calderón stadium. Atletico Madrid vs. Schalke 04. 18 minutes into the first half.***

On this night, just as in those far-off days of his childhood, Kun demonstrated that the idea of getting tired was not something he particularly cared for. And also that nothing could diminish his desire to compete in every game possible. Three days earlier, he had returned to Spain from Beijing where he had won the gold medal at the Olympic Games with the Argentinian team, following a season that had itself started without a pause for breath the previous year after his participation, and starring role, in the Under-20 World Cup in Canada. Without the merest sign of jetlag, he put in a memorable performance to ensure that Atletico classified for the Champions League for the first time in 11 years. He opened the scoring with a header in the box after a perfect cross from the right by the Colombian Amaranto Perea, before providing two further assists in the 4-0 victory. The 55,000 people packed into the stadium, seeing him off the field of play with the cry of "Kun, Kun, Kun", shook in recognition of the commitment of this 20-year-old boy who gave his absolute all for the shirt that they so cherished.

Sergio's energy was apparently inexhaustible. In February

2001, he played in the fifth 'City of Ayacucho National Youth Football Tournament' for Independiente, 330 kilometres from Buenos Aires, which they dominated from first to last, unbeaten with 18 goals for and only one against. The final was against River Plate from Uruguay, who they defeated by one goal to nil, thanks to a free-kick by Kun.

Furthermore, this great performance led to the *Olé* newspaper printing an article about Independiente's 1988 *categoría* on February 23rd. With the headline of 'Summer Happiness', it told of a 'spectacular campaign'. The report has a photograph showing a smiling Sergio Agüero alongside Néstor Rambert. *Olé's* journalists were right to dedicate the column inches to that Independiente team. Soon afterwards, they would be talking about them again. And, in particular, about Sergio Agüero, who was already demonstrating a maturity on the pitch rarely seen in a boy of his age.

At 12 years old, Kun's physique was already starting to develop the traits that would become his trademark. The way that he walked with his shoulders seemingly starting each step before the rest of his body, his strong legs, and a body that seemed to have been sculpted from a model of the archetypal footballer… all endowing him with an invisible but unavoidable magnetism that ensured he would never pass by unnoticed. And how.

The following months would see Kun start to really come of age as he started to compete in his first major tournaments.

'The Family Stone'

Off the back of the title victory in Ayacucho, and led by Kun, Independiente's 1988 *categoría* squad went into the AFA *pre-novena* championship full of confidence. This competition was contested by teams representing clubs from the top three flights of Argentinian football.

Naturally enough, the sides that always reached the final stages were from clubs at the highest level of regional football. During the first phase of the championship, *El Rojo* scored successive and comfortable victories over Excursionistas, Atlanta, Ituzaingó, Boca Juniors, Yupanqui, Comunicaciones and Laferrere.

On a personal level, Kun's stand-out performance came against Ituzaingó, when he scored five of his team's seven goals.

In the second phase, which started on July 5th, the *pre-novena* team continued with their winning streak, broken only by two defeats against San Lorenzo and Lanús. Kun's best match came as he scored twice in a 3-0 victory against Vélez Sarsfield – a side featuring Damián Escudero, who would go on to be his team-mate in the Argentinian Under-20 national team.

As the league came to an end, Independiente were exactly a point ahead of the two teams that had beaten them: San Lorenzo and Lanús. With one game remaining, whoever finished top would win through to play in the grand final against River Plate, who headed up the other half of the tournament. *El Rojo* had to travel to Gimnasia y Esgrima, who they had already beaten by two goals to one in Avellaneda, while a Lanús team featuring an old acquaintance of Sergio's, Lautaro Acosta, were to face San Lorenzo.

The games were scheduled for Tuesday, December 12th, 2001 against the backdrop of unprecedented political, economic and social crisis across the country. Oblivious to all of the turmoil, the boys in the 1988 *categoría* of the AFA leagues prepared to settle what, for them, was far more important. The match in La Plata turned out to be anything but easy for Kun's team, who were beaten by three goals to nil.

"Gimnasia were on a poor run of form," recalls the manager Rambert, "but we didn't play well and they put three goals past us in 15 minutes. And to cap it all, the referee sent Kun off because he reacted badly when he was kicked for the umpteenth time. He never complained, but on that day it was too much. We were totally dejected because we thought we were out of the title race. Until we found out that Lanús and San Lorenzo had drawn one-all, which meant we were all level

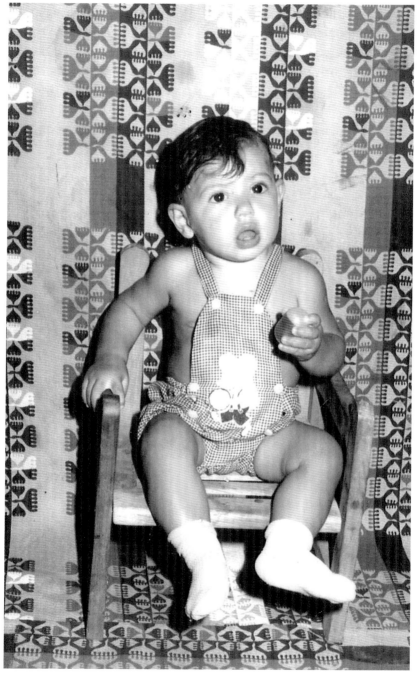

This is me, aged six months, in December 1988

This is our house at Los Eucaliptus – which couldn't be much closer to the *potrero*

My fourth birthday party

At the age of two,
standing with my father
Leo and his friend

My sister and I at our Holy Communion ceremony, held on the football pitch outside our house, in December 1997

At Don Bosco kindergarten in 1993

With my sisters in 1993 at the Independence Day celebrations at kindergarten

Me (left) with one of my first pieces of silverware, won with Loma Alegre in 1995

Another trophy presentation, with my friend Cristian Formiga (left) in 1996, this time with my club 1° de Mayo de Bernal

That's me on the right, with my Loma Alegre team-mates in 1993

And here I am when I played for Los Primos de Berazategui in November 1998 (bottom row, second from the left)

Me and Emiliano Molina
with Colombian goalkeeper
Faryd Mondragon in 1998

By 2000 I was playing for the Independiente youth
teams. Here I am with the ball in the front row

In March 2002, aged 13, I was training and playing with the Independiente *novena* team
(Courtesy of Olé/Gustavo Ortiz)

My debut for Independiente came against San Lorenzo when I was aged just 15 years old and my entrance onto the field was captured on TV

My first goal for *El Rojo* came on November 26th, 2004, against Estudiantes
(Courtesy of Olé/Marcelo Genlote)

Independiente legend Ricardo Bochini hands me the famous number 10 shirt in 2005
(Courtesy of Olé/Fabián Urquiza)

I dedicated my goal against derby rivals Racing to my friend and former team-mate Emiliano Molina, who tragically died after a car accident
(Courtesy of Olé/Juan Manuel Foglia/Sebastián Pérez)

I was officially presented as an Atletico Madrid player in June 2006

(Courtesy of Atletico Madrid)

I scored lots of goals during my time with *Atleti*, including this one in a 4-3 win against Barcelona in 2009

(Courtesy of Atletico Madrid)

on points. We had to play a triangular play-off to decide who would get through to the final," recounts the manager, with the same excitement that he must have felt at the time.

The games took place in the midst of *cacerolazos*[1] protests, social unrest and a subsequent repression that left 25 dead and more than 400 injured in Argentina and forced President De la Rúa to resign from his post on a fateful December 20th, 2001. Against this backdrop, Independiente played their first game against Lanús – which finished 1-1 – without Kun, who was not able to play because of a one-match suspension. He would return for the clash with San Lorenzo.

"And how!" says Rambert. "What a show the little guy put on that day! We won 3-0 and he scored twice. When the game ended Gabriel Rodríguez, who at that time managed the youth teams at San Lorenzo, said to me: "All it is, is that you've got that kid... he won the game for you on his own." And so we qualified for the final against River on goal difference."

The AFA set a date of Sunday, December 30th, 2001 for the deciding match, with Club Atlético Atlanta's stadium as the venue.

In a peculiar end to the year for Argentinians, those who met up to attend the final heard rumours through the media indicating that the new President of the Republic – De la Rúa's successor Adolfo Rodríguez Saá, who had only been in the job a week and had announced that Argentina had defaulted on its

---

[1] *Cacerolazos* was the name given to the popular protest against the financial crisis where people all over the country, mainly at night, would take to the streets or beat on saucepans in their homes and create a huge din in an attempt to make their feelings heard.

external debt – would also be handing in his resignation that evening.

While the very same media were busy explaining the constitutional mechanisms for succession in a leaderless nation, which would result in the unprecedented occurrence of Argentina having five separate presidents in just one week, those involved in the final were getting ready for kick-off. It seemed somewhat strange to play under those circumstances, but only football could provide a certain respite and a reason to come together in the face of such desperation.

On that hot morning, Leo Del Castillo and his companions anxiously awaited the start of the match. Without knowing who they were, nearby, two young men – one of them a businessman and owner of a private postal service, the other a lawyer – who were associates and invested money in buying the rights to footballers, took their seats ready to watch Sergio Agüero, who had been earmarked as an outstanding prospect.

Hernán Reguera and Gonzalo Rebasa, the men in question, had met in 1996 at a gathering of mutual friends, many of them connected to the world of rugby. On that particular day, Gonzalo was paying more attention to his radio – and specifically to a football match involving Chacarita Juniors, a lower league club fighting for promotion – than what was happening around him.

It was in those circumstances that he met Hernán, whose attention was drawn towards this man who, despite his surroundings, was listening to a game of lower league football, something that he also followed.

Conversation flowed naturally enough, as both were interested in the representation of sportsmen and took hours out of their respective professions to follow lower league footballers.

A few months later and despite neither of them having reached their 28th birthday, or perhaps because of the youthful drive of their tender age, they had already got five players on their books from the Colegiales club in the B Metropolitana league of Argentinian football.

Weekends would find the two of them at different football grounds in the lower leagues, trying to discover new talents and immersing themselves in something that was still really in its infancy in Argentina: the representation of athletes. In this way, they became regular but atypical spectators at clubs such as Flandria, Luján, Berazategui, Morón and Excursionistas, among others. Through these initial dealings, they increasingly integrated themselves into the world of football and moved closer to the country's top clubs.

Four years on from that first encounter, at the end of 2001 and by that time already fairly renowned as agents, Hernán and Gonzalo met up at Atlanta's ground to watch this promising young talent about whom so much was being spoken back then.

Although they had a rule not to sign players of such a young age, they could not resist the urge to get together to see him in action. Not only would they not regret having made that journey, but the occasion would mark the start of a much longer pursuit that would result, a little over a year later and following much hard work, in a significant achievement: the signing of Kun Agüero to the IMG stable, the international sports agency to which they had been recruited by Jorge Prat Gay, president of the group in Argentina.

The appearance of Hernán and Gonzalo in Kun's life is important, as in time they would become somewhat more than just his agents. The combination of their flair for business and legal experience would resolve the majority of the circumstances in which the Agüero-Del Castillo family would find themselves in the future.

Yet additionally, and perhaps of most relevance, is the place they would occupy as they participated in the family's growth and maturity as people, providing a kind of daily fraternal companionship during the early days of Kun's sporting development.

Also present on that peculiar December 30th, 2001, blending in among the spectators that had made the journey to Atlanta's ground as part of a ritual that he would never stop performing, was Miguel Ángel Tojo. The manager of Argentina's national youth teams, accompanied by national goalkeeping coach Ubaldo Matildo Fillol, sharpened his gaze to pick out the eye-catching players who could eventually make it to his teams.

For Tojo, watching these finals was a real pleasure. He tried not to miss any of them because he considered, and with good reason, that what could be witnessed among those boys was an unadulterated purity of football and a true amateur spirit, not yet tarnished by the pressures and ambitions of the professional game.

On that morning, Néstor Rámbert and 'Luli' Ríos named the customary line-up that Independiente had fielded in their recent matches, with Emiliano Molina in goal, Nicolás Torresán, Bruno Mora, Leandro Torres and Leonardo Talpini in defence; Emiliano Ferreyra, Daniel Molina, Ricardo Gómez and Rodrigo Breard in midfield; and Luis Morelli and Sergio Agüero in attack. Facing them, the manager of *Los Millonarios* Galdino Luraschi picked Sand; Ávalos, Gallardo, Sotomayor and Alvarez; Dul, Libramento and Palermo; Pereyra Monsalvo, Corvalán and Ruiz.

Independiente went ahead in the first half with two goals in two minutes, with Kun playing a vital role in each of them. The first was scored by Gómez in the 26th minute, the second by Ferreyra in the 28th. *Los Millonarios* went for broke after the interval and halved the deficit three minutes in, thanks to a goal by Alba, who had come on at half-time together with Diego Buonanotte, one of River's young prospects who years down the line would be transferred to Málaga in Spain.

'The River manager brought on the players who changed the game,' reads the Buenos Aires newspaper *Crónica* in its January 4th, 2002 edition. 'They got one goal back but could not find the equaliser. They created countless scoring opportunities but failed to make them count, and so Independiente were crowned as AFA *pre-novena* champions. A quick word also,' *Crónica* underlined, 'for a magnificent performance by *El Rojo's* number 10, Agüero, a player who you would put your mortgage on going on to a successful future. When they had to defend, the team also had goalkeeper Emiliano Molina to thank for a spectacular display which, in the final minutes, protected his team's advantage to ultimately secure the victory.'

A photograph of the triumphant squad, with Kun holding the cup, accompanies the newspaper's report. *The Crónica* journalist's opinion was shared by Miguel Ángel Tojo who, eight years on from that day, recalls that it was the first time after a youth final that he went to the changing rooms to congratulate the players.

"How well those boys played," he says. "Look, I must have seen so many of those finals… I was always there on the lookout for new talent. But on this occasion I went down to both changing rooms afterwards to show my appreciation for their standard of play. That was the first day that I laid eyes on Sergio. Because of the way he played and his physical strength, he was the best. He was tough, strong and great with the ball at his feet. And Emiliano was there too, the goalkeeper. The team was built around the two of them, one stopping the goals and the other scoring them."

Three goals in two minutes

The 1988 *categoría's* success in the *pre-novena* tournament saw expectations naturally raised by the time the full *novena* championship itself kicked off in March 2002. They grew further still after it became known that *El Rojo* had appointed Alberto Tardivo as youth team coordinator and Jorge Rodríguez as coach of the *octava* and *novena* teams.

Rodríguez boasted vast experience of youth football. He had been the director at this level at both Platense and Argentinos Juniors where, in addition to bringing in Juan Román Riquelme after discovering him at seven years of age in the San Jorge de Don Torcuato neighbourhood, he was also the coach of the *novena* team.

True to his status as an expert in these matters, Rodríguez – who would go on to become the general manager of youth football at Boca Juniors – remembers having spotted Kun before his arrival at Independiente.

"I saw him play during his first year in youth football, in 1999, when I was at Argentinos Juniors and the two teams played each other. I remember that I was with my brother, and we said to each other that we were in the presence of a phenomenon. On that day he jinked past every opponent he came across, took it past the goalkeeper and ran all the way into the goal with the ball at his feet. And he was no more than 10 years old. He was already impressive. When, a few years down the line, Independiente offered me the job, I knew that he was going to be at the club. I wanted to manage him. And I was lucky enough to be able to do so."

After assessing the championship-winning *pre-novena* squad, Rodríguez understood that he had to strengthen in certain positions. He did so at the back in the shape of Juan Caracoche, who he brought in from a club affiliated with Independiente. He also brought in Diego Campos, a battle-hardened central midfielder who he had seen at a tournament in Córdoba and who played for a *baby fútbol* team in Ciudad Evita in the Greater Buenos Aires area, from where he originated. Rodríguez's eagle eye also picked out José 'Pepe' Sosa, a potent, goalscoring striker who arrived from the province of San Luis and who he considered to be the ideal partner for Kun up front.

"We had to consolidate the assets that we had, and strengthen in certain areas throughout the team. As for Sergio," he says, "I played him as a link-man between the midfield and the attack, rather than as an out-and-out striker. I liked him to pick the ball up from deeper. And I looked for a more goalscoring number 9 – Pepe Sosa – so that Sergio could play in that slightly more withdrawn role.

"He still scored goals from back there. He would take hold of the ball in the midfield and they couldn't get it off him, and he was also a great provider."

In fact, Diego Campos and Pepe became great friends with Kun, companions on and off the field.

"Sergio was the one who most warmly welcomed me to the dressing room," remembers Diego. "I didn't know anyone, and he helped me an awful lot. Playing with him was a pleasure, but the friendship that we struck up was even better. I also spent many days with his family, who always gave me such a warm welcome…"

Diego and Pepe would later be present at some key moments in Sergio's life, like his first holiday by the seaside and even in his new life when football took him abroad, firstly to Spain and then to England.

There were Diego and Pepe, to accompany him and help make the settling in process in these new countries more manageable.

The air of expectation surrounding Rodríguez's team led to the *Olé* newspaper dedicating two sizable reports to them in its 'Juveniles' (Youth) section in the month of March 2002. The first of these, on Friday, March 1st, carries the headline 'Now they have to win here too' and is accompanied by a photograph of the squad with the following caption: 'The line-up of the champions. Wearing the white shirt is Sergio Agüero, a *super-crack* according to Bochini'.

The second report, penned by journalist Demian Meltzer, was published a week later, on Friday, March 8th, and is entitled 'The Family Stone plays in the *novena* league'. Meltzer went on to explain that Sergio Aguero scored three goals on his debut in the *Novena* youth league, in a 6-0 victory for *El Rojo* over Estudiantes, and assured that 'at only 13 years of age, this *pibe* is the club's biggest hope for the future'.

Within the article, Kun expressed his admiration for Ortega and Riquelme, and spoke of his dreams.

"Like everyone, my dream is to play in the Primera Division. And to play in a World Cup. To do so, I have to keep on going like I have so far and keep training, so that I don't lose my place."

The headline chosen by the journalist, Meltzer, turned out to be a premonition. A few years later, the 'Family Stone' would indeed appreciate so much in value that Independiente would sell him for millions of euros, a sum that would allow the club to escape the grasp of their creditors and modernise their home ground.

With the new name of Libertadores de América, the renovated stadium would be unveiled in November 2008 with a party and a match between some of *El Rojo's* old favourites and rising stars. Taking the ceremonial kick-off would be Mauricio and Gastón Del Castillo, Kun Agüero's younger brothers who were playing in the youth teams and who, having resolved the administrational problems that their older brother experienced, bore their father's family name like their sisters. The stadium was officially reopened with a competitive first team match in October 2009, which saw Independiente defeat Colón from Santa Fe by three goals to two.

The boys in the *novena* team really started their AFA league campaign on the front foot. They followed up the March 2nd thrashing of Estudiantes with a 2-0 win over Lanús, a two-all draw with Newell's and a 4-0 victory over Nueva Chicago.

In that game, Diego Campos – nicknamed 'The Missile' or 'The Tractor' due to his style of play – scored his only goal of the whole campaign.

"And I think that it was the only goal of my short career in football," he recalls with a smile. "The thing is, I never was much of a goalscorer. Quite the opposite. But I'll never forget that day. We were playing on Pitch 1 at the Villa Domínico training ground. Kun dribbled round almost all of the opposing team and passed the ball to me, and all I had to do was knock it in…", says Diego who cannot, and nor would he want to, forget this anecdote out of recognition of his friend's generosity.

The *novena* team's initial purple patch was ended by a 3-0 defeat at the hands of River Plate and a one-all draw at home to Gimnasia y Esgrima.

The chance to get things back on track came with their trip to Banfield on May 4th, 2002, where a positive result would see them back in the title race. It is worth following manager Jorge Rodríguez's passionate account of what happened on this Saturday, to find out in detail about the events that took place from 11:15 in the morning, when referee Daniel Romano sounded his whistle to start the match.

"The game had barely started and they came right at us with everything. And right away they forced a corner. In came the cross, a header, and in it went. One-nil to them. When we kicked off, Sergio burst between two players and played a one-two with Pepe Sosa at unbelievable pace. Pepe played the ball back to him and as soon as he latched onto it, from outside the area, he struck a shot of such precision and power that it was unstoppable. So fortunately we were quickly back on level terms, but Banfield had a very tough team and the game became very tight.

"In the second half they didn't create any chances against us, but neither were we able to get out of our own half. At one point, I looked at the clock and saw that only five minutes were left. I shouted to the boys to play the ball on the floor, and not to keep hitting it long. But it was no use. With two minutes to go, Sergio won the ball on the edge of our area. And he started to take it past their players. Tiqui, tiqui, tiqui, tiqui, tiqui… all the way up to the corner flag.

"Right then, he could have crossed the ball with his eyes closed and it would have been a certain goal. He'd taken it past everyone… and Pepe and Campitos were arriving in the middle.

"There were only 90 seconds of the game left. But instead of playing the pass into the centre, he cut back inside from only a metre away from the touchline and the corner, then hit a bullet of a shot that went in off the far post. It was one of those amazing goals… We all just looked at each other in disbelief. Even Banfield's coach looked at me, as if to say 'you can't do anything about that'… And my brother was saying to me, 'tell him that he should have played it back, tell him…' That put us 2-1 up, and all that was left was the referee's final whistle. But, do you know what the final score was? Four goals to one… Sergio scored twice more, in less than a minute-and-a-half.

"You see, I always tell my players to press the opposition as soon as they kick off, because they're a bit distracted. After the second goal they immediately pressed up, and won the ball. Kun took possession and smashed it in from outside the box. Goal!

"When they kicked off again, the boys carried on pressing and won a throw-in. It was Kun, he took it, they laid it back to him and 'pum', another rocket into the top corner. Three goals in two minutes. It was incredible… That's why I never understand it when they sometimes take Sergio off in a match that hasn't yet been decided. At any stage in the game, he can make the difference. Sure, sometimes it may seem like he's gone missing. But only until he puts his hand up… Then watch out! And to think that some coaches or journalists following youth football had doubts over whether Kun was the real deal.

"They said that he spent a lot of time standing still on the pitch. But if they were suggesting that he play like that the whole time, we would have won all the matches 18-0…" concludes Rodríguez's comprehensive account, covering each and every last detail.

*Saturday, April 8th, 2006. **Buenos Aires. The José Amalfitani stadium. The Clausura championship. Velez Sarsfield vs. Independiente. 37 minutes into the second half.***

On this day it was once again clear to see just what the people who knew Sergio Agüero best had been pointing out. El Rojo had arrived in Liniers hoping to break a run of five matches without tasting victory. However, it was a tight encounter, low on precision, and neither team could break the deadlock. Until eight minutes from the end Kun popped up with a little bit of magic, dancing past Claudio Enría and Hernán Pellerano and into the area before gently stroking the ball with his right foot past the advancing goalkeeper Gastón Sessa. A beautiful goal to make it 1-0, but he was not finished yet. Four minutes later he scored a second, seizing on a rebound on the edge of the 18-yard box to masterfully place the ball once more to Sessa's left, proving that his mere presence on the field of play is enough to change the flow of a game right up until the very last minute.

The lap of honour

The win over Banfield kept Independiente's *novena* team in the running for the title, and meant that they approached the rest of the season in high spirits. Wins over Chacarita Juniors, Vélez Sarsfield, Huracán and Argentinos Juniors followed, as well as a draw with San Lorenzo. The latter match featured various players who had been called up a few days previously by Miguel Angel Tojo for the Argentinian Under-15 national team. Four of them were from Independiente: Emiliano Molina, Bruno Mora, José Sosa and Sergio Agüero. The other three played for San Lorenzo.

Meanwhile, around this time the full Argentinian national team managed by Marcelo Bielsa, who had qualified in style for football's premier event, were eliminated from the first phase of the 2002 World Cup in Japan and South Korea, a source of much anguish for Kun who could not get his head around what had happened.

Having played 14 matches, manager Rodríguez and Agüero's side had racked up 30 points which left them in second place, only two points behind Boca Juniors on 32 and three ahead of joint third-placed San Lorenzo – who had a game in hand – and River Plate on 27 points.

The 15th round of fixtures, the third from the end, would see a decisive match-up, almost like a cup final, pitting, as it did, the league's top two teams against each other: Boca and Independiente.

The match took place on July 13th, 2002 and *El Rojo*, playing away from home, secured a crucial victory by two goals to nil, thanks to strikes by Pepe Sosa and Luis Morelli, a victory which saw them overtake Boca and lead the table with 33 points. Their next match, the following Saturday against Rosario Central, would be their last as they had no game scheduled for the final round of matches.

If they won in the city of Rosario and San Lorenzo – who had moved to 30 points after winning their game in hand – failed to win, Independiente would become champions of the *novena* division a week before the end of the tournament.

For this game, the technical coordinator of Independiente's youth teams, Alberto Tardivo, asked the board of directors whether, in a change from their normal routine, the boys could travel a day before the match and stay the night in the same hotel in Rosario as the first team usually did.

The request was accepted and, unprecedentedly for these 14-year-old boys, on this occasion they were to be treated like professional footballers. They felt this even more keenly when, on Friday, July 19th, they arrived at the hotel and were shown to double rooms while the *octava* and *séptima* teams, who also had matches the next day, were spread out in makeshift dormitories on the ground floor. Kun and his team-mates were over the moon.

"We were very motivated," says Sergio. "We knew that we had to get our rest, because it was a unique opportunity. Arriving a day in advance, and then sleeping in hotel rooms, was something new for us."

His team-mate and friend Pepe Sosa remembers that he shared a room with Kun that night. "We wanted to play the match the next day, and win it. But we were very anxious. So to kill time we played cards until it was late with Ismael Sosa, who was in the *octava* team at the time, and another boy. We wanted to go to sleep early… but we couldn't…" says José.

It was a fresh morning as dawn broke in the city of Rosario on July 20th, 2002. The cool temperature of seven degrees, which would rise to 14 degrees during the match, helped the boys to wake themselves up after a night during which they had struggled to get to sleep.

As for Sergio, his arrival at the Rosario Central reserve team pitch overlooking the River Paraná convinced him that the morning could have the sweetest of possible endings. He felt no particular pressure, despite knowing that he would be under the gaze of many who considered him to be his team's central figure. What he did feel was a responsibility as captain to give all that he had to win the match. And, if results went their way, the championship too.

However, any such thoughts faded away when, leading out his team with the number 10 on his back, and followed by Emiliano Molina he stepped on to a playing surface that was in many areas quite worn out. The rest of the team was made up of Bruno Mora, Leonardo Talpini, Nicolás Torresán, Yair Soloaga, Juan Caracoche, Luis Morelli, Diego Campos, Pepe Sosa and Luis Farías. For their part, Rosario Central named a starting eleven of Federico Rodriguez, Gastón Ale, Walter Godoy, Nahuel Valentini, Renzo Funes, Andrés Peralta, Emiliano Vechid, Guillermo Chiquetti, Milton Caraglio, Mauro Maya and Ezequiel Vera.

Out of all the boys who played in that match, and as another example of how difficult it is to reach the professional game, only three others would join Kun in playing, with varying success, in the Primera División: *El Rojo's* Juan Caracoche, and Rosario Central's Milton Caraglio and Nahuel Valentini.

Independiente would play the first 30 minutes from left to right. Leo Del Castillo – who, along with the rest of the boys' families and friends, got ready to watch the match from behind the railings that stretched alongside the touchline in front of a cement stand and close to the substitutes' bench – positioned himself as close as he could to Central's goal. In this way, he thought, he would be able to get the best view possible of his son's play. And he was not mistaken.

Shortly after referee Diego Colombo had given his signal for the game to commence at precisely 11 o'clock in the morning, Leo found himself in the perfect position to watch his son create the first clear opportunity to open the scoring. Kun received the ball on the left side of Independiente's attack, close to the penalty box, marked by Andrés Peralta, Central's number 6. He squared up to him, dribbled into the area and, after various dummies, reached the by-line where he cut back and beat his marker. The opposition number 5, Renzo Funes, attempted a desperate challenge that Kun resisted by sticking out a strong leg to keep possession of the ball. Knowing that he was beaten, Funes then tripped Kun's right foot and fouled him. The referee, following the attack closely, pointed to the penalty spot without a moment's hesitation.

Sergio, left spread-eagle on the ground, could see as much as he lifted his head and looked towards him. It was a sequence of events that had been seen in other matches: Kun had taken on the opposition, a penalty had been awarded and Emiliano Molina – up to that point unerring from 12 yards – was to convert it.

However, that morning would not have the same ending. Emiliano struck the ball low and powerfully, towards the corner, but the ball rebounded off the Central goalkeeper's left-hand post. Leo, from behind the railings, and the manager Rodríguez, standing on the chalk touchline, held their heads in their hands after that failed attempt. But they did not have too much time to dwell on it.

The next action, after 13 minutes, saw Luis Farías preparing to take a free-kick from just in front of the halfway line. Almost all of Independiente and Central's players were waiting in the penalty area. The powerful, lofted cross cleared all of the defenders and Kun, tight to the dead-ball line on the left-hand side of the attack, managed to get his head to the ball and send it back towards the centre of the box, where Luis Morelli stole in to win another header that sent the ball into the back of the net.

That made it 1-0, a scoreline that still stood at the end of the first half. At the start of the second half, a searching pass left Central's number 8, Chiquetti, one-on-one with Emiliano. The goalkeeper managed to keep out a powerful shot but was unable to prevent the rebound being headed in by Milton Caraglio, who had followed the attack into the area. The one-all scoreline was not enough for Independiente to win the title on that morning.

Now throwing caution to the wind, the boys – led forward by Kun – threw themselves into all-out attack. "But the ball refused to go into the opponents' net," recalls the manager, Jorge Rodríguez. "We missed so many chances... I said to Tardivo to keep calm, that we were going to win. But the minutes ticked by and we didn't finish off any of the chances that we were creating."

As if the situation was not dramatic enough already, a player from each team was sent off: Ezequiel Vera from Central and

Diego Campos, Kun's friend. Now 10 against 10, the game opened up. Shortly before the end of the regulation 30 minutes, referee Colombo added three minutes of stoppage time. There was little time left for the decisive blow to be struck. For the first two-and-a-half minutes, Jorge Rodríguez incessantly urged his players on. And in the last 30 seconds – for all that took place out on the field of play – he could not stop gesticulating.

Six years after the event, Sergio's account of the last 30 seconds of the match only goes to show the capacity that certain players have for remembering in detail each one of their goals, no matter how long ago they scored them.

"We had thrown ourselves forwards in search of the goal, but they won the ball and launched a counter-attack with us totally exposed at the back. Central's striker carried the ball forward with three of his team-mates up alongside him, against only one from our team, Bruno Mora, who was backpedalling. At the perfect moment, Mora took advantage of the striker not playing the pass, stopped suddenly, stuck a leg out and won the ball from him. And obviously, their counter-attack now became ours, only they had more men back.

"'Morita' gave it to the number five and he passed it to me just over halfway," remembers Sergio. Entirely focused on the play, Kun could not hear his manager Jorge Rodríguez – who could not stop jumping up and down on the chalk touchline – calling for him to keep hold of the ball and to dribble towards the opposition goal.

However: "I spin," continues Sergio's account, "and I quickly open the play out to the right for another team-mate who sprays it out to Sosa who was further out on the right. As Pepe breaks forward I start to shout 'Pepe, Pepe, play it, play it...' He's already in the box when he goes to cross it and a defender tries to take it off him, but he feints back and beats him, continues forward with the ball, sees me and crosses it. All I remember is being in the six-yard box, just in front of the left-hand post and I had one of the centre-backs tight alongside me and the goal-keeper in front. The ball came to me, I stretched out my leg, got a touch to it before the defender, and the ball went through the goalkeeper's legs and in.

"All of this happened in the six-yard box. When I saw the ball in the net, I started to celebrate like a madman. I ran away, took off my shirt and started to swing it around, with all my team-mates running after me. I stopped just short of the corner flag, still swinging the shirt around, and when they got to me I threw it up into the air. The shirt flew up, fluttered about and slowly fell to the floor near to the shirt belonging to Morelli, who'd done the same. I was stuck in the middle of everyone, squashed but happy."

Central still had to take the kick-off, so that the referee could blow the final whistle. Before this, the referee decided to show a yellow card to Morelli – who had already been cautioned – because he considered his celebration to have been over the top. The red card would follow.

However Morelli, on realising what was about to happen, instead of replacing his own shirt intentionally put on Kun's number 10 jersey, and gave his one to Sergio, in order to avoid being sent off. "In the middle of our celebrations," says Sergio, "he grabbed my shirt and gave me his. When the referee showed him the yellow card, he had the 10 on his back. He did it to avoid being dismissed. But one of Central's players spotted what was happening, and they ended up sending him off."

That initial error is still recorded in the official account of the match, which is still in the Argentinian Football Association archives. Under the heading 'Dismissals', the names of Exequiel Vera, Diego Campos and Luis Morelli appear. And between the last two names, crossed out by a pen, the name of Sergio Agüero can also be made out.

As soon as the home team played the ball out from the centre circle, the referee signalled the end of the match. The boys from Independiente quickly celebrated the dramatic victory in their usual manner, by crowding around the figure of Emiliano Molina, who stood out among all of them. The Kun-Molina partnership had borne fruit. Sergio had scored 11 times in the league and Emiliano six, all from the penalty spot.

Complete euphoria broke out a few minutes later when a member of one of the boys' families, who was still in Buenos Aires watching the match between San Lorenzo and Lanús, informed them over the telephone that the match had been drawn and so the 'Santos' could no longer catch them.

Independiente were the new champions, a week before the end of the season. The lap of honour and subsequent run from the centre circle to dive onto their bellies on the touchline were just the start of a party that would continue in the changing rooms. There, the cameras from ESPN Report – enjoying privileged access and already having recorded images of the game itself – sought out the man of the match.

"I thought that the game was getting away from us, but I told my team-mates to stay calm. To give it to me, and that I would put it away..." said Sergio Agüero, still in a state of undress and with a beaming smile on his face, as he uttered only a few innocent words that nevertheless showed the same assurance he had demonstrated on the field of play. "To become champions when playing well is the best thing that can happen to you," he added, in a plain declaration of what he believed the principles of the beautiful game to be.

What Sergio did not know at this stage is that the feat of scoring a dramatic goal in the dying stages to win a championship was one that he would go on to repeat 10 years later, in contrasting circumstances and with entirely different repercussions, but with the same celebration: furiously swinging his shirt above his head, in this case the light blue of Manchester City, in the most enthralling climax to a Premier League campaign of all time and for a historic coronation as champions.

A godfather for Sergio

The championship won by Independiente's *novena* team also made waves in the written press. 'A final worthy of Hitchcock' said the *Olé* newspaper in the youth section of its Sunday, July 21st edition, in reference to the match against Rosario Central. *Clarín's* local edition in the Avellaneda and Lanús area on July 24th ran with the headline 'Thanks to Agüero, *El Rojo's novena* team celebrate the title', making reference to the last-minute goal scored by 'the division's stand-out player' and to the 'talent of Agüero, a deep-lying forward with goals, ability and elegance'.

In a box of text accompanying the article, the technical coordinator of Independiente's youth teams Alberto Tardivo stated that "what those kids did was really spectacular. They played as if it were a final, and they should have won it comfortably.

There are *pibes* in this squad with a big future ahead of them, especially Agüero, who really is one of a kind: only 14 years old, he already plays like a seasoned footballer".

Sergio's joy, however, was not unbridled. Six days after winning the championship, his mother Adriana was admitted into the Quilmes Hospital, where she had to stay for a fortnight. Despite having felt unwell, she had continued to go to work so as not to miss out on the little money she earned. Accessible employment was not in abundance in those days in Argentina. What Leo made from his sporadic work was still not enough to support such a large family. Adriana was neglecting to look after herself, and it was to lead to an even more serious relapse.

"I just let myself out," says Adriana. "I was in the hospital for a fortnight, but I left without being discharged and without a precise diagnosis. My weight dropped from 63 to 55 kilos. I wanted to look after my children, so I went home. But I didn't gauge the possible consequences. It was at the Argerich Hospital that they finally diagnosed me with a very serious anaemia, and I was only able to recover from it with pills and injections. But I went a whole month without being able to walk. It was really hard because I wanted to care for my kids, but I couldn't."

Leo had to stand in for his wife, and during this time he was therefore unable to stay at Sergio's side as before. It was at this point that someone appeared in their lives, and who helped and supported the Agüero-Del Castillo family through those difficulties.

It had all begun a short time previously when, by chance at a practice session for Independiente's *novena* team, first contact was made between Kun and somebody with whom he would go on to share an obvious affinity. During those days, Darío

Fernández – the man in question – had been taking his son Lucas, who was a year younger than Sergio, to trials at Independiente. While waiting for a brief moment, he decided to go and watch a practice session that the *novena* team were holding on an adjoining pitch. He walked towards the fencing and watched the game alongside someone else, who was already watching from the same spot. He was thinking of quickly heading off to see his son, but was mesmerised by a boy out on the pitch who seemed to be doing whatever he pleased.

"That dark-haired lad can really play, can't he?" he asked the man standing alongside him. The person in question turned, looked at him and answered: "He's good, isn't he?" And they carried on talking for a while longer.

When training was over, Darío watched as the boy who had impressed him so much walked towards the fence carrying his boots and, addressing the man who was standing next to him, said: "Dad, I'm going to get changed and then I'll be right back." Darío, in a response indicative of his friendly and good-humoured nature, said to him: "That's your son? Well you're set for life, then…"

The hearty laugh he then shared with the father of that boy – none other than Leo Del Castillo and his son Sergio Agüero – proved to be the first of many during a conversation that continued that day at the buffet, and also represented the start of a friendship that has stood the test of time. Firstly with Leo and quickly with Sergio too, for whom Darío became a sort of guardian while Adriana went through her health issues.

During those difficult times for the Agüero-Del Castillo family, Darío took Kun into his own house as if he were one of his own without asking for anything in exchange. The foundations of mutual trust having been laid, Sergio's bond with Darío – as well as with the rest of his family, and particularly his son Lucas – went from strength to strength. As well as his striking, messy mane of hair, Darío's smile and his excitement shine through when he speaks about Kun.

Every memory that he shares comes accompanied by the inevitable tear, indicative of the love that he feels for him, a feeling that became mutual and that was never expressed more clearly than years later when Sergio himself chose Darío to be his godfather at his belated baptism.

"It became a sort of partnership based on care, where the currency invested was that of affection. I was there to fuss over him and protect him. And he used to love coming to my house. He would sleep over at ours, and then I'd take him to his training. From that time we saw each other at Independiente onwards, we were never apart," says Darío.

This was very much the case, to the extent that he became a loyal companion of Leo's during the fledgling career of Independente's number 10, in both the youth teams and the Primera División.

Darío also holds the privilege of having been the first to spot the similarities between Kun's physique and playing style, and those of the Brazilian Romario. It is a comparison that would later be made by none other than César Luis Menotti, provoking a huge media response.

"One day after a match, I said to Leo: 'This one's just like Romario. He's a little Romario.' A few years later, we heard Menotti saying the same thing. 'You see? Just like I'd told you,' I said to Leo," he smiles with pride when he remembers the anecdote. Darío, an expert in attributing nicknames, also called

Sergio 'the right-footed Maradona'. Although the less widely-known moniker, but one used more often by Darío, was 'Rottweiler'.

"For the way he walked, the way he ran, and, in particular, his speed off the mark, he was like a Rottweiler. He would take them on with so much power that he left a trail in his wake, making him unstoppable. Indeed, just like a Rottweiler dog. But a good one, you know?" says Darío.

This nickname ended up becoming a war cry during Kun's matches, after a particularly good piece of play or a goal. And it was also a good way of letting Sergio know from where exactly in the stands or the crowd he was watching, along with Leo and the rest of those who knew him. Darío would cup his hands to his mouth and, in his trademark hoarse voice, bellow out "Rottweilerrrrr!" with all his might.

The *pibe* out on the field of play would almost immediately recognise the call, responding with a knowing look, a smile, or even a goal especially dedicated towards where his loved-ones were gathered. Darío's love of life was infectious, and would start to rub off on Kun as he entered his adolescent years.

Agüero, the talisman

While Adriana was still in hospital, on Saturday, July 27th, 2002 and only a week after their lap of honour in Rosario, Independiente's *novena* team, led by their captain Sergio Agüero, would have the thrill of celebrating their title in no less a venue than Independiente's home ground in Avellaneda, at Alsina and Cordero, although this second street would eventually be renamed after the legend Bochini. They would parade their title before a Primera División encounter that *El Rojo* were to play against Lanús as part of the opening round of Apertura championship matches. Some 27,000 excited fans, packing out a colourful Doble Visera stadium, fervently applauded those boys whose triumphs allowed them to dare to dream of new golden eras to come in the future.

In fact Américo Rubén Gallego – or 'El Tolo' as he is known, at the time the first team manager – had a brand new team on show that night that also had the fans dreaming, but of more immediate success.

Marshalled at the back by a defender of the calibre of Gabriel Milito, with Lucas Pusineri, Federico Insúa and 'Rolfi' Daniel Montenegro in the midfield and a goalscorer like 'Cuqui' Silvera up front, Independiente's fans appeared to be full of hope that this would be the team to bring an end to their eight-year trophy drought.

The scenes in the stadium on that Saturday left a lasting impression on Kun. Although he had already stepped onto the turf at the Doble Visera in that benefit match against Tinelli's team, this night was different. He was moved by a crowd that cheered its team on incessantly.

The red smoke that the fans had let off accompanied the cry of "Champions!" that reached them from the stands. And while he completed the lap of honour with his team-mates, the love that he felt for *El Rojo's* red shirt grew even stronger.

Playing football for their first team had always been his dream. But witnessing the fans' passion – the same that burned inside him – only intensified and heightened that desire, which he nevertheless felt was still a long way from becoming a reality.

"It's difficult to explain how it feels to play for a club that you also support. The thing for me is that I arrived at Independiente when I was nine years old. And then I left when I was 18. In other words, I had spent half of my life at El Rojo. For that reason, when I wasn't able to say goodbye to the fans on the pitch at Independiente before going to Spain, I got so upset. I was on four yellow cards and after that match against Olimpo, we were to play against Boca at home. Maybe I got it wrong on that day at Bahía Blanca when at half-time I said to the referee Abal not to give me a yellow card, because I would be suspended for the one home match we had left. He said to me that if I didn't foul anyone, then I wouldn't have any problems. But at the first opportunity, after a normal incident, he goes and books me. At first I was angry at myself for having spoken with him. And then I just went crazy. And right there, out on the pitch itself, I started crying. The tears were just streaming out of me. I was a bit embarrassed, but I couldn't stop. The thing is, the realisation that I wouldn't be able to say goodbye to the club at the Doble Visera, and to the people who had supported me so much, was too much for me. Now I'm a bit older and when I remember that moment, I think that if it happened to me again today I'd cry again. These are feelings that come from within, and you can't hold them back."

SERGIO AGÜERO

As kick-off time approached, so Kun's anxiety grew. The wait for the match to start seemed like an eternity. He wanted to watch it in peace and enjoy the sense of hope that the team inspired in him. The same hope shared by all of the fans. Because a good start to the championship, he thought, would be the best way to keep the dream of winning it alive.

However, after completing the lap of honour, they asked him to stay out on the field of play because they needed ball boys.

"I didn't want to, but they insisted so much that I had no option but to say yes," says Sergio. "They gave me the clothes and sent me behind the goal where all the Lanús fans were."

If Kun's idea had been to watch the match in peace, then no sooner had he got to where they showed him than he realised that this was not going to be the case. "And there I was, wearing clothes that marked me out as an Independiente fan. The things they said to me. There wasn't an insult that they didn't throw at me…" he remembers.

Independiente's attack struggled in the match, and they even missed a penalty. The fans' impatience became tangible. The first half, and almost all of the second, had gone by and the match was still goalless. Until after 87 minutes, Independiente won a corner.

"The ball had gone out of play on my side. I ran quickly to get it, so as not to waste any time," tells Sergio, with the same enthusiasm as back then. "I grabbed it, placed it down for the corner and thought to myself: 'let's see if I bring them luck, and they score with this ball'… and back I went to see what happened. Serrizuela took the corner, Cuqui Silvera jumped unchallenged, got his head to it and scored. I couldn't believe it. I screamed my head off, as if it was me who had scored…" says Kun who, without wanting to, ended up contributing to Independiente's first win in the championship, eventually by the scoreline of two goals to nil after another goal scored by Juan Eluchans in stoppage time.

That win on the first week – and that luck that Kun thought he had provided for the corner – was the starting point of a great campaign for Independiente, who ended up becoming champions after a final head-to-head with Boca Juniors.

"It was the only time in my life that I was a ball boy. It didn't go so badly for me, did it?" smiles Sergio, who was unaware that in a little under a year's time he would be sharing the same pitch with many of those players who he had watched from the sidelines that day, only by this time he too would be part of the first team.

Kun did not have too much time to continue the celebrations. One Saturday on from the victory parade at the stadium in Avellaneda, the *novena* team began their campaign in the Clausura championship with a 2-1 victory over Estudiantes. The order coming from manager Jorge Rodríguez, and from the boys themselves, was to try and do the double.

From this first win up until the seventh round of matches, their record read three wins, three draws and only one defeat against Nueva Chicago, all of which kept expectations raised. Just like the previous championship, River Plate and San Lorenzo were shaping up as the other contenders for the title. The derby against Racing Club, which even at youth level was considered to be a unique fixture, was scheduled for the eighth round of matches.

It was played on September 21st, the first day of spring, and to the boys from Independiente, and Kun in particular, on that morning the sun appeared to be bigger than ever. They won 1-0 thanks to a great goal by Sergio from outside the area that Leo, present on that day at Racing's home ground at Deportivo Español, greeted with screams of joy.

"I remember that goal well," he says. "He feinted in from the left and then struck a high shot that flew into the top corner."

The September 22nd Sunday edition of the *Olé* newspaper backs up Leo's recollections. "A right-footed shot from outside the area by Sergio Agüero left those present with their eyes as wide as an owl's. A wonderful goal. No more yawns, just sit back and enjoy the football played by *El Rojo's* 1988 *categoría*, champions of the Apertura. Independiente 1–Racing 0."

It was Sergio's first goal against Racing at youth level. It would not be the only one that he scored against the eternal rival, including when he'd turned pro. All of them out of the top drawer, and all celebrated with the same intensity.

Saturday, February 25th, 2006. **Clausura championship. Avellaneda. The Racing Club stadium. La Academia vs. Independiente. 9 minutes into the second half.**

On this afternoon El Rojo's fans were left in no doubt that there was no better assassin to shoot down their eternal rivals than this 17-year-old boy, who in barely three minutes and with two strokes of genius scored two exceptional goals to once more etch his name into the history books. For the first, he received the ball from Bustos Montoya on the edge of the area and hit a low shot with his less-favoured left foot, which beat Campagnuolo and nestled sweetly in the left-hand corner of his goal. Three minutes later Oscar Ustari, El Rojo's goalkeeper, cut short a promising Racing attack and with a quick punt downfield fed Kun, who was on his own, up against José Schaffer. He won the header, continued running although tightly marked by the defender, and burst into the penalty area at pace. Campagnuolo desperately tried to close him down but Agüero, with two sensational side-steps, caused goalkeeper and marker to collide before opening out

towards the right and this time with his favoured right foot struck
a powerful shot that beat two other desperately retreating defend-
ers. Two goals to nil, and the fans in red were sent into a state
of almost unbridled joy. The result also thrust Kun into the lime-
light, overshadowing Diego 'Cholo' Simeone's debut as the coach
of La Academia.

The *novena* team followed that victory against Racing in 2002 with four more wins and two draws. One of the victories came once more against Boca Juniors, in week 15 of the fixture calendar, with Kun again the star of the show. 'Agüero, the main man for Independiente's *novena* team,' said *Olé* on Sunday, November 24th. "When he does not score himself, he tees it up for a team-mate. Kun, as he is known to one and all, was involved in all three goals and drove Boca mad."

That comfortable win kept Independiente dreaming about a second successive title. River Plate were first in the table but, after drawing the following week against Vélez Sarsfield, they held only a two-point advantage over Independiente and San Lorenzo, who had a game in hand against each other. If either of the two won, they would be champions. If they drew, it would gift the title to River.

There were two free weeks between the Boca match and the finale against San Lorenzo, which Kun took advantage of to travel with Los Primos to Mar del Plata where the Buenos Aires Games were being held, in which they would represent the area of Berazategui. The experience was an enriching one because, in meetings such as this, there were competitions in not just football but all sports.

"It brought kids from all over the province together, boys

and girls competing in many different disciplines," says his coach Cacho Barreiro. "There were 250 youngsters travelling from Berazategui alone. There were a lot of temptations for those children of only 14 years of age. The hotel where we were staying was next door to the one hosting the girls, who competed in the dance competitions. They popped round to chat with my boys. And some of them were swarming around Kun, and I had to chase them off…"

But Barreiro knew that they were growing up, and understood the process that they were going through. By now fully adolescent, they obviously had other interests aside from football.

"But I told them not to forget that they were there to compete. And, in particular, I said to Sergio that, with the potential he had, he would have to look after himself even more, as someone who wants to go far in the sport has to make sacrifices. In any case, I also knew that football wasn't the only thing in his life. In fact the first time that he went out dancing – with advanced permission granted by his mum Adriana – was one Saturday when he had slept at my house. He went with Mariano, who was the son of Adriana Iácono, the president of Los Primos, and who was two years older than him. We asked him to take good care of him. They went in a minicab, there and back, to a nightclub in Quilmes called Elsieland. But right at that moment, in Mar del Plata, it was another story. We were in full competition mode. And all of us wanted to be champions," explains Cacho.

While Sergio was in Mar del Plata, the Apertura championship of the Primera División reached its climax. Kun, who had watched all the matches in Avellaneda up until that point in the lower tier behind the home dugout alongside Leo and their irreplaceable mechanic friend Mario Portinari, would not be able to attend.

"The last but one game was against Boca Juniors. And there I was in Mar del Plata… We were losing 1-0, and if it stayed like that they would draw level with us at the top with only one game to go. But Pusineri equalised only four minutes from the end. I remember that day and that moment very well," says Sergio.

"I was walking down the stairs at the hotel because we had to go and play. I heard shouting and asked what had happened, and they told me about the draw. There and then, I started celebrating like mad."

A week later, on December 1st, 2002, Independiente won the title after beating San Lorenzo by three goals to nil. Kun remembered on this occasion the day that he had been a ballboy – on that first weekend of the season – and had placed the ball down for the corner that led to the first goal for his Independiente. And he knew that it was a sign of what was to come. And that luck would remain with him, and with *El Rojo de Avellaneda*.

Sergio's disappointment at not having been able to attend the match at which Independiente were crowned champions was balanced out by his happiness at having won the Mar del Plata tournament with Berazategui.

The final – which they won comfortably – was, paradoxically, against the team representing Avellaneda. The setting was spectacular, the stands full to the brim with people who wanted to see the boys who everyone was talking about in action.

"Once more," says Cacho, "Kun made the difference. He had a genuinely spectacular turn of pace, devastating. And it was in his nature to be cunning. When he had a free-kick on the edge of their area and they formed a wall to try to block his powerful shot, he would purposefully place the kick lightly and precisely so that the ball hit the wall and then broke to one side for a second bite of the cherry. And then, with the wall dismantled, he would hit it into a corner. He scored so many goals like that…"

Barreiro points out that nobody had taught him these moves, that he came up with them intuitively. And he recognises that, although Kun knew to take his instructions on board, he himself also had much to learn from Sergio.

"I told him on many an occasion not to stand so tight to the touchline, because I saw that he was boxing himself in. And he would answer me in a very curious way. He said to me that 'the line is my friend, I dribble better beside the line'. And he was right. Because he would knock the ball past his opponent's leg and head straight towards the opposition goal, unchallenged. The two of us learned a lot from each other, to listen to each other and respect each other," says Barreiro.

That year would be the last that Kun played for Los Primos. However, he never lost contact with Cacho. And even today he expresses gratitude towards him as one of the coaches who taught him most about football and life.

Sergio was unable to finish the year 2002 as he would have liked. He had won the Apertura championship with the *novena* team, the Buenos Aires Games title with Berazategui and *El Rojo's* first team had also won their title.

All that was left was the game in hand against San Lorenzo, which would decide the Clausura championship for Independiente's *novena* team. The winners would become champions or, in the case of a draw, the glory would all be River Plate's.

The match was played at *El Rojo's* ground at Villa Domínico on Saturday, December 7th. At this point, Sergio had adopted a new hairstyle that made him stand out even more. "He had let his hair grow long at the back, and also had part of it dyed blond," recalls Gonzalo Rebasa, who attended the match on that day, with a smile.

"But what really caught the eye was the way that he played, confirming all the while that we were in the presence of a true phenomenon. Just seeing him on the ball was enough to realise that he was a *crack*."

But Gonzalo, who had not yet met the inner circle of the Agüero-Del Castillo family back then, was also taken aback by the group of people that had gone with Leo to watch Kun in the final. They were headed up by a man who he didn't know at the time, but somebody he could tell was utterly unique: Darío Fernández, who would later become Sergio's godfather.

"I recall seeing someone with a dyed blond mane of hair, who arrived throwing fireworks and bangers, and who cheered Kun on throughout the match by shouting 'Rottweiler'. This wasn't a common sight in youth level matches. Right there, I realised that there was a phenomenon on the pitch, but that there was another one off it too," says Gonzalo, who on that day was also witness to one of the first sporting frustrations of Sergio's life.

Because, after only 10 minutes of the first half, San Lorenzo went ahead through Ángel Rodríguez. Nine minutes later, Kun equalised by making the most of a rebound off the post from a shot by his team-mate David Orellana. However, on this occasion there was to be no miracle ending like in Rosario.

The game finished as a draw and River were crowned champions. The photo of Kun sat on the halfway line with his hands on his knees, published by the newspaper *Olé* on Sunday, December 8th, was indicative of the frustration that he felt on that day. This new experience would prove to be very useful for him in the future.

Thanks to that disappointment, he would start to understand that as much, or even more, can be learned from a defeat as from a victory. It would also go on to demonstrate to him, a short while later, that in football there is always room for revenge.

A Debut For The
Record Books

At only 13 years of age, Sergio Agüero had already made a name for himself in the football world. Well-known club officials, agents and scouts from abroad made no secret of their attempts to lure a player who they believed had a big future ahead of him. As such, the attention and pressure that Leo, his father, had to deal with started to become even greater. And harder to resist.

However, despite insistence from the Agüero-Del Castillo family and José María Astarloa, Independiente gave no firm indication of their intentions to keep hold of their most promising young player, or to put his contractual situation in order.

"We had come to the agreement with his parents in 1998, and we let Independiente register him as a player with the AFA in 1999, without causing a fuss or raising objections," states Astarloa. "But every time we wanted to sit down and discuss the player's economic rights, we didn't get a reply. I had been informed that Boca Juniors and other big clubs had already tried to sign him, but I always told Leo that I was more inclined to keep Sergio at Independiente. That was also the club's wish. But no offer was forthcoming. There was an unhelpful lack of clarity coming from those in charge at *El Rojo*," says Astarloa.

On a monthly basis, Leo travelled to the lawyer's office at Puerto Madero. "I often went with Sergio. While we chatted, he'd have a fizzy drink and biscuits. And as we were on one of the top floors of a tower block, he would spend his time gazing at the river. He loved that."

One such visit to the Puerto Madero office took place in October 2002, only on that occasion Leo was accompanied by Adriana and their friend, the mechanic Mario Portinari. On that day, Astarloa heard from Leo himself that representatives from the great Italian club Juventus were trying to take Sergio to Italy to join their club.

The offer included – in addition to a significant sum of money up front – monthly payments to be made in Italy and Argentina, an apartment, travel, all expenses paid and the option for one of his parents to go with him. Leo and Adriana knew that it would be a difficult decision to make but, at the same time, the offer – which also included sizable payments to those who had helped them out so much up until then – remained attractive.

They were torn two ways: on the one hand, they believed that it would be best for Kun to complete his development as a player in Argentina but, on the other hand, they saw it as a firm offer that would remove any uncertainty over the future of their son, and their family.

For Astarloa, the situation presented to him by the Agüero-Del Castillo family was extremely delicate. He had a closely-held belief that, for Sergio, it would be better to stay in Argentina to complete his development, and that uprooting him prematurely might stunt his growth both as a person and as a footballer. But he also understood the concerns of his parents. For them, it was very difficult to turn down an offer that would remove the uncertainty from their future. However, and although he and his partners stood to benefit financially from the offer, Astarloa decided to advise them on what he firmly believed would be best for Kun's future. Once they were alone, he spoke to them from both his head and his heart.

"I told them," recalls Astarloa, "that I felt that Sergio was very young to be going to Europe; that he was 13 years old, and that I felt it was important for him to complete the learning process at Independiente. For him to carry on growing and developing in Argentina. That it was important for him to be able to identify with the club and with the country. I tried to visually explain as best I could, and I said that for me it was like taking a tree that wasn't yet fully grown from one place to another. It meant going to another country, with another language and another culture, and that they would run the risk, if they did so, of the boy not developing as he should.

"I even said to them that I couldn't give them the money that those people were offering and that, if they decided to accept the offer, I understood and I would make no objections, and that the agreement that I had with them would not be affected.

"They replied," says Astarloa, "that they were going to think about it."

It was not easy for Leo and Adriana to come to a decision. They were faced with two risks. If they rejected the offer, they would miss out on a very real opportunity to immediately secure a better life for the whole family, because nobody could guarantee that the future would bring another proposition like it. But they also knew that, by accepting the offer, they would run another risk: that of making a decision that might impact negatively on Sergio's development as a person.

They did not have to take too long to think about it. The following day, they returned to Puerto Madero to tell Astarloa that they had decided to turn the offer down and that Sergio would remain at Independiente, in Argentina.

Following this episode, José María Astarloa was certain of three things. Firstly that, regardless of what would happen with Sergio in the future, both he and the parents had chosen to do what was best for him. Secondly that the time had arrived to suitably clarify their relationship with Independiente in order to avoid future issues. And, thirdly, to find the appropriate people and the best experts to represent him and look after him during the next stage of his development.

Not until March 2003 – following various failed attempts, a media campaign that tried to paint him as the villain of the piece, and several days when Sergio did not attend his team's training – did Astarloa manage to fix a meeting with Andrés Ducatenzeiler, then president of *El Rojo*, at his offices on Avenida Santa Fe to discuss Kun's situation.

"We knew that it was going to be difficult to get them to accept what we were entitled to. Through third parties, they had already let us know that they were claiming that we would have to pay the club to keep a percentage of the player's economic rights. It was such a hard meeting. They argued that we had got a really good deal out of the sale of Forlán and that they needed the money because of the difficult times that the club was going through.

"We explained to them what our role had been with the Agüero family during those years when Independiente hadn't given them anything, and what our rights were. After much toing and froing, and intense talks, we agreed to pay them 70,000 dollars for 25% of the economic rights. What we did seemed paradoxical. But we preferred to do it like that to lay the situation to rest, once and for all. And that is what happened, as two contracts were signed. One which put everything in writing, and by which Independiente recognised the sale of the 25% in exchange for 70,000 dollars. And another, between the three parties, in which we committed to continue supporting the family, together with a break clause in case they wished to exercise parental authority over Sergio's future."

After that meeting, Astarloa was more certain than ever that the time had come to find the best people to professionally handle Sergio's fledgling career in football. Things were moving on fast, and decisions had to be made accordingly.

Astarloa's new resolve coincided with an era in which IMG, the world leader in sports marketing and representation, started successfully developing their operations in Argentina. The international company, established in the 1960s by Mark McCormack and which counted Roger Federer, Michael Schumacher, David Nalbandian, Tiger Woods, Serena Williams and María Sharapova among those on its books, had opened its Buenos

Aires office in 1993. It started strongly, but only gained real momentum from 1998 onwards after the arrival of lawyer Jorge Prat Gay as head of office.

Sure enough, one of his best moves was to open a division in the company to focus on football, an area that IMG had not explored in Argentina up until then.

Prat Gay had been passionate about sport since his childhood, firstly as a rugby fan and later as a player at all levels for Cardenal Newman. At a young age, just as he was finishing his law qualification, he had set up his own business involved in horse racing, raising and commercialising thoroughbreds, and events management.

Fate would have it that he crossed paths with two businessmen and international icons: the magnate and tsar of Australian television Kerry Packer and none other than the inventor of international sports representation and founder of IMG, Mark McCormack. The latter chose him, at only 36 years of age, to head up the Latin American branch of IMG. And it was not a situation he lived to regret.

To develop the football division, Prat Gay resolved not to persist with the methods that were in practise at the time, such as acquiring established agencies and placing them under the company umbrella. On the contrary he decided to put his weight behind the formation of a new division from scratch, one with a solid base respecting the country's unique characteristics, and the implementation of a serious, long-term project. He believed this to be the best way to enter a highly competitive market. So long as he chose the right people to take on this project, the scope was there to claim a share of the market through the professionalism of their operations and by offering potential clients the best possible level of service. Over the years, this model would prove to be highly successful.

By winning its market position organically, and not through acquisitions, IMG earned a privileged status in the world of footballer representation in the country. One of the iconic signings associated with that initial decision would be that of Sergio Agüero in 2003, when he was only 14 years of age and had a promising, although not trouble-free, future ahead of him.

Kun's talent, the way he burst onto the scene, and the work carried out by Jorge and his team, all paved the way for his transfer three years later, in 2006, to Atletico Madrid for 23 million euros, the highest transfer fee in the history of Argentinian football.

In the early days of the IMG Football Division, Prat Gay recruited journalist Darío Bombini, and together they embarked on a first stage consisting of representing players who had already turned professional. The successes and failures of that initial stage served as a great apprenticeship for both of them.

Coinciding with the Under-20 World Cup held in Buenos Aires in 2001, they began a second stage: signing younger players, many of whom had already made their debuts in the Primera División. As a result, players of the stature of Maxi Rodríguez, Leonardo Ponzio, the brothers Diego and Fernando Crosa and Maxi López joined the company's roster.

Having set this platform, they threw themselves into establishing a third stage: the creation of a youth football structure to identify talented footballers at an early age and to sign players from the youth leagues. Against this backdrop, and following a strict selection procedure, Jorge Prat Gay recruited two scouts in October 2002. They were none other than those two young business partners Hernán Reguera and Gonzalo Rebasa, the former a businessman and the latter a lawyer, who were involved in buying the rights to young footballers and who, in December 2001, had been present at Atlanta's stadium to witness Kun's Independiente 1988 *categoría* side becoming champions of the *pre-novena* tournament. With the two of them on board, results were not slow in coming.

The application of this model for acquiring talent, followed by the professional levels of service and personal attention offered to the clients, proved to be the winning formula that was to underpin IMG's strong standing in the world of footballer representation in Argentina.

"With the arrival of Hernán and Gonzalo, we embarked on the third stage that we'd envisioned back at the beginning," says Prat Gay. "Shortly after they arrived, and having already signed some young players, they started talking non-stop about Sergio Agüero. According to them, he was a *crack*, one of a kind."

Despite the boy's tender age – he was only 14 years old – and the natural doubts that this may have generated, Jorge preferred to stick to his guns by delegating and keeping faith in those who he had chosen to do the job, and gave the two of them the all-clear to make the necessary approaches that would lead to the player's signing.

"We had followed him throughout the whole of 2002," says Hernán. "We saw him in memorable matches. He was different, talented. The best by far. We really stood firm on this, because it would be worth the effort to get him signed. And Jorge understood that."

Hernán and Gonzalo went to work and, through their

knowledge of the media, knew that the businessman Samuel Liberman, via his lawyer José María Astarloa and the journalist Eduardo González, had links with the boy. And they wasted no time in approaching them.

Their meeting came at the precise moment that Astarloa was also looking for the best option to take with regard to Sergio's future.

"I always said to Leo and Adriana that we had to find people who were serious, who would take care of Kun and handle his affairs in every sense. And as he was earmarked for Europe in the future, it would have to be someone who could accompany him throughout the whole process. I had interviews with the most prominent names around. But when I met Gonzalo and Hernán, about whom I'd heard only good things, they seemed to me to be sound guys, untarnished by an industry where you really do find all sorts. What's more, they worked for a recognised company."

The meeting where Astarloa sat face-to-face with Gonzalo Rebasa and Hernán Reguera for the first time took place at a bar in the centre of Buenos Aires.

"It was important because it allowed us to conclude the first stage, which was the pursuit, and start the next which we had been working on for some time: that of being able to represent him. The thing is, there were no precedents for the company having invested in such a young boy," say Hernán and Gonzalo. "But we always believed that we had no choice but to sign the boy. That's why we kept on insisting, and in the end we got the green light."

Adriana Agüero remembers José María's exact advice on how Sergio's career should be managed. "He told us that, at that stage, we already needed someone who could represent him, and that he wasn't a specialist in that area. And that what mattered was that they were good people. He explained to us that the least he could do was to look for the right people for the job.

"A short while after, he introduced us to Hernán and Gonzalo. It was on April 20th, 2003, in a café on the corner of the IMG offices."

On that Monday, on the corner of Calle Pueyrredón and Calle Enrique Levene in the Recoleta district of Buenos Aires, José María Astarloa and Eduardo González made the customary introductions. There, various faces who would shortly form a close-knit team saw each other for the first time: the Agüero–Del Castillo family, and Hernán Reguera, Gonzalo Rebasa and Darío Bombini from IMG.

Four days later, on Friday, April 24th, the papers were signed at the company's office in the presence of IMG president Jorge Prat Gay.

"For us it was the end of an era," says José María with a hint of nostalgia, but with satisfaction. "The only thing I asked is that they carried on looking after the boy. And they stepped up to the mark fully."

Sergio sat calmly through the meeting. He preferred to let his elders speak, although he listened to every word that was said. He couldn't gauge the scale of what was being agreed. But he felt that he had taken one step closer to his family being able to live a better life thanks to his football. That better life started to materialise immediately following the signing of the agreement. Because, from this moment on, Leo and Adriana enjoyed unconditional support that allowed them to deal more easily with the complexities of such a large family, whose life changed so drastically in such a short space of time.

The typical duties of an agent took a back seat to the emergencies that they had to help out with. Each day, by resolving simple everyday issues or some setback or other, a mutual trust built up, underpinning a relationship that grew closer and closer.

Hernán Reguera recalls that "up until that point we had never spoken with the parents. We knew Leo from having seen him at matches. But we'd had no contact with him. The same with Kun. We met him in person on that day. We exchanged some words but he was very reserved and, what's more, in the company of people that he didn't know... But a strong, mutual bond formed quickly enough. There was good teamwork between the different parties. It was like they needed us, and we needed them. And it was all to make a success of Kun's professional career. And it turned out to be a marriage made in heaven."

Once again, and as always seemed to happen for Leo and Adriana, the right people appeared at just the right moment. Many big challenges were waiting around the corner. And, once more, time would go on to prove that the right choice had been made.

Great strides forwards

One of the first repercussions after signing the agreement was a new change of home for the Agüero-Del Castillo family, their second since leaving Los Eucaliptus.

At the insistence of Kun's new agents, they left the house at Calle Carlos Pellegrini in Quilmes to move to another located in Bernal on Calle Moisés Lebensohn.

"It was bigger than the other one. On the ground floor there was a living room, bedrooms, the kitchen and a bathroom. And another two bedrooms and a second bathroom upstairs. It was very important for us, to carry on growing. We had all the amenities that such a large family like ours needed," says Adriana.

Also around that time, after initial work by Sergio's manager in the Independiente *novena* team Jorge Rodríguez – and in an unprecedented move for someone who was still yet to make his debut in the Primera División – Kun was signed up by Nike Argentina. The contract had both a national and an international option, which the North American company exercised when Sergio burst onto the scene, to extend mutual ties that, while they lasted, brought both parties ample benefits.

Another pertinent matter was Kun's return to training with Independiente's *octava* team. And, from that moment on, an incredible succession of events that brought him much happiness but, equally, left him with strangely mixed feelings. He played his first game back, after an enforced break due to the contract problems, the day after signing with his new agents.

El Rojo won the game in question by a goal to nil against Unión de Santa Fe. However, Kun's spell in the *octava* team was short-lived. Because at the same time as Oscar Ruggeri took charge of the first team – replacing Américo Gallego, who had not been able to repeat the success of the previous year – Guillermo 'Luli' Ríos, who Kun knew from the youth teams, took over the management of a team that acted as the Avellaneda outfit's reserve side.

On June 5th, 2003, three days after his 15th birthday, Luli called Sergio up to train for the first time with that team.

"He told me that he wanted to bring me in to train with the senior players. And by Thursday I had already started training on the pitch beside the one where the first team trained at Domínico. I was over the moon. Just imagine. They were all there: Pocho Insúa, Gaby Milito, Rolfi Montenegro, Lucas Pusineri… And as we had a match the following day, we spent the night together as a team, just like they did. Emiliano Molina had also been called up. We looked at each other and we could not believe it… The only downside was that I couldn't carry on with my studies. I didn't have the time."

On that Friday, June 6th, he made his debut for the reserve team against Nueva Chicago in the Avellaneda stadium. He came on after 10 minutes of the second half, wearing the number 16 shirt. According to the *Olé* newspaper, "he brought clarity to the home team's attack and had a one-on-one opportunity saved by goalkeeper Jorge De Olivera."

A week later, in between matches, Sergio's belated baptism took place. The ceremony was held in a church in Don Torcuato, and at the same time they took the opportunity to celebrate the baptisms of Mauricio and Gastón, the two youngest sons in the family. Darío Fernández was chosen by Sergio to be his godfather.

"It was very close to my house, so we walked to the church. As well as Kun and all of his family, my wife, my children and Emiliano Molina were all there. Sergio had recently turned 15, and was already a strapping young lad. And I said that instead of me lifting him up in my arms for the ceremony, he should lift me up," says Darío Fernández, laughing heartily.

An intimate party to commemorate the event took place at Darío's house, at which point they were joined by Sergio's maternal grandparents and Daniel, one of Adriana's brothers. In this way a friendship was sealed, one that would grow stronger as the years went by, as Darío continued to bellow "Rottweiler!" at him with his booming voice during matches after particularly good bits of play. Darío had the chance to display his war cry on Saturday, June 21st when Kun, in his second game for the reserves and only three minutes after having come on in the second half, scored his first goal at this level.

The following two weeks would be absolutely intense for Sergio. On Monday, June 23rd, while training with the reserves, Ruggeri brought him over to join in with the first team's session. Almost without realising it, he was playing a practice game of attack versus defence with the same players who he had been fetching balls for in that match against Lanús six months earlier.

"I was impressed by how powerfully Montenegro struck the ball. But I stayed quiet… I played, I watched and I didn't say anything," says Sergio.

On Tuesday, June 24th, he played in the starting 11 of the *quinta* team that drew one-all with Colón from Santa Fe. On Wednesday, July 2nd, he was back practising with the first team and played for the substitutes, who lost 3-0 in a game against the starting eleven. That very same day, at the end of training, Ruggeri approached him and asked him: "Are you up for being named on the bench on Saturday against San Lorenzo, or are you frightened?"

Sergio could only respond in a barely audible voice, shyly but with genuine assuredness: "No, not at all… scared, no," he managed to reply.

The coach also confirmed to him that on Friday night he would be based with the rest of the squad. It would be their 19th and last fixture in the 2003 Apertura championship. The season had brought more pain than glory for *El Rojo*, and a squad overhaul was envisaged once it was over.

Leo, who was at the training complex on that day, felt a deep sense of happiness when an excited yet serene Sergio relayed to him his conversation with Ruggeri.

Father and son quickly set forth back to the house to pass on the news to the rest of the family. Cue total pandemonium. Adriana was excited, but worried about the kicks and blows that her son might receive from players who were bigger than him, in terms of both age and physique. The explanations from the men that "that's what referees are for" fell, once more, on deaf ears.

"On that day, Leo was absolutely buzzing. Just imagine. He almost never left Kun on his own at Independiente. If he did so on four occasions, that seems a lot. What he did was incredible. And what's more, he did it without putting pressure on him, like other parents do. He just went with him and looked after him. When he had to point something out to him, he always did it at home, never in front of others. And Sergio listened to him. It could seem like he was away with the fairies, but he took it all in. He thought about it and a few days later he would surprise you with a thoughtful reply. Sergio used to win things, used to bring home trophies but he didn't talk about it much. All of that seemed normal to us. But that day was special. At that moment, we remembered about all the sacrifices that we had made. About the times when we didn't have enough money even for a cup of coffee. About everything that

Leo did to get him good boots. But I never imagined that he'd get as far as he did. Never. Now I see him on the telly and I say: 'that's my son…' No, I can't believe it."

ADRIANA AGÜERO

Debut time

The media quickly reported Ruggeri's decision to give a Primera División debut to a 15-year-old *pibe*.

The *Olé* newspaper, in its section on Independiente on July 4th, confirmed that 'at 15 years, one month and three days, Sergio Agüero, the brightest prospect in the youth teams, will make his Primera División debut' and clarified that he would be on the bench, but that Ruggeri had announced that he would bring him on in the second half.

Olé's report gave details on Kun's short career. But an insert penned by the journalist Eduardo Castiglione under the title 'He was unstoppable' best described Sergio and the expectations that he had created.

After making reference to the time that Kun and other prospects had spent in the FADI *baby fútbol* leagues in Avellaneda, Castiglione indicated that "this Kun always was a rascal. We suffered against him, and admired him, at my beloved Unión de Crucesita when he was playing for Primero de Mayo, when he would win games at will.

"I saw him score goals by dribbling from one end to the other, taking it around everyone. He used to hit free-kicks into the wall, and then smash in the rebounds.

"I saw him nutmeg defenders with his back to them, and cross the ball with a *rabona*[1]. He was impossible to mark. And for good measure, when he is given some stick, he is tough like the *potreros* demand. Here's hoping," he foretold, "that on a full-sized pitch he is able to do half of what he came up with on those small pitches, where he will never be forgotten."

On that same Friday, Kun stayed overnight in the first team camp for the first time. He travelled from the Villa Domínico training complex with the rest of the squad by bus – on the front seats, as custom dictates for the youngest players – to the Hotel Presidente in Buenos Aires, an experience which was similar, but also very different, to the one that he went through a year ago in Rosario when he won the title with the *novena* team.

Once they had arrived at their accommodation, he was assigned a shared room with the defender Rubén Salina and the substitute goalkeeper Lucas Molina.

"I know that I wasn't very aware of everything that was happening to me. To be there, with the first team players… It sunk in a bit at dinnertime when they sat me on a table with Pocho Insúa, Lucas Pusineri and other more senior players. And what really struck me was that they weren't talking about football, but about other things. Ruggeri was on another table with the rest of the coaching staff. I looked at him and thought 'what am I doing here?'" remembers Sergio.

To kill time, that night he went to the room where his teammates Pablo Guiñazú and Hernán Franco, who were twice his age, were staying. They played on the PlayStation until

---

[1] A *rabona* is trick where players kick the ball by flicking their strong foot round the back of their standing leg.

midnight. And despite his talent for video games, he could not win. If he was anxious or nervous about his debut, it was not obvious. More than anything, he was angry at having lost the games. Then he returned to his room and slept soundly until morning came.

At midday he received a visit from Gonzalo Rebasa, who travelled down especially to find out how he was feeling. It was not normal – and less still for the player himself – to be making his debut at such a young age in the Primera División. Gonzalo still remembers that moment.

He probed him from every angle possible, to try to find some sort of doubt or worry. But he could not pick up on anything that betrayed any concern. Quite the contrary. He was even surprised by the reply when he asked him what Ruggeri was like. "He answered: 'good…good…' Incredible. He was 15 years old. That night he was going to make his first team debut, he was surrounded by already established players and he was acting as if it was nothing… And he even told me that the coach seemed okay to him. I understood right then that the boy was unflappable. He just took it all in his stride, in such a way that really made him stand out from the crowd. It was something which I later found out would be a feature throughout Kun's entire career."

Sergio was calm in the hours leading up to the match. But as kick-off approached, scheduled for 21:10 on that Saturday, July 5th in the Doble Visera stadium in Avellaneda, his anxiety did start to increase. After all, it was not a normal day. Neither was it for Adriana, who would sense great excitement in addition to her own anxieties. It was to be the first time that she had been to watch her son in a football match. She had never done so previously, and she did not see anything strange in that. That had been Leo's role, while she stayed to look after their other children. She had thought about maintaining that custom of not going, but they convinced her in the end. And off she went, together with Leo and Rubén Amarilla and his wife, their friends from Los Eucaliptus.

They positioned themselves in the lower tier, behind the Independiente substitutes' bench, to get a better view. She was struck by how many women were there, and the way they shouted. "More than the men," she thought.

She looked at the pitch all lit up, the grass that seemed greener than ever, and she thought about Tucumán, about her teenage years, about the moment she met Leo and about the unfulfilled desire of her husband to play in the Primera División. She looked at him and understood that he too was going to fulfil a dream. He was proud, and you could see it.

At almost exactly the same time, in the home changing room, Kun received the shirt that had been assigned to him with the number 34 and his surname Agüero on its back. He had already decided that, after the match, he would give it to his parents as a gift.

He started completing the taping up ritual that Leo had taught him when he was little. The bandage, he had told him back then, must not be at all tight so that the feet did not hurt afterwards. To fasten it, sticky tape must be used but in such a way that it does not catch in order to keep it tight. When the time came to put on his shirt, Sergio realised that, paradoxically, he would make his debut for the team of his dreams – *El Rojo de Avellaneda*, or 'The Reds of Avellaneda' – in a white shirt. For on that day, Independiente would play in a different colour kit so as to avoid a colour clash with the visiting team.

Whether coincidentally or not, the shirt that he would wear on that night – all white, with blue in a band around the top of the sleeves and down the sides – was in the same colours as he had worn in his first steps as a footballer with Loma Alegre.

Once out of the tunnel, Sergio looked for his family in the stands. When he found them, the look that they exchanged said it all. Gonzalo Rebasa and Hernán Reguera, who had also gone to the Doble Visera, saw Adriana overcome with emotion, and unable to hold back the tears.

Their heartbeats all quickened in the second half when they saw Kun starting to warm up with the rest of his team-mates beside the touchline. Sergio's own pulse was throbbing even more vigorously, as he glanced at Ruggeri in anticipation of a sign to indicate to him that he was going to come on.

The boy from San Luis, Pepe Sosa – Kun's friend and team-mate from the *octava* team and who, in the *novena* team, played the pass for his championship-winning goal in Rosario – was a ballboy on that night. He positioned himself, as always, near the substitutes' bench. He chose this position because, if the television cameras focused on that side of the pitch, his relatives back in the province of San Luis were able to see him. But on that day he had an extra bonus, for it was he who Ruggeri asked to let Sergio know that he was coming on.

"It was thanks to me that Kun made his debut," recalls Pepe with a chuckle. Sergio, who in between his warm-up sprints was alive to everything, saw the sign that Ruggeri made with his hand: with his palm facing downwards, he made the gesture for 'the smallest one'.

He ran towards the halfway line and, while he was trying to

take his blue training top off, the coach put his arm round his shoulders and started to talk to him. For most people watching the match, this was the debut of a *pibe* who everyone said had a big future ahead of him. But the fans' main concern was over the current state of the team, as the curtain was drawn on a championship that had ultimately brought neither pain nor glory, and as they bid farewell to one of its last true leaders, Gabriel Milito, who was about to be transferred to Spanish football.

However, for a few others – watching in different locations but united by the common thread of a boy who inspired deep emotions in them – this was an almost sacred moment. Mario Portinari, the mechanic, felt prouder than ever to be a fan of *El Rojo*. Two self-confessed Racing Club fanatics were at that moment the most passionate of Independiente supporters: 'Luigi', Sergio's coach at 20 de Junio, was with his children in the stadium among *El Rojo's* fans at their home end, this time without the 'nuisance' of his video camera; and Jorge 'The Baker', who had taken Kun to Primero de Mayo after winning that bet with Leo, watching on television at his house in Bernal, could not hold back the tears.

Very close by, in Los Eucaliptus, televisions were tuned only to *TyC Sports*, the channel that was broadcasting the match live. In particular at Gustavo and Any's house, the old neighbours of the Agüero-Del Castillo family who could not hide the pride that they felt for their friends. And further into the *villa*, at Cristian Formiga's house, Kun's childhood lieutenant had to make a special effort to control his parents, who were crying as if it were their own son making his debut.

Further south in Berazategui, Cacho Barreiro, his coach at

Los Primos, accompanied by his children and grandchildren, trembled at the sight of the little face looking back at him from the television set, of that *pibe* who he had helped to grow.

Meanwhile, 300 kilometres north of Avellaneda, a 16-year-old boy at his house in Rosario – where he was spending his holidays with the permission of Barcelona, the club for whose youth teams he played his football – was surprised to see somebody a year younger than him on television, about to make his debut in the Primera División.

Lionel Messi, the boy concerned, would not forget what struck him as such a remarkable event, unaware that their paths were soon destined to cross.

On the other side of Buenos Aires, in Don Torcuato in the north, Jorge Rodríguez, the manager of the *novena* team, followed attentively as the cameras zoomed in on Sergio's young, agitated and excited face while Ruggeri spoke to him before he went on. Jorge guessed what Sergio would be thinking: "Stop talking and put me on, I want to get out there…"

This was pretty much how Kun was feeling, and all he managed to take in was the manager telling him to "play like you do in training, play your own game, and have fun".

The rest of the words went over his head. His gaze was fixed on the match and, although he nodded his head, his focus was already on the field of play. He just wanted to get on. He thought about Leo and Adriana and all the other people he knew watching them… And after being waved on by referee Rafael Furchi, after 24 minutes and eight seconds of the second half, on he went in place of Emanuel Rivas.

"History is made in Argentinian football. A boy who has only just turned 15, playing in the Primera División," remarked the ever-precise journalist Alejandro Fabbri in the televised transmission. It was indeed a historic moment: the Argentinian football archives had never recorded a player making his debut at the age of only 15 years, one month and three days.

Kun had achieved the feat at a younger age than Diego Armando Maradona, whose debut came at 15 years, eleven months and twenty days. He was younger too than Javier Saviola, Carlos Tévez and Pablo Aimar had been in the Argentinian game, or than Pelé and Ronaldo internationally.

*Monday, August 15th, 2011. **The Etihad Stadium. Premier League. Manchester City vs. Swansea. The 68th minute.***

On this evening, a restless Sergio Agüero again demonstrated that every first time is an opportunity, and one that must be seized with both hands. He had joined City 19 days previously, following his record transfer from Atletico Madrid. After 60 minutes, and with the Citizens leading Swansea by a goal to nil, Mancini gave the order for him to come on for the Dutchman De Jong. And in only 30 minutes he made a mockery of the speculation over how long it would take him to settle in, demonstrating that he had not come to the Premier League to slip past unnoticed. His first touch was a shot that forced the visiting goalkeeper Vorm into a testing save. And eight minutes after his introduction, he scored his first goal by ghosting in on the left to classily finish off a centre from the right by Micah Richards. Barely two minutes later, he set up David Silva for the Spaniard to make it 3-0. And to complete a perfect evening, with stoppage time being played, he scored his second goal and his new team's fourth with a powerful and precise right-footed shot from outside the area. It was his first game for the Citizens, and it marked the start of a long-standing love affair with City's fans, sealed by the 30 goals he would score in that first season and rounded off by a historic league title triumph.

Learning to fly

Sergio enjoyed the little-over 20 minutes that remained for him to play, although – perhaps due to nerves – his first involvement was a foul committed against a player from San Lorenzo, the opposing team featuring Pablo Zabaleta who would later be Kun's team-mate, friend and captain in both the Argentinian Under-20 national side that were crowned world champions at Holland 2005 and in English football.

The newspaper *Olé*, in its Sunday, July 6th edition, stated that seven minutes after having come on "he produced a lovely feint and quickly set off on the attack. And then a one-two with Insúa. Best of all: a burst past the defence and a cross that Ayala could not quite reach. Pretty good, no?"

For the record, the result on the night was 1-0 to San Lorenzo. It left *El Rojo* in 17th place in the table with 18 points, only three above last place and 25 behind River Plate, winners of the Clausura championship with 43 points under the stewardship of Manuel Pellegrini, who years later would be Kun's coach at Manchester City.

After that match, Sergio did not hold down a place in the first team. Seven months would go by until he played again. For some of that time he carried on playing for the reserve team, for whom he scored seven goals. It was around that time, in August 2003 to be precise, when he read in the *El Gráfico* magazine about another Argentine, a year older than him, who was considered to be the next big thing at Barcelona in Spain. What they said about Lionel Messi – for that was the boy's name – grabbed Sergio's attention: they predicted a bright future in the first team for him, and made comparisons to Maradona because he was also left-footed.

Although he would not easily recall his surname, neither would he forget what he had read. But he was paying more attention to what was happening at Independiente, where Oscar Ruggeri – after encountering opposition from the fans, who questioned his style of play – resigned as manager in October 2003. He was succeeded by Osvaldo Chiche Sosa, who also had to relinquish his duties in December due to poor results.

The constant upheaval and the club's erratic progress were obvious signs of confusion at senior management level at *El Rojo*. Sergio still hoped to play more of a role under the newly-arrived José Omar Pastoriza, a legend at the Avellaneda club who, at 60 years of age, began his fifth spell as the Independiente coach in January 2004.

'Pato' Pastoriza started pre-season with a squad of 30 players, many of whom had come from the youth set-up, including Kun. On the evening of January 4th, 2004, the squad were to set off by plane towards the province of Salta where the majority of their groundwork for the new season would take place.

Sergio took advantage of the free time to accept his godfather's invitation to have a midday barbecue at his house in Don Torcuato. The festivities were spoiled by his godfather Darío's pet Belgian shepherd, who reacted badly to Kun and bit his thigh. After the customary checks – the dog's vaccinations were up to date – but in some pain, he left for the Metropolitan Airport and arrived just in time to make the flight.

It was Sergio's first time on an aeroplane, and he really enjoyed it. He could even see Tucumán, his parents' province, from the air because the plane stopped off at its capital, San Miguel. The experience did not disappoint, and neither did those days spent in northern Argentina as part of the senior squad. Sergio was not spared from having his head shaved, however, a ritual administered by his team-mates to those who, like him, were starting a pre-season for the first time.

'Pato' Pastoriza's idea was to slowly introduce him to play alongside more experienced players. He even gave him some game time in the 3-1 defeat in a friendly against Boca Juniors. The arrivals of Fernando Navarro Montoya, the Chilean Rafael Olarra and the Colombian Jairo Castillo strengthened the coach's conviction.

"It doesn't take much to see Sergio Agüero establishing himself in the first team. There's a reason why he made his debut when he was only 15. You can see he's got what it takes," Pastoriza told the newspaper *Olé* at the time.

True to his words, on February 12th, 2004 he selected Kun for what would be his second competitive match and his debut against a team from outside of Argentina. This came in the 4-2 home win over Cienciano from Peru in the Copa Libertadores. He came on wearing the no.25 shirt after 69 minutes, replacing Alberto Sebastián García.

He would repeat the trick a month later, on March 2nd and again in Avellaneda, coming on after 74 minutes for Hernán

Losada in the 2-0 win over El Nacional from Ecuador.

Kun's appearance in the first team at 15 years of age had generated a heated debate over whether it was appropriate to give a debut to such a young player. Not just in Sergio's case, but for other young prospects too.

This phenomenon was becoming more commonplace in Argentinian football because of the urgent need for teams to replace their most valuable assets, who were sold to clubs abroad in order to alleviate financial woes. At other times, it was more a case of clubs searching for a 'saviour' to give their teams a much-needed lift. The most severe critics argued that it did not fit in with the players' process of maturing and that, ultimately, it conspired against their natural development.

Opinions were divided over Sergio's case. There were those who maintained that one so talented and precocious must start acquainting himself with the world of professional football at first hand, and that nothing should have stood in the way of his emergence, which came about naturally enough. Others, on the other hand, suggested that he should logically go through a spell in the youth teams first.

Keeping away from this controversy, Kun just made the most of every experience that came his way. Having contact with established players, being part of the team camp, listening to the team talks and, in a nutshell, experiencing professional football, all helped him to better understand a world in which he would soon be fully immersed.

Furthermore, what he was going through helped him to understand a number of things: that the best path to establishing himself in professional football would involve an inevitable and enriching apprenticeship; that, thanks to his hard work and talent, his time would come naturally enough; that he was at the start of a long career and that he had everything ahead of him; and that he had to make the most of that time in order to find his feet in preparation for when the opportunity came his way. That was the key. He now knew that it was not just about reaching that level, but being able to stay there. And in order to do so, he would firstly have to grow both as a person and as a player.

He would receive part of that tuition from the man who coached Argentina's youth teams: Miguel Angel Tojo. From the time that he saw him at Atlanta's stadium in the *pre-novena* final, Tojo had closely followed Kun and always called him up for the Under-17 team, even though he was still young for this level.

"Those boys who stand out in their age groups," says Tojo, "have natural, innate class. But they also have much to learn. For example, what most caught my eye about Kun, just like Carlos Tévez or Lionel Messi, is that they were so different to the rest. But they only started playing when the ball was at their feet. When they didn't have it, they stayed still waiting for someone to pass to them. They had to be taught, there-fore, that football is also played without the ball. They have to start moving to draw their marker out, to find more space or to create space for a team-mate."

The importance of Tojo's presence at this time cannot be underestimated for Sergio, who eagerly met up for the national youth team practice sessions at the AFA training complex at Ezeiza from Mondays to Wednesdays. Away from the pressures and demands of the first team, there he received – like the other boys who had been called up – personal guidance. Tojo played the role of the tutor, and Kun welcomed it.

"He always had something to tell me," he remembers. "At the end of a game – be it competitive, a friendly or just a training session – he would point out the things that I had done wrong. Even if we had won, you know? For him, what you did never went unnoticed. When I dribbled too much, he would say to me: 'When you have two or three defenders on you, it's easier to take a touch and then look to play a one-two or to pass forwards or back. You'll still get the ball. If you want to take everyone on, at best you'll manage it but the alternative option is simpler'. He taught me to trap the ball, to take free-kicks. It was incredible, because we'd take 30 free-kicks and we'd be dead. And he'd take 200 and still be as fresh as anything. 'I can do it because I'm used to it. You're still not,' he'd say."

Just as with his other coaches – each at their respective stage – Kun demonstrated the same capacity to take from his national youth team coach what was best for his development. Tojo knew how to teach, and Sergio knew how to learn. That was his finest virtue: a rough diamond who allowed himself to be polished. Proof of this can be found in the numerous times that he chose to stay overnight at the Ezeiza complex.

On those days, it was customary at the end of dinner for Tojo to approach him and say that he would pass by his room in half an hour's time.

"He used to come at eleven o'clock at night," says Kun. "And he would explain to me how the South American teams played: Paraguay like this, Uruguay like that…"

During these night-time chats, Tojo took the opportunity to outline the best way for him to make the most of his great potential. Alone in the bedroom, he would draw an imaginary football pitch and, with his hands, would show him the positions of the defenders and the attackers, and the movements that he should make.

"I tried to be as instructive as possible. I would speak with him and say: 'Once your midfielders have got hold of the ball, you simply have to make a move to go looking for it. You have to look to see if anyone's coming with you to be able to receive the pass or, if not, just halt your run and then go again. If the centre-backs are on top of you and applying pressure, you can't receive the ball. If you drop off to receive the ball and the defender follows you, knock the ball ahead and you'll beat him in the sprint. Or you'll have a lot of space to play the ball to a team-mate. And if the defender doesn't follow you, you receive the ball and then you'll take him on and beat him. Because the attacker knows what he's going to do. On the other hand, the defender doesn't know what the attacker is going to do. And if you take advantage of this, it can create a goal.'"

Years after those chats, Sergio Agüero, by now established in international football, remembers Tojo's words. And he repeats them – when asked to relate his experiences with him – with a curious precision, even using the same imaginary pitch and moving the fingers of his hands to imitate the movement of the defenders and attackers in the same way as his coach from those early adolescent years did.

"I learned a lot from him," he says, with heartfelt appreciation. "And I was then able to apply those lessons on a football pitch."

*Wednesday, October 1st, 2008. **The Vicente Calderón stadium. Atletico Madrid vs. Olympique Marseilles. Three minutes into the first half.***

After 11 years waiting, the fans could finally bear witness to a home match in the Champions League. And the red and white celebrations were not long in coming. The architect was Sergio Agüero who, putting into practice the teachings of his mentors, threatened to drop deep to look for the ball and then burst between his markers down the middle of the pitch. His team-mate Maxi Rodríguez spotted him and played an inch-perfect pass that fell between three defenders. Kun majestically brought the ball down on the edge of the area, beat a defender with a move to the right and – with the goalkeeper rushing out and another opposition player closing him down – hit an angled shot inside the left-hand post to send half of Madrid delirious. He ran off in celebration of the goal, finishing up with a thumb in his mouth in dedication to his unborn son. At 20 years of age, and without realising, he had already initiated his fatherhood with an unspoken message to the baby who he would name Benjamín: that it does not matter what you say but what you do, and that knowing how to listen is always the first step to learning.

The waiting game

Sergio had to wait until June 19th, 2004 – just under a year after his first team debut and 17 days after his 16th birthday – to be named in the starting eleven for the first time. It came in the 2-1 defeat away to Atlético Rafaela in the province of Santa Fe.

On that day, *El Rojo* lined up with Fernando Navarro Montoya, David Abraham, Darío Caballero, Hernán Franco and Raúl

Damiani; Cristian Zurita, Fernando Lorefice, Sergio Agüero, Cristian Giménez; Jairo Castillo and Emanuel Rivas. It was the penultimate fixture in a Clausura championship that ultimately saw River Plate crowned as champions.

Independiente had endured another campaign to forget with 22 points from 19 games, by way of five wins, seven draws and seven losses.

José Omar Pastoriza announced back then that he would seek to strengthen his squad, but that he would also put faith in youngsters from the youth teams. It therefore came as no surprise that a few days later, in July 2004, Kun signed a contract for the first time with Independiente and became a professional footballer. But the shock death of the manager on August 2nd, following a heart attack, changed those plans. Pato Pastoriza's passing brought deep pain to the football world, where he was a respected and much-loved figure. It also caused great anxiety among *El Rojo's* fans, for whom he had been a true idol.

For Sergio – who held Pato in the highest regard – this was a first loss and one that would soon be followed by others, causing him much pain.

"I will never forget that day. It was early in the morning. I was sleeping, and my dad woke me up and told me that Pastoriza had died. I couldn't understand. I turned on the television and they were reporting the news on *Todo Noticias*. I had a very good relationship with him. He called me 'Kan' instead of 'Kun'. There was good chemistry. When they told me, I couldn't believe it," he recalls.

The man chosen to succeed Pastoriza was Daniel Bertoni, another legend at the Avellaneda club and a team-mate of Ricardo Bochini's throughout all those championships won in the 1970s, as well as the scorer of Argentina's final goal in their 3-1 victory over Holland in the final of the World Cup in 1978. But Sergio had little time to put himself at Bertoni's disposal, as in a few days he was called up to join the Argentinia team for the South American Under-16 Championship that was to be played between September 11th and 26th, 2004 in Paraguay. It was to be his first experience as an Argentinian international.

As was already customary, his goalkeeping friend Emiliano Molina was also in a squad that additionally included: Juan Caracoche, his team-mate in the championship-winning *novena* team at Independiente; Diego Buonanotte from River, who was on the opposing team in that match in December 2002 when he won the championship with the *pre-novena* team; Juan Forlín, the Boca Juniors defender; Alejandro 'Papu' Gómez from Arsenal in Sarandí; and Mauro Formica from Newell's Old Boys.

Argentina progressed from the first phase without a hitch. Drawn in Group B, they beat the United States 2-1, Ecuador 3-0 and Uruguay 2-0. In the quarter-finals, they knocked Peru out by a goal to nil.

Just when they seemed certain to reach the final, Colombia eliminated them 2-0 in the semi-finals.

"That tournament was a disgrace," remembers Tojo. "We later found out that some Colombian players were 20 years old. It wasn't legal. At that age, it's a huge difference. I remember them kicking lumps out of Kun. It was terrible."

Sergio still had the consolation of having been one of his team's best players, the scorer of three goals in the tournament, and of having gained experience that he would be able to call upon in years to come, when he would claim two world titles and an Olympic gold medal with Argentina.

Furthermore, that championship marked the start of more concerted attention on the part of international scouts, who underlined his name and surname, in order to bear him in mind for future transfer deals.

On Sunday, November 21st, 2004, two months after returning from Paraguay with the national team, Sergio went back to the Monumental stadium in Nuñez, where he had attended his first ever football match. A little over eight years had passed since that moment.

On this occasion, however, he was not there to watch but to play. He was part of the Independiente reserve team managed by Pedro Damián Monzón, the former Independiente player who had been part of the Argentinian national squad that was runner-up at Italia 90.

For Monzón and his charges, it was a very important match. It was played during the warm-up to the first team match, against a spectacular backdrop. They wanted to make a good impression and, above all, to win the derby. On the bench, Monzón was a bundle of nerves and smoked cigarette after cigarette.

Before the referee's whistle sounded to start the match, he saw Kun approaching him and, with the impudence of a 16-year-old but respectfully all the same, he pinched one of his cheeks and very calmly said to him: "Moncho, don't smoke so much. Don't be nervous, I'm going to score two goals and we're going to win."

Monzón, a firm believer in *El Rojo's* great prospect, then watched from the best seat in the house as Sergio put in a magnificent performance, proving to be almost as good as his word by scoring one goal and setting up another in a 2-1 victory for the team from Avellaneda.

"I'll always remember what he did on that day," says Monzón. "The thing is Kun was already special; the kid was a winner. With that comment before the match, he confirmed that he had enormous confidence. And without arrogance, you know? He was already demonstrating, back then, that he had a gift for doing everything very naturally, both on and off the pitch."

Leo Del Castillo, godfather Darío Fernández and his son Lucas, friends Emiliano Molina, José Sosa and Diego Campos, and Hernán Reguera and Gonzalo Rebasa, who followed Kun wherever he played, also enjoyed Kun's outstanding performance at the Monumental on that afternoon. But on the same afternoon, the Independiente first team suffered a painful defeat by three goals to nil that led to Bertoni – who alleged a lack of support from the club's management – handing in his resignation three days later.

His successor would be none other than Pedro Damián Monzón – *El Rojo's* sixth coach in a year-and-a-half – who would arrive with Guillermo Luli Ríos as his assistant, who was also familiar to Sergio. It was no surprise, then, that Monzón immediately put his faith in Kun in attack.

"He was the best. And all that I did was what had to be done: give him a starting place. I grew up at Independiente, and I know what people at *El Rojo* like. Sergio ticked all the boxes. He had talent, played well and loved the club's colours."

There were only three matches left of that championship, and Monzón picked him in the starting eleven for all three, kicking off Sergio Agüero's short but successful campaign in Independiente's senior team.

The first of those matches was on Friday, November 26th against Estudiantes de la Plata in Avellaneda. The game did not start well for Monzón's charges. After six minutes they were already trailing 2-0, thanks to goals by José Sosa and Marcelo Carrusca. But after 22 minutes, and following a spirited response from the team, Kun – who had chosen to wear the number 20 on his back – advanced from left to right near to the Estudiantes 'D' and unleashed a powerful right-footed shot that flew into the top left-hand corner of Herrera's goal. It was his first goal in the Primera División.

"Monzón filled me with confidence," says Sergio. "And it did me good. He asked me to go out there and have fun, and to play right up front. And he told my team-mates to support me when I got the ball so that I could dribble. He always asked me to take people on. And that's how the goal from outside the area came about," remembers Sergio, whose words are backed up by Monzón.

"Before a match, I always speak to each player with a specific instruction. And on that day I did the same. But I only told Kun what you tell a *crack*: to have fun, to take the opposition on and to do what he knew best."

Sergio's performance in the match – which ended up as a two-all draw – was worthy of the most generous comments from the press, who adjudged him to have done enough to keep his place in the team.

Two days later, on Sunday, November 28th, the Independiente squad suffered another blow following the sudden death of substitute goalkeeper Lucas Molina after a cardiorespiratory arrest at his home. With all the emotion caused by a life lost so inexplicably – after Pastoriza, the second time that this had happened in three months – everyone at Independiente paid tribute on Saturday, December 4th.

Before the start of the match against Arsenal de Sarandí, all of the players in the squad, wearing grey sweatshirts with the number 12 on their backs and black armbands as a sign of their mourning, stood hand-in-hand around the centre circle and dedicated a minute's silence to him as a tribute.

In such a climate, the match did not go Independiente's way and they ended up being beaten by two goals to one. *El Rojo's* only goal was scored by Kun, a minute into the second half.

"I couldn't celebrate. We were all upset. What happened to Lucas had affected us," recalls Sergio, who on that evening received his first personal chants of encouragement from fans who were already excited by his play. The call of 'Agüero, Agüero…', which had almost subtly emerged on that Saturday, would soon become a universal and powerful chant.

A final win on December 12th, 2004 against Newell's of Américo Gallego – who, despite the defeat, were crowned champions in Avellaneda – was the last match of a year that ended with many people convinced that more opportunities lay in store for the young 16-year-old. Opportunities like the ones given to him by Monzón who, owing to a strange decision by the club's management of the time, was sidelined from the coaching staff after those matches.

Monzón was forced to hand over the running of the first team, but nothing and nobody could take away the intimate satisfaction and pride that he feels from having been the first coach to have given Kun a run of games in the first team. It paved the way in 2005 for that strong, crafty and talented kid with the bandy legs from the *potreros* of Quilmes to establish himself in the Primera División, and to become in no time an Independiente idol and an Argentinian footballing revelation.

Menotti, Messi
And Molina

The start of 2005 gave Sergio the chance to consolidate what he had hinted at in those last matches with Independiente. Even more so, given the arrival of César Luis Menotti to take up the first team reins.

The experience of 'El Flaco', the World Cup-winning Argentinian national team coach in 1978, could really help rubber stamp his progress. The timing just happened to be appropriate, too. *El Rojo de Avellaneda* was celebrating its centenary that year and the sense of a good team coming together, in addition to Kun's emergence, could only help to get the festivities off the ground.

The 15 international titles that Independiente boasted, from which they took their nickname of the 'King of Cups', deserved a player who represented the quality and finest footballing traditions that had always been a feature of the Avellaneda team.

The Buenos Aires newspaper *La Nación* reflected as much in a special feature for their January 2nd, 2005 edition, for which it brought seven of the club's all-time greats together. Pepe Santoro, Osvaldo Mura, Oscar Sastre, Ricardo Bochini, Roberto Ferreiro, Mario Rodríguez and Rodolfo Micheli posed for photographs alongside the young prospect Sergio Agüero, who represented the club's future.

There was further good news for Kun as the year got underway, as he was called up once more for an Argentinian national team, this time the Under-17 side that was preparing for the South American Championships, to be played at the end of March in Venezuela.

It was always a source of great pride for Sergio to return to the Ezeiza training facility. He liked being part of the Argentinian national team set-up, or the *Albiceleste* as it is also known, and sharing the dreams of many other boys who came together there at the different levels.

On that particular occasion a meeting took place, of no great significance at the time, but which would nevertheless be the starting point for a bond that would cause a considerable stir in the future. For, in addition to the boys in the Under-17 team that Kun joined, the Under-20 side that would take part in the South American Under-20 Championship in January in Colombia were also preparing at Ezeiza. They were all lodged at the same venue, and regularly came across each other at meal times.

On one such occasion Sergio went up to a group at dinner including Lautaro Formica, from the Under-20 team and whose brother Mauro he played with in the Under-17s, and Ezequiel Garay, also in the Under-20 squad. They were both from Rosario and played at Newell's Old Boys, and they were chatting with another boy, who he did not recognise, about some eye-catching boots that the latter had brought back from the USA.

Sergio followed the conversation with interest for a good while, before looking at the stranger and asking him: "Sorry, what's your name?" The youngster replied simply: "Leo". Sergio persisted: "Leo? Leo what…?" As they exchanged glances, the reply came quickly back from that third boy, who was also from Rosario and had roots at Newell's. "Lionel. Lionel Messi," he said. The surname rang a bell, but he could not immediately put his finger on where from. But a quick intervention from Formica and Garay, making the customary introductions, helped to clear any doubts.

He would later remember having read an article in the *El Gráfico* magazine, following his debut for Independiente in 2003, about an Argentinian who was playing at Barcelona and for whom a big future was predicted. And who also became, a few months later, the youngest player in history to make his debut for the Catalan club in a competitive game.

The surname Agüero also sounded familiar to Leo, and he quickly made the connection with that boy who he had seen on television while he had been on holiday in Rosario in 2003, making his debut for Independiente against San Lorenzo, and who had become the youngest player to play in the Argentinian Primera División.

Without knowing each other personally, both had heard a lot about the other and been surprised at what each had achieved at such a young age. They were not to know back then what further achievements awaited them, and less still that, a short time after that first casual encounter in Ezeiza, a close friendship would be formed between the two of them off the pitch and a great understanding on it.

There was also an extra spice to Sergio's satisfaction at having been called up for the Under-17 squad: it gave him the chance to be a part of the group of youngsters who would act as sparring partners for the senior team. In this way, at 16 years of age, he could get a taste of training with the established figures of an *Albiceleste* side managed by José Pekerman, the successful former youth team coach who had won three Under-20 World Cups – in Qatar 1995, Malaysia 1997 and Argentina 2001 – and who had succeeded Marcelo Bielsa as senior team manager in October 2004.

Pekerman was preparing his team for the Confederations Cup to be played in June, for the World Cup qualifiers for Germany 2006 and, of course, for the main tournament itself.

Miguel Ángel Tojo, who was a member of the coaching staff at youth levels, recommended Sergio and some others to Pekerman to put the senior team through their paces.

"I recall," says Tojo, "that to motivate him even more I said to Sergio that no player from the youth teams had ever managed to score a goal against the senior squad. 'I'm going to do it,' he replied. And he did exactly that. The goal is etched in my memory. They played the ball out to him on the left-hand side of the attack. He was marked by Facundo Quiroga. He cut inside with his right foot and, as he advanced, Gaby Milito came at him like a steam train. The two collided straight into each other, but Sergio kept possession. He dribbled the ball to the right and, as Leo Franco came out, he knocked it past him. What a goal."

Tojo's memory is not playing tricks on him and Kun corroborates his account, adding that "Tojo took me out of the game straight after the goal. He told me he did it because, if he hadn't, they might have taken it out on me. And he congratulated me on the goal."

Kun took a knock to his right knee as a result of the collision with Milito and, during a training session with Independiente a few days later on Thursday, February 10th, he felt it again. The initial prognosis came on the Friday: he had torn his outer meniscus.

"My leg had seized up. I couldn't move it. To begin with I couldn't stand up and, when I did, I couldn't bend my knee. And as I was always joking that something was hurting me, at first they didn't believe me. The arthroscopy confirmed the tear, and I had to have it operated on."

Because of the injury, the first significant one of his short career, Kun would miss the beginning of the campaign as well as the chance to play at the South American Under-17 Championship that was getting underway on March 26th in Venezuela. His representatives therefore sought the best specialist to take charge of the operation. They settled on Dr. Sebastián Rosasco, considered as a leading figure in the area. As such on Saturday, February 19th – in the company of his family and his agents Hernán Reguera and Gonzalo Rebasa, who oversaw everything down to the last detail – Kun underwent the procedure.

"I was a bit scared. I'd seen how other team-mates who it had happened to had trouble coming back afterwards. And I didn't want the same thing to happen to me. All I remember from the operating theatre is the bubble going down the tube. And after, when I woke up. I didn't even know where I was," says Kun. "Luckily everything went perfectly. They gave me a suture stitch and discharged me. They told me to relax and that in 25 days I'd already be on the mend."

Sergio followed all the instructions that they gave him for post-operation, although he found it hard to walk on crutches.

"After the operation I was more relaxed. And as I got better, all my confidence came back. I went to the gym, where they put me on different routines, applied ice and then got me jogging and running. The biggest shame was to miss out on the South American Championship, which acted as a World Cup qualifying tournament for that age group. I wanted to go at all costs. But the time frame was too tight and in the end they wanted me to stay in Argentina to complete my rehabilitation."

Miguel Ángel Tojo had listened to the doctors whose advice was that Kun should not travel so as not to take any chances. As normal, given the chance of a relapse, he decided not to include him on the list – he would never rush a player's return after injury. It was Tojo himself who called Kun by telephone at his home in Don Bosco – the Agüero-Del Castillo family had moved house again – to explain to him the situation.

"I had a good team and Sergio was my trump card," remembers Tojo. "But Menotti called me at the last moment and told me that the doctors didn't want to risk it. For me the most important thing is always the player. I couldn't take a chance with an injury that might affect him in the future. In any event,

I sent Daniel Martínez, the national team doctor, to examine him. He told me that the knee was fine but that there was still a danger. Then I called him and explained to him why I wasn't going to take him. And that, if all went well and we qualified, he'd have another opportunity."

Sergio did not know it at the time, but in two months' time he would receive another call-up that would more than make up for that disappointment.

At the same time as the start of the South American Under-17 Championship in Venezuela, and around the time of the Centenary Parade where nearly 100,000 Independiente fans celebrated 100 years at the club, Sergio returned to training and, quickly, to the first team.

This decision created no small amount of controversy, as some believed that his comeback had been too hasty. The argument went that, given that he had not travelled with the national squad, then his return to action should not be rushed. Despite this, Menotti confirmed that Kun would be in the starting line-up for Independiente's game against Gimnasia y Esgrima from La Plata, to be played on Saturday, April 2nd, 2005.

It was, in fact, in the week leading up to the match against Gimnasia when Menotti drew the comparison between Kun and Romario, the great Brazilian striker. He would not be the last distinguished coach to make such a comparison.

"We're in the presence of one of the best players to have emerged from Argentinian football, and one with enormous potential to keep getting better. In appearance he reminds me of Romario, for his playing style in and around the box," said 'El Flaco'.

Sergio found out about the coach's comments from his team-

With Atletico Madrid I was able to get my hands on the UEFA Cup after we won the
Europa League final against Fulham in 2010

(Courtesy of Atletico Madrid)

Winning the Europa League meant a lot to me and the fans of Atletico Madrid
(Courtesy of Atletico Madrid)

My son Benjamín was on hand to help me celebrate
winning the European Super Cup with *Atleti*

With the Argentina U17 squad in Paraguay in 2004, wearing the number nine shirt

I won the Golden Boot and was voted the best player at the U20 World Cup

I got to lift the trophy after our U20 World Cup success in Canada in 2007
(Courtesy of Olé/Fabián Urquiza)

As a 17-year-old I helped Argentina to win the U20 World Cup in Holland
(Courtesy of Olé/Sebastián Pérez)

Success also came in the 2008 Beijing Olympics. Here I'm celebrating a goal against Brazil in the semi-finals as we went on to claim the gold medal

And here I am with an Argentina flag and a gold medal around my neck in Beijing
(Courtesy of Olé/Fabián Urquiza)

With my mother Adriana at the 2010 World Cup in South Africa

Leo Messi and I help Gonzalo Higuaín celebrate a goal against South Korea at the 2010 World Cup

More action from the 2010 World Cup as we took on Greece

My dad Leo was with me as I completed my medical before joining Manchester City in 2011

I was able to score on my Premier League debut against Swansea City (twice). This is the first of them

As you can see, I enjoyed getting off to a goalscoring start for Manchester City

Mario Balotelli did some crazy things, but I got on really well with him

Carlos Tevez was one of several Argentinians at Manchester City

I scored at Old Trafford as we thrashed Manchester United 6-1 in October 2011

My goal at Norwich earned me the City goal of the season award in the 2011/12 season

I had a good relationship with City manager Roberto Mancini

As the clock ticked down in injury time of the final game of the 2011/12 season, I managed to stay on my feet despite a strong challenge to hit the back of the net against QPR and help City win their first league title in 44 years

(Courtesy of Manchester City FC)

mate Nicolás Frutos, who he was rooming with at the time. "I was sleeping and Frutos tells me to 'wake up, *Chapulín*[1]'. And he shows me on the internet what Menotti had said. My godfather Darío had been telling me the same thing for some time. But obviously, that hadn't reached the press.

"After those comments and the impact they had, some people started to call me *Chapulín* or *Chapu*. I never saw him play but I've watched him on the internet, and I do have a very similar running style. And physique too, although I must admit that at the time I was more impressed by another Brazilian: Ronaldo. I watched his videos every day. He was tremendous…" says Kun.

In addition to the physical resemblance (Sergio was 5ft 7" tall at the time and wore size six boots, Romario 5ft 6" and a size five), there were many other similarities in the way the two of them played: the feints and pauses while dribbling, the use of the body, the ability to hold the ball up and, above all, their finishing. What was certain is that Kun had only just started in the game, whereas Romario was already into the final stretch of a successful career in which he was said to have reached, when he retired in 2008 at the age of 42, the landmark of having scored more than 1,000 goals – like the great Pele.

Sergio, at only 16 years of age, had scored 19 goals in the *novena* team, a dozen between the *octava* and reserve sides, and two in the Primera División. Yet the comparison did make sense in terms of the significance of Kun's emergence, for he had already started to display in the senior game the qualities that had stood out so much at youth level, showing early promise

---

[1] Brazilian striker Romario is known in Argentina by the nickname *Chapulín*, meaning 'grasshopper'.

that he would comfortably fulfil in the years to come. Competing at increasingly demanding levels did not hinder his talents but, on the contrary, allowed them to flourish even more. In this way, the stage was being set for his inspiration, ability and quality to be fully expressed.

Saturday, November 17th, 2007. **Buenos Aires. The Monumental stadium. South Africa 2010 World Cup Qualifying Tournament. 40 minutes into the first half.**

On this afternoon, Sergio Agüero joined the privileged list of Argentinian footballers who have scored in a full international for their country. He had made his debut a year and two months previously in London in a friendly match against Brazil, coming on in place of Carlos Tévez after 20 minutes of the second half. But on this Saturday in Núñez he was named in the starting line-up, forming part of a fearsome attack alongside Lionel Messi and Carlos Tévez. The midfield supply was also of the highest order, thanks to coach Alfio 'Coco' Basile's decision to entrust playmaking responsibilities to Juan Román Riquelme. However, aside from the occasional spark from Leo Messi, the Argentinian team was unable to break down a tenacious Bolivia side. That was until, towards the end of the first half, Argentina won a corner on the left. Tévez played it short to Messi, who lifted his head and played a cross with his right foot that Martín Demichelis managed to get on the end of, sending the ball back into the six-yard box. Kun applied the finishing touch with a header from only a few inches out underneath the crossbar, once more proving the old adage in Argentina that "two headers in the box equals a goal". The ball rippled the back of the net to make it

1-0, sparking off celebrations among the whole team and opening up a match which would ultimately see Argentina emerge victorious by three goals to nil. He was 19 years old and this was his first – but would not be his last – goal for the senior Argentinian national team.

Glory and Pain

The foundations of César Luis Menotti's team were built around players from the previous year's team. And he surrounded his young players with experience brought in from elsewhere, in the form of José 'Turu' Flores, formerly of Vélez Sarsfield, Fernando Cáceres, formerly of River Plate and Boca Juniors and a long career in Spain, and 'Mono' Fernando Navarro Montoya. All of them were twice Kun's age.

The arrivals of Nicolás Frutos, a goalscorer from Gimnasia y Esgrima, Franco Cángele from Boca Juniors and Lucas Biglia from Argentinos Juniors, completed the squad. However, the team never got up and running in the Clausura championship and on April 19th – following four defeats, three draws and two wins – Menotti handed in his resignation.

During that period, because of his injury, Sergio only played in the last three matches, although in one of them, against Gimnasia y Esgrima, he scored his third goal in the Primera División. Menotti nevertheless had a notable influence on Sergio during his spell at Independiente.

"He was among those who had the biggest influence on me. 'El Flaco' knew how to talk to me. He pointed out a load of ideas to me that would be helpful for any footballer, but even more so for someone like me who had only just taken my first steps in the Primera División. Without a doubt, I wouldn't have turned out the same if I hadn't had him as a coach," declares Kun, who also indicates that some of his best teachings came through his work with the ball.

Menotti's departure led to another caretaker manager. On this occasion Miguel Angel Santoro, a former Independiente goalkeeper and club legend, took charge.

For Sergio, it was like starting from scratch again. He was named on the bench for six consecutive matches, without coming on. This was frustrating, but he found solace in being named as part of a provisional 42-man squad for the Under-20 World Cup to be played in Holland during the month of June. The team was led by Francisco 'Pancho' Ferraro, as Hugo Tocalli had left the role to become one of José Pekerman's assistant coaches with the senior national team.

Sergio kept the faith, even though he knew that it would not be easy to make the final 21-man squad. He was the youngest of a group that included some very good players. He demanded the absolute maximum from himself in training sessions, as he did in one of the friendlies – in which he played, although not from the start.

He needed to show what he was capable of, and the opportunity came just in time.

"I had just got back from Chile, for a preparation match with the national team that I didn't play in, and I went straight from the airport to a training session with Independiente. I arrived half an hour late. The practice game was already underway. When Pepé Santoro saw me, he told me to warm up and in the second half he put me on the team with the other starters.

I was raring to go… I'd been so long without playing… That was how I secured my place in the starting line-up for the next match, which was against Argentinos Juniors."

The match took place on Sunday, May 22nd, 2005, a few days before Ferraro was to name his final squad. And, once again, Kun was able to make the most of his opportunity. Thanks to his two goals, and another by Federico Insúa, Independiente won 3-2.

'Manrique intercepted the ball in midfield. Agüero set off with a change of pace, took on Medero (who fell), burst into the area and the 16-year-old finished à la Romario,' was how the report in the newspaper *Clarín* described the goal.

"I think that those six matches on the bench helped me to nail it against Argentinos and that, in the end, it was thanks to them that I was picked to go to Holland with the national team," recognises Sergio.

And so Kun was indeed included on the list of 21 players who would travel to Holland, announced by Ferraro on Friday May 27th. Sergio was in Córdoba where Independiente had played out a goalless draw with Instituto. As they were staying the night in the province, he returned to the hotel with the rest of the squad.

"We were having dinner when the news came through over the radio. I celebrated like mad, and everyone started to congratulate me. It was a really happy moment," he remembers.

Alongside Sergio the squad featured, among others, Oscar Ustari, the Independiente goalkeeper who was still yet to make his top flight debut, and defenders Ezequiel Garay from Newells, Fernando Gago from Boca Juniors and Pablo Zabaleta from San Lorenzo. The latter had played against Kun in his first match in the Primera División and, as fate would have it, Pablo would also become an important figure for Kun in the future when their footballing paths crossed once more at Manchester City.

The team also included one sole player who plied his trade at a foreign club: Lionel Messi of Barcelona, that boy that Kun had casually met in person for the first time a few months previously at Ezeiza, and who was all but unknown in Argentina because the Catalan club had signed him when he was only 13 years old.

Leo had made his first team debut for Barca on October 16th, 2004 and on May 1st, 2005 – at the age of 17 years, 10 months and 7 days – he became the youngest Barcelona player ever to score a goal in La Liga, in Barcelona's 2-0 defeat of Albacete. Messi, who was wearing the unusual number 30 shirt, scored with a lob after a great pass by Ronaldinho. The image of the Brazilian giving Leo a piggy-back in celebration hinted at a partnership that would subsequently pay great dividends for the Catalans.

Exactly a month after that first goal for Barca, Sergio and Leo saw each other again, although on this occasion out on the field of play. It was on June 1st, 2005, at the last training session for the Under-20 national team before they travelled to Holland.

The *pibes* from the national team played an informal warm-up match against their counterparts from Arsenal de Sarandí, who they defeated by six goals to one. Messi scored three of them, and Kun one.

'These last two players displayed a very good understanding and were the morning's stand-out performers at Ezeiza,' said *Olé* in its Thursday, June 2nd edition. That understanding and those good vibes out on the pitch immediately spread off the field too.

Part of the credit must go to Miguel Angel Tojo who decided that the two should be room-mates at team camps, an arrangement that remained in place in the future.

Curiously, Agüero and Messi were the youngest players in the squad by some two or three years: Kun was 17 years of age and Leo 18, while the majority of their team-mates and opponents were already 20 years old or just under this age.

"We became friends very quickly and went everywhere together. We immediately got on well with each other, maybe because we were the youngest. There was an immediate affinity, and it helped us to settle in to the group better," remembers Leo Messi.

"Tojo told me that he put me in with Leo so that he would tell me what it was like to live and play in Europe," says Sergio. "I think that he knew it wouldn't be long before I left Argentina too, and he wanted me to be well prepared. And it's true. We spoke a lot about it. About the differences between our football and European football."

Tojo got it spot on. Fast forward a year and, having just turned 18, Atletico Madrid would be presenting Kun as their new star signing.

A day after celebrating his 17th birthday, on June 3rd, Kun and the Argentina Under-20 squad left for Holland. However, and despite their initial enthusiasm, the team started off on the wrong foot. Their first match on June 11th against the USA ended in a 1-0 defeat. Sergio was on the substitutes' bench, but was not brought on. And Messi was only introduced at half-time.

Defeat hit the group hard, but would bring the best out of each of them. The excellent bond that had formed between the players was the basis for a quick recovery. Pablo Zabaleta, the team's captain and leader, orchestrated a series of classic practical jokes on the youngest players, including Kun, who he called by telephone at one stage, pretending to be a radio journalist from Argentina. Kun did not realise that it was all a practical joke.

"I respected him a lot," says Sergio. "He already played in the Primera División. He was the captain. I followed him and did what he asked of me. But all the jokes were in good spirit. It was a very good group."

Pablo Zabaleta describes Kun back then as a boy "who you could tell was a character but, being the youngest, knew his place, spoke carefully and had a lot of respect for us all".

One of the linchpins, when it came to developing a tight-knit group, was Professor Gerardo Salorio, the squad's fitness coach, who knew how to balance the necessary discipline with a fun side that helped team-building and allowed the players to let off steam. He always had a game to hand to bring the squad closer together. One of them was to call the boys' rooms in the mornings with music or a song to wake them up, then to have them guess what it was.

"Imagine how sleepy we were," explains Sergio. "Plus Leo always asked me to answer it, when really neither of us wanted to get up. I never got it right because all I knew was *cumbia*[2] music, and I didn't have a clue about those songs…"

---

[2] *Cumbia* is a music genre popular throughout Latin America.

278

Another of Salorio's favourite hobbies for the boys was a drawing competition with a World Cup theme.

"He set the task on Monday and they had to be presented on Thursday. Ever since I was little I'd liked drawing, but the fact of the matter is that, on this occasion, I couldn't find any inspiration. On the last day – Wednesday night – I started trying. Then I saw a picture of Ronaldinho on a PlayStation box. He had his hands together, looking upwards. I copied it and I wrote 'I want to win the World Cup'. Leo couldn't think of anything either, and he asked me to help him out. The hotel booklet was on the table in our room. I looked through it and I found a sort of small Mexican-style mariachi figure sat down alongside a cactus with a guitar, and I drew that. Messi wrote 'if we win the World Cup, I want you to shave off your moustache'. I won the competition with my drawing of Ronaldinho. We ended up winning the World Cup too, but the Prof didn't shave his moustache off," recalls Sergio, laughing.

Another preferred way to pass the time were the games, fought 'to the bitter end', on the PlayStation. Particularly against Messi. "We were pretty loud. We would scream when the goals went in and whoever won would drive the other mad. We'd each win in turn. Those games became true clásicos."

However, Sergio's spirits were dealt a serious blow when, on Monday, June 13th, he heard about a worrying piece of news coming from Argentina: his friend Emiliano Molina – his buddy for so many adventures with Independiente and the national teams, and together with whom he had shared such vivid dreams for the future – had been involved in a terrible accident and was fighting for his life in the Fiorito Hospital in Buenos Aires.

The car that he was driving had crashed into the back of a lorry on the Pueyrredón Bridge, which links the capital city with Greater Buenos Aires.

"I had gone to ask our kit man, Patricio Auzmendia, for some kit," relates Sergio, still affected by the memory despite the passing of the years. "It was he who told me. 'Have you heard about Emiliano?' he asked me. And he told me, there and then. I couldn't believe it. It was a real blow. When I then saw the state of the car on the internet, with its front all smashed up, I feared the worst. I called home immediately and my mum told me that they had already gone to hospital and that Emiliano was doing better. They all said the same to me, because they knew that I was such a good friend of his and they didn't want me to find out about the state he was in."

Tojo, one of 'Pancho' Ferraro's assistants for the tournament, was someone who helped to keep Sergio calm.

"We had to take care in dealing with the matter. We had to be very tactful when we spoke with him. Because they had been such, such good friends since they were little… Imagine being dealt a blow like that…"

Sergio's agent Hernán Reguera was also helping to reassure him at this time, having travelled with him for this first phase of the tournament.

The following day, Sergio had the chance to play his first few minutes of the World Cup. It came in the 2-0 win over Egypt, with goals from Messi and Zabaleta. He came on wearing the number 19 shirt after 65 minutes in place of Gustavo Oberman. It was a substitution that would be repeated in the third match, but this time after 73 minutes, in the 1-0 win over Germany.

Sergio did not play a part in the 2-1 and 3-1 victories against

Round of Sixteen and Quarter-final opponents Colombia and Spain – the latter side featuring amongst others Cesc Fábregas, Fernando Llorente and David Silva, a player with whom he would form a great on-field partnership in the future. But he would appear in both the semi-final and the final. Even though, before that penultimate match, he received the news that he feared most: the death of his dear friend.

Despite the surgical procedures that he had undergone, and as a result of the serious injuries suffered during the accident, Emiliano Molina passed away in Buenos Aires on the night of June 25th. He was 17 years old, the same age as Kun.

The experience of waking up on June 26th – the day after the match against Spain – was one of the worst that Kun can remember.

The coaching staff, who were informed of Emiliano's death at four o'clock in the morning, had taken the precaution of asking the hotel to disable the internet access. They wanted to communicate the sad news themselves. However, something went wrong and the service remained available in certain rooms.

In the morning Messi, who had risen a little earlier, went through the ritual of checking the news on the internet. While his room-mate updated himself with what was going on in the world, Kun started to change for training. "No... no...," Sergio heard Leo say, with a fearful look on his face. "No, no...," he repeated, not knowing how to tell Kun that his friend had died. Until he finally found the words.

"We started crying together," remembers an emotional Sergio. "For a long time. Leo knew him too, having trained a few times with him. But he knew that he was a great friend of mine. It was very hard for me. And I was so far away, too... I couldn't believe it. The semi-final against Brazil was coming up… Brazil no less. We had to win. I just remembered all the dreams we'd had, and said to myself that the best tribute that I could pay him would be to beat Brazil and then win the World Cup."

Leo remembers those difficult moments that he went through with Sergio well. "He was shaken. I hadn't known Emiliano so well, but I knew how important he was to Kun. And we all promised to give everything, agreeing that it was the best way to pay tribute to him."

On June 28th, Argentina – with deep sorrow in their souls, which they would try to convert into energy – took on Brazil in the semi-final. All of the *Albiceleste's* players and coaching staff walked out onto the pitch wearing black armbands on their left arms in memory of Emiliano.

The match could not have had a more dramatic conclusion. In the last minute, with the match level at one goal apiece, Leo Messi – scorer of the first goal and the game's stand-out performer – beat two defenders on the left wing and pulled back a cross that Kun, who had been introduced in the 81st minute, failed to fully connect with. The ball fell to Pablo Zabaleta in the six-yard box. His shot cannoned off a defender, the ball agonisingly crossing the goal line protected by Renán. It was a goal, the end of the match and Argentina's ticket to the final. And also relief.

'There they are in a huddle. All jumping. Nobody keeping still. The match is won, but it has been a real struggle, the sort that triggers a total release of emotion. Argentina are in the final. They've knocked out Brazil and it's time to celebrate, to relax. There goes Kun, jumping up and down, the kid Sergio

Agüero, the youngest of them all who still qualifies to play for the Under-17s. The *pibe* is letting it all out, more so than anyone. He was a friend of Emiliano Molina's, and he's crying. He can't stop. The others go up to him to console him. Miguel Angel Tojo approaches, and embraces him to stop the tears. But he is unable to…,' wrote Hernán Castillo, *Clarín's* special reporter in Utrecht, Holland.

The comments that Sergio gave to the reporter from *La Nación*, Martín Castilla, speak volumes about what he was going through: "In the tunnel I saw Emiliano's face, his jokes, his pranks. What happened can't be true. If it helps in any way, this is for him."

Only one match stood between them and what they so longed for. "I wanted to dedicate the World Cup to Emiliano. So then I got them to write 'For you Emiliano' on a white t-shirt that I had. And Oscar Ustari, who also knew him very well, got one done just the same. I wanted to be able to show it off to the world. For him, for me, for everyone…"

Standing in the way of glory was a powerful Nigeria team. The game was played on July 2nd, 2005, a few days after Brazil had thrashed Argentina's senior team 4-1 in the final of the Confederations Cup played in Germany, and a year before the World Cup would be played in that same country.

Argentina lined up with Oscar Ustari in goal, Julio Barroso, Ezequiel Garay, Gabriel Paletta and Lautaro Formica in defence, Pablo Zabaleta, Juan Manuel Torres, Fernando Gago and Rodrigo Archubi in midfield, and Lionel Messi and Gustavo Oberman in attack. Kun, who had started the match on the bench, came on for Oberman 12 minutes into the second half with the match delicately poised at one apiece.

Messi had opened the scoring in the 40th minute, with a penalty that he himself had won and then taken with aplomb. Nigeria then equalised eight minutes into the second half with a header from Ogbuke. Eighteen minutes after having come on as a substitute, and having received the ball from Messi, Kun ran into the area and knocked it past his marker, James, who brought him down. Messi once again executed the penalty perfectly. That made it 2-1, which would soon be the final score.

The referee's final whistle was the cue for unparalleled celebrations and relief among the Argentinian boys. According to Victor Hugo Morales on *Radio Continental*, Zabaleta was in tears on his knees while Messi and Kun were locked in an endless embrace.

That title was Argentina's fifth youth World Cup triumph. The first came in 1979 with the memorable lap of honour in Japan, led by Diego Armando Maradona. That was followed by the teams managed by Pekerman, in Qatar 1995 with Juan Pablo Sorín and Biagini; in Malaysia 1997 led by Pablo Aimar and Juan Román Riquelme, and in Argentina 2001 with Javier Saviola and Maxi Rodríguez.

In 2005, it was the turn of the gifted Messi, the great captain Zabaleta and the fledgling figure of Sergio Agüero, who played a decisive role in the final match. There the three of them were, alongside the rest of the team, down on the playing surface at the Galgenwaard stadium in Utrecht. Arms around each other in a huddle, endlessly jumping and dancing. Overcome with emotion, knowing that they were making history. With Professor Gerardo Salorio carried aloft. With head coaches Francisco Ferraro and Miguel Ángel Tojo and their colleagues, physio Raúl Lamas and doctor Daniel Martínez. And the kit man

Patricio Auzmendia, a friend to all the boys, who could not be left out. Every last one of them with a medal hanging proudly around their necks. And Leo Messi rejoining his team-mates with both hands full, having been awarded two prizes. In one hand the Golden Boot trophy, awarded to the top scorer, and in the other the Golden Ball, for having been chosen as player of the tournament. Ready to receive the congratulations of all concerned. Firstly Kun, squeezing his arm, unable to imagine that in two years' time he himself would be awarded with the same distinctions. Kun, who was experiencing a bitter-sweet sensation. An overwhelming joy, and an unrelenting pain. Wearing the white t-shirt which read 'For you Emiliano', there for all to see. A worthy tribute to his friend, for whom he had another homage in store, one that would touch everyone and, if only in part, soften the pain of his absence.

A worthy tribute

One of the first things that he did on returning to Argentina was to visit Emiliano's parents. He missed his friend, and even more so now that he was back in the places where he used to regularly enjoy his company. On the field and off it. He remembered the fiercely competitive games of cards they played, the trips away, the matches, the jokes.

His sense of loss felt all the more prominent now that he was facing up to reality back in his own country after having returned from abroad. He promised himself at that point that his moment would come soon, that he would be able in some way to fulfil one of the dreams that they had shared together.

He reported almost immediately to the new head coach of Independiente, Julio César Falcioni, the former Vélez Sarsfield goalkeeper who had arrived after recently taking Banfield to second place in the championship.

Part of the team's pre-season preparations took place in the town of Open Door, the same place where Kun had won the title with Loma Alegre's 1987 *categoría* seven years previously. Those were, of course, very different times. And the incoming boss had prepared a great surprise for him: Independiente's senior management had decided to give him the number 10 shirt, to wear in the Apertura championship that was soon to get underway. He received the jersey from none other than Ricardo Bochini himself, an extremely symbolic moment: a legend from Independiente's past bestowing upon their great new hope the responsibility of gloriously sporting such a mythical shirt. The number 10 could not be in safer hands. The traditional 'exquisite taste' of *El Rojo's* fans was assured with Kun. And he would not let them down.

Sergio wore the number 10 for the first time on August 7th, 2005 at home to Lanús in the first match of the Apertura championship, which finished in Independiente's favour by four goals to two. And he did it proud. He won two penalties and was man of the match. He repeated the trick in the second match against Instituto from Córdoba, where he was the best player on the pitch and scored two screamers.

The chant of 'Agüero, Agüero' rang out around the stadium in Avellaneda when Falcioni brought him off five minutes from the end. Two 1-1 draws followed against San Lorenzo and Argentinos Juniors, and then a 3-0 loss to Gimnasia y Esgrima.

Back then, very few could have foreseen what would take

place a week later, on September 11th, 2005. Only one person really thought that it could happen, a 17-year-old boy who had spent many nights dreaming about it. He had dreamt of it in every way imaginable, although what he would experience a few minutes later would exceed all his wildest fantasies.

Sergio Agüero arrived at the Doble Visera stadium that morning with one thing in mind: he wanted to score a goal. This was not just any other match – this was the derby between Independiente and Racing. And not just any other derby game, which is why, once in the changing room, he took the white t-shirt out of his bag that he had had made in Holland with 'For you Emiliano' written on it.

He put it on slowly, as if searching for inspiration from that moment. Over the top, he pulled on the red shirt with the number 10 on its back. And with the rest of his team-mates, he headed out from the tunnel towards the field of play. They were taken aback by the spectacular scene awaiting them. The red in the stands stretched around all four corners of the stadium. The team: Bernardo Leyenda, Martín Pautasso, Marcelo Méndez, Fernando Cáceres, Eduardo Domínguez, Lucas Pusineri, Mariano Herrón, Lucas Biglia, Esteban Buján, Nicolás Frutos and, of course, Sergio Agüero.

Up against them, Guillermo Rivarola's Racing side, with the heart of Diego Simeone and Juan Manuel Torres, the creativity of Rubén Capria and the incisive running of Raúl Pipa Estévez.

The referee, Sergio Pezzota, signalled for the match to start 15 minutes behind schedule – they were playing at the strange time of 11 o'clock in the morning – due to some paper having been set alight in the away end. Kick-off had to wait until the firemen had finished putting out the fire. After 35 minutes, midfielder Chaco Torres was sent off after blocking Domínguez's goalbound header with his hand. Frutos converted the resulting penalty to give Independiente a one-goal lead. With the score-line in their favour and a one-man advantage, the game was perfectly set up for *El Rojo's* counter-attack.

During the half-time break, and much like every time he had touched the ball in the first half, Kun could not stop thinking about the goal that he wanted to score. A goal that was not for him, but for someone else. He continued thinking about it at the game's resumption. After 11 minutes of the second half, a Frutos header made it 2-0. Nineteen minutes later, Kun beat Cabral in the area and was brought down. Another penalty, which Frutos again converted to make it 3-0. The third goal was the cue for unbridled celebrations. Kun looked around, and said to himself that there could be no better moment to realise his dream. And 37 minutes into the second half, with nobody aware of what was running through his mind, Kun started a counter-attack in his own half from the left touchline.

This was his moment and, as he set off, he felt as if his past and his present were colliding. With Leo's passion coursing through him, carried in his genes. With Adriana's never-say-die tenacity. With the spirits of La Soledad and Los Eucaliptus dancing around him. With the wise words of Jorge 'The Baker', Coria and 'Correntino' Ramírez ringing in his ears. With the love of life 'Luigi' had. With Cacho Barreiro whispering for him to take his chances, with his calls of 'go on Sergio… put it away…' With Jorge Rodríguez, certain that with Kun on the pitch, anything is possible until the very last minute. With Tojo's guidance paving the way. With his godfather Darío Fernández, his arms around Mario Portinari, crying out 'Rottweiler' to motivate him. And, above all, with the face of Emiliano shining down on him, inspiring him to sparkle brighter than ever as he moved into Racing's half.

Martín Vitali, the Racing defender, has now been left behind. There is a huge expanse of open field ahead of him. He advances majestically. Diego Crosa lies in wait at the edge of the area. Sergio twists and turns, feints, pauses and then cuts past him. He pauses again, rolls his foot over the ball, cuts past him once more and, by now in the area, leaves the defender chasing shadows. One last touch of the right boot leaves him one-on-one with Campagnuolo. And all the while the voice of his friend is telling him "it's against Racing, it's in the Primera División... put it away and we'll celebrate together..."

And, with an angled left-footed shot into the far post, Kun scores a goal for the history books. But also a goal in memory. In memory of Emiliano who, up on high, receives an embrace from Kun, who is celebrating down on the field of play by taking off his number 10 shirt, revealing to the world his white t-shirt emblazoned with the dedication 'For you Emiliano'. A goal that has set his soul alight with pure emotion. That has won everyone's affections. That finds him carried aloft by his team-mates. And looking upwards, his hands pointing towards the sky, a goal that offers Emiliano a long-promised and richly deserved tribute, one that they had dreamt of together.

Explosion, expulsion and revelation

"Wait, there's someone here who wants to talk to you," said Leo Del Castillo over the phone, that Sunday afternoon. In a few seconds, the person on the other end of the line would hear a voice that he immediately recognised. He had heard it for the first time seven years earlier, although on that Sunday it sounded different, more forceful. "Did you like my goal, José María?"

From the other end of the line, Astarloa could not hide his emotion. As a huge fan of Independiente, he had enjoyed watching the thrashing of Racing on television with his son, and had been reduced to tears of joy by the goal scored by that talented young kid who he had had the honour of helping out. And hours later that boy was calling him over the telephone to speak to him about the goal, to ask him if he had liked it.

"A goal like that, scored by you, is a gift from above," José María answered.

Deep inside, he felt great pride at having played his part in keeping Kun at Independiente and, more specifically, giving *El Rojo's* fans the chance to enjoy having him in the team. It resulted in Kun establishing a bond of affection with those fans, and meant that – having laid down his roots and shaped his identity in the best footballing traditions of the club – he would then be able to make the leap ahead to his inevitable destiny in European football. With these experiences behind him, he thought, anything would be possible.

The next day, the front pages of Argentina's main newspapers showed images of Sergio looking towards the heavens, with his arms pointing upwards and his red shirt in one hand, while being carried aloft by his team-mates.

Kun had the chance to look through those papers that morning at home in Don Bosco, surrounded by his parents, brothers and sisters, and his friend Pepe Sosa. He still could not

...that he had scored. But that was not going to ...ng it, nor could it get in the way of the feeling ...the happiest days of his life.

...view his dialogue with Ricardo Bochini on ...

"...ous goal," said Bochini. "But I saw him ...goals like that for the youth teams. I've ...little, and I knew that he was also going ...the Primera División against Boca, ...own words: "I never imagined that I ...rt like he had. It's a shame I never ...s. When he

goodbye to ... the white t-shirt with his dedi-
his second ...orner under his wardrobe. He
would look for it ag... while later to give it to Jesica, his friend's sister, who had asked for it especially. And then he returned to the routine training session, although this was not just any other day. It would end – after a stop-off in Don Torcuato to see Darío and Lucas Fernández, and an intimate party with friends at a bar in Martínez – on Diego Maradona's television programme *La Noche del Diez* ('The Night of the 10') on Channel 13, where he was to appear as a guest.

Sergio had the privilege of being one of the players to pay tribute that night to Diego – who was hosting his own show – with a song based on a recording by Juanse, the lead singer of the Ratones Paranoicos, and Andrés Calamaro.

The line 'I want to watch Diego forever…' was sung by, among others, Diego 'Cholo' Simeone, Ezequiel Lavezzi, Mariano Pavone, Federico Insúa and Kun, drawing heartfelt thanks from the legendary number 10.

"This is the most beautiful surprise of all. I a⌐
debt. I am a footballer and I will die a football⌐
you," he told them. In the television studios that⌐
briefly crossed paths with Gianinna, Diego's eld⌐
who was 16 at the time. They did not speak with ea⌐
they would have another fleeting encounter a sh⌐
when, at the end of the year, Maradona appeare⌐
presented by Marcelo Tinelli, on which Sergio was⌐

A game of head tennis on the studio terrace sa⌐
Tinelli-Maradona taking on a team made up of S⌐
and Lucas Lobes, who played for Gimnasia y Es⌐
Plata. The youngsters prevailed over the veteran⌐
popped his head into the dressing room to say⌐
Diego, he bumped into Gianinna once more. ⌐
occasion found them chatting together for a few minutes, with
neither imagining that from these beginnings, an unforeseen
future relationship would be born.

Kun's devastating performances for *El Rojo* caused a conspicuous rise in enthusiasm among their fans. And proof of these
new levels of excitement could be seen in the club's ticket sales.
Seven fixtures into the Apertura championship, and without
being at the top of the league table, Independiente were nevertheless top of the pile in this regard with more than 100,000
tickets sold, ahead of San Lorenzo and Racing. The increase
in the number of Independiente fans attending their matches,
with numbers resembling their last championship-winning
season in 2002, was sustained in spite of Sergio being sent off
on September 24th, 2005, in their eighth fixture against Tiro
Federal. Sergio recalls that red card, the first he received in the
Primera División, with precision.

"You learn from everything. I remember that my marker, Germán Basualdo, spent the whole match kicking me. I never reacted to treatment like that. But it was driving me mad right from the beginning on that day. For starters, he fouled me for a penalty that Frutos converted. And then every time I touched the ball, he insulted me or spat at me. It got to the point that I couldn't take it any more, so I insulted him back. The referee's assistant saw us and told us to calm it, and that if not we would be sent off.

"Julio Falcioni, the coach, realised what was happening and decided to substitute me to avoid a sending-off. And when I was already on my way off, Basualdo started to insult me again. He told me that I was a faggot and that I was going off because I was scared. And I had already seen red, so I squared up to him and pushed him, but not hard. But he made a meal of it, threw himself to the ground and the referee Juan Pablo Pompei sent me off.

"I became even madder because I wasn't going to be able to play the next match, against River Plate. Falcioni told me that I had to take it as a lesson, that I had to learn not to become embroiled in the opposition's games. I still remember what my team-mate Lucas Pusineri said to me in the changing room when he saw my eyes, all swollen from having cried so much: 'I told you, stupid, that any time an opponent is having a go at you, you let me know...' Lucas always looked out for me. Even that night, when he had to do a drug test and so did Basualdo. They told me that he wanted to kill him..."

Sergio has a special memory of Pusineri, one of the squad's most experienced players, who was 12 years older than him and 29 at the time. He was one of the players who looked after Kun most in his first clashes up against bigger, more experienced opponents. Kun can also recall some of his jokes, which demonstrate the mutual affection between the two of them.

"When we were all sharing accommodation before games, and we went up to the second floor for the team talk, he would grab on to the staircase banister like it was a crush barrier and then start to sing the song that the fans sang to us when we weren't playing well: 'Players, let's see if you've got the balls; let's see if you're up for it; you're up against a load of mugs…' and then he'd look at me and he'd immediately start the 'Agüero, Agüero…' chant, as if to say that they're having a go at everyone apart from me. Then he'd carry on with another song, the one that went 'you have to sweat for the red shirt'. Before changing to 'Agüero, Agüero…' again. Lucas is a star, he used to kill me with laughter…"

Sergio returned with a bang after his suspension. He scored both of Independiente's goals in a 2-0 win over Newell's on October 6th, 2005.

"I hit one of them with bend and placed it just inside the far post…" recalls a player who received an ovation from the fans on both entering and leaving the field of play on that day.

The cry of 'Agüero, Agüero…' had already become a healthy habit in the Libertadores de América stadium, as Independiente's home ground had by now been renamed. Next would come goals, and noteworthy performances, against Banfield, Colón, Arsenal and Olimpo, that crowned a very good year personally and kept Independiente in the hunt for honours until the final fixtures of the season, even if they ultimately fell short. Sergio was his team's joint top goalscorer with nine, the same number as his team-mate Nicolás Frutos.

As had been the case when he played as a child, and also in the youth teams, the out-and-out striker who played alongside him ended up near the top in the goalscoring charts.

The Apertura champions for 2005 were Boca Juniors who, under the stewardship of Alfio Basile, racked up 40 points. In second place were Gimnasia y Esgrima with 27, third Vélez Sarsfield with 33 and fourth Independiente with 32, their best campaign since 2002. Sergio was considered by the critics to have been the year's great discovery. The newspaper *Clarín* awarded him the 'Golden Newcomer' prize, alongside Lionel Messi.

A few days before being awarded the prize, and for a feature in that same newspaper comparing him to Ricardo Bochini, journalist Sergio Danishewsky wrote a perfect summary of what the football world in general – and Independiente fans in particular – felt about Sergio Agüero: 'It's curious because Agüero never saw Bochini play, and because they have different styles. One more the provider; the other closer to goal. But it is also obvious: both represent a feeling for football, which has bestowed greatness on a shirt that one will be wearing a little longer, and that the other will light up forever. There are little details that prove that this 'feeling' still exists, regardless of modern trends and tactics: Agüero, just like Bochini before him, is respected by all football fans. Kun shyly admits as much himself, when he tells stories of the people who he meets in the street who want him to play for the national team and at the World Cup in 2006. There is not much to say about Bochini that has not been said before. Another little detail that might escape the attention of those who do not frequent the Doble Visera stadium is that, 15 years down the line, the Independiente fans once more applaud the intention to play a through-ball, even if does not come off. They managed to applaud Bochini when the ball slid under his foot and out of play. And Agüero only has a few months left, before his magic takes him to Europe, to write another chapter in this love story. They are lapping it up while they can: the audacity, the mythical 10 on his back and the old, yet vital feeling that he has for the game.'

The newspaper *La Nación* also chose him as one of the best players of the Apertura championship with an average score of 7.17 from 18 games, the highest of any of those playing in the competition.

Journalist Nicolás Balinotti wrote in the December 21st edition: 'He was fundamental to *El Rojo's* play, with the team at times Agüero-dependent. The striker never lost his cool, nor did it weigh down too heavily on him that he was responsible, at 17 years of age, for being the mainstay of their play, the driving force and soul of a team that lacked renowned figures. In just six months, Agüero's life was turned upside down. The figure-head of everyday life at Independiente almost immediately, his name circulated all around the world as fast as broadband. He went from being that kid that dazzled at Villa Domínico, to becoming the realisation of everyone's impossible fantasies and one of the most coveted players on the planet. He is the boy of the moment.'

Catching the eye of Tony Muñoz

Neither journalist, from *Clarín* nor *La Nación*, had got it wrong. Kun had become one of the most coveted players in the world, and his magic was destined for Europe. For after his appearance at the Under-20 World Cup, and the subsequent rubber-stamping of his promise in the Primera División for Independiente, the stories that first emerged during the South American Championship in Paraguay – about the interest among the world's biggest clubs in signing him – started circulating again. His representatives were inundated with enquiries. The rumours, echoed in the media, spoke of approaches from English, Spanish, German and Italian clubs, and of figures in the order of 20 million dollars.

What is for certain is that observers from different clubs were keeping tabs on those prospects who they considered to be the main emerging talents. One such interested party was Tony Muñoz, then sporting director of Atletico Madrid, who had had Sergio in his sights since the South American Championships in Paraguay. At that time, his scouts had singled him out as a prospect to bear in mind. But Muñoz preferred to watch players in person, not on video. For this reason, and in order to have an uninterrupted view of Kun on the field of play, he travelled to Argentina.

The first time was in April 2005. On that occasion, he was able to follow him in two games: against Gimnasia, when Sergio returned after his knee injury to score his second goal in the Primera División; and against Racing, a match Independiente lost 3-1, shortly before Menotti resigned as manager. Tony returned to Buenos Aires seven months later, in November 2005. This time, he was able to witness – on November 13th in Avellaneda – Independiente's first win over Vélez Sarsfield in 17 years, by one goal to nil, in which Kun was the game's stand-out performer.

"In that match," Tony recalls, "every time the ball was at his feet, the crowd went quiet in anticipation. That's not a common sight in Argentina, where supporters are fanatical about their teams. But Sergio was not just any old player. He was even more polished than the time before when I had seen him play. That season had done him good, because he was stronger. Despite a bottom-heavy physique that might make mobility an issue, everything he did, he did well."

Once back in Spain, he produced a detailed report for Miguel Ángel Gil Marín, the chief executive of Atletico Madrid, in which he advised the club to sign Kun. The report made it clear that it would be a gamble – because of his age, and the size of the transfer fee – but at the same time suggested that he should be brought in.

Soon the hierarchies of other clubs around Europe would be experiencing the same dilemma, over his age and his price tag. Tony's recommendation to the directors at *Los Colchoneros* would later have a key role in an acquisition that would be finalised in 2006, and that would ultimately bring *Atleti* – as they are known in Spain – the best possible results.

Moving Times

Attempting to distance himself from the rumours of possible offers coming in from abroad, Independiente's president, Julio Comparada, took it upon himself during those months to clarify that Kun would be there "a while longer" and to claim that he would be playing at *El Rojo* for the whole of the year 2006.

What is for certain is that the state of the club both institutionally and financially – they had filed for bankruptcy protection with an initial debt confirmed at 36 million pesos, later rising to 59 million – could only lead one to assume that such a claim was a long way off the mark.

If rumours of the multi-million pound offers for Sergio were proved to be true, they would not be able to hold on to him.

Back then, and as stories of the potential sale of Kun to an overseas club gathered momentum, various media sources reported that Independiente owned 100 per cent of the rights to Sergio Agüero, failing to acknowledge the pre-existing agreement between José María Astarloa and the Agüero–Del Castillo family that had been signed by the previous administration at Independiente. It was claimed that the transfer of 25 per cent ownership to a business group was not legal. Recent history repeated itself as, once again, the role of those people who had helped Kun from the start was called into question.

"For us it was like a terrible betrayal," says Astarloa, "because they were unaware of everything that had taken place up until then. The true story was not being told."

Leonel Del Castillo and Adriana Agüero decided at that point to take the bull by the horns and to honour the commitment they had made alongside José María Astarloa in 1998. And, via the media, they made clear their stance.

Leo and Adriana spoke of the links that tied them together, and the assistance that they had received from Samuel Liberman ever since Sergio was 10 years old. They explained that the percentage that the group held came as a result of this context, and reaffirmed that they were not prepared to tolerate the agreement not being respected. To avoid all doubt, they were very explicit: if their interests were not recognised, then they would not authorise Kun's sale.

"The gesture made by Leo and Adriana, to honour everything that we had been through together," says Astarloa, "seemed to me indicative of their tremendous moral stature. It speaks volumes of that family's values, which were found wanting in many people around the time."

Astarloa revealed his thoughts and feelings at the time in a letter addressed to Leo and Adriana on November 4th, 2005, which the Agüero-Del Castillo family have kept to this day: 'I want to write a few words to you, because I wish to express how happy I was yesterday after speaking with you. After the unpleasant situation that the club has put us in, it was a welcome opportunity for me to have an insight into your guiding values and convictions. Neither fame nor fortune have been able to undermine the inner beliefs of those people that I first met seven years ago. Regardless of the fate that will befall the group I represent, I feel proud at having been able to help you. The support has not been lent in vain. On the contrary I saw a stable Agüero-Del Castillo family, their feet on the ground, and with the same compassion as always. I congratulate you for all your achievements, and I hope that many more will come your way in the future. You deserve them. Keep going as you are, and here's hoping that the money helps each and every one of you to continue to be good people. Yours with affection. José María Astarloa.'

For Leo and Adriana, making their position public was only fair. As such they also informed Samuel Liberman, who they finally met in San Antonio de Areco, at the football ground that belongs to the businessman.

"I was always thankful for all the help they had given us" says Adriana. "Not just anyone would have opened doors like they did for us. Because what's more, they did so at a time when Sergio was not even well-known and nobody knew what sort of future lay ahead of him. That's why it was unfair of Independiente not to value everything that they had done for him. We spoke about it with Leo and Sergio. And we said to each other that we had to be good to our word. We had given them our word, and we had to make good on what we had promised."

Leo and Adriana's public declarations – which revealed details of what, for the majority of people, was an unknown past – triggered a wide-reaching media response and had the desired effect. A few days later, a call from the senior management at Independiente paved the way for a new round of negotiations.

"They proposed to pay us 400,000 dollars and, in addition, to transform our 25 per cent of the player's economic rights into 15 per cent of the economic rights, as recognised by the buying club," says Astarloa. "We didn't think it was the best outcome, but perhaps that it was the wisest. We responded in the affirmative, and that was how an agreement was reached."

Sweet seventeen

Along with the growing recognition coming his way, Kun had the opportunity to start treating himself. One such treat was the purchase of his first car. It was a brand new black Chevrolet Astra, which he was able to buy with the money that he had set aside from the bonuses he had been paid throughout 2005.

"It was money from his bonuses, money that he gave me to keep safe," confirms Adriana. "He would say to me 'this is for the car but, if you need it, use it'. But I never so much as touched it. And that was how he bought it."

He also treated himself by having it kitted out. In order to do so, he turned to his friend Mario Portinari, who installed everything he requested, including the best and most powerful sound system for listening to music – *cumbia*, of course, his favourite.

The Agüero-Del Castillo family also had the chance to spend their first holiday all together, to which Diego Campos and Pepe Sosa – Sergio's friends from the Independiente *novena* team – were also invited. It was in December 2005 and, for many family members, it would be the first time that they had seen the sea.

The chosen destination was Pinamar, 360 kilometres from Buenos Aires. They stayed in a first-class hotel belonging to the businessman Liberman, and to this day they remember how they enjoyed those days spent on the beach, in the sun and listening to music.

Sergio's fledgling fame brought him more attention from fans, who then requested photos or autographs. To begin with, his signature was simple and somewhat shy. He would write 'Agüero Leonel', without his first name. He did not add his nickname, and on signing it he would simply print his surname underneath.

He soon realised – and it was also pointed out to him – that he could not sign autographs in the same way as he did when signing for legal reasons. He decided, then, to try out other options. He tried and tried again, prodding and probing almost in the same way as if he were trying to deceive an opposing defender with a dribble. Firstly just with his name, 'Sergio'. Then with the word 'Kun' on its own. And afterwards just with 'Agüero'.

And after crossing out various attempts in that quest for his own style, he found the one he liked the most and adopted it definitively. And so, from that simple signature, he was able to develop a new one. He had, by now, said to himself that it absolutely had to feature his surname, his nickname and the number 10, which had, at the time, become like a trademark, just as the 16 would be later in his life.

The definitive signature was developed from those attempts on blank sheets of paper. On one of them, the vertical line of the letter 'R' in Agüero stretched down below the rest of the name. It was to this line that he added the two diagonals, one upwards and one downwards, to form the letter 'K' and therefore be able to write Kun. The finished article had 'Agüero', with 'Kun' underneath the 'R', to which he would then add a '10' in brackets, an arrangement that would characterise his autographs from that moment onwards. Autographs, furthermore, that would become more and more commonplace as he started to take part in different advertisements. Because Kun's image had started to become an appealing one for sports advertisers.

Through the work of his agents, and at only 17 years of age, he had already secured contracts with Gillette and Pepsi, and had filmed commercials that were broadcast on television.

One of his first adverts was for Nike's 'Jogo Bonito' campaign, in which images of his goal against Racing are accompanied by commentary from Kun himself: "Agüero, brings it down superbly. Off goes the number 10. The crowd goes 'Oléeeee'. Still Aguero. Ta, ta, and he's squaring up to the defender. He takes him on. 'Oléeeee'. Takes him on again. 'Oléeeee'. Still Agüero, Agüero, Agüero. Ta, ta, ta... Gooooooooooal by Agüero..."

These are the words spoken by Kun while the images show the feints and finish of a goal that had already gone down in history. The clip finishes with Sergio in the foreground, imitating the supporters' chant of 'Agüero, Agüero' as if it were filling the stadium, a hymn in tribute to the finest football. Afterwards, the caption 'Never stop playing' appears, a premonition of the feelings that many would have towards Sergio in the future.

This 'Agüeromania' was also there for all to see during Independiente's pre-season preparations during January 2006, spent in the city of Mar del Plata. Sergio attracted more attention than anyone, including from fans of other clubs, even those of Racing Club who – according to the reports from journalists from around the time – waited for him at the doors of the hotel where *El Rojo* were staying. And even more so after his brilliant performance in the Torneo de Verano (literally 'Summer Tournament'), as Independiente beat River Plate 2-1 with two more goals for the Agüero scrapbook.

*Wednesday, January 11th, 2006. **The Mundialista stadium at Mar del Plata. Torneo de Verano. Independiente vs. River Plate. Thirty-eight minutes into the first half.***

It was on this night that the admiration that Independiente's fans held for Kun Agüero would first spread to opposing supporters. Agüero, who had promised so much throughout 2005, was to start the following year with a bang. He had already scored an equalising goal after 25 minutes, caressing a precise right-footed, first-time shot from outside the penalty area narrowly past the opposition defenders and beyond the reach of goalkeeper Germán Lux's dive. Thirteen minutes later, he was to crown the night with another memorable strike. Receiving the ball from Lucas Biglia on the edge of the area, he turned away from goal to escape the attentions of Oscar Ahumada. Now faced with Gabriel Loeschbor, he cut back towards goal, leaving the defender sprawling on the turf.

He advanced into the area, with Lux desperately rushing out in an attempt to close him down. This time Agüero finished with his left foot, planting the ball just inside the goalkeeper's right-hand post. Seconds later, he was buried under a pile of team-mates unable to contain their elation at the goal they had just witnessed. He was 17 years old and, for the first time, he heard the chant of a whole stadium echo one of his most burning desires: 'borombombón, borombombón, Agüero for Argentina…'

In his report for *Clarín* magazine on January 12th, Fernando Gourovitch chose the following words to describe the second goal against River: 'This teenager, who is elevated above the men surrounding him whenever the ball is at his feet, conjured up a moment of pure Maradona. Or Bochini, bearing in mind that he was wearing the number 10 of Independiente… He set the play up like a right-footer and finished like a left-footer, almost in homage to both Bochini and Maradona, those two football wizards.'

It was no surprise that Kun received an ovation from all four corners of the stadium, and that they were demanding his involvement with the national team. The World Cup would soon be held in Germany, and there was no small amount of clamour for him to be called up.

The partnership between Messi and Agüero, which had worked so well the previous year at the Under-20 World Cup in Holland, had given many people new hope. José Pekerman, Argentina's head coach, was cautious but did not rule out the possibility of a call-up. He had up until May 15th, and he would wait until the last moment to name his final squad. The *El Gráfico* magazine, in its February 2006 edition, asked the question of whether Kun should go to the World Cup.

'The great enigma' was the title of an extensive article which compiled the opinions of various figures from the world of football, those both for and against his inclusion. Furthermore, the report outlined what it defined as the 'past errors' of players not having been selected, such as Diego Maradona in 1978 and Javier Saviola in 2002, and provided reminders of other cases internationally where players had been taken by their countries, such as Pele, Eto'o and the Brazilian Ronaldo at 17 years of age, Owen at 18, and Beckenbauer and Kaka at 20. But it was not just the sports publications that were focusing on Sergio.

The children's magazine *Billiken* had him on their front cover for the month of February under the headline 'Idol!' Kun was winning admirers of all ages, including the very youngest who saw him as someone who liked the same things as them, and shared the styles of their generation.

At 17, Sergio had the same off-the-field interests as any other teenager. He was fascinated, for example, by video games. He played against his team-mates in do-or-die games, as if they were for real. He would choose to play as Arsenal, Juventus or Chelsea. Or as Liverpool, who he would line up on the pitch with four at the back, two central midfielders and two pushing on out wide, then a forward in the hole behind an out-and-out striker.

"I play Gerrard just behind Cissé or Morientes. With that team, I put six or seven past my friends," he told the *Un Caño* magazine in February 2006. Or he would spend hours on his handheld console, a treat from his godfather Darío Fernández.

The friendship group formed by the latter's son Lucas along with Kun, Pepe Sosa and Diego Campos, had become inseparable. It was with those friends that, footballing commitments permitting, Kun would go out dancing or to the cinema. And in doing so encounter his first young romances, and his fair share of new experiences, all of which helped him to find a more relaxed path through that period of greater media demands and exposure.

He could also count on his sisters Jessica and Gabriela, trusty companions for nights out, or extended breakfasts or morning *mate* sessions.

At this stage, in early 2006, the Agüero-Del Castillo family had moved house once more, the last time that they would do so as a full family. For the first time they left the south of Greater Buenos Aires to settle down in a two-storey house in the northern neighbourhood of Martínez.

There would no longer be any problems with space, like there had been in days gone by. There was even room for two cousins of Pepe Sosa, who was already considered as one of the family, to live with them. And last but not least Atila, a Rottweiler given to Kun as a present by his godfather Darío Fernández, who had the back of the house to himself. There was also space for the numerous trophies and souvenirs that were starting to pile up. Like the number 34 shirt that he had worn on his debut in the Primera División, which was framed and occupied a place of honour on the living room wall, a source of daily pride for the whole family.

In a surprisingly natural way, Sergio's 18th year passed by in a whirl of on-field successes and adolescent experiences. Indeed, 'Agüero: sweet seventeen' was the headline chosen by journalist Juan Pablo Varsky for his column in the *La Nación* newspaper on February 6th, 2006.

'We've discovered that he has the charisma of an idol. From his knowing, mischievous smile to his innocent, frank comments, not to mention his friendly nature and, even, his renowned drawing ability. He likes signing autographs, and a very important national title has already been bestowed upon him: he is the people's player.

'His own fans worship him and, in turn, opposition fans applaud him. Other players respect him, due to the purity of his play...

'He has just started his second year as a footballer, crucial in discovering whether an unfinished article will end up on the shelves of the finest department stores, in the sales section, or straight to the bargain bins. Surely time will see him rise to a status reserved only for the chosen ones, where we all want to see him.

'It is not his problem if our anxiety is moving faster than his own development. He is captivating us with wonderful feats. Here's hoping that, faced with higher levels of expectation, he continues achieving those same wonderful feats, like his friend Messi, who has already made the leap forward at Barcelona and in the senior national team.

'Let's have a bit of patience. At only 17 years, Sergio Agüero is showing us how important it is to slow down and pause before finishing.

'There is no need to put a time or a place on his coming of age. The moment will come naturally. That much we know too…'

Just a few months down the line, Juan Pablo Varsky's convictions would be validated. Kun's coming of age was drawing ever nearer.

Decision time

Falcioni's Independiente got off to an inconsistent start in the 2006 Clausura championship, with a draw, two wins and two losses. The stand-out match in the sixth round of fixtures, to be played on Saturday, February 25th, was the Avellaneda derby. It was to mark another milestone in Kun's career.

Racing, who had only one point from their first five games, desperately needed a victory. Much as *El Rojo* did, if they were to sustain their title aspirations.

In a match where the on-field exchanges reflected the personalities of the two coaches involved – the courage of Racing's 'Cholo' Simeone and the caution of Independiente's Julio Falcioni – Sergio made the difference with two goals in three minutes, which ended the match as a contest.

The first came nine minutes into the second half with a diagonal run from right to left past the central defenders, followed by a low left-footed shot from outside the box which crept inside Gustavo Campagnuolo's left-hand upright, the hapless goalkeeper once again beaten by Kun. And three minutes later in the 57th minute, Independiente goalkeeper Oscar Ustari – with Racing on the attack – launched a quick counter-attack with a long punt downfield that Kun latched onto in the opposition half. He stole a march on José Shaffer and, once in the penalty area, feinted back away from the onrushing goalkeeper, dummied again to leave the backtracking defender and Campagnuolo out of position, and sent the ball into the back of the net with a right-footed shot.

Kun's celebration, including a few steps of *cumbia*, showed his immense happiness at having scored the goals – all the sweeter still for having been at the home of their old rivals – as well as the passionate love he felt for that music.

"With the celebration, I was imitating the one that Carlitos Tévez does," he announced to journalists after the match. "I saw him on TV and, as he's one of my idols, I copied his moves."

Already by that time, Kun had appeared on different television programmes with the Santa Fe *cumbia* group Los Leales, who were promoting their gigs with the slogan 'the music Kun listens to'. Two months later, with the same group, he would have the pleasure of recording a song that summed up his feelings for football.

In March 2006, while Sergio carried on leaving his mark on the football pitches of Argentina, offers were being fine-tuned in the offices of the world's biggest clubs. Those offers would later be made in an attempt to lure a player who was managing to change the course of matches in a matter of minutes, whose play aroused happiness and excitement.

This was a time when the decisions were being made that would determine Kun's short-term destiny within the game. In Italy, where Inter, Milan and Juventus were showing interest. In France, where the directors at Olympique Marseilles were sharpening their pencils in preparation of the battle for his signature. In Germany, where the senior management at Bayern Munich were among the most convinced, even resolving to send a delegation to Buenos Aires for negotiations. In Spain, where Real Madrid – who were going through a turbulent presidential election process at the time – and Atletico Madrid had decided to make own their moves in pursuit of the signing. In England, where Manchester United, Chelsea and Liverpool were not to be left behind.

Born To Rise

The message coming from sporting directors everywhere was the same: there was a very strong interest in signing him, but there were reservations over what was considered to be a very high price for the transaction, bearing in mind that this was a 17-year-old kid who would still have to adapt to European football.

Indeed the Spaniard Rafael Benítez, years later in October 2008 – while still manager of Liverpool and in the days leading up to the Champions League clash between the English club and Atletico Madrid – recognised that they had contemplated signing Sergio during those months in 2006, but that they had preferred not to take the risk of such an expensive transaction involving such a young footballer.

Against all the odds, it was Atletico Madrid who left all the doubts to one side and played their hand with an offer that drew closer to Independiente's asking price. Tony Muñoz's recommendation to club director Miguel Ángel Gil Marín had had its effect. At the start of April, a first offer was initially refused by the Avellaneda club. However, negotiations were now underway and it would not be long before they were concluded.

During this time, one of his agents' main priorities was to decide upon the best destination for Kun during his first stage in Europe. There was a wide range of options, and those provided by the biggest clubs in the world were extremely tempting. But they believed that a full analysis was required for them to then be able to indicate their country and club of choice.

As had been the case throughout the years that they had been with Kun, Jorge Prat Gay, Hernán Reguera, Darío Bombini and Gonzalo Rebassa knew that the most important thing – beyond all other factors – was to recommend a destination where Kun could complete the process of his training and development. Sergio was still only 17, and the wrong choice here could knock him off course.

With this in mind, they all agreed that language was a critical factor. As was the culture of the country. Therefore, Spain became the priority. And in terms of the opportunity to settle into European life and its football, to develop further and be given the chance to prove himself, Atletico Madrid emerged as the preferred option.

Additionally, the Argentines Maxi Rodríguez, also from the IMG stable, Leonardo Franco and Luciano Galletti played for *Los Colchoneros*, which might help him to settle in. As such, they relayed their conclusions to Leo, Adriana and, of course, Sergio.

"I wanted to stay a little longer at Independiente," remembers Kun, "but I also knew that it was a very good opportunity for me and for the club, because the money would be very useful for them in putting an end to their state of insolvency. Everyone agreed that the best bet was Atletico Madrid because of the language and the customs, and because I would have more opportunities there. I knew about the history of the club and I knew the team from having seen them on TV, but from that day on I watched them more closely. And the suggestion seemed to make sense to me. What's more, they said that Madrid was similar to Buenos Aires… I'd never been to Spain. The furthest I had ever been was to Holland for the Under-20 World Cup. I didn't know whether things would turn out well for me, but I wasn't scared. I was convinced that I was going to do everything I could for things to work out as best they could. And if it didn't go well for me, I'd come back, I'd take the return flight."

"He wanted us to decide. He asked us what we thought, and what we wanted. We replied that he had to ask himself the same questions. He then told us that he wanted to go to Spain. But that he wanted all of us to go and live there. We didn't reply to him straight away. But afterwards, we explained to him that this would not be possible. That it was his life, and that the rest of the family moving out there with him was not an option. We couldn't uproot everyone, and have everyone start a new life. We promised to support him as best we could. I looked at him, and it made me so sad. I said it to him through tears. He was so young… To begin with he didn't understand, and he was insistent. But then he realised that what we were saying made sense. And we agreed that, out of all the options, Spain was the best one. At least for a first step. Because of the language and customs being similar to ours. We thought that it was the best way for him to be able to settle in to life in Europe and that, come what may, he would be able to change again in the future."

ADRIANA AGÜERO

By the middle of April, and after Comparada had sent a representative to Spain to close the deal, a pre-agreement was signed between Independiente and Atletico Madrid. In doing so, the two clubs had settled on the terms of the transfer.

The final amount: 23 million euros, a record transfer fee for Argentinian football and the highest in *Atleti's* history. At the same time as this took place, and in separate negotiations, the agents agreed Kun's personal terms with the club.

Journalists reported Kun's transfer abroad as a done deal, but they still did not know the name of the buying club. However, and just when it seemed that there would be no more surprises,

Sergio's agents were contacted for a last-minute meeting in a hotel in the centre of Buenos Aires.

A representative from Real Madrid was ready to go to any lengths to sign him. His instructions were clear: to equal any existing offer, and to significantly improve the wage packet. The response from the agents was that a pre-existing agreement with another club would be respected, although they would not specify who it was at this stage as it had not yet been made public.

With that last attempt dealt with, all that remained was to make the official announcement, which would take place shortly after the conclusion of the domestic championship. Miguel Ángel Gil Marín and Julio Comparada would make the announcement at a joint press conference to be held in Buenos Aires towards the end of May 2006.

For IMG, beyond having been involved in Argentinian football's record transfer, what Sergio Agüero's move represented was the highest transfer fee paid for one of their footballers anywhere in the world. And for Jorge Prat Gay, their president in Argentina, and his team, it also confirmed the success of the system that they had implemented with the initial creation of the football department.

The professional and personal satisfaction involved only served to ensure that they did not rest on their laurels, instead spurring them on with their policy of efficiently seeking out talent, signing it up and then giving the best service to their clients.

Securing the best contracts for them always went hand-in-hand with a tight control over all other related aspects, in order to allow them to become the best professionals they could be.

The decision to remain close to the clients, not just on the sporting side but personally too, was one of their best. Kun's case also represented a learning process, putting their model to the test by representing an elite sportsman. The results were – and would continue to be – more than satisfactory.

In any case, the transfer would be just another step on the road, and there was still much work to be done. Indeed, while the transfer was still being finalised, a new agreement was concluded with Nike, because the one originally signed in 2003 was coming to an end on March 31st, 2006. As with the transfer between clubs, there was firstly a fierce struggle between the world's other most iconic sports equipment manufacturers, from which Nike prevailed by triggering a clause from their first agreement, which gave them the right to equal any other offers. The decision to gamble, just at the right moment, when Kun was only 15, now bore fruit for Nike, who were then able to hold on to their star.

The enthusiasm of the North American brand was there for all to see when both the head of their legal department and the head of sports marketing travelled down from the USA to Argentina, in order to negotiate the final deal with IMG. It took three days of intense discussions with Jorge Prat Gay and the company's lawyers which resulted, on the morning of Saturday, March 25th, 2006, in a contract being signed.

Kun himself was of course called to that final meeting, held in offices in the north of Greater Buenos Aires, although he needed a last-minute change of clothing first. An unconcerned Sergio had headed off to the meeting wearing trainers belonging to a rival brand. With this little issue settled – and sporting some newly-borrowed trainers – the meeting could take place.

It was a cordial meeting, where the satisfaction of all parties at having reached an agreement was clear to see. The customary introductions with Nike's representatives, via a translator, went pleasantly enough. The North Americans, soon to return home, put themselves at Sergio's disposal for anything that he may need.

At this stage, they were used to many of their clients requesting souvenirs or merchandise related to the brand's other celebrities such as LeBron James, Kobe Bryant or Roger Federer.

However, Kun did not interpret their offer in this way, and instead innocently asked whether they could get him a PlayStation 3, which had still not been released on the Argentinian market.

The request – which was naturally accepted – showed Kun as he really was: a boy, still developing and still maturing as a sportsman and a person, despite being on the lips of the world's biggest brands and clubs and having multi-million dollar figures swirling around him.

Music and tears

In the Clausura championship, Independiente continued to show a lack of consistency, which saw any title ambitions slipping further away.

In the 10 matches since that win over Racing in the sixth round of fixtures, Falcioni's team only claimed two wins. The remaining games comprised of four wins and four draws.

Throughout the period Kun, like the rest of the team, performed inconsistently. However, he did score five goals: against

River, Banfield, Colón de Santa Fe and a brace against Vélez Sarsfield. In this last match, Sergio once more intervened decisively with two goals in four minutes towards the end of the second half, in the 82nd and 86th minutes.

Only three fixtures were left in the championship and, on Saturday, April 29th, *El Rojo* would travel to Olimpo in Bahía Blanca for their 17th game. It would prove to be a fateful night for Kun, who knew that he would have to take special care because he had already received four yellow cards and a fifth would exclude him from the next match against Boca Juniors in Avellaneda, which was going to be his last opportunity to play at home for his beloved team.

Quite simply, it would be a farewell to his fans in their own stadium. That it would indeed be his last match at the Libertadores de América was confirmed and made public when, the day before the Olimpo clash, Spanish newspapers published momentous news: Sergio Agüero had been transferred to Atletico Madrid for 23 million euros. Although nobody officially acknowledged the move, different journalistic sources confirmed it as such.

Despite the disappointment that came from knowing that Kun would only play three more matches for Independiente, *El Rojo's* fans greeted him on that night in Bahía Blanca with various songs in his honour: 'Olelé, olalá, Agüero is a *Rojo* and always will be'; 'Borombombóm, borombóm, Agüero for Argentina', roared the away end. Sergio kept reminding himself that he had to be careful, in order to remain eligible for the next match against Boca Juniors.

The latter were on course to become champions, and he did not want to allow them to secure the title and perform their lap of honour in Avellaneda. Meanwhile, he was dreaming of a farewell goal. Therefore, once on the field of play and shortly before kick-off, he approached referee Diego Abal to explain to him the situation.

"I told him that I had four yellow cards to my name and that, if he gave me another, they were going to suspend me. I explained that I may well catch someone, but that it wouldn't be on purpose. He said to me that if I didn't foul anyone, then I wouldn't have any problems," remembers Sergio.

A few minutes into the game, and Kun was receiving more of the same treatment that the opposition had been dishing out to him in every match: a crunching slide tackle by Uruguayan defender Máximo Lucas, who was booked, left stud marks on his right thigh and forced him off the pitch on the first aid buggy. Despite his anger, he promised to himself that he would not react to any more potential kicks or provocations.

He limped back on, but was able to recover and after 30 minutes slipped the ball through for Emiliano Armenteros to beat goalkeeper Roa. Ten minutes later, in trying to sprint past his marker Lucas by the left touchline, he made minimal contact with the defender, who fell dramatically. Referee Abal not only awarded the free-kick to Olimpo, but also walked up to Sergio with a hand in his pocket. When Kun realised that he was going to be booked, he held out both hands and desperately pleaded for the referee to reconsider. Abal was not moved and, to Sergio's desperation, he showed him the yellow card. Kun walked angrily away, grabbing at his hair.

Seconds later television cameras caught images – despite his efforts to cover it with his shirt – of a face covered with tears.

He was an image of desolation. His despair became everyone's despair. He was inconsolable. His team-mates tried, as did his opponents, to console him. Lucas Biglia and Emiliano Armenteros both attempted to. But Kun carried on, unable to stop crying. He alternated between blaming himself for having spoken with the referee, and the sense of injustice over an unmerited yellow card.

"For the defenders to be booked they have to kick me time and again, and for me a tiny bit of contact and I get a yellow card… it's just not fair…," he said in the changing rooms.

Sergio was able to vent some of his frustration in the second half when, after a fine piece of individual play, he was fouled for a penalty that he himself converted. He knocked it softly down the centre and, on seeing it go in, let out a cry of anger and frustration. It would be his last goal in the red of Independiente. He sensed as much and, after celebrating, went up to *El Rojo's* fans and dedicated it to them by kissing the club badge on his shirt.

Despite the resentment that he felt over that fifth yellow card, he did attend the match on Sunday, May 7th against Boca Juniors, watching from the director's box at the Doble Visera stadium. He endured Independiente's 2-0 defeat, goals by Martín Palermo and Rodrigo Palacio securing the title for their opponents with one fixture to spare.

Sergio's bitterness was only softened by the acclaim that he received from *El Rojo's* fans who, knowing that they were witnessing the imminent departure of their idol, paid tribute in every way possible. He was inundated with chants, flags and ovations throughout the 90 minutes.

Sergio still had 13 minutes of a match against Banfield that had to be completed behind closed doors, and the season's final fixture against Rosario Central in the Gigante de Arroyito stadium on May 14th, which also ended in defeat by two goals to nil. It was hardly his dream farewell.

Furthermore, Independiente failed to qualify for the South American competitions. However, the sadness caused by leaving a club for whom he felt such passion was compensated for by the affection that he received at all times from *El Rojo's* fans.

The flags hung up at pitchside, true symbols of their love, demonstrated as much. 'Thank you Kun', 'Thank you for your magic and your tears', 'Kun, may *El Rojo* always flow through your veins', '*El Rojo* will always be your home – thanks'. More and more dedications sprouted up among the fans. They were just pieces of cloth with handwritten messages from people who could not let their idol leave without paying tribute, for each one of them, without exception, felt that he had represented them through the way he played, his craft, his dribbling, his commitment and his goals. He had enthralled them time and time again. Never before had a player managed to inspire such a depth of feeling in so little time. Kun's charisma and charm had made it all possible. And as only appropriate in the presence of such passion, and with 'Agüero, Agüero' ringing out, he slowly approached the stand, as if absorbing for one last time a chant that moved him so deeply. He took off his shirt and rolled it up and, while contemplating the intensity of all he had been through in such a short period of time, offered it to his people. They went crazy for him once more.

He had pulled on that Independiente shirt 54 times in local tournaments, as well as twice for international matches, and had scored 23 goals. It was days before his 18th birthday and, more than ever, he felt like a sacred understanding had been formed during that time. And he felt certain that he would be back, in the same way as one always returns to a first love.

That bond between Kun and *El Rojo's* fans – unique and unconditional, as only a bond between an idol and his people can be – was summed up perfectly by Matías Linetzky, a musician and Independiente fan the same age as Sergio. He composed a song for him, which he named 'From one heart to another'.

It was through music, Sergio's other passion, that he was also able to express what he felt for football. More specifically through *cumbia*, one of his favourite styles of music.

He accepted an invitation from Marcelo Agüero, the leader of the Santa Fe cumbia group Los Leales, to attend a rehearsal session. Despite sharing the same surname they were not related, although later Ezequiel, Marcelo's son, would marry Gaby, Sergio's sister.

The *cumbia* rhythm is very popular in Argentina. Its roots are in the music of the same name from Central America, but the Argentinian version is uniquely fused with other local styles, as well as being influenced by Caribbean music. Particularly from the 1980s onwards, *cumbia* enjoyed a strong renaissance, penetrating firstly among the poorer sections of society and then spreading to all social classes.

Marcelo, the singer of the band who had followed Kun's career, dedicated a song to him which, in accepting their offer, Sergio agreed to sing with the group.

"The idea first came about at a barbecue that we had together at his house in Martínez," says Marcelo. "We suggested that he sang it with us. He jumped at the chance, and so we did the lyrics together with my brother Sergio. All we did was to quite simply write down everything that he relayed to us, about his passion for football and the emotion that he felt when the fans sang out his surname."

The song was recorded in one afternoon. Sergio had the chance to get used to the microphone, and appeared unfailingly relaxed and smiling for the cameras that were filming him. He had never done anything like it before.

His thing was obviously football. But in the same way as he entertained himself with the ball, he also enjoyed himself during that recording.

A few months later, the video was already appearing on television programmes dedicated to *cumbia*, and on the internet.

"About who? About who? Kun Agüero, papa…" Sergio says at the start of the recording.

In the verses that he sings, he makes the lyrics written by his friend his own.

"Because of the desire that I cannot contain. Because it is always in my blood. Because of the emotions that it inspires in me.

"Football is my passion, my life-force. Football flows through my veins, it's a part of my soul, the fans shout 'come on Kun Agüero!' Have strength, for the world wants to see you, showing your courage, making people happy with your football. It's my dream come true…"

He happily emerged from his brief foray as a singer unscathed, although having shown somewhat less aptitude with a microphone than with the ball at his feet.

The experience led him to claim afterwards – jokingly, but also expressing a barely-concealed desire – that "if I hadn't been a footballer, I could have been a singer".

Best wishes

The day after the conclusion to the Clausura championship, on Monday, May 15th, 2006, Argentina's national team manager José Pekerman named his final squad for the World Cup which was starting in Germany on June 9th. Sergio did not receive the call-up. The coach opted instead for Julio Cruz, the veteran Inter Milan striker who had had a noteworthy season with 21 goals in 45 matches. At 31 years of age, Cruz would play at his first World Cup.

The other five attacking places, out of the six forwards Pekerman took, were occupied by Lionel Messi, Hernán Crespo, Carlos Tévez, Javier Saviola and Rodrigo Palacio, the Boca Juniors striker and only one among them who played in the Argentinian domestic league.

"Of course I would have liked to have gone. I was a bit angry. But it didn't bother me too much, because I knew that it would be very difficult to make the squad. I was very young, and I knew that I'd have other opportunities. It was still very painful, watching from afar," recalls Sergio, who went through the end of that month of May and the start of June on a rush of pure emotion. Because once the championship was over, and after enjoying a few days of rest, the time to complete his transfer was upon him.

In order to do so, Atletico Madrid's chief executive Miguel Ángel Gil Marín travelled to Buenos Aires. One of the first things he did on arrival was to meet Sergio and his family. The meeting took place at Samuel Liberman's football ground in San Antonio de Areco. There was good chemistry between the Spaniard and the Agüero-Del Castillo family from the off.

"All I want is for you to look after my son," Adriana Agüero told him. "Nothing else. He's very young, and I don't want you to put him under pressure. It's important that he doesn't lose the happiness that he feels at the moment when he plays his football, so that he keeps his desire and carries on enjoying what he does…"

Gil Marín's response was immediate: "Don't worry, the boy will be well looked after," he replied, still impressed by Adriana's character. The meeting was barely over when he telephoned Emilio Gutiérrez, the head of marketing and communications at Atletico Madrid, who he told to look after the player as if he was his son. With gusto, Gutiérrez took it upon himself to make good on Atletico's promise.

On Tuesday, May 30th, Gil Marín and Independiente's president Julio Comparada announced in a press conference that Kun had been signed by *Los Colchoneros*.

According to their statements, the Avellaneda club was going to receive 23 million euros, or 28 millions dollars, for 90 per cent of the player's rights and, in the case of a future sale, the right to 20 per cent of anything received above 18 million euros.

"This is not just any other signing," declared Gil Marín. "It is a strong statement of intent by *Atleti*, one of the most important signings in the club's history. We are all excited by Agüero. I don't think that there was a coach in the world who didn't want him."

For his part, Comparada stated that "the financial gulf made it impossible to keep hold of the player, and we all hope that one day he will return to Independiente. I have no doubt that Agüero will prove a great success in European football."

Sergio did not speak at the press conference. His words were being saved for six days later when he would be unveiled in Madrid, to sign a contract that would tie him to the club for the next six seasons.

Before that imminent departure, Kun celebrated his 18th birthday, which simultaneously became a makeshift farewell party.

"We had to prepare it at the last minute," says Adriana. "The thing is, we didn't know if he was going to be called up for the World Cup or not, so we hadn't planned anything. On top of that, the next day we had to travel to Spain for his official unveiling."

The party was held on Friday, June 2nd at a function room in the Martínez district of northern Greater Buenos Aires.

Originally conceived of as an intimate gathering, it ended up being a great celebration. Sergio himself, wearing a brown shirt and light yellow suede-effect trousers, was at the door welcoming the guests one by one.

There was hardly anyone there from the world of football, but his nearest and dearest were all in attendance. His parents Leo and Adriana. His brothers and sisters Jessica, Gaby, Maira, Daiana, Mauricio and Gastón. His maternal grandparents Rodolfo and Ana. His uncle Daniel and aunt Maggie. His godfather Darío Fernández and his wife Lili. His friends Pepe Sosa, Lucas Fernández and Diego Campos. From Los Eucaliptus, a specially-hired minibus carried his old neighbour Gustavo Castillo and his wife Any; Rubén Amarilla, his wife Elena and their son Toto; Cristian Formiga and his parents Daniel and Patricia. And from Lanús, 'Luigi' and his family. Emiliano Molina's parents and family were also there. José María Astarloa and Eduardo González were not missing out, and neither were his agents Hernán Reguera and Gonzalo Rebasa.

The night was largely sound-tracked by the music of Los Leales, with the group itself performing on stage. Sergio took the initiative and grabbed the microphone to sing with them. There was time for a specially prepared surprise video for the occasion, which started with images of the cartoon of 'Kum Kum the Caveman' and contained testimonies from different people who had played their part in shaping him as a footballer, among them Néstor Rambert and Alberto Tardivo, and also a message from his sisters Jessica, Mayra and Gaby.

An emotional Adriana carefully followed every last word. She could not help but remember those early days when they were not even able to celebrate Sergio's birthdays. She looked at her son and saw part of her smile in his, the dimples which formed on his cheeks – just as on hers – when he expressed happiness. She looked at her son and at Leo, and she could see the passion that united them. And she felt thankful for life, and that God had rewarded them. Not because of what they now had, compared with harder times in the past, but because of her family and the miracle of that boy who, above all else, was a good person. And because of all those who had helped them to reach this moment. And she expressed as much in a letter that she read to him on that night, on behalf of Leo and the rest of the family.

"You are already becoming a man, and with so much up ahead of you," she read to him in one of the passages. "Although the great majority of your desires have already been fulfilled, there is still a lot to come. May you always have that happiness and that twinkle in your eyes. And may you never lose the humility and modesty that make you such a wonderful person. We congratulate you and we are happy for you, for all that you have achieved. You are an excellent son. Never forget that we love you."

The majority of the guests at the 18th birthday party could guess at least one of Sergio's wishes as he blew out the candles. For a few hours after the end of the party – which went on until six o'clock in the morning of Saturday, June 3rd – he had to travel to Madrid to start a new chapter in his football career. And many of them travelled to the airport in Ezeiza to bid him a unique farewell.

The emotion shown by everyone, and particularly his godfather Darío who could not stop crying, only served to heighten his sense that this was the perfect dawn to a new era that was drawing ever nearer. In those spirits, he boarded the Aerolíneas Argentinas aeroplane which was to take him to Spain. His parents went with him as well as, on behalf of IMG, Jorge Prat Gay, Hernán Reguera and Gonzalo Rebasa.

It was his second trip to the Old Continent. The first had been on the occasion of the Under-20 World Cup in Holland. Only on this occasion he was travelling in Business Class, and therefore enjoyed a greater and unexpected level of comfort.

What with all the commotion of the last few hours, he wasted no time in relaxing and falling fast asleep. The same could not be said for Adriana, who was travelling on an aeroplane for the first time.

"Leo had already travelled by plane a few times and he wanted to talk to me. But I couldn't concentrate on anything. Even when it started to move, I thought I could smell petrol. And once we were up in the air, I said to myself 'this isn't for me'. I didn't even want to eat. I saw Sergio sleeping peacefully, and everyone else so calm. In the end I was able to relax, and when I awoke we were about to land.

At Barajas Airport, Atletico Madrid's head of marketing Emilio Gutiérrez started fulfilling the responsibility given to him by Gil Marín. His first task was to welcome Sergio and his family. He was surprised by the stir created by Kun's arrival. More than 500 people, an unprecedented number – among them Spaniards and Argentinians, some of them residents in Spain and others in transit towards Germany to watch the World Cup – had crowded together in anticipation of Sergio making his way out of immigration.

The plane had landed at 18:40 on Sunday, June 4th, 2006 and the crowd, which exceeded all expectations, had already been waiting impatiently for an hour. The mixture of chants to be heard made the situation even more unique. One which went 'come, come, sing with me and you'll find a friend, Kun Agüero's going to lead us round and round' could be heard alongside the more traditional '*Atleti, Atleti, Atleti…*'. There was also 'clap your hands, clap your hands, don't stop clapping, Agüero's goals are on the way' and 'Kun Agüero, laralalala, laralala', all sung in a unique blend of accents from Spain and Buenos Aires.

Sergio, dressed in a white shirt and a black corduroy jacket that a prudent Gonzalo Rebasa had managed to buy just before boarding the aeroplane, could hear the shouts as he went through the formalities at immigration. His exit from Terminal 1 was delayed even more as he stopped to sign autographs for the Civil Guard officials who requested them.

At that moment Emilio Gutiérrez, having already introduced himself to Kun, explained to him that under the circumstances it would be very difficult to stop and speak with the press, who were also waiting for him in their droves. They had the option to leave via another exit, but that did not seem appropriate to them. They decided to exit where everyone was waiting for them, although they never for one moment envisaged the chaos that awaited them as they walked through the door. There was such an avalanche of bodies that they all practically lost each other. Only Sergio and Emilio managed to stay together. Leo and Adriana stayed to one side and looked on, witnessing a journalist who fell on to a luggage trolley, and then one of Emilio's colleagues rolling on the floor, having been pushed over by the fans.

"We lost sight of them," says Adriana. "It was like the people had gone mad. I never thought that there'd be so many people waiting… And naive old me, having asked Sergio to acknowledge the people and sign autographs for those who asked him. It was impossible…"

To the cameras that came and went, Sergio managed to give the journalists a brief soundbite: "I'm coming to Spain with much hope and excitement, I want to do well and be successful". At last, they reached the cars that were waiting for them. One of them – a top of the range Kia Opirus, used for official club purposes – had room for Emilio, Sergio and, lagging behind, Leo and Adriana.

Still shocked and a little overwhelmed by the welcome he had received, and as their driver headed off towards the Hotel Foxa M30 where he would stay for the next five days, Kun asked Emilio: "All of this is for me?" Emilio smiled and replied, "And who else would it be for…?"

Emilio Gutiérrez did not leave Kun's side for one minute on

that day. He explained to him all about Spain, about *Atleti*, about his team-mates and the media. He wanted to give him a good feel for his new surroundings, although without overwhelming him. Especially so, bearing in mind that it was his first day in a new country. Sergio listened attentively, and he even had time to accept radio interviews with *Cadena Cope* and *Cadena Ser*.

When they asked him how he had felt at making his Primera División debut at only 15 years of age, if he had felt much pressure, Kun unflinchingly responded: "Pressure? Pressure is living in a *villa*. I'm here because I want to be, what pressure could I feel?"

Emilio, who had been running Atletico's marketing and communications departments for 15 years, knew that night that he was faced with someone different, someone who presented him with a challenge that he had not experienced with any other player: that of helping to nurture him so that he could continue developing as a person. He considered it to be a personal duty. All of a sudden, he felt a protective instinct towards a boy who, providing he managed to settle in well, could become one of the world's best. It struck him as a great privilege to have the opportunity to help him on his way.

"My first impression was of a very humble kid with a striking glint in his eye. I looked at him and I thought that it was going to be wonderful working with him. Because he knew how to listen and because he seemed so full of hope and excitement about everything that was happening to him."

The expectations generated among the fans of Atletico Madrid – considered as the most loyal and fervent following in Spain – could well have surprised Kun, even though there were various explanations for it.

Only Real Madrid and Barcelona had historically won more La Liga titles than *Los Colchoneros* but, by June 2006, 10 years had gone by since the club's last title and they had only won one championship out of the previous 29. They had also suffered a painful relegation to the second division in the 1999/2000 season which lasted for two years, in the first of which the team finished a lowly fourth place.

In addition, they were going through a seven-year drought without a win over Real Madrid and even the big name arrivals of the Italian Christian Vieri, the Brazilian Juninho or the Argentinian coach Carlos Bianchi had been unable to pull the club out of its doldrums.

For Atletico's senior management team, led by president Enrique Cerezo, it was a time of institutional overhaul. The creation of a new, 140-hectare 'sports city' complex, a projected stadium move and the building of a competitive team were the main goals for the club to reclaim its historic place at the top table of Spanish football.

In this context, Kun's signing only served to further increase optimism among the fans. The devotion that he had inspired, without having even kicked a ball, was on display on Monday, June 5th when he was shown off at the Vicente Calderón. Some 2,000 fans, an amount previously unheard of, welcomed him alongside the 170 journalists covering the event. After passing a medical, he was unveiled at a press conference, flanked by president Enrique Cerezo and sporting director Jesús García Pitarch.

A somewhat nervous Kun got himself ready to answer the journalists' questions. Showing her maternal instincts Adriana, who was sat in the front row next to Leo, his agents and the rest of *Atleti's* senior management, noticed her son's unease. When Sergio looked in her direction, and in an effort to calm him, she blew him a kiss from her hand, which drew a smile. Gil Marín, who observed them at this very moment, was touched by the gesture. Quite simply, this was a mother trying to boost her 18-year-old boy's confidence. To try to remain calm, Sergio looked into the eyes of each one of the journalists who asked him a question, detaching himself from the others. And in his own style, speaking in a low voice, he managed to get some comments out.

"I hope to give my best for the club. I really wanted to come to *Atleti*. I'm here to score goals. Hopefully I can win the title, the fans will enjoy my play and I'll be free of any pressure."

In turn Cerezo, after handing him his club membership card, declared that "Spain, thanks to Atletico, will come to understand that it has a marvellous player on its hands. We are putting together a young, fearless team that wants to win everything."

Once the press conference had finished, Sergio headed to other surroundings in which he felt much more at ease: the dressing room, where he pulled on, for the first time, his new team's red and white striped shirt, with his surname on the back in blue letters. Wearing it, he went out on to the field of play where the fans greeted him with cries of 'Agüero, Agüero' and '*Atleti, Atleti*'.

He delighted those present for 15 minutes, playing keepy-uppies and signing countless autographs, until one of the fans was rewarded with being able to take that first shirt home. The love affair had begun.

From Madrid
To Canada

After staying in Spain for five days, Sergio returned to Argentina with his family on Friday, June 9th, the same day that the World Cup started in Germany.

In the time that remained before he was to return to Madrid to start pre-season training with Atletico, he followed the fortunes of the senior national team. He took pleasure from the 2-1 win over a tough Ivory Coast team and the 6-0 thrashing of Serbia and Montenegro, and reassurance from the 0-0 draw against Holland that secured top spot for Argentina in Group C.

He endured the tense round of 16 tie against Mexico, where a wonderful strike by his future team-mate Maxi Rodríguez –

later chosen as the best goal of the World Cup – gave Argentina a 2-1 victory which qualified them for the quarter-finals. And he could not hide his disappointment on June 30th, watching on as his countrymen were reduced to tears out on the pitch at the Olympic Stadium in Berlin after being knocked out 4-2 on penalties by the hosts Germany.

He had followed the game on television at his house in Martínez, with his father Leo and other friends.

"We were all sad, upset… And to try to put it out of my mind, I decided to go to the gym to carry on with my everyday routine. I took a taxi and the driver started telling me how terrible he felt because of the defeat, about how his mother hadn't stopped crying. And I could sense the sadness among people in the streets. I knew what it meant to wear the national team jersey.

"Ever since I was little, I went every time they called me up for the national teams. I always reported for duty when the call came, because it's an honour and, as a player, you can't aspire to anything greater. And I always wanted to be there. But on that day I realised what the national team meant to the people…"

Sergio had learnt to love the national team from a very young age. Ever since his first call-up from Tojo – after that *pre-novena* final at the end of 2001 – he eagerly reported every time he was invited to join the national youth squads. He had grown to enjoy the training sessions at the AFA complex at Ezeiza, the nights spent in team camps, the one-on-one chats with the coaches and being able to practise with established players. He represented his country with pride at the South American Championships in Paraguay and tasted glory at the Under-20 World Cup in Holland.

He may not have made the squad that went to the World

Cup in Germany, but he had faith that the opportunity to join the senior national team would arrive sooner or later. And that day arrived on September 3rd, 2006 when Alfio Basile, beginning his second spell as Argentina coach after having replaced José Pekerman, called Kun up for a friendly match that saw the national team fall to a 3-0 defeat against Brazil at the Emirates Stadium in London.

Sergio's dream then became a reality, and at only 18 years of age, when he came on in place of Carlos Tévez after 65 minutes. A shot that missed the target by a couple of yards following Juan Román Riquelme's pass, and an assist which Federico Insúa was unable to take advantage of, were his best moments. And he even picked up a yellow card after a tough challenge on the Brazilian Lucio, who consequently left the match with a 'souvenir' from Sergio.

Beforehand, and having taken advantage of the time off to see his family and friends, Kun had returned to Madrid on Monday, July 10th to join the rest of the *Atleti* squad coached by the Mexican, Javier 'Vasco' Aguirre. Just like on the first day that he touched down in the Spanish capital, the fans swarmed to Barajas to welcome him back.

Despite landing at six o'clock in the morning, around one hundred fans were present, and their chants provided the background music to the images recorded by the ten television cameras that were also there to greet him.

This next phase included pre-season training in Segovia, some friendly matches and warm-up tours in Germany and China. He started to get to know his new team-mates, and to show glimpses of his potential. Furthermore, wearing the number 20 shirt and in his own inimitable style, he scored five goals.

They came in the matches against Atletico B, Energy Cottbus from Germany, Kashmiri Antlers from Japan, Shanghai Shenhua from China and Albacete. Agüero headed up a group of new reinforcements whose arrivals, along with the retention of star player Fernando 'El Niño' Torres – already a club icon at only 22 years of age – had filled *Atleti's* fervent and loyal followers with hope. There was reason to believe that they could turn around the poor results of recent years.

There was also a strong Argentinian presence in the squad, which featured Sergio's compatriots Maxi 'Fiera' Rodríguez, goalkeeper Leo Franco, defender Mariano Pernía and striker Luciano Galletti. This helped him to settle in.

The rest of the squad was comprised, amongst others, of the Bulgarian Martín Petrov, the Portuguese players Maniche and Costinha, the Greek Giourkas Seitaridis, the Colombian Luis Amaranto Perea, the Frenchman Peter Luccin and the Spaniards Pablo Ibañez, Antonio López, José Manuel Jurado and Mista.

Sergio had moved in to a house in the town of Majadahonda, 16 kilometres to the north-east of Madrid and only 300 metres from Cerro del Espino, Atleti's training complex. He had rented a seven-bedroom property in order to house everyone who had accompanied him for this first period in Spain, as well as those who occasionally visited him. His family sought the best way to remain close by, and to make it as easy as possible for him to settle in.

One of Adriana's brothers, Daniel, and his wife Maggie, moved out to live with Kun and to help make his daily tasks more manageable. Gonzalo Rebasa and Hernán Reguera – and later Maxi Lo Russo – alternated their stays at the house in order to handle any affairs linked with his professional activities.

Of his parents, Leo spent most time with him in Madrid, while Adriana stayed back in Buenos Aires looking after the rest of the family. By keeping in touch on a daily basis, the distances between them seemed shorter, and from time to time he would receive friends who travelled especially to spend time with him.

Meanwhile, the Argentines in the squad took it upon themselves to help out and make sure he felt at home – Maxi Rodríguez in particular, who was also one of his neighbours.

"From the moment he arrived, I spent a lot of time with him," says Maxi.

"He was very young, so I tried to pass on my experience from having already been in Spain for seven years. He was obviously going to find his own way of settling in, just as we all had. But if I could help him, all the better.

"Sergio is a very likeable kid, and it was noticeable what he brought out in others."

That first half of the 2006/07 campaign, Sergio's debut season at Atletico Madrid, was defined to a certain extent by controversy over how to best manage the process of settling him in to European football.

The debate over whether he should be introduced slowly – an option favoured by manager Javier Aguirre – or whether, because of his quality, he had to start every match, was instigated right at the start of the La Liga season as Sergio was left on the bench, to the surprise of many, for the first fixture against Racing Santander on Sunday, August 27th.

On that day at the Sardinero stadium, Aguirre put his faith in the Torres-Mista partnership for a match that ended up in a

1-0 victory to *Los Colchoneros*, thanks to a strike from 'El Niño' himself.

Kun came on after 67 minutes for what was his official debut in the red and white of Atletico. His second match came on September 9th against Valencia – in between times, there had been a FIFA international break in which, as already outlined, Kun had made his debut for the Argentinian national team against Brazil in England.

He was once again included among the substitutes against Valencia, a team managed by the future head coach of Atletico, Quique Sánchez Flores. *Los Colchoneros* quickly went one down following a goal by David Villa in the seventh minute. It would turn out to be the only goal of the game.

Kun, who entered the fray at the start of the second half, was his team's stand-out performer. This was an opinion shared by journalists and fans alike, who were persistently demanding for a starting place to be found for *Atleti's* new number 10, a starting place that finally arrived for the first time on Sunday, September 17th against Athletic Bilbao in the La Catedral stadium, in place of the suspended Torres who had been sent off in the previous match.

For that match Gonzalo Rebasa, who travelled to the match by car from Madrid with Uncle Daniel and Aunt Maggie, witnessed the surprise of *Atleti's* senior management when they saw the players get off the bus that had brought them from their hotel. The majority of the players were lost in their own thoughts, while Kun was smiling from ear to ear, enjoying the experience to the full.

"That kid feels no pressure," they said to Gonzalo, who replied that this was indeed one of Sergio's traits. The naturalness with which Kun instinctively approached those challenges was reflected out on the field of play. Kun's magnificent display in his team's 4-1 win, which saw him notch his first official goal in *Atleti's* colours after beating two defenders to score with a shot from outside the penalty box, earned him La Liga's player of the week award for the third round of fixtures.

"We were in the stands and we screamed our hearts out when he scored, right alongside the local Basque fans who wanted to kill us," says Gonzalo, who returned as quickly as he could back to Madrid after the match. Kun had returned by plane with the squad, and waited up for him until five o'clock in the morning.

"It's just that he wanted to tell me all about it, to find out what it had been like up in the stands. He was buzzing," says Gonzalo.

'A star is born', said the *As* newspaper the next day. 'Agüero's magnificence earns him the honours at La Catedral', was the headline in *Marca*. 'Kun is already causing *pañoladas*[1]', wrote *Mundo Deportivo*.

Maxi Rodríguez confirms that Kun showed much enthusiasm during those first months, a young man who was very excited by everything that he was experiencing, and who was making an effort to settle in to a new country and fit in with his team-mates.

"He had to get used to different customs, to a changing room environment unlike that which he had known in Argentina, to coming up against the best in the world out on the pitch. It took him some time, but he got there," underlines Maxi.

---

[1] A *pañolada* is a typical way in which Spanish football fans express either their satisfaction or discontent, by waving handkerchiefs in the air.

He also points out that Kun, still so young, had to learn to live with players who were already established internationals. "He had to win his place, and demonstrate what he was capable of. He managed to do that, too."

Sergio's personality also helped him to win over his teammates. The music of Los Leales proved to be an ally in this regard. He managed to get it played in the changing rooms, on the planes, on the buses and at team camps, and even 'El Niño' Torres had to take a CD off his hands that he listened to in his car.

In fact, he struck up a good relationship with his fellow striker. Torres was always on hand with good advice, both on the pitch and off it, and he always made reference to the responsibility of the whole team when the coach was pointing out something in particular to Kun. His positive influence was also behind the idea for one of Sergio's first tattoos.

Just as Fernando Torres had done with his name, Sergio had 'Kun Agüero' written on the back of his right arm in the 'Tengwar' language invented by writer J.R.R. Tolkien and spoken by the elves in 'Lord of the Rings'. Years later, another tattoo would appear on his other arm, the left, but this time in Spanish and in homage to his son.

Daniel Agüero, Adriana's brother who along with his wife had moved to Madrid to be with Kun, was in a privileged position to witness Sergio settling into life in Spain. Not just because they shared the same house and saw each other every day but because, by starting to work at Atletico Madrid's Cerro del Espino sports complex, he had an uninterrupted view of how he was getting on in all aspects of his life.

"He was able to get on with it just fine. Just imagine: he was very young and he was used to being with his family, surrounded by friends and loved ones. I thought that he would find it more difficult. But from what I could see, both at home and at training, it all came very naturally to him. The thing is, he was so keen to learn and to give his all for it to go well, that he made it easier for himself."

During those early days, Daniel and Maggie almost became like substitute parents.

"My wife cooked him his favourite food and, between the two of us, we tried to make him feel at home. Telephone calls and the internet made Buenos Aires feel a bit closer, and he also really enjoyed the visits from members of the family," says Daniel.

"I would say that between the agents, ourselves and his team-mates, we formed a network that gave him the best possible support base and helped create the right environment in which his own good attitude could flourish."

Emilio Gutiérrez adds details of how Sergio settled in to the *Atleti* squad.

"He was able to spread happiness around the changing room. His good humour was contagious. And as Kun doesn't have a nasty bone in his body, it was impossible for anyone to feel uncomfortable," he says, and adds that Sergio's willingness to learn caught everyone's attention.

"His eyes would light up. He was like a sponge, impatient to learn more, to increase his knowledge. And without losing an ounce of his humility."

Emilio, who at this time dined almost every Thursday at Kun's house, perfectly completed that support group which formed around him during his settling-in period.

AGÜERO

Born to Rise

MY STORY

He oversaw Kun's contact with the press and tried to protect him, so that he could concentrate solely on his football.

What is for certain is that Sergio felt at ease in Madrid. It amused him when fans in the street would come up to him and quite literally say "you're going to get out of there this year ..."

It was actually a local way of expressing encouragement, but he did not understand and had to ask his team-mates to translate it into 'Argentinian' for him.

In a short while, he stopped simply being surprised and admiring of the respect shown to pedestrians by road users, and instead became a part of it.

Driving a Kia estate car, which each member of the squad received from the Korean manufacturer who sponsored *Atleti* at the time, or the BMW 3 Series that he had bought, he got to know the best routes to the Vicente Calderón stadium and other regular destinations. Some of those were within Majadahonda, particularly when it came to buying Argentinian cuts of meat.

One of them was a shop specially recommended to him by Maxi Rodríguez, who knew the town inside out. "But what is certainly true," says Maxi, "is that at barbecue time I was the one who did all the work. There was no way Kun would come anywhere near the grill. Whereas he was first in line to sort out the music. He would always cheekily put on the Los Leales song, and you'd have to try and persuade him to stop singing."

Games of tennis or trips to the cinema with Maxi were frequent. As were the informal get-togethers in the bakery facing the sports complex, run by Argentinians, and whose croissants were the perfect accompaniment to their *mate*, for whenever they were missing Argentina.

Regaining confidence

The final third of 2006 found Sergio continuing down that same path: settling in to a new country, a new team, a new coach and, all the while, displaying his class out on the pitch. The dribbles, the feints, as well as what the Spanish press were already calling his 'strokes of genius', were all appearing in the stadiums that Kun graced.

One of the most significant dates came on Sunday, October 1st as Atletico took on Real, in what would be his first Madrid derby. Javier Aguirre once more opted to leave him on the substitutes' bench, continuing with the Mista-Torres partnership up front. In fact, it was Mista who put *Los Colchoneros* ahead after six minutes. Raúl equalised before half-time for the team managed by Fabio Capello, featuring Englishman David Beckham, Brazilians Ronaldo and Roberto Carlos, Dutchman Ruud Van Nistelrooy and Italian Fabio Cannavaro among their ranks, and later to incorporate the Argentines Fernando Gago and Gonzalo Higuaín.

Kun came on 15 minutes into the second half and, five minutes later, struck a low shot that almost beat Iker Casillas, who only just managed to keep it out. Sergio tried to take on and beat defenders with his dribbles, and in doing so was fouled on four separate occasions. He was on the end of some rough treatment in Spain, just as he had been in Argentina.

At this stage he had already received more fouls – 17 in 279 minutes of play – than any other player in La Liga. Sixty seconds from the end of the game against Real, he had the opportunity to rewrite history and put an end to *Atleti's* seven years without a win over their city rivals.

A wall pass with Torres left him one-on-one with Casillas. Closed down by the onrushing goalkeeper, he opted to chip it over him, but his delicate lob just cleared the bar. Gonzalo Rebasa was among the thousands of supporters in attendance, and he bore witness to the comments from some of those fans after Kun's missed opportunity.

"They weren't particularly generous towards him. But it took guts to do what he did, at that age, on that stage, in none other than the Bernabéu. I was sure that sooner or later he would do things that were just as good, if not better, than that. But the people didn't know that; they still didn't know him. That was a tough night for Sergio, he was completely gutted. And we stayed up very late chatting."

Kun remembers what his feelings were at the time. "I wanted to kill myself…" he says.

But the words that Gonzalo said to him on that night became etched onto his memory forever. "You became a great footballer by playing just like you did today… Do you know how many strikers, in the same position, just close their eyes and smash the ball? But there are very few who would do what you did. Don't stop doing it. Carry on, because that's your style. And it's how you're going to become even greater."

It was perceptive advice. And, in a short while, those who had said that his miss was an unforgivable error started to change their tune. Because that attempt – which he still regrets, in spite of the years which have gone by since – demonstrated Sergio's talent and his daring. He was only 18, and it was his first derby at the Bernabéu.

Two weeks later, on October 14th, 2006, he scored his first goal at the Vicente Calderón stadium, against Recreativo

Huelva during the sixth round of fixtures. It was the winning goal, yet one surrounded with controversy as – unseen by the referee – he had scored it with his hand.

Sergio, wearing blue gloves on his hands that night, pushed the ball in with his fist following a corner taken by Jurado and flicked on by Torres. What, for some, was cheating, for others was simply a matter of the *potrero*. There were plenty of references to Maradona's 'hand of God' goal against England in the 1986 World Cup in Mexico, and to the 'craftiness'; of the Argentines. They even joked that he had purposefully worn gloves, so as not to leave fingerprints.

Kun settled the debate in a frank, direct statement: "Yes, I scored with my hand," he explained after the match. "But it was purely a reflex action."

Sergio scored another goal in Atletico's 10th fixture against Manuel 'The Engineer' Pellegrini's Villarreal team in a victory by three goals to one, this time executing a lob to perfection. And he notched another against Levante in the Copa del Rey on December 13th, scoring in the dying minutes to send the tie into extra time and to ultimately pave the way for *Los Colchoneros'* safe passage to the round of 16.

The goal – a shimmy leaving a defender on the seat of his pants, followed by a powerful finish past Cavallero – intensified the debate over whether a starting place should be found for Kun, who had once more entered the fray in the second half of the match.

And on December 20th, in a 1-1 draw against Barcelona, he scored his fourth goal in La Liga and his first at the Nou Camp. He stole in behind Puyol and Lilian Thuram, before beating Victor Valdés when through one-on-one. Expectations were

high at Atletico Madrid as 2006 drew to a close, with the team on 28 points after eight wins, four draws and four losses. At that point Seville were top with 37 points, followed by Barcelona with 34 and Real Madrid with 32.

In the second half of the league season, played during the first six months of 2007, neither Kun nor Atletico were able to build on the promise shown before the New Year. Sergio only managed to score on two further occasions, against Celta Vigo in the 18th fixture and Athletic Bilbao in the 22nd.

Falling behind in a title race ultimately played out between Barcelona and Real Madrid – who, after a hard-fought comeback, drew level with the Catalans on points and were crowned champions on goal difference – *Atleti* finished up in seventh position on 60 points, having won 17 matches, drawn nine and lost 12. They were outside the Champions League and UEFA Cup places but did qualify for the Intertoto Cup, providing a route back into Europe after so many years.

Kun played a part in all of *Los Colchoneros'* official matches in La Liga and the Copa del Rey, starting 27 of them and making substitute appearances in a further 15. He scored seven goals.

During that first half of 2007, Sergio went through his most difficult months since leaving Argentina. He was also involved in more controversy – following the goal scored with his hand – against Villarreal in April, when he played a cross that his team-mate Fabiano Eller headed in to make it 1-0 while an opposition player, his fellow countryman Guillermo Franco, was laid out on the floor a few yards from goal. Sergio's protestations that he had not seen him fell on deaf ears, and criticism of a supposed lack of respect for fair play quickly followed.

Almost at the same time, and coinciding with Kun and

his team's poor run of form, questions were raised about a supposed lack of care for his physique and about his 'chaotic' lifestyle. The most severe critics questioned his multi-million euro transfer fee, and raised doubts over his progress, claiming that it was not what had been expected. Those defending him said that it was just the normal settling-in period that he would have to go through, and pointed out that even venerated players like Ronaldinho and Zinedine Zidane had endured inconsistent first seasons in Spain, at Barcelona and Real Madrid respectively.

Trying to shrug off that controversy, and instead seeking out the support of those who had his best interests at heart, Sergio made his own adjustments. For example, he changed his eating habits in order to keep his weight at the ideal level for his football. Although remaining in Majadahonda and close to *Atleti's* training ground, he moved to another, smaller apartment which afforded him more intimacy. He also organised his schedules better and looked to get sufficient rest. He knew that he was facing up to a vital challenge: he had to demonstrate what he was capable of, and that he could continue to improve. It was all about – as he had heard his closest confidants say – bringing out the player that lay within him.

"You will have to decide," Emilio Gutiérrez would say to him, "whether you want to settle for being Sergio Agüero, a good footballer who can make his living from the sport, or Kun Agüero, of whom great things are expected and who can go far in football. If you want to be Sergio Agüero, that's fine. But you have talent. And if you take care of yourself and act in a professional manner, you can reach the highest level and stay there."

Sergio trusted his instincts. One such hunch was telling him

that his participation with the Argentinian national team in the Under-20 World Cup, which was to start at the end of June 2007 in Canada, would be a good opportunity to get his football back on track.

Atleti's senior management and his agents were doubtful over whether he should even take part in the tournament. They feared him picking up a possible injury and argued, not unreasonably, that Kun should take a holiday that would allow him to rest up, so that he would be in the best possible shape for the following season.

"The doubts that had arisen were understandable," says Maxi Lo Russo, who was with him at the time in Madrid. "The thing is, he needed to rest up and put in a good pre-season in preparation for everything that was coming up. Sergio asked us what we thought. But he was already showing a determination and resolve to go to Canada," he affirms.

"I wanted to go, come what may," says Sergio. "I told them that I had made my decision, even though many people were arguing that if the team lost or didn't perform well, then much of the criticism was likely to be levelled at me. That didn't bother me. I could put up with that. I wanted to take the chance regardless. And that's what I did."

Kun's conviction meant that those closest to him supported his decision. "Keep calm, we're going to bring that cup home," he said to Maxi Lo Russo, who would travel with him to Canada.

Minutes after winning the tournament, Kun would not pass up on the opportunity to remind him of those words. Indeed, Sergio was overwhelmingly confident and assured in the lead-up to the tournament. This was something that Hugo Tocalli picked up on when he got word, via the kitman Patricio

Auzmendia, that Kun was keen to be involved. And when he called him in Madrid, he received a quick and positive response to his decision to call him up.

"I called him before submitting the list," says Tocalli, "and right away he said yes, that I could count on him. He had great belief. He was convinced that we'd be champions."

Double champion

Sergio, who celebrated his 19th birthday in Madrid, returned to Argentina on Monday, June 18th, 2007, a day after the conclusion to the La Liga season. He immediately reported for duty to Tocalli, who had put together a competitive squad.

The coach had all of the players that he had envisaged with him, with the exception of Lionel Messi – who was playing in the Copa America with the senior squad at the same time – and Gonzalo Higuaín, who ended up not joining the squad. The team featured, among others, Lautaro Acosta from Lanús – Kun's old rival in youth tournaments – Mauro Zárate from Vélez Sarsfield, Ángel Di María from Rosario Central, Claudio Yacob, Matías Sánchez and Maximiliano Moraléz from Racing Club, Éver Banega from Boca Juniors, Federico Fazio from Ferro Carril Oeste, goalkeeper Sergio Romero who already played his football in Holland, Emiliano Insúa from Liverpool and Pablo Piatti from Estudiantes de La Plata. After the tournament, many of those players would end up at clubs in Portugal, Spain, England and Italy.

Hugo Tocalli was surprised when he saw Kun at the national team's training complex in Ezeiza. He had known him since he

The unbelievable moment when we clinched the title in May 2012. After scoring the winning goal against QPR, I pulled my shirt off and swung it around my head until I was jumped on by my team-mates after a historic victory

Captain Vincent Kompany lifts the Barclays Premier League trophy above his head at a jubilant Etihad Stadium

(Courtesy of Manchester City FC)

My dad Leo and my son Benjamín enjoy the euphoria of an English championship trophy win on the pitch with me

My celebration after a headed goal against Chelsea in the semi-final helped City to reach the 2013 FA Cup final

Manuel Pellegrini took over as City manager in 2013

nother derby strike – this time in a 4-1 win against Manchester United in September 2013

I became a Premier League champion for the second time when City won the title in 2013/14

Holding my baby son Benjamín when he was only 21 days old

Benjamín with a ball at his feet and an Independiente kit on – just like his dad

Benjamín shows me how he will sign his autographs when he grows up!

As well as showing promise with a football, Benjamín also looks at home with a golf club in his hands

The whole Agüero-Del Castillo family

With my sisters Daiana, Mayra, Gaby and Jessica

With mum Adriana, dad Leo and Benjamín

With my brothers Mauricio and Gastón, who play in the youth teams at Independiente

Messi and me – Leo and I are very close and here we are with the Argentina strip I bought for his little boy Thiago
(Picture (left) courtesy of UNICEF/Ibáñez)

With tennis star Rafa Nadal

With my City and Argentina team-mate Pablo Zabaleta dressed up as Father Christmas
(Courtesy of Manchester City FC)

At an advertising campaign for PUMA
(courtesy of PUMA/ Manuel Schlueter)

was small, from when he had trained with Miguel Angel Tojo, and he could recall when he had been used to put the senior national team through their paces in training. But since he had moved to Spain, he had not seen him in person.

"I realised how much he had changed. How much he had grown. He was no longer the kid that I saw at the training ground who barely spoke. By then he had developed his own opinions, and considered ones, about football and life in general. I asked him if there was anything that he needed to change and he replied that sometimes he would go missing in a match, that he had to learn to keep up better with the tempo of a match for the full 90 minutes. I had known a boy and, there I was, starting to see a man," he states.

After the team had been together for a few days, and before they set off to Canada, he presented him with the iconic number 10 shirt.

"I realised that he was a player who could lead the team. That's why we gave it to him. He deserved it, not just because of how much he had grown as a player and as a person, but also because he hadn't deliberated over what he stood to win or lose by going to Canada with the squad. He had said yes straight away, that it was his priority. And he didn't disappoint."

Sergio was eager to get going and self-assured, and now he was backed up by the confidence bestowed upon him by his coach and the respect of his team-mates. It would also be the first time that he was not among the youngest players in the squad.

On the contrary, almost all of those who joined him in the group for that tournament were of his age. It was in these spirits that he approached the start of a competition where he would

be the centre of attention for the majority of the international journalists, who singled him out in advance, alongside the Brazilian Alexandre Pato and Barcelona's Mexican star Giovanni Dos Santos, as being a potential contender for player of the tournament.

Argentina were drawn to play in Group E with North Korea, Panama and the Czech Republic. They started against the Czechs on June 30th, 2007, in a match which ended goalless. The team's performance caused a certain amount of concern, although the doubts faded away three days later when they beat Panama 6-0 with two goals by Maxi Morales, one by Zárate, one by Di María and two by Kun, who returned to scoring ways after four months without a goal.

The team advanced to the round of 16 with a 1-0 win over North Korea, thanks to a goal from a free-kick by Kun.

"We hadn't played well in that match," says Tocalli, "so once it was over we had a meeting where I spoke quite firmly with the boys. I remember then that Sergio's attitude reflected his new maturity. He stood there and said 'Hugo, we're going to have a meeting among ourselves to discuss what happened'. He demonstrated real character, and his capacity for leadership. When he spoke, his team-mates listened. He was a positive leader. He got on well with everyone, and he also defended his team-mates. He was a very important player for us, for what he did on and off the pitch."

Tocalli's earbashing had the required effect, and Argentina played superbly against Poland in the round of 16, winning 3-1 with two great goals by Kun, who put in a magnificent individual display.

The FIFA website spoke of 'Agüero's great show' and eulo-

gised about his performance against the Poles. 'He needed less than 40 seconds to put his team ahead at the start of the second half. And only a chosen few can take a goal like the one he scored: a flick over the defender, a majestic spin, and an angled shot in to the back of the net. They do not come any better than that. He also scored the third after a skilful dummy that left the opposing goalkeeper on the seat of his pants, making the rest a formality.'

Christian Leblebidjian, covering the tournament for *La Nación*, described it in the following way: "The second half had barely got underway when he scored another one for his personal compilation: in the area, he flicked the ball over defender Adrian Marek with his right foot and, before it dropped, hit an angled shot with his left, across Bialkowsky and into the far post. The goalkeeper was to be on the wrong end of his cheek once more, when a dummy straight from the *potreros* of Buenos Aires left him sprawling on the floor, before Agüero tapped in to conclude a 3-1 win for the national team."

Fernando Gourovitch, writing in *Clarín*, chose words which were at explicit and foreboding.

'Agüero is shining bright, and the Under-20s are catching fire. If the 2005 team was Messi-dependent, then the 2007 team is Kun-dependent. And that is not a forced comparison. Agüero seems determined to repeat all of Messi's achievements from two years ago. Back then 'La Pulga' was Argentina's most destructive player, the top goalscorer and the tournament's best player. And Agüero is doing everything within his powers to emulate him on all three accounts.'

The quarter-final tie against Mexico was played on Sunday July 15th. On that same day, the senior national team had gone

down 3-0 to Brazil in the final of the Copa America in Venezuela. The Under-20 boys had the chance to bring some cheer to soften the blow of that painful defeat. And they did just that.

In a tough match, and thanks to a goal by Maximiliano Moralez, they beat Giovanni Dos Santos' team and won through to the semi-finals. Once there, they would have to take on a strong Chile team that had firstly knocked Portugal out and then eliminated Nigeria.

In a hard-fought, at times violent, encounter Argentina's *pibes* showed their superiority and clearly defeated their Andean neighbours by three goals to nil, with Di María, Yacob and Maxi Moralez all scoring. They would play the deciding match against surprise finalists Czech Republic, who had been Argentina's first opponents way back at the start of the tournament. The Czechs had won through to the final on penalties against a Spain side – containing Gerard Piqué, Mario Suárez, Diego Capel and Juan Manuel Mata – that had previously eliminated Brazil.

The sense of anticipation within the squad at the prospect of winning Argentina's sixth Under-20 World Cup was enormous. After that uncertain start, the team had played consistently in a style that made them everyone's favourites for the final.

The dependable Sergio Romero in goal, Federico Fazio's strength in defence, the subtlety and explosiveness that Ángel Di María and Maxi Moralez provided, and finally Kun's talent and leadership, all gave the team and its supporters reason to dream of glory.

"We had reached excellent performance levels, by playing to the strengths of each player," says Hugo Tocalli. "But what stood out with Sergio is that he could play as an out-and-out

striker, or could also drop off a few yards. Out to both flanks. Because he's a number nine who is very good on the ball. And he brought a lot to us on both sides, playing with Di María or with Zárate. But what stuck out even more was how his personality had grown. He was no longer the boy who only attempted the spectacular.

"The Agüero at that World Cup was an intelligent player, one who looked for space to receive the ball, who went looking for the pass. Beforehand, you would have to give him the ball to his feet and leave him to attempt the outrageous. The best example came in the final against the Czech Republic, where he shows Banega where he wants the ball, then latches on to it and finishes with remarkable ease."

*Sunday, July 22nd, 2007. **The National Stadium in Toronto. The Under-20 World Cup Final in Canada. Argentina vs Czech Republic. 16 minutes into the second half.***

On this day, Kun Agüero felt that he had to prove to himself and others that his game was influential enough to help carry Argentina to the top of the world at this level. He had had an excellent campaign, and there was one match left to crown it off. However, after a goalless first half, Martin Fenin beat the Argentinian goalkeeper to open the scoring for the Czechs. But Kun would not let the dream of glory fade away. The stakes had been raised, and he was prepared to go all in. Barely two minutes later, having shown Éver Banega where he wanted the ball and after an impeccable pass from the latter, he received possession four metres outside the penalty area. He let the ball run across his body and advanced decisively down the inside-right channel towards Radek Peter's

goal. After seven large strides, and without touching the ball, he entered the area, lifted his head, waited for the goalkeeper to come out and then stroked the ball into the back of the net with his right foot. With that quick equaliser, victory seemed within touching distance once more. His intense celebrations with the number 10 on his back were the prelude to an even bigger party later on when, with five minutes to go, Mauro Zárate scored the winning goal. In doing so, Argentina won their sixth title at this level and Kun – the pibe from Los Eucaliptus – became only the third player in history to win two world youth titles, and the first Argentine to win two consecutively. He was 19 years old and, on that day, he took home every available honour.

The final whistle, blown by Spanish referee Undiano Mallenco, was the cue for total delirium. Kun – armband on his left arm in the absence of regular captain Matías Cahais through suspension – was left face down on the turf with his head in his hands, overcome with emotion, unable to contain his tears. Neither could his team-mates, who clung on to each other in a celebratory huddle.

Up in the stands, the Canadian fans paid tribute to a group of youngsters that had given their absolute all for the triumph. Mixed among them were a handful of Argentines, the only relatives and loved ones of the players who had been there since the start of the tournament in Canada: Leonel Del Castillo, Kun's sister Jessica, his godfather Darío Fernández and Maxi Lo Russo delighted in witnessing Argentina's triumph and Sergio's brilliance. Just like millions of other Argentinians, who saw in that team a continuation of their nation's finest footballing traditions.

The cup was raised aloft by Sergio Agüero, the embodiment of a top class footballer from the *potreros*, the winner of the Golden Boot for finishing as top scorer with six goals, and of the Golden Ball as the player of the tournament.

Benjamín

The image of Kun, his hands full with all of his trophies, was seen all around the world. There was an air of serene joy and satisfaction about him as he posed for photographers while proudly sporting his captain's armband, the gold medal hanging around his neck and carrying the Golden Ball, the Golden Boot and the Under-20 World Cup trophy itself.

Thirteen years had gone by since he had lifted his first cup while playing for Loma Alegre in Quilmes, alongside a handful of boys who all dreamed of one day winning silverware at the very top level. And there was Kun, chosen by the 167 accredited journalists present as being the best of the 504 players from around the world who had competed in the Under-20 World Cup, and thus picking up the mantle from his friend Lionel

Messi in Holland 2005. And just like the squad from that year, the 2007 vintage celebrated to the full. Firstly out on the pitch, then back in the changing room, and together with a management team led by Hugo Tocalli, alongside assistant Jorge Theiler, doctor Daniel Martínez, Professor Jorge Kiriluk and physio Raúl Lamas.

But Kun had to quickly leave the celebrations behind. He had resigned himself to missing out on the triumphant homecoming back in Argentina with the squad, instead flying quickly to Madrid to play for *Atleti* on Sunday, July 28th, 2007. The match, a 1-0 victory over Gloria Bistrita of Romania, saw the team qualify for the second preliminary round of the UEFA Cup.

The only goal of the game was scored by Diego Forlán, who had recently arrived at Atletico from Villarreal and who had previously played for Manchester United. Kun partnered him in attack for the first time on that evening, the first outing for a duo who would offer *Los Colchoneros* an enviable goal threat.

On Thursday, August 16th, the squad took on Vojvodina from Serbia, in a match that marked Atletico's return to full European competition after a seven-year absence. Their comeback could not have gone any better. The Vicente Calderón stadium, full to the brim with the partisan support of 50,000 fans, witnessed an eye-catching 3-0 win in which Kun, the evening's stand-out performer, put on a show that included a wonderful move to set up Maxi Rodríguez for the first goal, in addition to one of his own – the third – with a diving header. It also included all the feints, backheels and dribbles to give the crowd no other choice but to offer up a rousing ovation when he was replaced after 30 minutes of the second half.

Soaking up the gratitude of his public while walking back towards the dugout, he felt that his decision to trust his gut feeling by competing at the Under-20 World Cup, and by following his instincts out on the pitch, had seen him mature. And that the renaissance of his football that he detected was linked to his decision, while out on the field of play, to remain true to the sense that he had always had for the game. He had rediscovered himself. And he now knew that he was back.

These impressions would begin to be confirmed at the start of the 2007/08 season, in an increasingly competitive Spanish domestic league.

Barcelona had brought in Frenchman Thierry Henry from Arsenal in England, another star to add to their existing constellation headed up by Lionel Messi, Ronaldinho, Samuel Eto'o, Xavi Hernández and Andrés Iniesta. Real Madrid, managed by the German Bernd Schuster, had signed the Dutchman Wesley Sneijder and the Portuguese Pepe. Atletico Madrid had incorporated Diego Forlán to replace Fernando Torres, who had emigrated to the Premier League in search of new horizons and silverware, where he would join Rafa Benítez's Liverpool. Forlán's arrival had the club dreaming about how far that team – featuring Kun's inspiration, alongside new captain Maxi Rodríguez, Simao Sabrosa and José Antonio 'La Perla' Reyes – could go.

Yet *Atleti* did not start the season as they had hoped, with their first fixture again leaving them frustrated by their old rivals. Despite leading 1-0 at the Bernabéu thanks to Kun's header in the first minute, Real Madrid turned the match around with goals by Raúl and Sneijder to ultimately claim a 2-1 victory. Kun again had the chance to draw his team level in the last

minute with another attempted lob which did not come off, this time Iker Casillas keeping it out.

Defeat to Madrid was followed by successive 1-1 draws at home to Mallorca and away at Murcia, where Kun was once more on target. Kun's fine form was underlined by his third call-up for the Argentinian national team. The second occasion had come in February in Paris, where he had played 10 minutes in the 1-0 win over France, secured thanks to a Javier Saviola goal.

That third opportunity then came on September 11th, 2007, against Australia in Melbourne, just two years after his memorable goal against Racing Club. The game, played during a FIFA international break between the Mallorca and Murcia fixtures, would demand a 35,000 kilometre round-trip from Kun. Even though he only played one minute, entering the fray in place of Messi in the 90th minute, the commitment he had shown would be rewarded with further call-ups for the official qualifiers for World Cup 2010.

Atletico Madrid's run without a win was ended on September 23rd, 2007 with a 4-0 win over Racing Santander at the Vicente Calderón, a match in which Kun won the hearts of all in attendance. And, just as with the supporters of *El Rojo de Avellaneda*, he was elevated to the status of an indisputable idol.

His outstanding performance – in which he scored a goal, played a part in two others and generally made the difference for his team – led to the new war cry of 'Kun, Kun, Kun...' sounding out around the Vicente Calderón. The crowd would have the chance to reprise that chant in the following two fixtures, as he scored twice more in the wins over Athletic Bilbao and Osasuna. And if, shortly after arriving in Spain, his

number 10 jersey had joined Fernando Torres' as one of the biggest sellers, from this moment on the official club store was inundated with requests for shirts with 'Kun Agüero' printed on the back. Sixty per cent of shirts sold were Sergio's, a figure that rose to 80 per cent among those sold in children's sizes.

A study carried out by *Atleti* in May 2007 to gauge the public perceptions of Sergio, shortly before his 19th birthday, revealed some surprising results: he had not yet spent a year playing in La Liga, and already 56 per cent of the Spanish population knew who he was. It was an extremely significant figure, when compared with the 92 per cent of people who knew who Iker Casillas or Raúl were, players who had already been playing at the highest level in the country for 11 years.

The same phenomenon could be seen with respect to the volume of interview requests he was receiving from both local and international media. Sergio was more in-demand than anyone. In fact, back at the start of 2007, the prestigious American magazine *Sports Illustrated* had produced a lengthy report on him, and even in China he was on the front cover of *Soccer Weekly* magazine.

In March 2008, it would be the turn of the BBC in London to focus on Kun with an extended report. Enquiries from the world's press were piling up in Emilio Gutiérrez's office, and it took a great effort to reply to them all.

"Requests and enquiries about interviews came in on a daily basis, from all four corners of the world," says Emilio. "And the volume increased further still after his return from the World Cup in Canada, when he rediscovered the spark and fresh-ness that are so much a part of his play. From the moment he decided to go, the kid went through a radical change. His

ability to lose a marker and his speed were remarkable. His confidence was back, he was in a great frame of mind. He was saying 'if I could do that at a World Cup, what's stopping me from doing it for *Atleti*?'"

In some of these features, a reflective and thankful Kun looked back at his early days and recognised that, were it not for football, his life could have gone down a very different route. He recalled how some kids from his neighbourhood, affected by their troubled surroundings, ended up behind bars or, worse still, shot by the police.

The memories of those days, and of his parents' struggles to make everyday life more manageable, came to the fore in an interview that showed a side to Sergio that the public rarely gets to see of its celebrities.

It took place in the early hours of the morning on October 1st, 2007 at *Punta Radio*, where Kun Agüero could be heard – and indeed seen, as the interview was also being filmed – in very genuine, frank form. A guest on the *El Mirador* show, hosted by journalist Josep Pedrerol, for an hour he analysed his performances in La Liga and *Atleti's* prospects, gave his opinions on his friend Lionel Messi and praised his former team-mate Fernando Torres.

Little by little, the questions led back towards his childhood, his life in Argentina and his bond with his parents. Sergio told of the sacrifices made by his family, and how his father had gone everywhere with him since he was small. At that moment, and without Sergio receiving prior warning, the producers handed the airwaves over to Leonel Del Castillo, speaking on the telephone from Argentina.

Kun's face was a picture of surprise on hearing his father's

voice, as he started to describe the happiness that the family felt for all that was happening to their son. And as he explained how they looked forward to match days so that they could listen to developments over the internet or watch the games on television, an increasingly emotional Sergio tried unsuccessfully to hold back the tears that had started to fill his eyes. And when he realised that he could not contain them, he held his face in both hands and remained that way for some minutes.

He was able to pull himself together for a moment and, timidly, managed to say "my dad was always with me… that's why…", before then hiding his face behind his hands once more, unable to carry on speaking.

"For 15 minutes, he couldn't say a word," remembers Emilio Gutiérrez, who was always alongside him at interviews and who was opposite him, just beside the video cameras, on that night. "His emotion was borne out of a deep sense of gratitude because, minutes before, he had publicly expressed how thankful he was for all that his father had done for him."

Sergio recalls that, on the way to the interview, he had mentioned to Emilio that he was missing Buenos Aires and that he wanted to visit his family for a few days.

"At that time, I was living on my own in Madrid," says Sergio. "And I was missing home. And then, in the interview, they put me on the phone with my old man. I couldn't stop crying. And when I left with Emilio, we carried on crying together."

On leaving the interview, they ended up having a chat at a bar before returning home.

"I was an idiot… crying like that," Kun said to him. Emilio – who was also emotional, inevitably associating what had happened with his own father, who he had lost when he was

young – replied: "On the contrary, Kun. Don't be ashamed, it was spontaneous. Don't feel bad. You don't know how wonderful it is that people can see that a famous star like you is just like them. Celebrities are often seen as being superficial, but you have shown that you have a set of values, that your family is important to you. You showed the real you. Just a person, flesh and bone, with feelings, to whom emotions matter much more than material matters. This is what makes you great, Kun."

Golden Boy

The last quarter of 2007 was particularly special for Kun. On Saturday, October 13th, he was able to make his first appearance in an official match for the Argentinian national team. It came against Chile at the Monumental stadium in Núñez, in the first match of the qualification tournament for the World Cup in South Africa.

The match ended 2-0 in favour of Alfio Basile's team, thanks to two Juan Román Riquelme free-kicks. Kun, who came on after 28 minutes of the second half, again in place of Carlos Tévez, received an ovation from the crowd and was able to link up on various occasions with his friend Lionel Messi. And towards the end of that month, on Thursday, October 25th, in Moscow, on Atletico's return to the UEFA Cup, he put in an outstanding display in the 3-3 draw with Lokomotiv. He scored the first goal, set up Diego Forlán for the second and scored the equaliser a few minutes from the end.

The headline in the *El Mundo Deportivo* newspaper the following day – 'Agüero was an artist in Moscow' – was not coinci-

dental. Indeed, after the match, Lokomotiv's coach Anatolyi Byshovets had claimed that "watching Agüero is like visiting the Prado Museum". The comparison led the *Marca* newspaper to publish a special feature based around an interview with Kun, who posed for the front cover with a ball at his feet in that very same museum.

On Saturday, November 17th, 2007, he made his first start for Argentina's senior national team, in a 3-0 win over Bolivia at the Monumental stadium. He scored the first goal after a Messi cross was knocked down into the six-yard box by Demichelis – who years later would be his team-mate at Manchester City – for Kun to head it in to an empty net.

The fact that Kun had scored with his head may well have come as a surprise to many. His 5' 8" frame did not suggest to fans that he would have a particular knack for scoring in this way. However, four of the seven goals that he had scored in La Liga that season had been from headers. One possible explanation for this could be found in the results of the physical tests that *Atleti* had carried out on their squad around the time. Sergio came top in speed and jump tests. With respect to the former, he managed to jump 59 centimetres from a standing start. And for the latter, he could run 15 metres in just over two seconds. His physical development went hand in hand with his growth as a footballer, leading in turn to the continued recognition that he was receiving for his performances.

In December 2007, he received the 'Golden Boy' prize, awarded by the Italian newspaper *Tuttosport* to the best footballer under the age of 21 playing in the European leagues. Kun was chosen after the voting was carried out among journalists from 30 media outlets around the world. In doing so, he became the

fifth winner of a title previously held by Lionel Messi, Cesc Fabregas, Wayne Rooney and Rafael Van der Vaart.

Kun's rousing finale to the year continued. On Tuesday, December 17th, as part of the same FIFA World Player ceremony in which the Brazilian Kaká was crowned as the best player in the world, with Lionel Messi and Cristiano Ronaldo second and third respectively, Sergio received the distinction as the world's best player under the age of 20.

Kun travelled to Switzerland with Emilio Gutiérrez, who had hired suitable dinner jackets to match the tone of a ceremony which took place at the Zurich Opera. It was the second time that Sergio had worn one. The first time had been in April, when he was involved in handing out the Laureus International Sports Awards alongside Maxi Rodríguez. On that occasion, it was Atletico Madrid's president, Enrique Cerezo, who had got hold of a dinner jacket for him.

"We were managing fine until it came to the sleeves, which we were able to sort out in the end. But we had no idea how to put on the bow tie. Maxi and I were killing ourselves laughing…" remembers Kun.

With that experience under his belt, Sergio's second time wearing a dinner jacket went well enough, although not without its difficulties. However, it was nothing in comparison to what he went through with Emilio on their return to Madrid.

FIFA had chartered a small private airplane so that he could get back in time for his next match. The only two passengers, Kun and Emilio, travelled in comfortable leather chairs backing on to the pilots' seats. The pilots explained how long it would take them to get to Spain, and kindly left them some quality refreshments for the journey. An hour into the journey, and as

they chatted away about animal documentaries, it occurred to Emilio to look out of the window. And he was not exactly enamoured by the sight that greeted him.

"It looked like we were flying over Afghanistan… there were flashes, and you couldn't tell what they were, nor where they were coming from. One of the pilots reassured us that it would only be 50 minutes until we landed, and that all was well. But five minutes later, I looked out again and I saw that we were in the middle of a storm over the Pyrenees. All those niceties from the pilots stopped right there. They would not so much as turn around. Kun was as worried as I was. We were looking out of the window and all you could see was snow, snow and more snow. It was a tremendous storm. We imagined ourselves crashing into a mountain.

"To take the tension out of the situation a bit, I said: 'Do you know what annoys me most about all this? That if anything happens, there'll be about 150 wreaths laid for you… and nobody's going to remember about me… there'll be one flower from my wife and kids. And nothing else.' At the very least I got a smile out of him, because we were having a pretty bad time of it. Those 50 minutes ended up being one hour and 20. It was horrific, the worst flight of our lives. We had only just seen the airport lights when we touched down. And when we stepped off the plane, Kun didn't say anything. He was speechless. But his shirt, dripping with sweat, said it all," remembers Emilio with a smile.

After suffering only two defeats in the final two months, Atletico Madrid entered the winter break at the end of 2007 in an encouraging fifth place in the La Liga table. They had 31 points, one behind Villarreal, two behind Español, three behind

Barcelona and 10 off the leaders Real Madrid, who already had 41 points. *Los Colchoneros*, with Kun as their top performer, had put together a record of nine wins, four draws and four defeats in 17 matches.

It was no surprise, then, that Atletico Madrid's senior management announced at the end of the year that Agüero's buy-out clause had been increased from 36 to 55 million euros. The aim was to shield Kun who, once again, was attracting covetous glances from the world's biggest clubs.

As well as reuniting him with his family and friends, Kun's festive season spent in Buenos Aires saw him further strengthen a bond that would result in him becoming a proud father in little over a year. What started as a chance meeting with Gianinna Maradona on the *'La Noche del Diez'* programme in 2005, had developed over the course of time and they had grown increasingly close. A little over two years had gone by since they had first met, and their occasional get-togethers and online chats had laid the foundations for a relationship that would become formal in December of 2007.

During January and February, *Los Colchoneros* claimed three wins, a draw and four defeats – the most painful coming against Real Madrid by two goals to one.

At the Vicente Calderón on March 1st, against a Barcelona side featuring Ronaldinho, Eto'o, Henry, Xavi and Messi – who came on in the second half – they had the opportunity to take revenge for the 3-0 reverse suffered during the first half of the season. It was also a chance to consolidate their chances of Champions League qualification, as at this stage Atletico held fourth spot in the table on 41 points, but with Sevilla and Español hot on their heels with 39.

*Saturday, March 1st, 2008. **Madrid. The Vicente Calderón stadium. Atletico Madrid vs. Barcelona. 25 minutes into the second half.***

On this evening, a dazzling Kun Agüero started to look at home among the heavyweights of world football. Dropping out to the left-hand side of the attack, he robbed Puyol of the ball in the final third and set off towards the goal defended by Valdés. With a body swerve he left Gabriel Milito on the floor, avoided his attempt to be bring him down, and from just outside the penalty area, while surrounded by five Barcelona players, he placed an inch-perfect, low, right-footed shot that crept inside Valdés' left-hand post, leaving the goalkeeper with no chance. As with his greatest and most decisive goals, he celebrated – along with a delirious crowd that shook the Vicente Calderón stadium to the rafters – by furiously swinging his shirt around his head. He had covered 35 metres in 10 seconds to score his team's fourth goal, against a Barcelona side featuring Xavi, Iniesta, Henry and Eto'o, and in doing so overshadowed Ronaldinho – who himself scored a goal from an overhead kick on that same evening – as well as impressing his friend Lionel Messi. Kun had scored the first, assisted Maxi Rodríguez for the second, won the penalty for the third and crowned his afternoon with that unforgettable fourth goal. An outstanding, coming-of-age performance to secure a historic 4-2 win. He was 19 years old, and on that day had the football world bowing down at his feet.

After the match against Barcelona, and during March and April 2008, *Atleti* played eight matches – resulting in three wins, three losses and two draws – which saw them retain their fourth position in La Liga. In various games, Kun came in for particu-

larly rough treatment from opposition players.

In the win over Seville at the Sánchez Pizjuán stadium on March 22nd, Kun was head-butted in the nose by Enzo Maresca, who received a straight red card from referee Delgado Ferreira. The picture of Sergio, his face covered with blood, was one of the day's defining images.

The last four games would be decisive in determining whether Atletico Madrid could secure their return to the Champions League after an 11-year absence, the target they had set themselves for the season. Three consecutive victories – 3-0 over Recreativo, 2-0 over Español and 1-0 over Deportivo – sealed their qualification. Their final league fixture, a 3-1 defeat at the hands of Valencia, was academic.

Real Madrid were again crowned champions with 85 points, followed by Villarreal with 77, Barcelona with 67 and *Atleti* with 64.

The fans celebrated wholeheartedly, and the fine achievement was mirrored in Kun's excellent season individually, his second since arriving in Madrid and in which he had scored a total of 27 goals: 19 in the league – emulating Fernando Torres' best tally in the 2003/04 season – in addition to six in the UEFA Cup and two in the Copa del Rey.

Recognition came not only from the fans, but also from the media. *Canal Plus* awarded him the Antonio Puerta Trophy, which goes to whoever is judged to be the season's most decisive player.

And the EFE agency declared him the league's best Latin American player after having tallied 242 points from 36 matches, his average of 6.54 placing him above Luis Fabiano (6.41) and his friend Lionel Messi (6.35).

Olympic champion

On both a sporting and personal level, the weeks following the climax to the 2007/08 season were among Sergio's most emotionally intense. After taking part in a friendly for the Argentinian national team against Catalonia, and as part of the preparations for the Olympic Games in Beijing, he then travelled with the senior squad to the USA to play against the locals and Mexico.

On June 2nd in San Diego, before the Mexico match, he celebrated his 20th birthday firstly with a rendition of 'Happy Birthday' from his team-mates in the middle of a training session, and later with his mother Adriana, godmother Liliana and partner Gianinna Maradona, who had arrived by way of a surprise. He was also able to celebrate during the match itself, two days later, when he was on target in a 4-1 win for Argentina. A 0-0 draw with the USA concluded the mini-tour, but not his football schedule.

While in Spain, *Atleti's* president Enrique Cerezo moved to deny – once more – a potential move to Chelsea, Kun played on June 15th in a 1-1 draw against Ecuador at the Monumental stadium in Núñez and on June 18th in the second half of a 0-0 draw against Brazil in Belo Horizonte, both qualifying matches for World Cup 2010 in South Africa.

Sergio planned to have some days of rest on the beaches of Cancún with Gianinna, before having to meet up with the national team squad that would travel to Beijing for the Olympics.

However, before travelling, news was confirmed that did not so much change their plans as alter their general outlook on life:

on June 26th, a quick pregnancy test revealed that they were expecting a baby.

"We were trying for it, and it happened," says Sergio. "I always wanted to be a young father so that when I was 40 the baby would be 20, and I'd be able to be there for him or her more. To be a father and a friend," he affirms. That same weekend, they informed their respective families of the news.

While Kun followed how the pregnancy was progressing day by day, the ball got rolling in Beijing. The majority of the squad were Under-23 players, complemented by three older reinforcements in Juan Román Riquelme, Nicolás Pareja and Javier Mascherano.

Also in the ranks were former team-mates of Sergio, such as Pablo Zabaleta, Lionel Messi, Oscar Ustari, Fernando Gago and Ezequiel Garay from Holland 2005, and Sergio Romero, Federico Fazio, Ever Banega, Lautaro Acosta and Ángel Di María from Canada 2007. The squad, managed by Sergio 'Checho' Batista, was completed by Luciano Monzón, José Sosa, Diego Buonanotte and Ezequiel Lavezzi.

It was during this tournament that Kun first wore the number 16 shirt on his back. It was the captain, Riquelme, who gave him the choice out of the remaining numbers available: 9, 16 or 17. Sergio did not think twice about choosing the 16, ruling out nine – which did not convince him – and 17, traditionally an unlucky number for Argentinians. That number 16 would bring him good luck, and Kun would enjoy some wonderful moments out on the pitch with it on his back, especially at Manchester City where his name would be so closely attached to it.

In the first round Argentina secured two tight, but well-deserved, wins against the Ivory Coast – 2-1, with goals by

Messi and Lautaro Acosta – and Australia – 1-0, with a goal by Lavezzi. Kun was not at his best during those first two matches but coach Sergio Batista, faced with enquiries from journalists, ruled out dropping him from the starting line-up by declaring that "he has to be kept out on the field of play, because technically at any moment he can settle a match for you."

Batista's words were not just a premonition but also demonstrated his absolute faith in such a special player, one who could alter the result in any passage of play. The 2-0 win over Serbia, featuring a much-changed team and goals by Lavezzi and Buonanotte, consolidated Argentina's place at the top of Group A and determined that their quarter-final opponents would be Holland.

The match was played in Shanghai on August 16th and Argentina, aided by a fine performance from Messi, won 2-1 with goals by Lionel himself and Di María. Once more Kun failed to find the target and, furthermore, missed four clear chances and was caught offside on seven occasions. The debate over whether Sergio should play or not dominated the sports pages as well as discussions on sports programmes on radio and television.

He acknowledged that he was not at his best, that he could offer more and that he was hoping for the opportunity to demonstrate that. And he also spoke out about his position on the field of play.

"I'm better playing further from goal," he stated at the time, "with more space to isolate players and take them on. I'm not saying that I'm uncomfortable, but I'm not used to playing as a nine. If I'm put in that position it's not easy for me, because I'm not a natural penalty box player."

And as the controversy over his starting place intensified, head coach Sergio Batista announced that he would indeed still be on the team sheet for the semi-finals. Argentina's opponents were none other than Brazil, who had been the scourge of the *Albiceleste* in recent tournaments: in the final of the Copa America in 2004, Adriano scored in stoppage time to draw the scores level at 2-2 in a match Brazil would ultimately win on penalties to take the title; in 2005, the *Seleção* thrashed the *Albiceleste* 4-1 in the final of the Confederations Cup; the final of the Copa America in 2007 saw another Argentina defeat, 3-0, with goals by Baptista, an Ayala own goal and Dani Alves.

For the national team, then, this was the opportunity to put an end to that bad run. Meanwhile, for Kun personally, it was the chance to show that great players always stand up when they are needed most. As this was all going on, Sergio continued to follow closely – although from afar – the developments with Gianinna's pregnancy and the plans for their future child. He was sent ultrasound images to his mobile phone or via the internet, and was kept up to date. He was already imagining the possible names that he might give to his future baby.

It was while in China that it occurred to Sergio, who then suggested, that if the baby was a boy he would like to call him Oliver or Benji, after the lead characters in the Spanish version of the Captain Tsubasa manga animation series that recounts the adventures of a group of childhood friends who play football and end up playing for the Japanese national team.

Kun thought about his future child non-stop, and he let the whole world know as much during the match against Brazil, played in Beijing on August 19th. With a great team performance and an exemplary showing by Kun – who claimed

two goals and won a penalty, scored by Riquelme – Argentina claimed a 3-0 win over the team managed by Dunga and featuring, among others, Ronaldinho, Alexandre Pato, Anderson, Marcelo and Diego.

For Argentinians, victory tasted particularly sweet, not just because they had eliminated Brazil, but because it represented a first win over their traditional rivals for three years and the first by such a wide margin in 44 years. On a personal note, for Sergio it meant being able to demonstrate his winning pedigree, to repay the trust placed in him by Baptista with his goals, and to be a part of one of the most joyful moments that Argentina had experienced in recent years. And he also had the opportunity to celebrate his goals just as he had dreamed: with his thumb in his mouth, announcing to the world that he would soon be a father.

'The Chest of God' is how Kun christened his first goal against Brazil, scored eight minutes into the second half by deflecting in a driven cross-shot from the left by Di María with that part of his body. The second goal came five minutes later as he touched in a cross from the right by defender Garay, this time with his foot.

"The celebration was for the baby which is on the way. I would have liked to have made the dedication before, but the opportunity came against none other than Brazil," was his reply when asked about the thumb that he had sucked like a dummy. And he added: "I broke the hoodoo. Things haven't been going well. They'd put a spell on me, or someone had taken away my mojo. But luckily I put a stop to it at the perfect moment, against an opponent that we all want to beat. I'm sure that the people back home will be very happy with this victory."

Argentina were to play the final against Nigeria, who arrived unbeaten after a draw in their first match against Holland (0-0) and then successive wins against Japan (2-1), the USA (2-1), the Ivory Coast (2-0) and Belgium (4-1). The 'Super Eagles', as they are known, had already won an Olympic gold in football at the Atlanta 1996 games, when they beat an Argentinian team managed by Daniel Alberto Passarella in a memorable encounter where the *Albiceleste* lost 3-2 after a failed offside trap in the last minute cost them the match. More recently, Argentina and Nigeria had met in the final of the 2005 Under-20 World Cup in Holland, when the Argentines won 2-1 with both goals by Messi, the second of them a penalty awarded for a foul on Kun. Messi, Agüero, Zabaleta, Gago and Garay were to find themselves face-to-face once more with nine members of the Africans' squad from that tournament.

It was August 22nd, 2008, the final of the Olympic Games in the National Stadium in Beijing. And things could not have gone any better for the Argentines. With a perfect finish from Di María, following a sensational pass by Messi, Argentina won by a goal to nil and in doing so claimed their second straight Olympic gold in football. Nobody wanted to miss out on so much as a second of the celebrations, both straight after the match and then following the medal ceremony.

Kun, his gold medal hanging from his neck and three international titles with Argentina under his belt, embraced Leo Messi. Oscar Ustari celebrated the triumph as exuberantly as anyone, despite having ruptured ligaments in his left knee in the match against Holland.

Javier Mascherano became the only footballer to have won two Olympic gold medals. They were joined by Juan Román

Riquelme, the team captain, and Ángel Di María, who had been a real revelation throughout the tournament and had chipped in with some vital goals.

Sergio Batista, meanwhile, was left with the satisfaction of having gambled on that group of players and backed them until the very end. The whole squad came together for a triumphant, collective celebration and then set off on a somewhat disorganised, but nevertheless intense, lap of honour which brought the sort of joy to their fellow countrymen that only football can give.

Twice around the world

The intensity with which they celebrated their title was then matched by the urgency with which each one of the players returned to their respective club sides. Kun was in as great a rush as anyone and on Sunday, August 24th, two days after the final, he was already making his way back to Madrid, to join an Atletico side whose defence had been strengthened by the arrivals of the Dutchman John Heitinga and the Czech Tomas Ujfalusi.

On Wednesday, August 27th, the team would be up against Schalke 04 in the second leg of their Champions League qualifier, having lost the first leg by a goal to nil. The fans welcomed Sergio back with open arms.

On that night, before the start of the match and from the hands of 'Kiko' (Francisco Narváez) and Juanma López, former *Atleti* players and Olympic champions at Barcelona 1992, Kun received one of the club's highest distinctions. They awarded him with a silver bar engraved with the club's three historic

crests, an honour reserved only for those who have helped and continue to help make the club great, and in recognition of his Olympic gold medal won in Beijing.

The ovation that rang down from the stands was repeated after 18 minutes of the match when, with his first clear sight on goal, Kun headed in to open the floodgates for what ultimately ended as a 4-0 win over the German team.

Following the start of the 2008/09 La Liga season in Spain on August 31st, and a 4-0 win over Málaga, Sergio returned to Buenos Aires where he had been called up by Alfio Basile to take part in two World Cup qualifiers with the national team. On September 6th at the Monumental stadium in Núñez, Argentina drew 1-1 with Paraguay thanks to a magnificent finish by Kun after an inch-perfect pass by Messi. The second match in Lima on September 9th, against a Peru side considered to be the continent's weakest, resulted in an identical 1-1 scoreline.

What is for certain is that Kun's demanding football schedule – at the time, he had more commitments than any other player – left him little time to lead what would be considered to be a normal lifestyle.

If, as a child, he used to travel from one side of Greater Buenos Aires to the other and into the capital city to play any number of matches for his different teams, at 20 years of age his routine was no less intense. But he was no longer carried between matches by cars and buses. Now he was taken by airplanes, and to play for *Atleti* or the national team.

Research by the Barcelona-based newspaper *El Mundo Deportivo* revealed that since the end of the 2007/08 season, on May 18th, and including just one La Liga fixture from the 2008/09 season, Kun had travelled more than 84,297 kilometres.

'Bearing in mind that a journey once around the world takes in just over 40,000 kilometres, this means that Agüero has already completed this distance twice over, plus 4,000 additional kilometres,' explained Chema Fuente in the September 12th, 2008 edition. The report also indicated that 'in the last 116 days, Kun has featured in no less than 18 games (16 with Argentina and two with Atletico Madrid). To do so, he has had to take 16 flights. If we add up the hours, Agüero has spent almost five days on a plane in the last three-and-a-half months.'

In another passage of the report, Fuente pointed out that Sergio had gone practically two years without a break. He detailed the following: the journey to Canada with the Under-20 squad and urgent return to Madrid for the Intertoto tie, both in 2007; the regular season that ended in May 2008; the friendlies for Argentina, the World Cup qualifiers and the journey to China – including a stop-off in Japan for a warm-up match – to compete in the Olympic Games. Such tumult, which neatly encapsulated his commitment to *Atleti* and the Argentinian national team, would not ease off over the coming months, but would actually intensify.

On September 13th, four days after the game in Lima against Peru, he was back in Madrid for *Atleti's* second fixture in La Liga, scoring the team's only goal in a 2-1 reverse at the hands of Valladolid. And three days later, he played in *Los Colchoneros'* comeback match in the group phase of the Champions League, a 3-0 win away to PSV Eindhoven. It was a dream debut for Kun in the competition, as he scored two goals and claimed the man of the match award.

Jorge Valdano, as eagle-eyed as ever, said to *El Mundo* that "Agüero has something of the Romario about him, an ability

to invent something in the most difficult positions. And what's more, there is a very noticeable raw quality to him, the sort that makes him fearless in the face of anything."

And there was no fear on show on October 1st, 2008, as he celebrated his 100th game for Atletico with a goal – accompanied by the customary dedication to his unborn baby – his 41st for *Los Colchoneros*, in the 2-1 win over Marseilles in the Champions League. But, of course, happiness is never complete.

Three days later *Atleti's* defensive failings were on full display once more in the 6-1 defeat to Barcelona, in which they conceded three goals from set-pieces in only eight minutes of play. The Catalans, who would go on to win the title that season, demonstrated their true prowess on that day with inspired performances by Messi, Xavi and Iniesta, against an off-form Atletico team.

The match, which had been built up by the press as a duel between the Argentines Lionel Messi and Sergio Agüero, ended with the former gaining the upper hand. Yet Kun would have his chance for revenge five months later and this time would come out on top, turning this fixture into a true South American clásico, fought out in Spain between two friends.

After that defeat, Kun's schedule of intercontinental flights continued, as he returned to Buenos Aires for two more rounds of World Cup qualification fixtures.

The national team's run without a win came to an end on October 11th, 2008, with a 2-1 win over Uruguay at the Monumental stadium in Núñez. Sure enough, the decisive goals came courtesy of messrs Messi and Agüero. But four days later, a 1-0 defeat against Marcelo Bielsa's Chile in Santiago sparked off a crisis that resulted in Alfio Basile's resignation and the arrival

of Diego Armando Maradona as the manager of the *Albiceleste*.

The year 2009 would see the national team get back on track for qualification for South Africa, which would be secured in October of that year after an extremely tough and exasperating climax, in which they beat Peru 2-1 in Buenos Aires thanks to a last-gasp Martin Palermo strike and won 1-0 in Montevideo against Uruguay with a goal by Mario Bolatti.

Towards the end of 2008, *Atleti* progressed to the round of 16 in the Champions League, having finished second in their group behind Rafa Benítez's Liverpool. Meanwhile, in La Liga they held a well-deserved third position with 30 points, the product of nine wins, three draws and four defeats. This left *Los Colchoneros* 11 points off the top spot, held by Pep Guardiola's Barcelona, but only one behind second-placed Seville.

Lurking expectantly behind Atletico were Valencia, with the same points tally but an inferior goal difference, then Real Madrid and Villarreal, a point away from the pair of them with 29.

By December 20th, and Sergio's last fixture with *Atleti* before the winter break, Sergio had scored 14 goals: nine in La Liga and five in the Champions League. Kun's superlative displays were once more generating strong rumours that Juventus, Inter, Manchester City and Chelsea were interested in signing him, prompting Atletico Madrid's senior management to once more raise his buy-out clause, from 55 to 60 million euros.

He took advantage of those months, spent more or less uninterrupted in the city of Madrid, to prepare the apartment in Majadahonda into one which the family would move shortly before the birth of the baby. Examinations had revealed that they were expecting a boy, so the baby's room, which they now

knew would be reserved for Benjamín, was predominantly decorated in light blue. The decision over his name had effectively been made. They already said Benja or Benji when referring to the baby, as did the future grandparents when they enquired as to how the pregnancy was going.

Although there was speculation in the media – which would continue up until the very last moment – over whether they would call him Leonel Diego or Diego Leonel, they never had a moment's doubt over choosing a name that would be his and his only, and which would not increase the burden of him carrying those illustrious surnames.

However, one thing that they could not avoid after the birth was that three football clubs – Independiente, Boca Juniors and Atletico Madrid – all claimed to have been the first to have made the baby a member of their organisations.

The birth

Atleti's good form severely suffered during the first part of 2009. Aside from having been knocked out of the Copa del Rey by Barcelona in January, by the start of February they had not even won a match. They had slipped, unchecked, from fourth place at the end of the year to seventh.

The last defeat – 2-1 at home to Valladolid at the Vicente Calderón – was one loss too many for Javier Aguirre who, after two seasons in charge, was relieved of his duties and replaced by a club legend, former goalkeeper Abel Resino.

The new coach was able to stop the rot in his first match with a 3-0 win against Recreativo, a match in which Sergio

returned to scoring ways after five fixtures without a goal. The next match, against Getafe on February 15th at the Vicente Calderón, ended in a 1-1 draw.

After the match, at a family dinner at the apartment in Majadahonda, photos were taken which would be the last before the baby's birth. At that time, anxiety was growing. Doctors had indicated a probable birth date of between February 20th and 28th. But by the end of January, Gianinna was already four centimetres dilated. In light of this development, Adriana predicted that the baby would be born on February 13th, Gianinna said the 16th of the month, and Sergio the 21st. On the night of Monday 16th and early hours of Tuesday, February 17th, they believed that the birth was imminent.

"That night, we couldn't sleep because the baby was moving so much. So in the morning we went to the hospital," recalls Sergio. Accompanied by both of their mothers, they headed off to the Montepríncipe university hospital in Madrid for a precautionary check-up. Sergio believed that this would be the day but, after the examinations, he was disappointed to find out that nothing had changed and that he would have to show a little more patience.

The wait went on until Thursday, February 19th, when it was decided that they would induce the birth. And at 9:30 in the morning, with Leo at the wheel, the full family headed off to the hospital by car. During the 15-minute drive from the Majadahonda apartment to the Montepríncipe hospital, the adults tried their best to reassure the inevitably anxious young couple.

"I bet we've forgotten something, and we have to go back for it," they said. The jokes made Sergio laugh, out of a mixture of anticipation and nerves. It was in these joyful spirits that they

arrived at the hospital, where Room 219 had been prepared for them.

While their companions settled into the waiting room, the obstetrician explained to Sergio and Gianinna how things would proceed from then on, and that it was just a matter of waiting for the right moment. Right then, those measured words from the specialist were exactly what was needed. And far from a solemn atmosphere, the overriding sense was that this was an opportunity to cherish the moment. This prevailing enthusiasm was especially evident in the adjoining room, where those present awaited developments in undisguised joy while sipping on *mate* and eating pastries, in typical Argentinian style.

Fortunately they had been able to settle in to the hospital without being hassled by the press who, although fully aware of the pregnancy, did not know the exact date of the long-awaited birth. It was Adriana who warned that the journalists would work out what was happening at 11 o'clock in the morning, on noticing Sergio's absence from training with *Atleti*. Sure enough, at 11:30 the hospital entrance was swarming with cameramen, reporters and photographers to announce the imminent birth.

In the confusion, and although the birth had still not taken place, the media in Buenos Aires were already reporting it as a fait accompli. In the waiting room adjoining number 219, the mobile phones of all present were not enough to reassure family members back in Argentina that Benjamín was still yet to be born.

Daniel Guzmán, an artist and friend of Sergio's who had also arrived on hearing news of the imminent birth, suggested that to kill time they should have a bet on what the baby would weigh. Diego Maradona went for 7lb 11oz, Adriana just less

with 7lb 8oz, Claudia for 7lb and Leo for 6lb 2oz. When it came to Sergio's turn, without hesitation he said 7lb 14oz, showing a hitherto unknown gift for guessing, as would be revealed moments later when he won the bet.

Throughout all the hours waiting in the spacious room at the Montepríncipe hospital – eight in total, from their arrival at the hospital to Benjamín's birth – and on witnessing the conscientious, caring and personal attention they were receiving on behalf of the staff there, Adriana could not stop thinking about her pregnancy with Sergio.

Twenty years had gone by since those months that she had spent alongside Leo, and since the extreme situations that they had gone through that had put the life of the baby she had been carrying at risk. In a flash, she remembered about the floods that they suffered while living in the 'Cave of the Vipers' neighbourhood in La Matanza, and then being forced to evacuate and subsequently return to their meagre little home, which had been destroyed by water.

She relived her period of prescribed rest in that humble shared room at the Piñero hospital in the Flores neighbourhood of the city of Buenos Aires, when she was only 18 years old and when her only company came from her husband and their little girl Jessica, who never stopped visiting throughout her extended stay there.

She also relived that momentous June 2nd, 1988 day when, together with Leo, and after a three-hour journey on two buses and a train followed by that long, agonising 200-metre walk, she had arrived at the maternity ward at the Piñero.

Silently, she recalled with anguish and surprise the strength that she had shown in not following the doctor's suggestion

that forceps be used, and instead in accepting that the baby's collar bone be broken so that the birth could continue without any further risks. She became emotional when that first image popped into her head of a tough, bald baby boy who the obstetrician passed to her following her final push, and who they would go on to name Sergio Leonel.

She recalled the words of that doctor – whose name she never knew – who told her that the boy had been born *con un pan debajo del brazo* and that he would bring fortune to his parents. And that miraculous sensation, inspired by Sergio's birth, returned to her. But not just because of the clear disparity between that birth and the one that was about to take place. But because, even despite such pronounced material differences between one birth and the other, the essence of what she felt was the same: profound thankfulness. For the life that she had been given. For her past and her present. For her family. For her children. For Kun, his good luck and the gift that God had bestowed upon him. And for the happiness that she saw in her son when they finally informed him that the wait was over.

At 18:30 and after one last check-up, Sergio put on the standard green gown and mask in order to witness the birth. Dressed in this way, smiling, calm and in good humour, he posed for photos taken by his family and, at 18:50, he got ready to experience the most sublime moment of all.

Once inside, he positioned himself to the left at the head of the bed, where he attentively followed what the doctor was indicating, without noticing the tears running down his face when he saw the little one appear for the first time, barely able to half-open his eyes, but making his presence felt with a sonorous wail. Benjamín Agüero had been born after three simple pushes. And

weighing 8lb 1oz, not far off what Kun had predicted.

Sergio was moved by the experience of having been present at the moment of the birth; of having been able to see and touch that little creature who meant so much to him; and of having been able to take him in his arms to the neonatal ward for the first check-ups, noting with surprise the skill with which the doctors took the baby by his legs for the initial examination. At that moment, Sergio looked at his son and knew, just like 20 years ago, that this baby, his own, would also bring much fortune to the family.

Neptune

No more than 10 minutes had gone by since they had entered the delivery room. But in the waiting room, where the family remained, the atmosphere was tense and anxious until they were told that Benjamín had been born.

And so the prevailing silence was replaced by rejoicing, an overwhelming happiness that grew even more when the new mother and Benjamín were pushed out in their bed to see them, unleashing feelings of pure emotion that would flow through all of them for the hours, and days, to come. Accompanied for Sergio and Gianinna with that strange feeling experienced by first-time parents: a mixture of shock, euphoria and an attempt to understand how they can best care for and attend to that young life entering their lives – having firstly warned them, yes, but not having allowed them to gain any previous experience first.

For Kun, Benjamín's arrival felt like the turning of a page to a

new chapter in his life, and he quickly understood what everyone had been telling him beforehand: that the arrival of a child changes your life. And he not only felt this with the everyday needs that he learned to incorporate in to his routine such as changing nappies, preparing the feeding bottle, the bathing ritual and having to wake up a hundred times per night… But he also felt it deep down, where he discovered what it meant to be a father, something inexplicable and more intense than he had ever experienced.

Proud of his son, he soon wanted to show him off to the world. And the occasion presented itself 10 days after the birth, on Sunday, March 1st, 2009, the day that Atletico were playing Barcelona at the Vicente Calderón. Due to the intensely cold weather in Madrid around that time, they were naturally cautious and ran their doubts past the paediatrician who told them that there would be no problems, so long as they took the precaution of wrapping the baby up nice and warm. And so they did. Sergio walked on to the pitch with Benjamín in his arms, sheltering him tightly with his hands. The baby was well wrapped up indeed, with cotton wool in his ears, two hats, various baby-grows and a mini Atletico Madrid shirt that the club had given him.

The shirt came down to his knees, and on its back there was only space for the word 'Kun' because, owing to its reduced size, they could not fit another word on. And if anything else was still needed, three blankets and a hood put the finishing touches to 'Operation: Protect the Baby'.

With all the cameras focusing on him, and despite the intense rumbling of the stadium, Benjamín carried on sleeping peacefully throughout, as if already used to the roar of the crowd.

Kun's pride and happiness were there for all to see. His look said it all. He is used to sharing his feelings in that way. Because Sergio says everything with his eyes.

The expressions on his face are more eloquent than any language could ever be. And it is a similar case with his football. He does not need to speak. The sport is his language. Just as it was on that very evening, when the presence of his son seemed to galvanise him. *Atleti* twice came from behind to ultimately beat the Catalan giants 4-3, with tremendous displays from both Kun and Forlán who scored two goals apiece, Sergio's second coming four minutes from the end.

The sight of Kun heading out on to the field of play, his son in his arms, was repeated a few days later on March 28th, but this time in Buenos Aires and at the Monumental stadium in Núñez with the Argentinian national team. The build-up to the World Cup 2010 qualifier against Venezuela – Diego Maradona's first match in charge of the senior national squad – found him posing for photographs with Benja, resplendent in the number 16 shirt just like his dad. In fact, preparing that little shirt for the baby had been a drama in itself. As they had not been able to get hold of one in a small enough size, great-grandmother Pochi – scissors and thread in hand – showed off her expertise by reducing the size of a bigger shirt which they had bought for the occasion.

After this, they just needed to print Kun on the back and it would be ready for the big night. And how resplendent the family's newest member looked once more, as he again inter-preted the cheers of the crowd as a curious lullaby. He remained asleep throughout the match, and not even Argentina's fourth goal – scored by Kun after leaving three defenders behind and

with the aid of an aberration from the Venezuelan goalkeeper – could disturb his tranquillity.

The same could not be said a short while later when Benja, by then 16 months old and a lot more restless, became the centre of attention for hundreds of photographers when, up in the stands, he waved his little hand at his father and grandfather before Argentina's matches at World Cup 2010 in South Africa. But much water was still to pass under the bridge before that moment. First and foremost, there was a successful end to the 2008/09 La Liga season with *Atleti* – featuring nine wins, one draw and three losses – which saw *Los Colchoneros* again finish in fourth place and qualify for the Champions League, with a stand-out contribution from Kun, who scored 21 goals that season: 17 in La Liga and four in the Champions League. That same season witnessed the finest Barcelona team in history claiming six titles after winning every competition that they entered.

The start of the 2009/10 season seemingly served to consolidate Atletico Madrid's fine conclusion to the previous campaign, as demonstrated by the wins over Panathinaikos in the Champions League preliminary rounds. The first match was played in Greece on August 19th, 2009, resulting in a precious 3-2 win thanks to stunning strikes by Maxi Rodríguez, Diego Forlán and Kun.

That laid the platform for the return leg, in which *Atleti* quickly pushed ahead through an own goal by Greek defender Loukas Vyntra and then sealed the result with Sergio's goal in the dying minutes. It was the 100th goal that *Los Colchoneros* had scored in the European Cup.

However, that promising start turned out to be just a mirage.

The following 10 games in all comptitions were a disaster for the team. In their first seven matches in La Liga, Atletico picked up only one win, two draws and suffered four defeats. In other words, they claimed five of the 21 points on offer.

Their form in the Champions League was similar, but the consequences were more immediate. One point, taken from a 0-0 draw at the Vicente Calderón against minnows Hapoel Nicosia, was all they had to show from the first three games they had played. A 2-0 defeat away to Porto and a conclusive 4-0 loss to Chelsea in London completed that dismal start, which practically sealed their fate in the competition. As well as that of coach Abel Resino who, on October 23rd, was relieved of his duties and replaced by Quique Sánchez Flores, the former Getafe, Valencia and Benfica manager under whom *Los Colchoneros* would enjoy a change in fortunes.

They had lost their way, yet the times up ahead would bring them the opportunity to get back on track, and their first European titles in 48 years would soon follow. Times which would also bring Kun the immense joy of winning his first silverware in an Atletico shirt, triumphs that he had dreamt of and promised on arriving in Spain in 2006.

Those tough few months midway through 2009 were not the happiest for Kun out on the field of play. Atletico Madrid's poor start to the season was coupled with Argentina's sticky progress in the qualifiers for World Cup 2010 in South Africa. Sergio never stopped travelling to join up with the national squad and, although he had not started many of the matches, he keenly felt the frustration of a spell in which results refused to go Argentina's way.

Defeats against Bolivia, Ecuador, Brazil and Paraguay had

Arena, taken over by more than 20,000 *Atleti* supporters who on that night turned the stadium into a home from home. The 14 trophyless years, and a European drought stretching back no less than 48 years, were all the motivation required.

The vocal support streaming down from the stands on to the field of play created a stirring atmosphere, and the sheer noise sent tingles down the spines of the Atletico team as they lined up in the tunnel. One by one, led by captain Antonio López, they awaited the instructions to walk out for the pre-match formalities. To their left, the English team were also waiting. Every player lost in his own thoughts. And up ahead, positioned halfway between the two teams, the Europa League trophy itself awaited, unsure of who would next have the opportunity to lift it triumphantly aloft.

Still grouped together, the *Atleti* players were aware of the superstition that applies to this type of situation. For, in the same way as popular belief determines that a groom must not see his future wife's wedding dress, the same can be said of footballers and the trophy at stake. Don't look at it, don't touch it. Quique Sánchez Flores himself took charge of reminding everyone at that crucial moment. He told each one of his players as he slapped them on the chest or the back, just as he did in every match before they ran out on to the field of play. Kun, eighth in line after Tomas Ujfalusi and in front of Reyes, had to make a supreme effort, like many others, not to succumb to temptation and sneak a glance.

It was so close... he had dreamt so much about it... but he nevertheless obeyed his coach's orders and faced forwards as he headed out on to the pitch, not looking from side to side but instead straight ahead, in an attempt to summon more magic

from a moment that placed glory within his reach.

It appeared that their dreams could have been becoming a reality when Diego Forlán opened the scoring in the 32nd minute. But those premature hopes were dashed shortly afterwards, as five minutes later Simon Davies equalised and, with the score at 1-1, it was back to square one.

The match became an uphill struggle for the team from Madrid who, despite their best attempts, were unable to break their opponents down. The end of the regulation 90 minutes saw the match move into extra time.

Throughout the whole encounter, Kun had respected superstition and had not looked at the cup, which remained on full display in front of the tunnel at the entrance to the dressing rooms. Not even once. But there were only 30 minutes left to make sure that he would get his hands on it. At that moment, he defied those unwritten laws and, as if to provoke fate, he approached the trophy, looked at it and in a barely inaudible whisper said that it would be *Atleti's*, that it would be going home to Spain, and that its destiny lay in Madrid. But in those final minutes, luck was evading them and they were unable to add to the scoresheet.

However, in the dying moments of the game and with the looming uncertainty of penalties only four minutes away, Kun's spirit and tenacity pushed him to race after a long ball down the left wing. He reached it before his defender, shrugging him off, and as he approached the penalty area, he played the ball between two covering defenders to Diego Forlán, whose majestic one-touch finish gave Atletico an ultimately decisive 2-1 lead.

The goal, and the victory, filled Kun with much joy. And he

knew two things for sure. The first was that his game is football and not rugby, as demonstrated during a wonderful sequence of celebrations when on three separate occasions he tried unsuccessfully to tackle the Uruguayan who, having stripped off his shirt, had started sprinting madly towards the substitutes' bench. In the end, it was Forlán's fourth team-mate who finally managed to catch up with him, and he was knocked to the floor before being buried – alongside all those years of frustration for Atletico – under a mountain of players, in a truly unforgettable celebration. The second was that Sergio had fulfilled his aim of winning a title with Atletico, a target that he had set soon after turning 18 at the press conference that followed his big unveiling to the fans in June 2006.

That winning goal against Fulham unleashed a collective outpouring of emotion, from those associated with *Atleti* at the stadium – players, coaching staff, management, fans – to the hundreds of thousands back home in Madrid, who initiated the celebrations that would reach their climax the following day at the Fountain of Neptune in the city.

"I ran and fought for the ball, then when I went to cross I showed Diego that it would go to the near post, and he had the class to put it away," said Kun in the midst of the general euphoria. Nearby, the Uruguayan Forlán himself was celebrating along with the Colombian Perea, the Brazilian Assunca, the Portuguese Simao and the Czech Ujfalusi, bringing an international flavour to an unmistakably Spanish party.

Running the show was captain Antonio López, who raised the cup – the first of his career, awarded to him by UEFA president Michel Platini with Prince Felipe of Spain at his side – to the skies, as silver confetti and tears of emotion rained down

around him. He was followed by Reyes, who thanked Quique Sánchez Flores for having helped him to regain the confidence in his own game. Then by De Gea, who spoke of a deserved victory "despite some sticky moments... but that's Atletico". And then, one after another, by each member of the squad, nobody wanting to miss out on kissing a cup that meant so much to them. Including Kun, whose turn came soon enough. And while he lifted the cup aloft – his fresh, natural and spontaneous smile speaking volumes – deep inside he remembered looking at that prize before extra time. The cup now belonged to him. To all of them, to a team that would go down in *Atleti's* long, illustrious history. This was recognised by all of the fans and the club's senior management, including club president Enrique Cerezo, who was visibly itching to get back to Madrid to start the celebrations at the Fountain of Neptune.

Meanwhile Miguel Angel Gil, the club's chief executive, admitted that at the end of regulation time he had left the hospitality box and found a room with neither a television nor a radio, from which he emerged only shortly after hearing the cacophony set off by Atletico's winning goal.

"I spoke with the heavens during extra time. My father would have loved this more than anyone. Diego and Sergio have conjured up a piece of history for this marvellous club," he said, still emotional.

Emilio Gutiérrez, the head of marketing and communications, has Atletico in his soul and on that night felt more *Colchonero* than ever. Sergio's family were up in the stands surrounding Benjamín, who had already started bringing fortune to his parents.

Everyone would then make their triumphant way back to

Spain for a historical gathering, starting with a parade that would leave from the Vicente Calderón, passing the Almudena Cathedral, then the Madrid Town Hall and that would end up at the Fountain of Neptune, the traditional destination for *Atleti* celebrations, which on that day was dressed in all its finery, particularly after Antonio López wrapped a red and white scarf around the neck of the God of the Seas. All of which was saluted by 75,000 souls incessantly cheering on the players, who were on board a bus specially decorated for the occasion, with the words 'Champions, the dream lives on' on its side. Players who returned the people's affections with their own heartfelt offering: one that had been the subject of everyone's hopes and dreams, embodied by the piece of silverware being passed around from hand to hand, covered by fingerprints leaving traces of a DNA of red and white talent that could now never be removed.

Time To Move On

The days and months to come only served to confirm to Kun once more that moments of joy are there to be enjoyed unconditionally, and that football – like life – can bring both glory and deep sadness. It was a case of the latter a week after the triumph in Hamburg when, in the city of Barcelona, Atletico Madrid were beaten 2-0 by Seville in the final of the Copa del Rey.

For Sergio, it was a painful defeat. He had so wanted to be able to play a part in winning that trophy, which both the squad and *Atleti's* impassioned supporters yearned for greatly. He was the last player to leave the field of play, having showed his gratitude to the thousands of Atletico fans who had made the journey to the Nou Camp.

The tears that flowed from his eyes until he reached the tunnel fuelled that sentiment. And they also marked the start of a necessary, but nevertheless short-lived, period of mourning following the loss. Because no sooner had the match ended, than he had to report for duty with the Argentinian national team, for whom he had been formally called up on that very afternoon, and who had already met up in Buenos Aires to prepare for the imminent start of the World Cup in South Africa.

For Sergio, returning for a few days to Buenos Aires also meant reacquainting himself with certain places that had played their part in his own professional development. One of them was the Argentinian Football Association's training complex in Ezeiza, a site he had first visited eight years previously in 2002 when, at the age of 14, he had been called up to join the Under-15 squad by Miguel Ángel Tojo, the coach of the national youth teams. From that moment, he had not missed a single one of the call-ups that he had received, endlessly travelling between Quilmes and Ezeiza to attend training, and alternating those sessions with the ones that he was already involved in with Independiente's first team. Or staying there to sleep over, in order to avoid such a long journey and, in doing so, benefit from the wise words of advice from his mentor, Tojo.

With each such occasion, he developed an increasingly keen understanding of what it meant to wear the light blue and white of his country. Not just when he had the chance to do so for the first time with the Under-16 team at the 2004 South American Championship in Paraguay, but also when he had opportunities to watch the senior team train and later to be in the youth shadow squad as part of those sessions, as had happened at the start of 2005 with José Pekerman's squad that were preparing

for the Conderations Cup to be played in June of that year.

It was there, at that training centre, and through the guidance of each of the in-house coaches, that he learned to love that shirt and came to understand that he had to prove himself worthy of it. And from that moment on, he had not wanted to miss a single opportunity to wear it again.

That is why he had suffered so greatly when injury prevented him from competing at the South American Under-17 Championship which was played in Venezuela in 2005. And why it was as if he had been reunited with his soul two months later when, at only 17 years of age, he was called up by Francisco Ferrara as part of the squad that would play in the Under-20 World Cup in Holland.

On that occasion, and also in the magical surroundings of Ezeiza, he met Lionel Messi for the first time, with whom he would form a close friendship, forged during the long training camps that they would spend together, alongside other young players who shared the same dreams of future glories, some of which would then come true. Such as at the Under-20 World Cup in Holland in 2005. And then at the follow-up tournament in 2007 in Canada, with Hugo Tocalli as head coach. And finally at the Olympic Games in Beijing in 2008, under the stewardship of Sergio Batista.

For Kun, returning to Ezeiza eight years after that first time meant reacquainting himself with those memories. Reliving them one by one; reinventing them. And from that moment on, alongside his 22 team-mates and led by head coach Diego Maradona, he would start to retrace familiar steps, but with a new ambition. The same ambition that was filling millions of Argentinians with hope and expectation.

Many of those fans showed evidence of that new hope on the night of May 24th, 2010, at the 5-0 win over Canada in a friendly that saw the national team bid farewell to their public before leaving for Pretoria. There, in front of a full house at the Monumental stadium in Nuñez, Sergio took full advantage of his time out on the field of play. He came on in place of Carlos Tévez in the 25th minute of the second half and scored with his first involvement, cutting past a defender with his right foot in the penalty area and finishing with a left-footed shot to goal-keeper Patrick Onstad's left.

Kun arrived in South Africa knowing that he would have to fight for his place, and certain that he was prepared to give it his all even if he was not in the starting 11. He would have to be ready to perform at his best in every training session, and whenever he had the chance to come on as a substitute. Argentina boasted one of the world's most potent collections of attacking talent, comprising Lionel Messi, Gonzalo Higuaín, Carlos Tévez, Sergio Agüero, Diego Milito and Martín Palermo. To be exact, goalscorers and star players from Barcelona, Real Madrid, Manchester City, Atletico Madrid, Inter Milan and Boca Juniors. Maradona's squad possessed such firepower that they went from initially not being considered as contenders, to soon becoming the team on everyone's lips.

These were exciting days for Sergio. On June 2nd, 2010, and four days after having arrived at the University of Pretoria where the Argentina camp would be based, he celebrated his 22nd birthday. Without prior warning, his mother Adriana had travelled out especially for the occasion. The surprise filled him with happiness and made his day even more complete.

He was faced with great challenges as he turned 22. As well

as experiencing a World Cup at close quarters for the first time, it just so happened that he was in a rather unusual situation whereby the father of his partner, Diego Maradona, was the head coach. It was a situation he handled very professionally, "out of respect to the coach and my team-mates", as he explained. He knew that he in no way benefited from any favouritism, even if he had to hide his annoyance when repeatedly fielding the inevitable questions from journalists about that unique situation.

Argentina kicked their campaign off in Johannesburg on June 11th, with a 1-0 win over Nigeria. Six days later, Sergio had the chance to start fulfilling his dream, by making his World Cup debut. And it could not have gone any better. It was on June 17th against South Korea at the Soccer City stadium. With a little under 20 minutes remaining and with Argentina 2-1 ahead, Maradona and his assistant Mancuso gave him the nod to indicate that he would be coming on.

Diego gave him his instructions as he pulled on the number 16 shirt. He was charged with adrenaline for the debut: he had waited so long and yearned so much for this, that the situation could only bring out the best in him. But, nevertheless, it was a debut unlike the others. He was no longer that 15-year-old kid who, almost without understanding what it meant, played in the Argentinian Primera División for the first time. Or even the 18-year-old who played his first game for Atletico. He had been through so much since then. And that precocious journey through football had prepared him for this moment, and nothing could stand in the way of him enjoying it to the full.

There was, however, just one similarity with another of his debuts. When he came on after 29 minutes of the second half,

it was in place of Carlos Tévez – just as it had been when he made his bow for the senior national team against Brazil in London. It was a coincidence that he would notice later, as for now, all his attention was focused on playing as well as he could. And talk about making an impact! In a matter of minutes he helped the team to consolidate the win by playing a part in their final two goals.

For the last, which sealed the 4-1 victory, he provided the assist for Gonzalo Higuaín's header following a sequence of touches from Lionel Messi, and in doing so a three-way partnership was reunited that had already proved so productive at Holland 2005 and at the Olympic Games in 2008.

Argentina, whose passage to the next round was by now all but assured, took on Greece on June 22nd, with Maradona making various changes to his starting 11. Kun, who started in attack for the first time alongside Diego Milito, put in a good display, particularly during a first half which featured his best moments.

He was replaced by Javier Pastore after 76 minutes of a match that would live long in the memory of all Argentinians due to the sight of the second goal scored by the indefatigable Martín Palermo, a strike which also brought much joy to the whole squad.

That 2-0 win over the Greeks meant that Argentina finished first in their group, setting up a round of 16 tie against Mexico, in a repeat of their game at the same stage of Germany 2006. And just as on that occasion, Argentina emerged triumphant once more on June 27th, by three goals to one.

Argentina, who turned in a rather uneven performance on the day, nevertheless made the most of the opportunities that came

their way to settle the match. Tévez, twice, and Higuaín scored the goals. Kun remained on the bench in this game, but he and his team-mates celebrated the team's passage to the quarter-finals where they would take on Germany, one of the revelations of the tournament, who had just eliminated England.

That July 3rd – when the quarter-final tie was played – ended up being one of the hardest days of Sergio's career. After three minutes of play the Germans went ahead through Thomas Müller, allowing them to sit back and deploy their power on the counter attack through their top goalscorer Miroslav Klose, while exploiting the spaces that opened up as Argentina went in search of the goals that would get them back in the game.

While Sergio was warming up to come on after 30 minutes of the second half, the Germans scored a decisive third goal. The game finished 4-0, leaving Argentina empty-handed and out of the World Cup.

It was a bitter blow, softened only in part the following day by the affection with which the team were greeted on arriving back home in Argentina, where a crowd was waiting for them at the airport in Ezeiza to accompany them to the AFA training complex. The squad and coaching staff soaked up the warmth of the people, to alleviate some of the anguish that they were feeling.

Kun was able to express those feelings via his new account on the social network Twitter, which he had opened before the start of the World Cup and which had been one of his main channels of communication with the public throughout the tournament.

'Sorry and thanks,' wrote Sergio, summing up what the whole squad was feeling at not having been able to live up to the hopes

of millions of Argentines and, at the same time, expressing the gratitude that they felt for that welcome on their homecoming.

For the duration of his World Cup 'mourning', Kun preferred to shut himself away with those closest to his heart. He did not even want – nor could he bring himself – to watch the final stages of the tournament, which saw an outstanding Spain team crowned champions. The frustration of the World Cup left wounds which were difficult to heal and an aching in his soul. But at the same time they made him stronger because, at 22 years of age, he had already acquired the sort of experiences befitting a veteran footballer.

It took a few days before Sergio could pull himself together. And when he did so, he was quick to express – via Twitter again – his recognition of Spain's triumph and also congratulate his team-mate Diego Forlán, chosen as the player of the tournament.

The time that had gone by had allowed him to review the experience in a more balanced way. And he was able to start feeling happier about what he had been through. Not about the result, evidently. But for his dedication, and that of his team-mates, many of whom were as young as him. They still had many years ahead of them to go for it all over again, and to seek revenge. Like that which he would take with *Atleti*, only six weeks later.

The return to Madrid after his holidays – the first three uninterrupted weeks that he had had just to himself in years – found Kun and his team-mates in full preparation mode for the 2010/11 season. And, before that, for the European Super Cup match against a powerful Inter Milan side that had won not only the Champions League that year, knocking out Pep

Guardiola's much-vaunted Barcelona en route, but also three other trophies in Italy.

Although the Portuguese José Mourinho had left to manage Real Madrid, the new head coach was none other than the experienced Rafa Benítez. Inter had held on to the core of their team – including the Brazilians Maicon, Lucio and Julio Cesar, and the Argentines Javier Zanetti, Walter Samuel, Esteban Cambiasso and Diego Milito – and were the favourites to lift the trophy. *Atleti*, who had quietly gone about their preparations despite a pre-season period that had left a few doubts, had also kept the heart of their team together, including Kun Agüero, who arrived in perfect shape, and Diego Forlán, the new winner of the Golden Ball at the World Cup.

Of the new signings, only Uruguayan defender Diego Godín played a part on that August 27th, 2010 day in Monaco. But Kun had his own 'reinforcements' off the field of play.

Gianinna, Benja and Leo, who had all been in attendance at the previous European final in Hamburg, were now joined by his mother Adriana, forming a group that was in the mood for a celebration. And their arrival in Monaco alone warrants a mention.

Although Kun's entourage had travelled on the same airplane as the squad – who had then continued by bus to their hotel – from the airport to Monaco, at the request of Leo, they had decided to travel by… helicopter.

The experience was a wonderful one for all except Hernán Reguera, who was also present and who, according to the rest, did not enjoy the best of times on board.

There were no alarms for Benjamín: he spent the whole of the short journey feeding, apparently summoning energy for

the day of the match, which would prove to be a particularly exciting one.

Quique Sánchez Flores declared in the build-up that his side were not there to make up the numbers, and how right he proved to be. With a fine performance, Atletico Madrid wrote themselves into the history books by beating Inter 2-0, and being crowned winners of the European Super Cup.

*Friday, August 27th, 2010. **Louis II Stadium, Monaco. European Super Cup Final. Inter Milan vs. Atletico Madrid. 36 minutes into the second half.***

Nobody could say that Kun scored the finest goal of his career on this night. All he had to do was to tap in an excellent cut-back from the left by the Portuguese Simao Sabrosa. But that simple touch into the back of the net made it 2-0 to Atletico and proved to be a decisive goal against the great Inter Milan, delivering another piece of silverware for Los Colchoneros, their second in less than three months. It crowned a perfect night, which had started with a Reyes goal scored after he had combined well with Sergio. The two of them were the game's stand-out performers, embodying a resurgent Atletico side that were putting an end to years of frustration. Kun was the catalyst for that resurrection, and he did not want this moment to ever end: in the midst of his team-mates, posing with the cup, with his son Benjamín in his arms, the baby boy who had already brought fortune to his father on two occasions. In this way, the little one could soak up that special feeling of victory from close quarters, while his dad experienced a wave of deep gratitude for the football that he was able to play and, more generally, for the hand that he had been dealt in life.

Strangely it was in victory, rather than defeat, that Sergio began to feel the page starting to turn on that chapter of his life. On that night back in Hamburg, when the celebrations made him feel like he could touch the sky with his hands, he began to understand that he had to push himself further.

Tasting victory, savouring it, and knowing that he had given his all to achieve it – none of this satisfied his hunger but, on the contrary, whet his appetite for more. And he was not getting ahead of himself. He was simply detecting something that he had felt ever since he was a child: the need to compete at the highest level, to raise the stakes, the desire to keep growing. This hunger for glory that he was feeling flowed through him naturally. It burned deep inside.

Back there in the changing rooms of that stadium in Monaco, he articulated those feelings to a friend via a text message which read: 'how beautiful it is to win'. A short and simple, yet meaningful, statement that expressed his satisfaction regarding what he had achieved, but also regarding what was still to come, in a future that would bring new challenges that he was prepared to meet head on.

A rounded individual

During his four years in Spain, Sergio had proved himself capable of rising to the enormous expectations which had been placed on his shoulders upon arrival.

They were four years during which he had demonstrated that he could play at the highest level internationally; that he could experience great pressure, withstand it, and emerge from those

ordeals unharmed; and in doing so he had matured more quickly, although his rapid rise had impaired neither his sporting nor his personal development. Four years during which he had learned to overcome the lows that inevitably accompany the process of adapting to life on a new continent; to implement the necessary changes in order to become a professional in every sense; and to go from being a boy of 18 to start becoming a man.

Those who had been with Sergio since the beginning detected a young man still anchored by the same values as ever, but now more intelligent and mature, not resting on his laurels, and unperturbed by his constant exposure in the media.

They had not always been the easiest four years, as success can often have an immense impact on one so young. One of his main feats was to have been able to adapt to all of this. During those four years he was repeatedly coveted by the biggest clubs in the world, and rated as one of the most valuable players around. And throughout these times, Sergio left nobody in any doubt as to his allegiance towards *Atleti*, identifying with the club's values and adopting them as his own, as for him only befits such a commitment.

His class endeared him to home and away fans alike. And thus he succeeded in holding a place within Spanish society – according to a market survey carried out by Atletico Madrid – as a player who created positive sensations, who transmitted exemplary values, who was a good role model and who inspired happiness in others.

Sergio had become an international icon who brought his club great benefits by way of television revenue, tours, shirt sales – the number 10 remaining one of the biggest sellers – and by his steadily rising market value. The perception of Sergio held

by society was no more than a faithful reflection of the reality.

Evidence could be found in his everyday life, where he demonstrated how naturally he was able to handle the status of being one of world football's brightest stars.

Kun had learnt to balance the obligations that come with such prominence with being able to enjoy his free time. The training, gym work and physical conditioning required of an elite athlete took up much of his days. As did meetings with friends, charitable activities and the fulfilment of his publicity and press obligations. As such, he would go from a campaign photo shoot for one of his sponsors – where he would pose as if he were a professional model, much to the delight of the photographers – to a dinner with family and friends, and traditional Argentinian games of cards during which he would fight tooth and nail, no differently to how he would in La Liga matches. Or from assisting the Atletico Madrid Foundation in putting together a charity calendar to help children suffering from achondroplasia, a genetic disorder that affects bone growth, to being invited to sing alongside famous artists to raise money for the victims of the earthquake in Haiti. To getting in touch via the internet or his mobile phones – he is quite the technophile – with his people back in Buenos Aires and closely following the progress of his younger brothers Mauricio and Gastón, who play in the 1996 and 1997 *categorías* of Independiente's youth teams, the former having already won the title with the *novena* team, just as he had done back in 2002. To overseeing his website and sending messages out on Twitter, the social network on which he would amass over four million followers in three years, to become the most followed Argentine on the site, or via Facebook, on which he would also break the

three million follower mark. To making a well-received cameo alongside some fellow footballers in director Santiago Segura's film Torrente 4, one of the highest-grossing films of all time at the Spanish box office. Or to go from enjoying a film at home – his favourite is Gladiator with Russell Crowe, which he never tires of watching over and over, crying without fail at the scene where the lead character dies – to receiving the visits of his family and friends from back in Buenos Aires. To making the most of the end-of-year breaks by travelling to Argentina to attend family events alongside Leo, Adriana, Jessica, Gaby, Mayra, Daiana, Gastón, Mauricio and all his other nearest and dearest linked to his roots.

He also put his time and energy into strengthening his bonds with that country which had made him feel so at home, forming new friendships that further integrated him into the society of his adopted nation. Such as the one that he struck up with Rubén Domínguez, a young man with a key position in the Majadahonda branch of a large Spanish electronics retailer, and who he fortuitously met one day when he went to buy some equipment for his house. What started as simply 'technical support' would naturally evolve over time into a close friendship.

Rubén, a Real Madrid fanatic, remembers that he was surprised at what a straightforward person Kun was and that, far from acting like he had imagined such a huge star would, he seemed to be just like anyone else and conversed with him in a very natural and spontaneous manner.

Sergio subsequently started to split the allegiances of this loyal Real fan, as Rubén would watch derby matches with an overwhelming sense of contradiction, unable to stop cheering for Kun despite his love for Atletico's great rivals.

Rubén describes the friendship that he formed with Sergio in the following way: "For me it was a surprise. Not because I had any preconceptions about him. But because I thought it was very difficult to have contact with people of his stature, who are so well-known. Most people see them as inaccessible, almost as if they were not even flesh and bone like the rest of us. Sergio demonstrated to me that it's possible to be an international star, while remaining natural and humble. And in a short time we formed a rapport that steadily grew stronger. And I'm not just talking about how he was with me. I could see it in his everyday life, in his relationship with his son, in his concerns for loved-ones and strangers alike."

Rubén became a good companion of Sergio's as well as, a short time later when his career took him to England, a loyal assistant.

In effect, those four years had served to enable Sergio – despite all the distractions – to keep his feet on the ground, and to continue his personal development while embarking on a new, more independent stage in his life, just like any other young person of his age.

All the while, he was experiencing something as personal as fatherhood, with all the natural fears that come with becoming a parent for the first time. But also the joy caused by Ben's first mutterings, his first steps and his cute habits that never failed to surprise him. And it was clear for all to see, as Benjamín had won him over from the very beginning. And he was able to enjoy those early years which, as we know, are unique and cannot be repeated. Like when at 10 months he started to walk, or when he said his first word: "Papa". It was a time to find out what he liked, to get to know his sweet personality and his

ability to bring out a tenderness in him that he did not previously know existed. And even to be amazed by how naturally he lived up to his unique genes and started choosing a football – or 'tita' as he called it – as his favourite toy.

Surrounded by other tempting games that he also took to with impressive ease, such as tablet computers, video games, books and films, Benjamín still preferred to play with a football from a very early age. With Sergio, his grandparents, or whoever else happened to be in front of him. On the patio or on the grass, at home or in the box at the Calderón where he and his mother would watch Sergio during his matches for *Atleti*.

Proof of this was there for all to see when Sergio uploaded a video to his official website, recorded in the living room of his house in Majadahonda one cold December day in 2010, which shows them partaking in an intimate game. Sergio throws the ball and Benjamín, walking as only a 22-month-old baby can, starts to run and then kicks the ball with striking power, even up into the air. And he then rolls different balls – including a basketball – under the sole of his foot with perfect balance, following the instructions from his experienced father.

The almost incomprehensible words coming out of Benjamín's mouth, the dialogue between the two and the looks that they exchange, all contribute to a touching scene demonstrating the tenderness between father and son. How natural it all appears on film perfectly replicates the time that the two spent with each other on a daily basis. All the camera did was to record a reality that had remained hitherto unseen by others.

The clip triggered a remarkable response from the public. In only five days the video attracted more than one-and-a-half million views, spending that period as a constant feature

on the YouTube home page and generating a record number of visitors to Kun's website. The images were also shown on news bulletins and television programmes in over 100 countries worldwide.

Kun's 22-month-old son was already showing an unusual ability with the ball at his feet. But more importantly still, the clip attracted a wave of empathy that went beyond that precocious talent, reflected in the thousands of messages and emails that they received and that made particular reference to the special bond between father and son exuded by the video. One of those messages in particular moved Kun. It came from a young couple who were unable to conceive a child, who were at one stage trying to adopt but had since given up. But who, after watching the video and 'seeing the connection that exists between the two of you', were going to try again.

'If uploading the video helped with this, then it was right to have uploaded it. We have been impressed by the warmth that it has generated. And it makes us feel very proud. Because, as I said, we were hoping that you could enjoy it like we do. Because it was just about playing his favourite game with him, like any father would with their son,' wrote Kun on his official website.

The fifth season

In August 2010, Sergio began his fifth season in La Liga with Atletico Madrid, the tone having been set with that triumph in Monaco – "we are the best team in Europe", he had declared following the win over Inter – and with the stirring sight of their fans' celebrations.

He was in impeccable shape, and he looked ahead with much interest to the prospect of striving to compete at the highest level in La Liga, the Europa League – as the holders – and the Copa del Rey.

The timing was also right to renew his ties with Atletico, as his existing contract was to expire in June 2012. As so often over the years, his on-field exploits had put him in the shop window for a potential transfer, with rumours circulating of multi-million pound offers from Europe's most prominent clubs. Sergio was very clear that he wanted to negotiate a new contract with *Atleti*.

He had arrived at 18 years of age and had always felt cared for and protected, by both the fans and by so many members of the club's staff and senior management. And he had faced up to both the tougher times and the recent successes with equal passion, giving his all even when his body, at times suffering, was asking him to slow down and allow it to recover.

For Sergio, renewing the contract, and doing so without making a big song and dance about it, was a part of that commitment. The fact of the matter was that, if he did not do it then, in a few months he would be free to potentially negotiate a contract elsewhere, and Atletico Madrid would not stand to receive a penny for his transfer. Sergio moved to end any possible speculation on that regard by informing his agents that, regardless of what could potentially happen in the future, this was his decision.

The time frame for a new deal to be reached with Atletico was made clear to those leading the negotiations on Sergio's behalf. And it was in that spirit that they entered discussions with the club's senior management.

The negotiations took place over the following months, and

were successfully resolved in accordance with Kun's wishes.

Atleti made a promising start in La Liga, with a 4-0 win over Sporting Gijón and a 2-1 triumph away to Athletic Bilbao, although in the latter game Kun was forced out of the action after 51 minutes following a strong challenge by Carlos Gurpegui. The resulting injury would keep Sergio out of the team's first Europa League fixture against Aris Salónica, where a 1-0 defeat did not bode well for their progress in the competition.

Kun forced himself back for the match against Barcelona at the Calderón but was unable to complete the 90 minutes, leaving the field of play six minutes after the interval of a game that Barcelona would go on to win 2-1. He was held back from the next two matches – consecutive 1-1 draws with Valencia at the Mestalla and Leverkusen in the Europa League – to avoid aggravating the injury. And just as he was coming back to fitness, he ruptured muscle fibres in his left buttock during training, leaving him sidelined once more.

Sergio aimed to return in the best shape possible and, as such, he followed the instructions from team physio Oscar Pitillas to the letter, making his 30 days out of the game more bearable. Kun shook off the niggle to make an immediate impact on his return after 65 minutes of the match against Rosenborg from Norway at the Calderón.

Sixty seconds after coming on, he had already scored to make it 2-0. He later set up Diego Costa for the third. That match was followed by a loss to Villarreal, a draw against Almería and a win over Rosenborg in Norway. Atletico could not break their curse against Real, falling to a 2-0 defeat at the Bernabéu, but wins over Osasuna and Real Sociedad in San Sebastián – their

first triumph in that city for 19 years, owing in no small part to a great two-goal performance from Sergio – seemed to get the team back on track.

However, at the start of December, rainclouds again started gathering over the club. The team firstly suffered two tough defeats by identical 3-2 scorelines, against Espanyol in La Liga and Aris in the Europa League, the latter leaving *Los Colchoneros* on the verge of elimination from that competition. A third consecutive loss, 2-0 against Levante in Valencia, saw further cracks formed that were only papered over by a 2-0 win on December 11th against Deportivo La Coruña at the Calderón, featuring an outstanding performance and another brace by Sergio.

Since his return from injury against Rosenborg, he had scored 12 goals in 12 games. However, *Atleti's* inconsistency was exposed by a 1-1 draw against Leverkusen in Germany, which finally put an end to their chances of defending their title in the Europa League, followed by a 3-0 win over Málaga and a 1-0 defeat of Espanyol before the end of the month, this time in the Copa del Rey.

The latter was to be the last appearance in Atletico's clolours by one of the icons of that year's double success: the Portuguese winger Simao Sabrosa who, approaching the end of his contract and lacking reassurances over a renewal, emigrated to Turkish football. The exit of Simao, a player who Kun had always admired as one of the team's key figures, followed José Manuel Jurado's departure to German football at the start of the season.

Sergio did not hesitate to publicly declare the high regard in which he held Simao. 'I want to say that I always looked up to

Simao, that he was an important member of the group, and that I learned a lot from him during our time together at *Atleti*. What's more, we had the good fortune of being rewarded for all those years of hard work with two European titles, during which he played a key role in the team.

'It was good to have been able to celebrate alongside him and the rest of the team. He is a great player and a great person. We're going to miss him. It's only left for me to wish him all the best of success for the new chapter that he is starting in his life,' he wrote on his website.

During those last days of December 2010, an agreement was reached between the parties involved by which the arduous negotiations over the renewal of Kun's contract with *Atleti* would arrive at a satisfactory conclusion.

The terms of the agreement, ultimately put together by Sergio's agents, tied him to the club until June 30th, 2014, significantly improved his wages, and reduced his buy-out clause from 60 to 45 million euros.

Before details of the agreement were officially made public, Sergio signed the contract in a face-to-face meeting with Miguel Ángel Gil Marín. In that meeting, Kun explained to the managing director the reasons that for him took precedence when it came to accepting the deal. He wanted to reassure him personally that his decision to re-sign owed everything to what the club had come to mean to him since his arrival in Spain. And that he would under no circumstances make use of the option to abandon the existing contract in order to allow himself to freely and unconditionally negotiate a move to another club.

The only personal commitment that Sergio asked of Gil Marín was that if, during the term of the new contract, an offer

came in that was suitable for all parties, or if he expressed a desire to leave the club, *Atleti* would not stand in the way of that departure. Sergio felt it necessary to make this last point clear because, although he harboured no desires to leave the club at that moment, he did not wish to close any doors that would prevent him, should the situation arise, from reversing that decision.

Gil Marín gave his word, and that was enough for Sergio to seal what he believed to be a gentlemen's agreement. An agreement that in the none-too-distant future would not be honoured, culminating – much to Kun's displeasure – in a painful exit from *Atleti*, the last way that he had wished or imagined for it to be.

On January 4th, 2011, via a press release, Atletico Madrid announced an agreement that was then officially presented at the end of the month. At the subsequent press conference, the reporters – who had travelled in their swathes to the Calderón – questioned club president Enrique Cerezo about the buy-out clause, which had been reduced from 60 to 45 million euros. They interpreted this as a route to Kun's potentially imminent departure.

Cerezo explained that "it was better to sign a renewed deal with a 45 million euro buy-out clause, than not to sign one with a higher clause", and emphasised that the reduced figure was of no great significance. And he explained that Kun "has been generous, he wants to stay here, lowering the buy-out clause is neither here nor there; he could have waited another 11 months to be able to negotiate his departure from the club as a free agent."

Cerezo had been quite clear in the face of an insistent press pack, who then asked Sergio about the rumours of his imminent

departure from the club. Kun replied forcefully: "Now is not the time to speak about that. The day I want to leave, it will be my decision and nobody else will take it for me. Now I am happy. The day that I want to go, I will say 'I want to go' and I will leave. It's my future, and I make the decisions. And if in June, the club and I decide that a change of scenery is for the best, then it will be everyone's choice."

The news that Kun would be staying at *Atleti* got 2011 off to a good start, inspiring high hopes among the club's passionate fans. Although their first match that year resulted in a goalless draw with Racing Santander in La Liga, *Los Colchoneros* advanced to the quarter-finals of the Copa del Rey when, aided by a determined Sergio Agüero, they salvaged a valuable 1-1 draw away to Espanyol to make the advantage that they had carried forward from the first leg at the Calderón count.

In the next round, they would come across none other than José Mourinho's powerful Real Madrid side. Their previous outing in La Liga against Hércules was far from the ideal preparation for that clash against their oldest rivals. A conclusive 4-1 loss away in Alicante left deep scars.

Three days after that defeat, Real showed a wounded *Atleti* no mercy at the Bernabéu and ran out 3-1 winners, meaning only a comeback of epic proportions a week later at the Calderón would do. A comeback that appeared increasingly improbable following confirmation that during the first match Kun had torn muscle fibres in his left thigh, which would keep him out of the return leg. Madrid won again, this time by a goal to nil, and *Atleti* were knocked out of the Copa del Rey.

And, to put the finishing touches to a January to forget, there followed two more defeats against Gijón by a goal to nil – with

Reyes and Kun both out injured – and 2-0 against Athletic Bilbao at the Calderón. They led to the supporters demanding answers of the club's senior management.

The dreams of repeating, or even improving on, the previous year's successes had started to fade away. Criticism coming from the supporters claimed that the club had not been up to job; that the management had not seized the opportunity to build on the strengths of the squad; that the additions brought in during both the summer and winter transfer windows had failed to replace the losses of José Manuel Jurado and Simao Sabrosa; and that the team had lost quality, with their level of play suffering as a result.

The hard facts showed that in a little more than a month, Atletico Madrid had been eliminated from the Europa League, a competition in which they had been defending their title, and from the Copa del Rey, in which they had been finalists the previous season. And to make matters worse, their position in La Liga was not at all what they had envisaged: those defeats had left them five points off the European places and with only a remote possibility of qualifying for the Champions League, the target that had been set at the beginning of the season.

In February, *Atleti's* dismal run went from bad to worse. Perennial champions Barcelona thrashed them 3-0 in the Nou Camp and then Valencia defeated them 2-1 at the Calderón. Sergio, who had worn the captain's armband for the first time, did not hide away in defeat and faced up on behalf of the team.

"It's been a few games now in which we haven't had the rub of the green. Especially in the last match, where we had no luck and ended up losing when we didn't deserve to. For that reason it's not the time to talk too much, and instead to go and get it

done out on the field of play. We have to prepare carefully, to give our all in every game and to fight for as high a position as possible until the last moment. It is the least that the history of this club deserves, as well as the fans who offer us so much support," he affirmed, in what almost amounted to a declaration of principles.

And Sergio then let his performances on the pitch do the talking. On February 19th, 2011, away to Zaragoza at La Romareda, Sergio scored a great goal that he was able to dedicate to Benjamín, who on that day turned two years old.

At that stage of the campaign, Kun was already Atletico's top scorer with 15 goals in all competitions. He had scored eight times in La Liga, three times in the Copa del Rey, three times in the Europa League and once in the European Super Cup.

The win over Zaragoza brought an end to the bad run. Draws against Seville and Getafe reinforced the feeling that a corner had been turned, consolidated further by a 3-1 win over Villarreal – featuring a chipped goal from Kun – that saw *Atleti* rise back into the European places. With that strike, Sergio clocked up his 90th goal in official matches in the red and white of Atletico, overtaking the mark set by another club legend: Fernando 'El Niño' Torres.

In the following match, a 2-2 draw against Almería, he scored his fourth brace of the season and his 15th since arriving at *Los Colchoneros*. In doing so, he moved on to 92 goals scored in official matches and into second place on the list of the club's all-time non-Spanish goalscorers, overtaking Mendonca.

Even a painful 2-1 defeat to Real Madrid – with Sergio pulling a goal back shortly before the end – did not slow down Atletico's revival, which in the month of April saw them beat Osasuna

3-2 in Navarra and Real Sociedad 3-0 in a match where Sergio scored his 20th goal of the season.

They then drew 2-2 against Espanyol with Sergio again on target, before defeating Levante 4-1 thanks largely to another brace by Kun. That made it eight goals in six matches, and the first time that he had scored in six consecutive games.

At the end of April, in the 1-0 win over Deportivo La Coruña at the Riazor stadium, goal number 98 in official matches for Atletico made him the 10th leading goalscorer in the history of *Los Colchoneros* in all competitions, overtaking another Argentinian and Atletico legend, Rubén Cano.

Sergio's impressive sprint finish to the season did not get in the way of him dedicating part of his time to his continued charity work. He actively participated in a campaign launched in Spain in support of the people of Japan following the fateful earthquake that had devastated the country, and he was present at the Royal Spanish Golf Federation course in Madrid for the biggest charity golf event to be held in Spain, organised by the Seve Ballesteros Foundation in support of research into brain tumours. Furthermore, he joined a campaign by the name of *'Dame vida'* ('Give me life'), devised by the singer Huecco, which aimed to generate electricity through sport and to then convert it into hours of light for families who do not have access to it.

Sergio took part in a video for Huecco, dancing the rumba and playing a percussion instrument – the guiro – alongside other international sporting icons such as Pau Gasol, Jorge Lorenzo, David Villa, Pepe Reina, Sergio Ramos, Fernando Verdasco and Vicente del Bosque.

"Kun is a big star and is perfectly at ease in that company, as you can see in the clip," Huecco said afterwards. "He always

has a smile on his face and has a big heart for charitable activities. It's an honour that he has taken part, alongside all the other champions."

Sergio was also invited around then by the Sánchez Vicario Foundation to participate alongside Rafael Nadal in the Precocious Champions cycle of events. The sportsmen shared the stage at the Ciudad de la Raqueta tennis complex in Madrid, where they spoke and analysed what it signified for their personal development to have had such early success in their careers.

The Mayor of Madrid, Alberto Ruiz Gallardón, who opened the event, stated that "because of their determination, work ethic and dedication, Rafa Nadal and Sergio Agüero are role models to society".

From a boy to a man

Having scored 24 goals in the campaign, only three off his most productive season with *Atleti* in 2007/08 and two off a century in the club's colours, Sergio prepared, along with his teammates, for the final stretch of the La Liga season in May.

However, two successive losses against Málaga (3-0) and away at the Sardinero against Racing Santander (2-1) threw the club's chances of qualifying for the Europa League into doubt.

The 1-0 win over Hércules put them back on track, but the final match of the season would still be decisive in determining their final position in the table.

Claiming fifth or sixth position would result in automatic qualification for the Europa League whereas, if they finished

in seventh, they would have to play in the preliminary round in July.

The last match would be played on Saturday, May 21st, against a Mallorca side fighting manfully to avoid relegation. Sergio came into the week leading up to the match in a more settled frame of mind, following a few days in which his feelings had started to become clearer. He found that the realisation that he had first experienced after the European Super Cup victory in Monaco was on his mind almost every day. His feelings were gathering momentum, and he knew at that point that he must not try to hold them back, even if that process would be painful and potentially misunderstood by some.

His thoughts alternated between, on the one hand, the desire for a change of scenery, to move on in search of new horizons that would allow him to keep developing as a footballer, and to step up the level of competition in an attempt to become an even better player. And, on the other, the desire to stay longer in a place that he looked upon as his home and where he felt very at ease, but at the risk of not fulfilling his strongest desires there.

He talked it through with those closest to him and with his agents. And he patiently listened to all of them. He had grown since 2006 when he decided to make the transfer to *Atleti*, and the situation was now different. He was on the verge of turning 23 and, more than ever, he realised that the decision had to be purely and simply his own, as if it were to mark the start of a new cycle in his life, leaving behind the boy who he no longer was in order to become the man who he was starting to be.

Weighed down by these feelings, he travelled with his team-mates to Mallorca for the match on May 21st, 2011 at the Ono Stadi stadium, where the home side needed a victory to distance

themselves from the drop. The local fans did all they could to encourage their team at such a difficult moment. However, they were silenced on no fewer than three occasions by Kun at his most ruthless.

Firstly on 12 minutes when, after a long clearance by Juanfrán, he won the ball on the right, beat his marker and – in the penalty area and with another defender bearing down on him – hit an angled shot with his right foot to beat the helpless Dudu Aouate in the opposition goal.

If it was striking that he did not celebrate that goal with his customary enthusiasm, then what happened in the 60th minute and with the match already 2-0 in favour of *Los Colchoneros*, seemed to carry even more significance. José Antonio Reyes sent a high ball down the left that reached Kun, who had run beyond a stationary line of defence. His immaculate control with his right foot killed the ball in the area, before two touches and a half-turn wrong-footed the three defenders who had tracked back in an attempt to dispossess him. He then squared up to hit the ball with his good foot, letting fly with a clean, powerful right-footed shot that flew into the top left-hand corner of the Israeli goalkeeper's net. Sergio saw the ball go in, turned and started to walk back, with his head almost bowed, towards the halfway line. Not even when his team-mates approached to congratulate him did his demeanour change.

That goal – a genuine work of art – was his 100th in the shirt of Atletico Madrid, but it also had a more profound significance that could be confirmed a few minutes later, when Kun scored another goal for his personal scrapbook. One that would, for a variety of reasons, remain etched on to the memories of all those who saw it.

TIME TO MOVE ON

*Saturday, May 21st, 2011. **The Ono Stadi stadium.
Mallorca vs. Atletico Madrid. 35 minutes into the
second half.***

*On this night a dazzling yet strangely subdued Kun Agüero left his
mark, once more, on a match in the top flight of Spanish football,
in the 38th and last round of fixtures in the 2010/11 La Liga
season. He had already scored twice, the second his 100th goal in
Atleti's colours, when he collected the ball on the left-hand side of
the attack and found a way past the four opposition players lying
in wait on the edge of the penalty area. He evaded the desperately
onrushing home goalkeeper by chipping the ball beyond him and,
with two more defenders trying to close him down, scored his third
goal of the night with an exquisite, inch-perfect lob. It was the
first hat-trick of his professional career and his 101st goal for
Los Colchoneros. Just like his first two goals, Sergio was unable
to celebrate his third. He walked back towards the halfway line in
a show of respect towards his opponents, for whom defeat could
mean relegation, but also with other, more personal feelings on his
mind. It had been one of his most successful nights on a football
pitch, but for the first time he had felt no sense of euphoria. Right
there, on that night, in that stadium, and with only a few days to
go until his 23rd birthday, Kun knew deep down that his time at
Atletico had drawn to a close.*

"What I have been through and what I am going through
have exceeded all the expectations that I had on arriving in
Spain in 2006, and for that reason I wish to dedicate it to all of
the fans who, from the very first day, have welcomed me with
open arms – I have never stopped feeling their encouragement
and affection.

"It's a shame that the three goals against Mallorca were not enough to avoid the preliminary round of the Europa League. But I'm still happy. Why did I not celebrate such significant goals? It's obvious... out of respect for a team that were fighting for their survival. But now nothing can take away the pride I'm feeling. Which of the goals was the most special? I really liked the second, because it was also number 100. But if I had to choose one, it would be the third. Because of how I scored it, and because it meant that I could finally break my duck and score a hat-trick. I'm also happy to know that I've finished as the third top goalscorer behind Cristiano and Leo."

These comments, which Sergio made after the match, expressed a large part of what he was feeling. He felt a very real satisfaction at having helped his team to qualify for the Europa League – which they would go on to win the following year – at having reached 101 goals for *Atleti*, at having been the third highest goalscorer that season in La Liga, and at having scored the first hat-trick of his career.

And indeed, he felt thankful towards the Atletico fans and had not wanted to celebrate the goals out of respect for the opposition who, despite the 4-3 defeat, were miraculously able to avoid relegation at the expense of Deportivo La Coruña.

But it was also true that he had not been able to celebrate the goals because his joy had been overshadowed by a sadness, triggered by the realisation during the match that a door was categorically closing and that his spell at Atletico Madrid was at an end.

He could not celebrate a farewell that was still painful, in spite of all the milestones that he had reached on an evening that also marked the end of a season in which he had equalled his

highest tally of goals, dating back to 2007/08: 27 goals (20 in La Liga and 7 in all other competitions).

It was in this state of mind that he returned to Madrid where, in a meeting with his family and agents, he outlined what he was thinking and the decision that he had come to. The unanimous show of support that he received sparked everyone into action on the various tasks that lay ahead. Sergio gave the green light for work to get started, but he made it very clear to those who were in charge of negotiating on his behalf that the decision over his next club would be purely and exclusively his.

The hours that immediately followed were more intense than any others that he could remember away from the field of play, but they would allow him to initiate the necessary grieving process that would strengthen him for what was to come. As things stood, Kun had to travel on Tuesday, May 24th to Argentina to join up with the national team, who were playing in the Copa America. His preference was to inform *Atleti* of his decision as soon as possible, to give them more time to find his new club.

However, the exchanges with Atletico's senior management, who did not attend a meeting that had been arranged for the afternoon of Monday, May 23rd at the Calderón, forced him to act quicker and to make his decision public. A statement, drawn up by Kun and his agents during those hours, was ready to be released.

While brainstorming ideas it was Sergio who, in his own words, came up with the title that would precede the statement.

"I think that it's time to move on," he said. And those were the words they settled on. Several tweets were sent out first. 'I have informed *Atleti* of my decision to leave. I have asked them

to receive, unconditionally, any offers that come in from other clubs. I always said that, when I wanted to leave *Atleti*, I would make it public. That moment has arrived and I am honouring my word.' A link then led to his official website, and a message entitled 'Time to move on':

"I have thought long and hard about it, and I'm convinced that I must be true to myself. I believe that I must not limit my chances of continuing to learn, continuing to grow. After five intense years, a chapter in my life has ended and I have to turn the page to start the next one. I am about to turn 23, and I have everything up ahead of me. Needless to say, this is not a financial decision but a strictly sporting one. Therefore I want to express my full appreciation towards the club, for the efforts they have made to keep me on with wages befitting of the biggest clubs in the world.

I also want to explain to you all that this decision has been brewing in me for some time. The matter was even discussed and agreed with Atleti last year when my contract was renewed. I wanted to sign and to renew the contract, as a way of giving back to the club and to everyone associated with it what they have given to me. If I hadn't done so, I would have been a free agent and the club would have stood not to receive any money for my transfer. At that point, I had the club's word that they would not stand in the way of a possible departure in June 2011. Therefore, in consideration of that commitment and in view of this, my final decision, I have asked the club to listen unconditionally to any offers that may come in from different clubs.

As for the fans, you have my eternal gratitude. I don't claim to be original, nor to say what's politically correct. I prefer to say what I feel, regardless of other considerations. Because I know that the

only way you'll understand me is if I write from the heart. That's the way that I feel you've all spoken to me over these years, with sincere affection and love. You are now a part of my identity, and of how I understand football. Scoring 101 goals and winning two titles after so many years without any silverware. I will never forget the celebrations at the Fountain of Neptune, and that night in Barcelona when we were unable to bring home the Copa del Rey. But it was worth it, wasn't it? For me, all of those experiences ended up confirming something that I have felt ever since I was little: the desire to compete, to win and to be among the best, offering all I have: my football, and my love for the game.

I don't want to fall into the trap of that old cliché that this is not a goodbye, just a 'see you later'. But I do want to mention something that I once heard a very famous Argentinian tango singer, Aníbal Troilo, had said, and which is very appropriate at this moment: "Who said I left? If I'm always coming back…"

A big hug for you all. I love you.

KUN

Now for number 16

Kun's statement announcing his desire to leave *Atleti* triggered a wave of reaction, from both press and fans alike, in the days immediately following its release.

Sergio's website registered over 120,000 hits in a matter of hours. The social networks also served as a sounding board for the decision and the controversy that it had sparked, particularly among Atletico's fans.

One target of choice was the club's senior management, who

were accused of not having done enough to build the rest of the squad to a level befitting a player of Kun's stature. They pointed to senior management figures as being the reason for Kun's departure and feared that any hopes of regaining the competitiveness that they had lost seemed more distant than ever, meaning that they ran the subsequent risk of not being able to fight for the league title and would instead have to settle, year after year, for qualification to one of the European competitions.

Sergio tried to steer clear of such debates. He had to travel to Buenos Aires to start preparing for the Copa America with Argentina. But the reaction of *Atleti's* senior management in the face of the avalanche of criticism that they were receiving from the fans started to stir mixed feelings in him. He did not understand the surprise expressed by many senior management figures at his decision to leave – a decision about which they were already aware – or their continued refusal to facilitate his exit, as promised in a succession of meetings leading up to the renewal of his contract.

Sergio had to make a conscious effort not to allow his feelings to become muddled. On the one hand – he said to himself – there were the directors to whom, in spite of everything, he was appreciative of their years together, and on the other there was the club itself and the fans. He made this distinction clear in comments made to journalists at both the Madrid-Barajas Airport, before boarding the aeroplane to Argentina, and on arrival in Buenos Aires.

"I think that my statement says it all. I want to leave. I have informed Enrique and Miguel Angel of that. On the day that I signed the new contract, I said to them very clearly that I would

make the decision over leaving, when I considered it appropriate. I also said that when I wanted to go I would announce it, as agreed. All that I can say now is that they knew I was going to announce my decision. The problem is that they don't seem to understand or remember what was agreed. The club has to respect what was agreed and the people have to understand that. I've had five wonderful years and I therefore wish to thank the club and the people for the love that they have shown me. It is mutual, but I have opted for a fresh start," he said.

Kun's words left no room for debate. But during the following days, as Sergio took advantage of the opportunity to spend time with his loved-ones back in his home country, the controversy would further intensify. This escalation was triggered by strong rumours of a supposed interest in Kun coming from Real Madrid. Such rumours – which cut deep with Atletico's fans – fanned the flames further and fuelled debates in newspapers, on the radio, on television and on social networks.

Faced with such a reaction back in Spain, Sergio concentrated on what for him was his priority at the time: the Copa America, to be played in Argentina during the month of July. His participation was dependent on being called up by the head coach Sergio 'Checho' Batista to an initial squad of 26 players, to be subsequently trimmed down to a group of 22 who would remain together until the start of the tournament. And two days before his 23rd birthday, on May 31st, 2011, he received the call.

'I can't wait to get back to Ezeiza to start training with my team-mates. I've said it before and I'll say it again: my commitment to the national team is total', wrote Kun on his Twitter account.

That commitment got its reward when, after various days of training and a friendly match against Albania – which Argentina won 4-0, Sergio coming off the bench in the second half to score a goal – he was confirmed by Batista in the final squad of 22 for the continental tournament. Kun was unrelentingly enthusiastic throughout those days. It would be his first Copa America, and nothing was going to get in the way of him enjoying the moment.

He also wanted to take advantage of the opportunity to carry out charitable activities. To this end, alongside Lionel Messi and Carlos Tévez, he took part in a UNICEF initiative where they were the first to sign the 'Commitment in favour of children and against discrimination'.

The aim of the campaign, which continued throughout the tournament, was to celebrate diversity and to raise awareness of the negative impact that discrimination has for thousands of children and teenagers, on their lives, growth, development and opportunities.

At the same time, Kun painted a picture that he auctioned off in support of UNICEF at a so-called Impact Art event, an initiative that brings together sport, art and solidarity through works of art produced by famous sportsmen that are auctioned off, with the money raised going to different non-governmental organisations.

Also at the start of the Copa America, and alongside Juan Carr's Argentinian Solidarity Network, Sergio initiated a campaign to find and provide aid to the lost children of Latin America. Each day, he uploaded photos and information on missing children on to his Twitter and Facebook accounts.

"It's a good way to try and make a difference by taking advan-

tage of the opportunities given to us by social networks. Hopefully it'll turn up some information. It's worth a go," Sergio said at the time.

Kun's attitude drew praise from Juan Carr at the Solidarity Network: "In Latin America, there are some 5,000 missing people, 1,600 of whom are under 18, and 440 of whom are Argentinian. I therefore appreciate it as a noble and admirable gesture that a young man like Kun, as successful as he is and in the glory days of his career, is still concerned about lost and underprivileged children."

All of these activities served to strengthen Sergio's desire to do his best for the national team and "to be able to bring happiness to all Argentinians", as he underlined in each and every one of his interviews prior to the start of the competition. However, the *Albiceleste's* showing did not live up to the pre-tournament expectations, and they were dramatically knocked out on penalties in the quarter-finals by Uruguay, in a match which ended 1-1 after 90 minutes and then extra time.

Argentina had not enjoyed an encouraging start to the tournament. They had drawn with Bolivia in their first match, thanks to a stunning strike by Kun who had entered the fray with 20 minutes remaining. A Di María cross, chested down by Burdisso and volleyed in by Sergio, ensured parity and calmed fears of an opening-day defeat.

However another draw against Colombia – this time goalless and with Sergio once more only coming off the bench in the second half – was not enough to silence the doubters over a misfiring team, and made victory over Costa Rica an absolute necessity to ensure the team's passage to the next phase.

For that match, Batista lined up with Kun in his starting

11 alongside Leo Messi and Higuaín. A 3-0 win, with Sergio scoring two goals, took Argentina through to the quarter-finals. But the aforementioned defeat on penalties to Uruguay, for whom goalkeeper Fernando Muslera was man of the match, was a sucker punch for a team experiencing yet more frustration, this time in front of their own public.

Elimination left Sergio with the bitter taste of not having achieved what he had set out to do. As on other occasions, he felt the pain deep down. Not even the fact that he was picked out by press and experts alike as one of his team's players of the tournament, and that he had been able to fulfil his potential in his country's colours, could help to ease his sense of frustration.

He had no option but to turn the page on it, but not without firstly resolving internally that this low had to serve as motivation for the *Albiceleste* to regain their lost prestige. He made a promise to give his all at every opportunity that would come his way, in order for the national team to be respected once more and to reclaim a status more befitting of the richness of their history and the talent of their players.

That need to quickly turn a page was entirely in keeping with his professional future. While he had been based with the Argentina team camp before and during the Copa America, Kun had left his departure from *Atleti* and the negotiations with interested parties in his agent's hands.

At that time, rumours of the different clubs in Europe drawing up offers for Kun were permanently circulating. Names such as Chelsea, Juventus, Paris Saint-Germain, Manchester City and Real Madrid were among those most frequently mentioned. Repeated references were also made to the finer details of the state of affairs left by Kun's departure from *Atleti*.

"There is only one way that Kun is leaving Atletico, and that is if a club triggers the buy-out clause, 45 million euros. A club that is not Real Madrid."

These comments, made by chief executive Miguel Ángel Gil Marín shortly after Kun's statement was released, and then reiterated throughout the process, pointed towards an unseemly departure that did not honour what had been agreed and bore no resemblance to what Sergio had envisaged. Sergio also felt that the senior management were trying to make him appear as the bad guy to avoid paying the price politically for his exit.

It was in this context that Sergio made certain comments to journalists in Argentina that hinted at his growing irritation with Atletico's senior management. In response to questions put forward by journalists on the *La Red* radio station in Buenos Aires, and when asked about his future and the interest from Real Madrid, he said: "I would be lying if I said that I was going to stay at *Atleti*. I don't see myself there and I'm not going to stay. Put your money on whoever you want, apart from Atletico."

Sergio went further still, wanting to make it clear that his footballing identity remained with Independiente in Avellaneda, the team "that I support", he said. And he added: "I have no idea which clubs are interested, but on a footballing level the English and Spanish leagues are the ones that appeal most to me."

Although some of his words reflected his thoughts about the attitude of Atletico's senior management figures, he also knew that they were not fully representative of all that he felt and that some of them could be misinterpreted. Although he certainly still felt a sense of belonging, in terms of his past and his

identity, to his first club in Argentina, he was also profoundly grateful to a club that welcomed him at only 18 years of age and gave him the platform to suceed in Europe. Everything that he had experienced during those five intense years with Atletico Madrid – and he had expressed as much both on and off the field of play – was genuine.

He decided then that it was not the time to fan the flames. And that, out of respect for those five years at the club, he would not say anything else that may in any way overshadow them. Even if it meant having to tolerate the truth not being told, and having to put up with unfair insults. He did not want to do wrong by himself, and neither did he want his words to betray him.

He decided to make no further comment on the issue, at least until everything was resolved. If others wanted to take that opportunity to dirty his name, then so be it – he would not rise to their provocation. Time, that 'great healer', would put things in order. On that basis, he steadied himself to await the results of operations which were already underway and which would go towards defining his professional future, before making the right decision for himself.

Since announcing his departure from *Atleti* and then travelling out to Argentina for the Copa America, he had let his agent get to work. Almost all of Hernán Reguera's time had been spent going from one corner of Europe to the next for talks with clubs that were showing an interest. He did so under the premise of listening to all offers, taking a note of them and then, following discussions with Sergio and those closest to him, moving things forward in the most suitable direction.

Atleti's determination only to let go of Kun if another club

paid his full buy-out clause meant that the situation required an offer that would be, without a doubt, the highest of that summer's transfer window in Europe. In this sense, the response that Sergio got from his agent was one of the utmost professionalism: to do everything necessary to secure the best for Kun's future and, regardless of the rumours circulating, to leave nothing to chance and consider every option.

In order to do so, he was constantly on the move, travelling through Italy, Spain and England to gauge the level of interest in Sergio. During two intense months of work, he was able to observe and hear at first hand, from conversations with those in charge at the various clubs, the scope of the offers. The idea – just as it had been for the transfer from Independiente to Atletico Madrid – was to assess every aspect of a move on which Kun's future career in football could hinge.

With this in mind, one of his trips took in a meeting with Roberto Mancini at his house in Italy. Manchester City's manager had invited him especially, to tell him about the project at the English club and why he believed that Sergio could have a crucial role to play in it. The meeting coincided with the 1-1 draw between Argentina and Bolivia in the Copa America on July 1st, in which Kun's stunning volleyed strike rescued a point for the *Albiceleste* in his debut in the competition.

Against that backdrop, Hernán had the chance to listen to the plans on an institutional and sporting level that were being implemented at City, a club which in 2008 – under the ownership of Sheikh Mansour Bin Zayed Al Nahyan from the United Arab Emirates – had initiated a concerted effort to position itself among the biggest in world football. The signing of players of Sergio's calibre fitted in perfectly with the aims of that project.

After that meeting Hernán was sure that, in the short-term, City would be one of the most serious contenders for Kun's signature. It did not take long for Mancini himself to declare as much publicly. In comments made to *Sky Sports*, he singled out Sergio as one of the players that he would like to bring in for the season that was soon to commence. Mancini's interest was thus added to that already expressed by Juventus, one of the first clubs to go on the charge for Sergio. The Old Lady of Italian football was undergoing a rebuilding process and wanted him to be the symbol of the club's new era.

In the last two weeks of July 2011, and with the outlook significantly clearer, it was finally decision time for Sergio. He was naturally anxious throughout those days, as only befitting someone who was deciding on his future, before diving head first into a new life.

The weekend of July 23rd found him in constant consultations. After listening to the detailed report from his agent, he settled on the decision to live in a new country, despite all the challenges that such a move would entail. He was on the verge of leaving Spain, where he felt very at ease. And also of leaving behind the process of moving to another house in Madrid, one which he had undertaken with such enthusiasm and which had already entered the final stages of decorations.

The act of starting a new phase brought with it much upheaval, but he approached it with all the enthusiasm required for it to go smoothly. He was prepared to embark on this journey focusing on the benefits, rather than the potential drawbacks. The series of discussions that preceded his final decision included a conversation with his parents Leo and Adriana, who knew just how to listen to him and hear out his points of view.

As the hours went by, Sergio seemed more and more convinced: his future lay in the Premier League. He liked the football played there, the high standard of the teams involved and the fact that it was so competitive, which all went towards its status as one of the most important leagues in the world.

Furthermore, he was attracted by the stance taken by Manchester City, the club that was showing the greatest determination not just to make the right noises about his transfer, but to show that they were prepared to take all the necessary steps to definitively move things forwards.

He was ultimately convinced when he learned more about the club's wider project, as well as about the quality of the squad that he would join, which made him feel certain – deep down inside – that the team would be in the position to fight for important trophies.

He took the time to make contact with his 'old' friend Pablo Zabaleta, who had been at the club since 2008. The words offered to him by Pablo – who, as fate would have it, had been playing against Sergio when he had made his Primera División debut for Independiente in 2003, and had then been his captain for Argentina's triumphant Under-20 team in Holland in 2005 – were a great help. As was the advice from Maxi Rodríguez, Kun's former team-mate at *Atleti* who was playing for Liverpool at the time.

The ideas that the two of them outlined, each from their own perspective, helped Kun to gather a more complete overview of what would be awaiting him. The pair of them, Pablo and Maxi, would also soon offer important support as he settled into this new phase of his life.

With Kun's green light and full backing, the negotiations

between the two clubs gathered pace, as did the final details of the deal that Hernán Reguera was in charge of penning with City's directors. And on Tuesday, July 26th, alongside his father Leonel, Sergio flew from Buenos Aires to Manchester, via London.

By then, the press were already anticipating that an agreement was to be reached imminently, although they still had no clue as to when it would be tied up. It was Sergio himself who, during the stop-off in London, announced via Twitter that he had arrived in England 'to finalise the details of the move to City' and that everything was going 'very well'.

City's people were waiting for him when he landed at Manchester Airport on Wednesday, July 27th, and they immediately took him to the private hospital for his medical, before moving on to the offices at the Etihad, the club's modern stadium, where he signed the contract.

'I am now a City player. Happy to be at this club and in this city. Thanks to everyone for the welcome and the reception!!!', he wrote on the social networks afterwards.

Despite a dizzying few hours, he was able to enjoy every minute of what was happening. He was impressed by the level of organisation at the club, by the facilities, and by the treatment he was receiving. Those first impressions underlined to him the importance of having trusted his instincts. And regardless of how it all turned out – although he was absolutely sure that he would have no problems settling in – he felt entirely motivated by what he was on the verge of starting.

They were feelings that were captured in his first interview since setting foot on English soil. It was in front of the cameras for City TV, Manchester City's official television channel,

which produced an extended profile on him. The chosen venue for his interview was the changing room, where the light blue shirt with the number 16 and the name 'Agüero' – at this stage without 'Kun' alongside it, something which would be added later – featured prominently in the background.

Sergio had chosen the number 16, the same number that he wore for Argentina.

"We're going to fight for important trophies. City is one of the biggest teams in England. I obviously said to my agent to do everything possible to get me here – it's a good club, I like it and I wanted to play in the Premier League," he spelt out regarding his expectations.

In terms of settling in, he explained that he would have no problems acclimatising. "I have only heard good things about the team and I'm looking forward to meeting them," he affirmed.

He displayed the same calmness and contentment at his first public appearance as a City player. It came in the city of Dublin, where his new team were taking part in a warm-up tournament, the so-called Super Cup in which Celtic, Inter Milan and an Airtricity XI were also involved. At a press conference alongside the manager Mancini, Kun – who did not play in the tournament – promised to work towards winning titles. "And if that comes this year, all the better," he said, which in time would prove to be something of a premonition.

His time at Manchester City was upon him. And he would give his all, just as he had done at every one of the clubs where he had played.

With that attitude, Sergio threw himself into trying to make the natural settling-in period – to a new country, a different city,

a different league and a different club – as short as possible. He felt confident that he could do so. He felt that knowing about and being a part of a different culture would also see him grow as a person. He had a great opportunity ahead of him, and he was certain that he would not waste it.

Citizen Kun

Sergio's settling-in period got off to the best possible start with the arrival of his family in Manchester, only a few days after he himself had got there. He chose to live in the village of Alderley Edge, located some 19 kilometres from Manchester and where other City players also had their homes. The calmness of the location, and its proximity to a small but charming shopping centre, made it all the more welcoming.

Sergio's enthusiasm was there for all to see as he started, almost immediately, to take English classes three times a week, a rate that later slowed up due to the countless commitments and trips away that he had to undertake with the team. And, against all expectations, he easily got used to the English custom of driving on the left.

In fact, the change barely registered with him. This made getting around much easier, above all to Carrington, the site of Manchester City's training ground and some 20 minutes from his new house. Initially his sat nav would provide directions but later, once he was sure that he knew the way, he started making the trip without the help of the device.

During those early days, he also took the opportunity to find out more about the history of the club, about its present situation and about its plans for the future, which impressed him more and more. He learned of the enthusiasm of City's fans, of their glory days at the end of the 1960s, and of the subsequent years of struggle when the team was relegated on several occasions.

Considered as the 'noisy neighbours' of Manchester United, their traditional rival and serial champions over recent years, City were looking to find the path to glory once more. He was told of the intensity with which the Citizens had celebrated winning the FA Cup a few months earlier, their first silverware in 35 years. And he also knew that City's main ambition was to win the English championship, a title that had eluded the club for 44 years.

They explained to him that the recent success, as well as those genuine aspirations for the future, had a lot to do with the arrival in September 2008 of Sheikh Mansour Bin Zayed Al Nahyan from the United Arab Emirates, armed with a project that was to revolutionise the club, the city and football in general.

Sergio could tell that the project went much further than what could be seen on the surface. He was pleasantly surprised by how seriously the club dealt with all professional issues, by the comfort of the sporting facilities, by the plans that had been

conceived to improve them, by the organisation in general and how attentive they were to the needs of the players, who only had to concern themselves with doing what they knew best: playing football.

Furthermore, he familiarised himself with the Etihad Campus, the complex that City had designed and started to build on 80 acres of land beside the stadium. The aim was to turn it into one of the world's most modern training centres for their young prospects, including a stadium for youth teams with a capacity of 7,000 people.

In this way, the good feeling that he had picked up on arrival in Manchester became even stronger, and would intensify even more when he was able to witness the passion of the fans at first hand. The opportunity came at the new Wembley Stadium on August 7th, 2011 with the Community Shield. It just so happened that, on this occasion, City would be taking on United in a passionate derby encounter.

Sergio, who was an unused substitute on the day, could savour at close quarters the quality and technical riches found in the squad, as well as the respect and support of the fans who, even in defeat – United came back from two goals down to win 3-2 – appreciated their team's efforts and intensified their support for a squad of players that had it within themselves to make their wildest dreams a reality.

Despite not getting his first game at Wembley, Sergio had a taster of what he would then experience on August 15th, 2012, only 19 days after having arrived in Manchester, in the first round of matches of the 2011/12 Premier League season.

The opponents were Swansea, the first Welsh team ever to have played in the Premier League. And the venue was the

Etihad Stadium, City's home ground since they left Maine Road in 2003, a stunning stadium with a capacity of 47,726 spectators and which, on that day as throughout the rest of the season, was full to the brim.

For their first league fixture of the season, manager Roberto Mancini selected a team made up of Joe Hart in goal; the powerful, home-grown Micah Richards and the Frenchman Gael Clichy as right and left full-backs respectively, and the Belgian Vincent Kompany and Joleon Lescott as partners in the centre of the defence. In the midfield, he went for Dutchman Nigel de Jong, Ivorian Yaya Toure, Gareth Barry and Spaniard David Silva. And in attack, the Bosnian striker Edin Dzeko and the left-footed Adam Johnson. The substitutes' bench included goalkeeper Stuart Taylor, Pablo Zabaleta, the Serbians Stefan Savic and Aleksandar Kolarov, James Milner, Kun himself and the Italian Mario Balotelli, a player he would come to adore through good times and mad.

From the dugout, Sergio – who felt some butterflies at making his debut, as Mancini had told him in advance that he intended to bring him on for the final minutes of the match – was able to see the stunning Etihad Stadium completely full for the first time, and the unique rituals of supporters who were clearly passionate but whose methods of support were very different from those to which he was accustomed.

Firstly, he was taken aback by the recital of 'Blue Moon', a classic song from the 1930s adopted by City's fans in the 1990s and henceforth sung in unison before matches. The latest version of the song – which had been recorded in the past by Frank Sinatra and Elvis Presley – was sung by Liam Gallagher, the former Oasis front man and renowned City fan, which

gave them even more affiliation with a song that was already a Citizen trademark.

Sergio was also struck by the way that individual songs were dedicated to each player, and he even allowed himself to imagine there being one especially for him in the not-too-distant future. He was also able to witness at first-hand the striking way in which the fans celebrated their goals. It was not until the start of the second half that City managed to break Swansea's resistance, and finally took a 1-0 lead thanks to Edin Dzeko. And there and then, Kun saw the fans turn their back to the field of play and put their arms around each other's shoulders to celebrate their team's goal.

The fans had adopted this custom, which they then christened the 'Poznan', after having seen it performed during a Europa League tie by the supporters of Lech Poznan, one of the most traditional teams in Poland. Accordingly, and to the cry of 'Let's do the Poznan', they repeat the ritual after each goal scored by their team. He did not know it at the time but, over the course of the next few minutes, Sergio would give the fans cause to repeat this most striking of rituals on a further three occasions. Because sure enough, 15 minutes into the second half, Mancini gave him the nod to enter the field of play.

When the television cameras zoomed in on him, he could even be seen taking the opportunity for a joke and a smile with the fourth official who, via his electronic board, indicated that number 34, Nigel De Jong, would be replaced by number 16, Agüero. Only some time later did he realise that, in one of those strange quirks of fate, this was the exact reverse of what had taken place at his Primera División debut for Independiente in 2003, when he was 15 years of age.

On that occasion he wore the number 34 on his back and came on for Emanuel Rivas, who wore number 16. But at that precise moment, his mind was a long way from picking up on this minor detail. He was fully concentrated on wanting to play. Just by the way that he ran onto the Etihad pitch, it was clear to see that he was particularly pumped up – something that would be demonstrated for all to see in less than two minutes. His first touch was a shot that forced the visiting goalkeeper Michel Vorm into a testing save. Seconds later, he was unable to successfully finish off an excellent run from the left. And after only eight minutes of his debut, he scored his first goal by ghosting in behind his markers to classily finish off a low centre from the right by Micah Richards. Barely two minutes later, following an attempted chip over the Swansea goalkeeper, he touched the ball back for Silva to place it into the back of the net and make the score 3-0.

The electric glance exchanged between the highly talented Spaniard and Kun after the goal acted as the prelude to a partnership that could answer the prayers of City's fans. In barely 10 minutes, Sergio had demonstrated his class and won admiration for what was already considered to be a dream debut, both for City and in the Premier League. But to complete a perfect evening, with the game already drawing to a close and stoppage time being played, a magnificent right-footed shot from outside the box left Vorm with no chance. It was a second goal for his personal account, and made the final score 4-0.

That wonderful strike drew an ovation from all four corners of the Etihad Stadium and gave City's supporters reason to let their imaginations run free, to dream about imminent glories and to start a new footballing love affair that would bring real

success. In keeping with those feelings, and still excited by such a promising start, Sergio put the hope that everyone felt into words. 'Hopefully it's the start of something big,' he wrote on Twitter. Words that nine months later would become a tangible reality.

On the road to records

Reaction to such a remarkable debut was not long in coming. At the end of the match, Roberto Mancini praised Kun's performance.

"He is young, I think that he'll be a fantastic player for us," he said, while also pondering the partnership that he struck up with Silva: "They speak the same language and they play very, very good football," he indicated.

The Swansea coach, Brendan Rodgers, was not to be left behind and described Sergio as a 'world class player'. The eulogies also came from the written press.

Such a promising debut coincided with the start of Sergio's relationship with Puma, the sports brand with whom he chose to sign for this new stage in his professional career. Christian Voigt, the Senior Director of Global Sports Marketing for the German firm, classed Kun at this stage as "one of the most exciting strikers to watch in world football" and expressed his satisfaction that he was now one of the faces of the company's global sports marketing campaigns.

"We are delighted to have him as a Puma player," indicated Voigt, who also said that he had "no doubts that Sergio Agüero is going to become a genuine legend".

The timing of Kun's association with Puma could not have been better. In a short space of time, Voigt's prophecy would be fulfilled by Sergio's performances for City, his goals and, above all, the team's achievements.

The strike power that City had demonstrated in their Premier League debut that season was substantiated in the following games. They firstly won away at Bolton by three goals to two and at Tottenham by five goals to one, with four goals by Dzeko, another by Kun and a great debut by the Frenchman Nasri.

On September 10th, 2011, Sergio scored all of his team's three goals, and the second hat-trick of his career, in the 3-0 win over Wigan. Kun lived up to the comments of Wigan's manager, the Spaniard Roberto Martinez, who in the run-up to the match had said that "Aguero has the ability to play between lines, he is explosive over the first five yards and defenders will have a real shock when they see just how quick he is".

And to complete his description, he described him as "a complete player and probably as close to Maradona and Messi as you will see".

City's fourth victory on the bounce, with a haul of 15 goals for and only three against, left the team at the top of the Premier League table and captured the attention of the football world. The team's solid play, based around a strong defence, high possession of the ball and convincing power in attack, won admiration. But it was also a cause for concern among their rivals.

In a little under a month, and having played only four games, Sergio could tell that he had joined a talented squad playing at a very high level.

From a personal standpoint, he knew that his own success in adapting to his team-mates and to the competitive brand

of football in the Premier League would be critical for him to maintain his level of play for the whole season. For although he had felt at ease during those first matches, he understood that he was now playing a quicker, more direct style of football which was forcing him to run a lot more.

One of the challenges was to remain switched on in matches for as long as possible. He therefore made himself work on this aspect of his play. If he could become more attentive, his contribution to the team would go from strength to strength. He was convinced that he could make City better, and was sure that City could help him to become a better player.

Throughout their next run of games, that hunch became a certainty. A 2-2 draw against Fulham (with another brace by Sergio) and three consecutive wins against Everton (2-0), Blackburn Rovers (4-0) and Aston Villa (4-1), left City on top of the Premier League with 22 points, two more than their local rivals, United, who would be their next opponents at Old Trafford.

Sir Alex Ferguson's team came into the derby on the back of a very good run of home form, consisting of 24 wins in their previous 25 games at their ground. Their objective for that game was clear: to take back first place from a team that was already shaping up to be the most likely challenger to their recent dominance.

City, on the other hand, were presented with the opportunity to increase their lead and consolidate the title-winning form that they had shown thus far during the first half of the season. For both teams, this would be an acid test, given an extra edge by the fact that it would be played out against their local rivals.

Additionally, the match would see a duel between their two top marksmen, who at the time led the league's scoring charts:

Wayne Rooney with nine goals and Sergio with eight. However, neither the most optimistic City fan nor the most pessimistic of United supporters could have foreseen what took place on the field of play that Sunday, October 23rd, 2011.

Thanks to a great team performance, in which they made the most of their one-man advantage from early in the second half following the dismissal of Evans, City consigned United to a historic defeat by six goals to one, with two goals from Balotelli – on the day that he revealed his 'Why Always Me?' t-shirt as a show of discontent at always being in the press because of his eccentric behaviour – one by Kun, another by Silva and two more from Dzeko.

It was a scoreline to send shockwaves through the international football world as Manchester United had conceded six goals at Old Trafford for the first time in 85 years. The other precedent for a loss of this magnitude took place back in 1955, when Manchester City won by five goals to nil away from home against their neighbours. The impact of such a heavy defeat was so great that Sir Alex Ferguson himself described that day as "the worst in Manchester United's history".

"Mario was crazy when he wanted to be. He'd do daft things whenever he felt like it because he thought he could," explains Sergio. "We'd go out on the training pitch and he'd kick the balls away in different directions just to be silly, or he'd throw cheese over people when he was sat in the dining room. A lot of his behaviour, I feel, came from a feeling he had that he was somehow different and maybe a little insecure. I couldn't help but wind him up from time to time, calling him silly names and toying with him but he knew it was always in an affectionate way because I loved Mario – everyone loved him, though he

CITIZEN KUN

drove us nuts at times. He used to say that nobody loved him and I'm sure he believed that was true, though it was anything but.

"Nobody knew he had that t-shirt on when we played United at Old Trafford – he must have hidden it beneath a vest or something, but later when I looked at the 'Why Always Me?' message on the front, I told him that if he was calmer and didn't do so many things, it probably wouldn't always be him. If we'd have known he had it on, we'd have told him to take it off. He'd say things like, 'The police have just followed me all the way to the training ground and want to talk to me,' and I'd say, 'No wonder! You've probably just broke the speed limit or bumped into somebody!'

"Sometimes he'd get a message from reception saying the police wanted to speak to him and he'd say 'F*** the police!' Then he'd say that he may have driven past the police pretty quickly and that could be the reason. He was always seeking attention.

"We were having breakfast at Carrington one day and I was sat near Mario who was reading the paper and it had a big picture of him in the 'Why Always Me?' t-shirt and along each side it had numerous reasons why it was always him – girls, smoking, police, red cards, parking fines, fireworks – it was endless. He'd say, 'Nah, I never did that,' and I would say, 'But there's a picture proving you did!' He didn't really take notice of anyone, but I always told him straight and he listened to me.

"His relationship with Mancini often made me smile. They would fight like cat and dog during training and then walk off with their arms around each other's shoulders. They would swear and shout at each other, but later they'd be like father and

son. Quite often we'd have five-a-sides in training and Mancini would join in. He would make sure he was on the opposite side to Mario so they could wind each other up. He'd tell Mario and the rest of us that he wasn't the manager in the game, just another player.

"He said we could say what we wanted to him and it would be fine so the game would begin and Mancini and Mario would be at each other, kicking lumps out of one another and shouting abuse until the final whistle when Mancini would say, 'Right, I'm your manager again, now!'

"Mario would say, 'You were sh** when you were a player... and it was a lot easier then than it is now.' Mancini would say, 'You wouldn't have been able to play then or now!' It was comical. Mario would go away and sulk for a couple of days and he was just like a little kid. I miss him being around the place because even though he was a little crazy, he was a great character to have around the dressing room.

"I was sorry to see Mario leave because I think the world of him and I'm happy that we are still regularly in touch. I was injured when we were playing Barcelona at home in the Champions League and watching the game from the stand when my phone went off. I didn't recognise the number but I answered it and heard, 'Hey! It's Mario! How's it going dickhead? Come on City, come on City!' – and then he just hung up!"

City now had a five-point lead in the league table and greater momentum in the race for the title.

The three consecutive victories that followed against Wolves (3-1), QPR (2-3) and Newcastle (3-1) meant that the team had made the best start to a campaign in the history of the league, their 11 wins and one draw breaking Arsenal's record from

2003/04, and had scored 42 goals in 12 games, the best total in the previous 50 years.

The Citizens' unbeaten run stretched for two further matches: a 1-1 draw with Liverpool and a 5-1 win at the start of December 2011 over Norwich in which Kun opened the scoring with a beautiful goal after receiving the ball at the edge of the six-yard box, surrounded by defenders and the goalkeeper, and coming up with a toe-poked shot that worked its way through his opponents' legs to end up in the back of goalkeeper John Ruddy's net.

For Sergio, that was his 11th goal in 13 Premier League matches. The victory enabled City to stay on top with 38 points, and they still boasted the league's most lethal attack with 48 goals in 14 matches.

As a reminder that nothing would come easily for them, and that the path to achieving their goals was still lined with many an obstacle, their first defeat duly arrived. It came against Chelsea at Stamford Bridge, in a match that had been going their way at the start but that became increasingly complicated towards the end.

The game was not even two minutes old when Sergio took possession of the ball in the midfield, surrounded by three opposing players, and threaded an inch-perfect pass through to Balotelli who beat his marker, took the ball round Cech and rolled it into the open net. Raul Meireles equalised before the end of the first half. And in the second half, with Clichy having been sent off for City, Chelsea claimed the victory with a well-taken penalty by Frank Lampard.

Despite the result, City remained two points ahead of United in first place, a lead that they preserved with two more wins.

The first by one goal to nil over Arsenal and the second by three goals to nil against Stoke, with two goals for Kun that took his Premier League tally to 13.

Those results meant that Manchester City were able to celebrate Christmas Eve and Christmas Day as they had been unable to for some time previously: for the first time in 82 years on those dates, they stood at the summit of English football's top flight.

However, their happiness over the Christmas period would not be complete. A 0-0 draw away at West Brom on December 26th, coupled with United's thrashing of Wigan, left the two Manchester sides level at the top of the Premier League table with 45 points.

Although goal difference was in the Citizens' favour, this parity at the end of 2011 sounded a clear warning to them: achieving their goals would not be a walk in the park, and was going to require them to give everything they had.

January blues

Kun's 2011 end-of-year report made for satisfactory reading. He had been selected by the experts on the FIFA Football Committee, the FIFA Technical and Development Committee and by a group of specialists from France Football among the 23 candidates for the 2011 Ballon d'or alongside: Éric Abidal (France - Barcelona), Karim Benzema (France - Real Madrid), Iker Casillas (Spain - Real Madrid), Cristiano Ronaldo (Portugal - Real Madrid), Dani Alves (Brazil - Barcelona), Samuel Eto'o (Cameroon - Anji), Cesc Fàbregas (Spain - Barcelona),

Diego Forlán (Uruguay - Inter), Andrés Iniesta (Spain - Barcelona), Lionel Messi (Argentina - Barcelona), Thomas Müller (Germany – Bayern Munich), Nani (Portugal - Manchester United), Neymar (Brazil - Santos), Mesut Özil (Germany - Real Madrid), Gerard Piqué (Spain - Barcelona), Wayne Rooney (England - Manchester United), Bastian Schweinsteiger (Germany – Bayern Munich), Wesley Sneijder (Netherlands - Inter), Luis Suárez (Uruguay - Liverpool), David Villa (Spain - Barcelona), Xabi Alonso (Spain - Real Madrid) and Xavi (Spain - Barcelona).

And despite having only played for half of the year in Spain, he was chosen by the *Marca* and *As* newspapers for the Liga BBVA team of the year, joining Leo Messi and Cristiano Ronaldo in attack.

That recognition – which Sergio eagerly lapped up – was, for the most part, reflective of Kun's output in 2011, a year in which he had played 53 games and scored 34 goals. In the first half of the year with Atletico Madrid, he had played 21 matches and scored 14 goals.

With the Argentinian national team, between the Copa America (4), friendlies (3) and qualifiers for Brazil 2014 (1), he had played eight matches – although he was in the starting 11 for only two of these – scoring five goals. And with City, in 24 appearances in all competitions (Premier League, Champions League and Carling Cup), seven of them as a substitute, he had scored 15 goals.

Sergio's impressive personal account in 2011 had brought him moments of huge satisfaction, as well as others which had left a more bitter taste. Among the former was to be found his first appearance for the Argentinian national team in the qualifiers

for Brazil 2014, after recovering from injury. He had not been able to take part in the draw with Bolivia in Buenos Aires or the defeat to Venezuela in Caracas, which made it critical that the team secure victory over Colombia in Bogotá on November 15th, 2011.

Head coach Alejandro Sabella brought him on in the second half, with Colombia ahead by a goal to nil, to take his place as part of an attacking trident alongside Messi and Higuaín, in an attempt to find more consistency going forward.

Sabella's decision was proved to have been 100 per cent wise. The trio would go on to produce the goods, not just on the field of play that night but in the future, as they formed a deadly strike force whose firepower would go a long way to restoring Argentina's reputation as one of the best national sides in the world.

*Tuesday, November 15th, 2011. **Estadio Metropolitano in Barranquilla. Qualifiers for World Cup Brazil 2014. Colombia vs. Argentina. 84th minute.***

On this night, La Albiceleste won back the respect of their rivals and, conjuring up their talent, restored pride in a team that had drawn with Bolivia at home in the Monumental stadium and then lost for the first time in a World Cup qualifier against Venezuela. As a result, they came into this match against Colombia wounded, and fell one goal behind as the first half drew to a close. In the second half, with Kun now on the pitch, the Argentinians carried more of an attacking threat. Firstly, they equalised through Messi after 60 minutes. And then, six minutes from the end, the Agüero-Messi-Higuaín combination paid handsome dividends.

Sergio, who had received the ball in his own half from Clemente Rodríguez, fed Leo on the edge of the opposition penalty box with a searching, measured pass. Recognising the threat that he posed, defenders were drawn to Messi who then played in Pipa, whose powerful shot was kept out by goalkeeper Ospina. Kun, who had kept up with the attack from the start, beat the defenders to the ball and forced it into the back of the net to give Argentina an ultimately decisive 2-1 advantage. Sergio's celebration – including a twirl of his shirt – was accompanied by a general feeling of relief, but also highlighted something that was already felt by many: the need for the national team to turn over a new leaf, to enter a new phase in which they would win back the respect of the football world and reconcile themselves with the Argentinian public, to whom they felt indebted. It was time for Kun to demonstrate, out on the pitch, the new maturity that he and many of his team-mates felt after their experiences at youth level World Cups, the Olympic Games and the last World Cup itself. A new era was dawning, and he felt certain that he wanted not only to be a part of it but to be one of its key figures.

He experienced quite an opposite, sinking feeling, during the second half of 2011 with City in the Champions League. He was particularly eager to play in this competition and for both him and his team to give the best possible account of themselves. However, different factors conspired to prevent them from doing so.

A less than fortunate draw – leaving the Manchester team in the so-called 'Group of Death' alongside the powerful Bayern Munich from Germany, Napoli from Italy and Villarreal from Spain – the team's inexperience in this competition and a suc-

cession of matches where they failed to come up with the answer to the challenges set by their opponents, all saw them knocked out at the group stage. It was also that very first match against Bayern Munich in which the controversy flared up between manager Roberto Mancini and Carlos Tévez for which Manchester City sanctioned the Argentinian striker.

"I was on the pitch at the time so I had no idea what was happening on the bench in that part of the field. It was obviously very heated in the dressing room after the game and Mancini was going mad at Tevez telling him to go back to Argentina and then he told some other players to go back to their countries. I was sat next to Carlitos and at one point I thought Mancini was telling me to go back to Argentina! I was thinking, 'What? Me as well? okay, I'll go and see my family for a few days.' Of course, he wasn't speaking to me," recalls Sergio.

"As for speaking to Carlitos afterwards, he didn't really say too much and the next day, he had gone back to Argentina as the manager had suggested and it was maybe four months before I saw him again when he came back to Carrington for a meeting. I believe there had been a number of fall-outs between Carlitos and Mancini in the past so this was the straw that broke the camel's back. Tevez can have a short fuse at times, just as Mancini did, so it was perhaps inevitable that it would explode at some point.

"Carlitos and I were team-mates and had a good working relationship and both being Argentinian meant we were a bit closer, but he wasn't someone I was really close to. Pablo Zabaleta has always been someone I consider a very close friend. We were both in the Under-20s World Cup together and there is the age difference to consider because Carlitos is four years older

than me and I only really knew him from my time here. We'd chat in the canteen at Carrington and played the odd round of golf together but we didn't chat on the phone when he was out of the country, whereas I would have done had it been Pablo because we know each other much better and talk all the time about all kinds of things."

That elimination from the Champions League in the month of December 2011 proved to be the forerunner of a January to forget for the Citizens. They would be dealt a double blow on New Year's Day: a one-nil defeat away to Sunderland, who scored the winning goal in the third minute of stoppage time after City had dominated the whole match, meaning that they had also failed to take advantage of a slip-up by United, who had also lost.

The 3-0 win over Liverpool at the Etihad stadium two days later was a rare high point in a month that held various headaches in store for City, not just in terms of their poor results but because it also saw the start of a series of incidents and mishaps that would affect their performances in the immediate future.

The first of them was a 3-2 defeat at home to United in the FA Cup. The defeat and elimination were all the more painful, coming at the hands of their local rivals, and in addition, City would also have to make do without their suspended captain Vincent Kompany for four games following his sending off. Kompany's unavailability was compounded by the temporary absence of Yaya and Kolo Toure, who headed off to join the Ivory Coast squad to prepare for the African Cup of Nations.

Eliminated from the Champions League, the FA Cup and subsequently the Carling Cup by Liverpool, City were left with two competitions to contest for the rest of the season: the

Europa League, which would start up again in February, and the Premier League, where they were still neck and neck with United for first place in the table. And it was in the domestic league that, despite struggling for form, they enjoyed two successes.

The first was a win by a goal to nil away at Wigan and the second was at the Etihad against Tottenham, one of the season's surprise packages, in an encounter that saw Spurs come back from two goals down but City ultimately strike with a last minute penalty by Mario Balotelli to secure a 3-2 win.

However, January would end for the Citizens in the same way as it had begun: with a defeat. On this occasion it came against Everton by a goal to nil, leaving the two Manchester clubs level once again at the top of the table on 54 points, followed by Tottenham, fighting not to lose ground on 49 points.

Irritating injury

Sergio was convinced that, by finding their ruthless streak once more in attack and putting right certain mistakes that they were making as a team, February could be a very different month to the one before. And he was spot on.

The starting point was a memorable match in the snow at the Etihad on Saturday, February 4th against Fulham, in which Kun, later chosen as man of the match, scored the first goal with a penalty, had a part to play in the second and, after a great piece of individual play, set up Dzeko for the third.

That result, coupled with a 3-3 draw between United and Chelsea, allowed City to once more pull ahead by two points

from their old rivals, a lead that they consolidated when Joleon Lescott's goal handed them a 1-0 victory over Aston Villa.

With Yaya Toure – who had already returned from the African Cup of Nations – back in the team, and with Kompany and Silva available again, the Citizens were making it quite clear that at full strength they would be in the position to continue making strides forward in the Premier League.

Proof of this came in the shape of a 3-0 win at Blackburn with goals from Balotelli, Kun (his 16th in the league) and Dzeko. A further two wins in February, in the Europa League against Porto (2-1 and 4-0, with Sergio scoring in each leg), helped restore the team to a much healthier frame of mind.

Back then, Kun was making waves off the pitch as well as on it, for at this time in England – and later in different countries around the world – the new Pepsi Cola advertising campaign started to be broadcast, featuring him as one of its stars alongside Leo Messi, Didier Drogba, Fernando Torres, Frank Lampard, Jack Wilshere and the prestigious DJ Calvin Harris. In the advert entitled 'Kick in the Mix', and in the backstage clip, Kun can be seen looking as at ease on an advertising set as he is on a football pitch.

The better vibes that the team had picked up on the field of play in the month of February unfortunately faded away, and the season's final straight was to prove an altogether bumpier road.

Eliminated from European football by Sporting Lisbon, all that was left for City was to fight for the Premier League title against a United team newly emboldened and confident after managing to reassert its strength – Ferguson had reassembled his team with the return of club legend Paul Scholes – and now

able to look down once more on its historic rival.

Despite their absentees, City had no margin for error and, to make things worse with 10 games to go, the fixture list seemed to favour United.

Their first big test came against a Chelsea side who, having replaced the Portuguese Andre Villas Boas with the Italian Roberto Di Matteo as their manager, were going through something of a renaissance on the pitch and were shaping up as fearsome opponents. A win was absolutely crucial in order to keep their title ambitions alive.

A full house at the Etihad Stadium on the night of March 21st looked on as their team produced a fine performance, one already deserving of victory at half-time. A shot against the crossbar by Nasri and a one-on-one chance for Balotelli that goalkeeper Cech finger-tipped away from goal had been the most presentable chances.

However, following a corner in the 60th minute, Cahill shot for goal and opened the scoring via a deflection off the Toure brothers. Trailing by a goal, Mancini had to try to inject more power into the City attack, and so brought on Carlos Tévez – on his return to the City first team after the dispute – for De Jong and Dzeko for Silva.

During this spell of the match, an incident took place that went unnoticed at the time, but which would in the coming days go on to cause a real setback for the Citizens. In open play Kun received a knock on his right ankle, forcing him to leave the field of play to receive treatment.

At this point, he was sprayed with a local anaesthetic that caused him discomfort as soon as it was applied. Sergio felt that something was not right. Not only because they were spraying

his instep, which was not where he felt the pain, but also because the spray did not alleviate the pain and, quite the opposite, created a burning sensation on this area. He asked them to stop applying it and quickly returned to the field of play to continue playing the match.

His team was searching for an equaliser and this was no time to be elsewhere. And indeed the efforts of the Citizens, in front of a set of fans whose support did not let up for an instant, were rewarded with the victory, firstly through a penalty scored by Sergio in the 77th minute to temporarily draw level and then, four minutes from the end, through a subtle finish by Nasri after Tévez had done well to keep possession of the ball on the edge of the area and thread him through, to make it 2-1 right at the death.

Once back in the changing rooms, Sergio noticed signs of irritation on his instep which, after being treated, was bandaged up by the medical team in an effort to cure it more quickly. Nobody, including Sergio, could have imagined that this episode would lead to more serious consequences.

At this point there seemed to be no cause for concern and, what's more, everyone was more than satisfied by a victory that had not only denied United the opportunity to extend their advantage, but that had also left one of their supposedly stronger rivals trailing behind.

Both the management team and the squad were confident about taking home three points from the following fixtures against Stoke, at the tough fortress of the Britannia Stadium, and against Sunderland, at the Etihad. Those matches would precede a tricky visit to the Emirates to take on Arsenal.

However, what at first appeared to be a minor detail became

a problem of some magnitude. For over the following days the initial irritation on Sergio's instep, caused by the anaesthetic spray, became a serious burn. The scale of the problem was not so much due to the burn itself, but to the uncomfortable blisters that it caused and that prevented him from training and running as normal.

On the morning of Saturday, March 24th in the hours leading up to the match against Stoke City, at the nearby hotel where the Citizens were staying, Sergio had another check-up. Upon first examination, any hopes of an improvement faded away. The blisters remained, and showed no signs of healing definitively. Sergio's face said it all. He found it hard to believe that this could be happening.

He talked it over with his friend and assistant Rubén Domínguez who, on that morning, was with him at the hotel. Rubén had joined the team at Eleven GT, the company that took over the football division of IMG when the latter decided to relinquish this area of business. The representation and supervision of Sergio – as with all the other footballers from the same stable – remained the responsibility of Jorge Prat Gay, and with Hernán Reguera and Darío Bombini as points of reference, although it now carried the name of the new company.

Hernán himself, who had left England just after the match against Chelsea due to other commitments with Eleven GT and who was preparing to return immediately to Manchester to be with him, spent that day in permanent contact with Sergio and Rubén over the telephone, to keep up to speed with any developments about the injury.

Father Leo and mother Adriana offered their thoughts from Buenos Aires. All agreed that the most important thing was to

look after his body, not to risk aggravating the injury and to preserve himself for the title run-in. The doctors reached the same conclusion and advised him not to play. Sergio could not help but feel bad about not being with his team-mates on the field of play and worse still because of a situation that could be described, at the very least, as unusual.

Kun's discomfort was shared by the management team, who had to indicate that Sergio would not feature in the match due to 'a light foot injury'. But there was no time to dwell on it; only to raise the team's spirits and help them to get over the loss of another player, in addition to Kompany and Lescott who were both still injured.

Sergio remained with the team and followed the match from behind the substitutes' bench. From that vantage point in the Britannia, he watched on as Stoke sat back for the draw, their firm defence preventing City from creating any threatening openings. From the same position, he also witnessed the amazing goal scored by Peter Crouch after 15 minutes of the second half.

After a couple of headers following a long clearance played upfield by the goalkeeper Asmir Begovic, he dispatched a thunderous and precise volley from the edge of the left-hand side of City's penalty area that flew into Hart's top right-hand corner, leaving the goalkeeper powerless to stop it. Such a goal – considered afterwards to be one of the best of that season – dealt a heavy blow to City's ambitions, although they did at least draw level 15 minutes later via a Yaya Toure strike from the edge of the penalty area.

The celebrations on City's substitutes' bench were measured, as they had been looking to take more than a solitary point

away from the Britannia. This result ran the risk of United stretching their lead over City to three points, something they did with a victory in their next game.

According to their previous calculations, and supposing that United would win all of their matches until the end of the Premier League season, that three point gap was the maximum that City could allow. The reason for this was that the third from last fixture would see the two teams face each other at the Etihad, and a victory then would leave them equal on points. And if City let nothing else slip, their better goal difference would come into play and would win them the title.

However, the end of the month did not bring good news. Firstly there was the confirmation that Sergio, with his persistent blisters, would also not be able to take part in the match against Sunderland on Saturday, March 31st. Secondly, on that very day, City were losing 3-1 until the 84th minute.

Just as it seemed that defeat was inevitable, a bullet from Balotelli and then another from Kolarov salvaged a draw that, once more, seemed to be worth very little. After all, another United win left City five points behind which, for many people, looked very difficult to pull back. However, the seven matches still to go before the end of the championship left cause for hope.

At this point in time, Sergio's was one of the voices that spoke up to underline that all was not lost. In an interview that he gave to David Clayton from Manchester City's official magazine, Kun took it upon himself to make it clear that he was not ready to abandon the dream of City winning their first title in 44 years so easily.

"Why wait for next year if we can win it now?" he said without hesitation, in response to a question about whether, if the title

did not come that year, they could possibly win it the following season. It was not a platitude. He sincerely felt that it was still possible.

"To win trophies you have to fight, and we're not going to stop fighting. We believe that we can win the Premier League and, although it won't be easy, we're going to do everything possible to make it happen."

And he made a promise: "We'll fight to the end." It was a promise that he would honour to the letter a month-and-a-half later, and that would become one of the team's calling cards and an anthem adopted by all of City's fans.

Time for a revival

'This is the real status of my injury. I got back from practice today and it's not bothering me. If it all goes well, I'll be at the coach's disposal next Sunday. I wasn't able to speak earlier – many unfounded rumours were published, and there were simply too many to deny. This is the one and only true story: during the match against Chelsea, I injured my ankle and it was sprayed with a local anaesthetic that caused a burn on the upper part of my right foot. The injury worsened after a few days and when blisters appeared I was told I wouldn't play against Stoke and then against Sunderland.

'You can imagine how I felt, being out of playing condition when my team is trying to take the championship! It's always worse from the bench. Especially after I started receiving incredible rumours about how it all happened. I've always respected journalists and I know my life is very public. I'm willing to take

criticism even if I disagree with it, but I will not sit quietly while lies are being spread - even more so if they cast doubt upon my professionalism.

'This is a simple injury and not a plot of intrigue. I've just laid out all of the facts. It's hard to believe it happened while we are fighting for the title. But it is what it is and it's no time for moping. I just want to recover as soon as possible to go back to giving the team my best every game. I've said it before and I'll say it again - we are going to fight 'til the end. That's our collective goal and I'm fully committed to it.'

Sergio chose these words for a statement published on his website on April 4th, to express what he had been feeling during the two-and-a-half weeks that had gone by since the spray episode. They were days filled with anger and ups and downs, during which he was largely dedicated to recovering from the burn and consulting the best specialists.

He had been enormously upset by some absurd versions of events put forward by journalists who, fancifully interpreting what Mancini termed as a 'stupid injury', had called into question the reasons for his absence. Sergio's declaration about fighting 'til the end, which he reiterated in his statement, seemed to be a far-off dream when four days later City went down to a 1-0 defeat against Arsenal at the Emirates and dropped eight points behind Manchester United, who took full advantage of the circumstances by winning their match against QPR by two goals to nil.

The Citizens had welcomed back Lescott and Kompany for that match. But Silva had been ruled out by injury and Sergio came into the match without having kicked a ball in almost 20 days. And if that was not enough, shortly after kick-off Yaya

Toure had to leave the field of play after being badly fouled. Arsenal were not about to apologise and, four minutes from the end, a shot by the Spaniard Mikel Arteta produced the only goal of the game.

To cap off a bad day at the office, Mario Balotelli was sent off for two yellow cards. The outlook was bleak, and Manchester United's eight-point advantage constituted a lead that seemed impossible to claw back. However, in an unspoken oath, everyone at City vowed not to let their heads drop. The campaign initiated by the club, based around the word 'Together', perfectly summed up the general feeling. The squad, the coaching staff, the directors and the fans, against all the odds, wanted to keep the dream alive.

The first opportunity to cling on to that hope came three days after the defeat to Arsenal. On April 11th, City dazzled, just like on their very best nights, in a 4-0 win over West Brom, featuring a great display by Kun, who was on the mark twice with his fifth brace of the season, taking his tally to 19 strikes in the Premier League, as well as laying on the other goals for Tévez, who was back in the starting line-up, and Silva.

Their joy was complete when it was confirmed that United had lost by a goal to nil at Wigan, which reduced the deficit once more to five points with five games to go, including the two rivals going head-to-head at the Etihad Stadium on April 20th. The win revitalised a City team that once more looked as convincing as it had done at the start of the season, something which was clear for all to see in their visit to Norwich City, to whom they handed out an eye-catching 6-1 beating with a hat-trick by Tévez – the first a stunning strike from outside the area – a classy brace from Kun and another by Johnson.

With these latest two goals – his first, City's second, after a one-two with Carlos who returned the ball with a back heel for him to shoot into Ruddy's top right-hand corner; and his second, City's fourth, after a great run from the halfway line leaving opponents in his wake before finishing with a magnificently-placed shot that gave the home goalkeeper no chance – Sergio hit his sixth brace, reached 21 goals in the Premier League and 28 goals for City in all competitions, and in doing so overtook his highest tally of 27 from his previous five seasons in Europe.

That thrashing served to raise spirits, but it did not close the gap to United, whose unyielding response was a 4-0 win over Aston Villa. With four fixtures remaining, the difference between the two teams still stood at five points. It would require a slip-up from United for City, who could not afford to drop any points, to be able to catch them in the table. The first opportunity presented itself on Sunday, April 22nd.

Manchester United were first up, hosting Everton at Old Trafford. And until seven minutes from the end of the match, City's hopes for that day appeared to have been dashed. The Red Devils led emphatically by four goals to two, giving no cause for hope at all.

However, once more football displayed its capacity for the unpredictable, and in two minutes, Everton, with goals from Nikica Jelavic and Steven Pienaar, were back on level terms at 4-4, which is how it remained at the end. With this result confirmed, Manchester City's match against Wolves at Molineux Stadium presented them with a window of opportunity. And after an opening spell where they lacked accuracy in the final third, any doubts were dispelled after 27 minutes, when an

excellent assist from Gael Clichy was finished off by Kun.

That goal put the team on course for a victory sealed when Nasri touched in following great set-up play by Tévez. And so, with three games left of the Premier League season, City were only three points behind the leaders, with an opportunity to do what had appeared unimaginable only three weeks previously: defeat their old rivals, draw level on points in the league and take back the top spot on goal difference.

And Manchester City did exactly that on April 30th, with a display of their true class in one of the biggest matches of the season. Ferguson, perhaps conscious of having conceded four goals in the previous match and knowing that a draw suited his team, sent out a very conservative starting 11 with Rooney on his own up front. He flooded the midfield with Giggs, Scholes, Park, Carrick and Nani, but Welbeck, Young and Valencia – who had played a crucial role up until that point – remained on the bench.

Mancini, on the other hand, chose a more attacking team with Kun and Tévez up front, creative support coming from Nasri, Silva and Yaya Toure just behind them, and Barry as a holding midfielder.

In defence, Pablo Zabaleta and Gael Clichy – both in fine form – patrolled the flanks, perfectly complementing the centre-back pairing of Kompany and Lescott. And, apart from the first few minutes of the opening exchanges, the Citizens' superiority for the rest of the match was there for all to see.

United's defensive strategy paid off until just before the interval, when Vincent Kompany, displaying all of his power and energy, leaped to head in a corner kick taken by David Silva. The image of the captain out-jumping the opposing defenders,

as if propelled by his team's thirst for glory and the yearning desires of an entire stadium, served as the clearest of signs that this was their moment to rise up, to scale the highest peaks and to almost touch the sky with their hands. United could not react and the home team could even have increased their lead on the counter-attack through Sergio, Nasri and Yaya Toure.

The 1-0 victory was the cue for wild scenes among the nearly 50,000 fans who had squeezed into the Etihad, and who now sang 'City' in unison to the tune of 'Hey Jude' by the Beatles in the sweetest of extended celebrations: their team had beaten their old rivals, maintained their unbeaten home record, pulled level in the league table and taken top spot on goal difference.

After that evening, only two steps remained on the path ahead of them. By winning their next two matches, they would be crowned champions. Their dreams now seemed at their fingertips, and glory within reach. Glory that they would indeed taste sooner rather than later, but only after an unexpected, agonising and emotional climax.

The people's goal

Over the few days leading up to the penultimate match of the 2011/12 Premier League season, City's fans felt a kind of positive anxiety mixed with the anticipation of imminent celebrations.

A unique opportunity lay before their team, the chance to win the title for the first time in 44 years, and to restore the pride that had ebbed away in recent years in the face of their oldest rivals.

Sergio, although only cautiously, counted himself among those who remained in high spirits and, in his careful public appearances, he could sense an overwhelming confidence coming from those around him. It was a mood he had already picked up on when he and his friend Pablo Zabaleta went to a shirt signing at the City Store, for which members of the public had been waiting in line for up to six hours before the scheduled start time.

The images subsequently broadcast by City TV, the club's official television channel, spoke for themselves: the players signing shirt after shirt, teenagers crying at being so close to the players, and parents excited at seeing their children, many of whom were still babies, photographed next to those considered to be among the team's most cherished players.

Pablo had already been with the team for four years and was very well respected for his professionalism, his people skills, and his influence in the changing room. The final stretch of the season had seen him cement his place in the starting line-up and consolidate his strong bond with the fans.

For his part, Sergio – after only nine months at the club – was already a real fans' favourite and his shirt, the number 16, sold more than any other.

"Thanks to his personality, his charm and his very nature, Sergio settled in very well with everyone. We mustn't forget that it was his first year in the Premier League and in a new country. And in very little time, he showed that he was special. It really stands out how he settled in, how quickly he managed it, how crucial he was throughout the season and how he earned an important role within the group," explains Zabaleta, who offered great company and support for Kun from his very first

days in Manchester. Pablo and Sergio would have the privilege of not only taking part, but of having a central role in the grand climax to the league season.

The admiration felt towards Sergio by everyone at City was demonstrated when he was chosen as the Supporters' Player of the Year, an award presented to him at a ceremony on May 3rd during which Vincent Kompany also received a prize for his contribution to the team, David Silva for Players' Player of the Year, and the Spaniard Denis Suárez for Young Player of the Year. Kun's first goal in the 6-1 victory over Norwich was also voted as Goal of the Season.

Sergio had already been nominated by the English Professional Footballers' Association for the awards of Player of the Year and Young Player of the Year (for under 23s), and all of those grand distinctions filled him with pride. The recognition only served to give him more strength and to confirm that, in the short time since his arrival at City, he had managed to make a positive impact and had developed a unique chemistry, in particular with the fans.

He especially liked the respect that they showed the players. Something to which he could testify when walking through the streets of Manchester or in a shopping centre, where he was recognised by a great majority of people who, despite being so close to their idol, nevertheless did not pester him.

"I feel very, very settled in Manchester," says Sergio. "I'm not one of these people who goes on about the weather all the time – I'm not bothered about whether it's hot or cold or whatever – if anything, I do prefer it to be a bit cooler, which is good seeing that I am playing for Manchester City. I'm lucky that my partner is the same – she likes the cold, too and I like nothing

better than sitting at home and listening to the raindrops on the window.

"Manchester is very quiet and a calm place to live. You can go for a stroll or a walk without any problem. There's a real difference between me living here and when I was in Madrid and particularly Argentina. When I first got here no-one really knew me so I could wander around the Trafford Centre or the city centre. If I'm wearing a cap, I don't get recognised as much.

"Maybe now I'm more familiar to people because of THAT goal, but I can go out for a meal and people are very respectful and if they can see you eating, they leave you alone. If they are sure you have finished, they may politely ask if they can have a photo taken with you, but in Argentina I can't do anything. I can't go out to eat, or to the supermarket or out shopping – it's just car and home. If I go out, word gets around and a crowd will gather in minutes and that's it. If I'm eating in a restaurant, people will come up and take a picture without asking – one guy came up once and wanted a picture so I asked him to wait for a moment and he said, 'No, no – I've got to go!'

"The people in England are so polite and respectful and that's something that really strikes me. They are warm and friendly but they keep their distance out of respect. I live near Alderley Edge and there are a few footballers that live in that area, but if I see any of the United players, I don't speak to them! Or say 'Oh, I didn't see you!'

"I don't see many United players because they don't like to leave their houses these days! If I saw any Liverpool players, I'd be okay with them – I've always liked Liverpool, maybe because I used to play for Independiente who also played in red. As a kid, I wanted to be Michael Owen and when I saw him score

that goal for England against Argentina I thought 'you little sh**'! Even aged 10, I knew they couldn't allow him that much space. He was a terrific player at that time."

Accustomed to the more demonstrative character of the Argentinians and the Spaniards, Sergio understood that the passion for football was the same but that it was expressed in a different way. Even at matches, where their habits of cheering on both the players and the team were different.

One example that jumped out at him was the way that his name was chanted by the fans. Whereas in Argentina, Independiente's fans had sung 'Agüero, Agüero' and, in Spain, Atletico's fans had preferred 'Kun, Kun, Kun', City's fans had chosen to chant 'Sergio, Sergio' during his time in Manchester. He found it strange that they did not call him by his nickname 'Kun', even though it was written on his shirt. But he had no problem – and on the contrary, he enjoyed the originality of it – when the fans sang 'Sergio, Sergio' in their strange accent after a goal or a worthy piece of play. It was a chant that had rung out after each one of the 29 goals that he had scored up until then. But, more than the goals, what Sergio really wanted was to cap off his first season in England with the league title, an aim shared by everyone, and even more intently than ever with only two matches still to be played.

The first of those matches was at St James' Park away to Newcastle, a team fighting for Champions League qualification. That midday on Sunday, May 6th, 2012, saw an intense and hard-fought match, in which City were only able to emerge victorious in the last 20 minutes. The 2-0 win meant that triumph and ecstasy were entirely in City's hands. They would not have to rely on anyone else to become the new Premier

League champions. Although both of the Manchester teams were left on the same number of points – United had beaten Swansea 2-0 and would then have to visit Sunderland – City's goal difference was so superior that a win in their next match at the Etihad against QPR would allow them to get their hands on the biggest prize of all.

In Manchester, the seven days leading up to the grand finale of the 2011-12 Premier League season went by in a haze of pure passion. Emotions ran high, and indifference was nowhere to be found. Sergio was confident about what was to come. But he could not shake off a certain apprehension at seeing how the potential celebrations were being organised.

There was certainly nobody at City wanting to tempt fate, but the inevitable preparations – in the same situation, any club in the world would have been doing exactly the same – made him feel uncomfortable. He preferred not to pay them any attention and instead looked to pass the time until Sunday, outside of the training sessions, doing all he could to help himself to relax and, at the same time, to concentrate.

He reviewed his eating routine which included, on the advice of the City medical team, a meal of fish at least twice a week – a way to noticeably improve his already excellent metabolism, they had told him – he spent some of his time playing golf, a sport that he had started to learn in Spain and that he had played increasingly since arriving in England; and he had the pleasure of spending the rest of his free time with his family, as on Thursday, May 10th his parents Leo and Adriana had arrived from Buenos Aires, especially to attend the last match.

He also took the opportunity, on Friday, May 11th, to celebrate his mother's 42nd birthday with a simple dinner in a

Japanese restaurant, where they were also joined by Pablo Zabaleta, Hernán Reguera and Rubén Domínguez.

Although it was something that the players only felt on the inside, just 48 hours before the final match Sergio and Pablo's fellow diners could see that the two of them were starting to experience that strange mixed feeling of responsibility, nerves and a desire to get started once and for all.

"The birthday celebrations were an excuse for them to relax a bit more. Because they were already a bit nervous. They looked fine but it's also true that they were saying it wouldn't be easy. I had a lot of faith that they were going to win and I told them as much, that I'd travelled especially to see them lift the cup. Also that they had to maintain a good energy, think positively, be relaxed and enjoy it," says Adriana, who also remembers that she said to Pablo that it was going to go well for him on Sunday and that he would score a goal.

The day before the big match, at midday on Saturday after training, Sergio wanted to regale his family and attempt to delight them with another of his new skills that also helped him to relax: cooking. Although he did not have a very wide range of dishes to offer them, he went for the one that had already become his speciality: beef in a cream sauce with mashed potatoes, from a special recipe that some friends had taught him and to whose preparation he gave his complete attention, which involved him personally choosing and buying every last one of the ingredients used from the shops near to his house in Alderley Edge.

It was in that atmosphere – which was relaxed, despite the permanent feeling that he was on the eve of a very special event – that Kun passed the time until seven in the evening, when he

punctually joined the rest of the playing squad and coaching staff at the Hilton Hotel, City's usual base for home matches.

Although everything seemed to be happening as on so many other occasions that season, this time there was a different feeling. None of the players spoke about the thoughts and emotions they were experiencing. But it was obvious that the countdown had triggered very similar feelings of anxiety in all of them.

The pre-match team talk took place on Sunday in that same hotel and in the same atmosphere, but this time, in contrast to other occasions, the players did not ask any questions or raise specific queries. The silence that reigned throughout the meeting demonstrated that they were focused on the game, but it also underlined the weight of everything that was at stake.

On the bus journey to the Etihad, with Carlos Tévez and Mario Balotelli in the front seats as usual, they were able to firstly see a city that had come to a halt because of the match, and then the intense activity in the stadium's surroundings, where thousands of fans were preparing for a party that had been 44 years in coming.

The match was scheduled to start at three o'clock in the afternoon and, from much earlier on, the stadium had started to fill up. Nobody wanted to miss out on a minute of the build-up or the spectacle. Certainly not the Agüero clan who, with Leo leading the way, made every effort to arrive nice and early. It was something that they managed, despite the heavy road traffic and a few diversions on the motorway.

Leo, Giani, Ben, Hernán Reguera, Rubén Domínguez and Nuno Vasconcelos from Puma sat in the comfortable seats reserved for them in front of the hospitality box. Adriana, on

the other hand, preferred to remain inside, in the room behind, especially equipped with a large table and a 40-inch television screen, and to peer out at the match through the glass that separated her from all that was going on, in an attempt to control the nerves which by this time were starting to affect her.

In Buenos Aires, on an unusual Sunday, the rest of the family and thousands of fans supporting Kun and City settled down in their houses to await the start of the match, a scene repeated in each one of the 200 countries in which the match was being televised.

Down below, in the Etihad's home changing room, once changed and ready to head out to the field of play with his team-mates, Sergio kept telling himself that everything would turn out for the best and that he had to remain calm. He joined the line behind Silva and in front of Toure and, on the officials' signal, started to walk towards the end of the tunnel to firstly reach the sign with the inscription 'Pride in Battle' that always greets them before stepping out on to the pitch. Then, to a thunderous roar, they found themselves below a human sea of light blue, spreading to all four corners of the stadium.

Although he already had plenty of experience in this type of match, he could not shake off that tingling sensation which told him that a unique event was about to take place. He did not have stage fright, but rather the exact amount of nerves to ensure that he was entirely concentrated on what was to come. And before the match got started he rubbed his hands together, an almost subconscious ritual that he carried out before matches as a way of immersing himself in the battle ahead.

The first few times he touched the ball set him at ease but, as the minutes went by, he realised that, like the rest of his team,

he was somewhat constrained and found it difficult to create threatening opportunities. One such opening did emerge when, with the clock showing 15 minutes played, Tévez and Silva combined for the first clear chance. The Republic of Ireland goalkeeper Paddy Kenny kept out the Spaniard's shot easily, showing that he was not intimidated and that City would have to work a lot harder than that to unsettle him.

After 20 minutes of play, the news coming in from Sunderland injected more urgency into the Citizens' situation: Wayne Rooney had put United ahead and, with that result, victory became imperative. And with the first worried faces starting to appear, after 39 minutes Silva and Toure linked together down the right and the Ivorian – already feeling some discomfort in his right leg – played it to Zabaleta in the area for a fierce strike by the Argentine who, in the most important match, could finally celebrate his first goal of the season.

The 1-0 scoreline calmed everyone's nerves although, due to injury, Toure needed to be replaced by De Jong before the end of the first half. The interval served to placate even the most pessimistic of souls, and helped to capture the collective imagination of all those yearning for that championship. QPR had barely got over the halfway line, had not created a single opportunity and, a goal to the good, the home team were able to play more freely and put the contest to bed.

A sign of this came when, shortly after the restart, Kun managed to connect with a ball in by Gael Clichy, and Kenny just about managed to avert the danger. But it proved to be just an illusion.

Immediately afterwards, an unfortunate lapse in City's defence caused the unthinkable to happen. The Frenchman

Djibril Cisse took advantage of a ball that deflected backwards off the head of Lescott, and beat Hart with a fierce shot. Three minutes had passed since the break, and City were back at square one.

Given the urgency of their situation, City's control over the game became even more suffocating, but so did the tension. Until, after 54 minutes, an incident took place that would be key to their aspirations. It all started when QPR's hot-headed captain Joey Barton elbowed Tévez, for which Mike Dean rightly showed him the red card. Far from calming down, Barton carried on protesting and, in the ensuing chaos before leaving the field of play, kicked out at Kun and left him sprawled out on the turf, seemingly in pain.

The match was held up for several minutes until the incident was brought under control. The episode was to have a great influence on the final result of the match. Not because QPR would have to play the rest of the game with 10 men following Barton's red card, but because the minutes lost during that commotion would be added on as stoppage time, a period which would produce an incident that would enter the collective consciousness as one of the most exciting moments in modern football.

What immediately followed the game's resumption went directly against what was expected. City could not make their one-man advantage count and, instead, QPR went ahead. After 66 minutes, a perfect counter-attack by the team managed by Mark Hughes – ironically the man who had started the whole process off as City's manager in 2008 – led to the Scot Jamie Mackie heading in a perfect cross by Frenchman Armand Traoré. If the equaliser had led to silence and surprise, QPR's

second goal sparked overt gestures of desperation all around the Etihad. A heavy feeling of unease and fear overcame everyone. On and off the field. The unthinkable was happening, and it was absolutely imperative for City to turn things round.

Mancini, showing clear displeasure after QPR's goal, brought on Dzeko for Barry and then Balotelli for Tévez. And goalkeeper Kenny, who had already kept out a goal-bound header from Carlos, shone again as he firstly deflected away a shot by Dzeko following Kun's low cross and then saved another powerful header, this time by Balotelli. At that stage, Kun's initial hope that his team could cancel out the deficit and then go for the victory seemed increasingly distant. And what he was going through was reflected back to him on the faces of the rest of his team-mates. They had almost completely frozen after going behind, and they could not find the required response.

They were controlling the game, they had possession of the ball, but they could not get close enough to the opposition goal. And when they did, each attack was repelled by their opponents – who were sat back in their own area – or by the goalkeeper who, up to that point, was looking like man of the match. Sergio could not believe what was happening. He looked at the clock after 75 minutes and told himself that it was 'now or never', that any later and it would be almost impossible. He did the same after 80 minutes, and after 85 minutes. But the moment never arrived. He watched as the minutes ticked by, and the championship slipped through their grasp.

Their lack of response was in direct correlation with the disquiet that could be sensed both on and off the field of play, where distraught faces, disillusionment and tears were already a common sight. The less time that remained, the less strength

they had. Something similar was happening up in the stands where, with the 90 minutes up and despite the five minutes of stoppage time added on by referee Mike Dean, many fans started to leave their seats and take refuge in the exits, as if in an attempt not to witness the collective despair, looking to retreat into their own anguish without being prevented from expressing all of their pain by the gazes of others.

Up in the box, Kun's family, Hernán and Rubén were a bag of nerves, experiencing the same sensations as all those other anguished City fans, with their heads in their hands, searching for an explanation that nobody could find. And all of them were looking inside the box where Adriana – in a display of her immense faith, with her medallion of Our Lady of Guadeloupe in hand – was kneeling down and praying for the Virgin to illuminate the team, to put on her robe and, even with so little time remaining until the final whistle, to find a way for the miracle to take place.

Down on the turf below, Mancini, on the edge of the touchline, went from crouching down and holding his head to rising up and rallying his players who, although weary, were searching for the strike that would at least allow them the chance to go for glory and apply the coup de grace. And after 91 minutes and 13 seconds, following a touch from Silva to Zabaleta that led to a corner from the right taken by the Spaniard himself, the Bosnian Edin Dzeko rose above the defence to powerfully head in and make it 2-2. The ball flew in with such power that it hit the back of the net and bounced back towards the goal line.

Kun, who had been standing on the line hoping for a rebound, headed towards the ball and the ball towards him, as if they knew that together the miracle was possible. He instinctively

caught the ball and, with it in his hands, ran and placed it on the halfway line, all the while precisely calculating that there were three minutes remaining and that the team could still create one or two more chances to score.

The first one, a Nasri cross that was cleared by the defence, used up the first of those remaining minutes. At the same time, United closed out their victory and were waiting expectantly and confidently on the pitch for the result from the Etihad to come through.

The clock was ticking louder and louder, counting down to glory for one team and misery for the other. There were only 120 seconds left and QPR were in possession of the ball, with a throw-in on the right in City's half. And Sergio was still experiencing an internal dialogue − without understanding where it was coming from − through which he told himself that he would still have a chance, that he would play a one-two and get on the end of it.

From the throw-in, Lescott won the ball back with a header that fell to the feet of De Jong. Ninety-three minutes and four seconds had been played. The Dutchman, unchallenged by the opposition, took eight seconds to cross the halfway line. Sergio, who had spent practically the entire match fruitlessly prowling around the penalty box, decisively dropped away from the area and showed for a pass from his team-mate. In only seven seconds, he would go on to change history.

After 93 minutes and 13 seconds he received the ball from the Dutchman, feinted away from his defender, initiated a one-two with Balotelli with the outside of his right foot, and headed for the return pass. The Italian received the ball with his back to goal on the edge of the area after 93 minutes and 16 seconds,

held onto it despite falling down and, when already on the floor, dragged the ball on with his right foot just as Kun was bursting at full speed into the area between two defenders. After 93 minutes and 18 seconds, Sergio received the ball and, with a great bit of skill, opened up his right foot to touch the ball past Taye Taiwo who, in a desperate attempt to stop him, launched himself to the ground and caught Kun's standing foot.

Never for a moment thinking of going down – although it was an obvious penalty – Sergio continued and, a metre away from the six-yard box, struck a shot after 93 minutes and 20 seconds that flew just inside Kenny's left upright and set off an explosion of emotion, of the sort that only football can produce, that spread like wildfire in every direction.

It was the same emotion that propelled Kun on as he continued running – as if floating on air, just like he had done after that other glorious injury-time winner for the first championship he won with the Independiente *novena* team some 10 years previously when he was only 13 years of age – as he flew off towards the right-hand side of the pitch, took off his shirt, held it in his right hand and started to swing it round and round, as if to frighten off the dark spirits that had tried to make their presence felt at the Eithad.

The goal had all of those present joining each other in a communion of emotion, tears and release, the likes of which had never been seen before in a Premier League finale. Including his family in the box, who were cheering to the rafters at that moment. Even Adriana, who only fully realised what was happening when she saw her son swinging his shirt in the air, which merely served to strengthen her faith even more. And Leo, who let the overwhelming pride that he felt for his son – 'my *pibe*' as

he likes to call him – show by way of unintentional but heartfelt tears. And Benjamín, trying to understand from his mum what Daddy had just done. And all of them huddled together in a celebration that spread outwards and at the same time fed back off the collective wave of feeling.

With Hernán and Rubén bearing witness to Liam Gallagher, the former Oasis singer and City fan, as he burst into the box to regale them with a cry of 'Sergio is my f***ing hero', a unique contribution to celebrations that allowed such over-exuberance. At the same moment, still screaming in celebration and wired with powerful emotion, Sergio started to be caught by team-mates who, in the same state of euphoria, managed to cut him off beside the field of play.

First came Edin Dzeko, scorer of the equalising goal that sparked off the revival. Then Mario Balotelli, who seconds before had for once been more Super Mario than Mad Mario. And after them the 'magician' Silva, De Jong, Kompany and Nasri who all threw themselves onto him for a type of cel-ebration that is without equal: that of one's own team-mates expressing their gratitude.

Barely able to breathe, and still bewildered, he was able to recognise their voices. He heard the captain Kompany and the Dutchman De Jong tell him in English 'thank you very much', 'I love you, Kun'; Balotelli in Italian and with an Argentinian accent, 'mate, mate, thanks'; the Frenchman Nasri in Spanish 'I love you, Kun'… All of them forming a pile of bodies that was laying to rest 44 years of frustrations, and opening the doors to a new mystical dawn, one that had only been made possible by such a dramatic climax.

And right there in amongst all of them, one of the pillars of

the structure, was Kun who – at only 23 years of age – capped off a remarkable season with the unanimous and wholehearted appreciation of all those around him.

Because there and then – more than 11,000 kilometres away from the *potreros* where he was born – inspiration, talent and a thirst for success had come together to form a perfect storm and create that most wonderful thing: that which is neither thought up nor planned but rather, through pure instinct, emerges spontaneously and takes shape only at the moment when a legend is born in the hearts of the people.

And a moment like that needs an exact amount of time, in this case only seven seconds, to take its place in history.

A Perfect Jigsaw

"People have commented that I never try to con the referee by feigning injury and why, when so many in today's game do dive and fool the officials, I don't do the same. There are moments when I am trying to use a burst of pace and maybe skip past two or three challenges and it's almost inevitable I will come up against a tackle or physical contact that would present the opportunity to tumble. But that's not how I play or want to play," reveals Sergio.

"It could come from my childhood when I used to play on the open ground that surrounded my family home where the pitch was uneven and bumpy and you had to learn to adjust your balance and keep going even when it was difficult to stay on your feet. Plus there were no referees to give you a free-

kick! There was no point in diving because the game would just continue.

"It's also a pride thing – if a defender catches me, I don't want to roll on the ground, just carry on and try and keep the run towards goal going. I've had friends and family ask me after certain games, 'Why didn't you go down? You would have won a penalty!' But the truth is, I wouldn't know where to start! I wouldn't know how to dive and think I would be rubbish at it and get booked if I even tried. The truth is, it's not in my nature and I can't and won't do it. I'd rather take my chances, carry on with my run and see if I can score or make a goal for a team-mate.

"I will always look back to that title-winning goal against QPR when I was challenged as I went past the last man – if I had been of a mind to dive, I could easily have gone down and maybe history would have been different. Maybe the ref wouldn't have given a penalty or maybe it would have been missed. No, I'll take my chances and always try and stay on my feet."

He was still in a daze when referee Mike Dean brought the game to an end. He saw Pablo Zabaleta approaching and they embraced each other for what seemed an eternity. Micah Richards joined them, thanking him for the goal, as did Gael Clichy, and this tightly packed huddle of bodies remained firm as Mario Balotelli and other team-mates from the bench began leaping on top of them. He could then make out the crowds of supporters who began streaming down from the stands to stage an unprecedented pitch invasion, which the stewards were unable to prevent, not that they could have imagined or foreseen such an explosion of people.

Men, women and children of all ages came up to him to touch, kiss or simply be close to the person who had just worked a miracle that had been unthinkable only a few moments earlier. He could hear a growing chorus of 'thank you' and 'I love you'.

Each one of the players was consumed by this surge of mass adoration, and were trying to find their way out of the sea of bodies as best they could. And so it was, in this state of shock, that he was 'rescued' by club stewards who then managed to escort him back to the dressing room.

City TV's famous 'Tunnel Cam', a static camera in the tunnel mounted just where the players pass on their way to and from the Etihad pitch, was able to show unstaged, authentic images that captured him at that special moment. This was Kun laid bare, his very soul on display, with a hazy expression on his face, full of emotion in his heart, yet still unaware of the significance of his deed. For it had triggered a whole series of reactions not only at the Etihad, not just in Manchester, in England or even throughout Europe, but also in Buenos Aires, in Argentina, in South America and all over the rest of the world.

Some were incredible, others were amusing and dramatic, and the majority of them were united by an unbridled joy triggered by that remarkable climax.

Neither during the celebrations in the dressing room with his team-mates nor during the title presentation out on the pitch did it really sink in for Sergio or did he end up understanding the magnitude of what he had achieved. Not even when he lifted the trophy while wrapped in an Argentinian flag emblazoned with the colours of his beloved Independiente, which his dad had brought over especially from Buenos Aires. Or even while he was speaking to the press and telling them how he was

really feeling ("I don't know what it was like, how I hit it, or where I got the strength from for that one last attack").

He was immensely happy and was enjoying the moment but he still felt like he was in a cloud, almost as if it were someone else experiencing all of this in his place. He needed a few hours to work out everything that had happened, and to take it all in. His first chance to do so came after the trophy presentation as he rejoined his family and, with a certain amazement, heard them relate one by one the full story of how their hearts had been racing over the last few minutes of the game.

Listening to his nearest and dearest describing just what they had gone through during those few minutes helped Kun begin to understand the wide range of emotions that he had engendered in so many people. He continued to complete the picture that night at the celebration gala dinner City had organised for the occasion. And again the following day, Monday, May 14th, during the open top bus procession that carried the squad of players and coaching staff through the streets of Manchester in a championship victory parade thronged by 150,000 people.

With every passing hour, the comprehension of what had happened slowly dawned on him. The same happened when his brothers back in Argentina told him about how excited they had been and how shouts celebrating the goal had been heard in the streets of Buenos Aires, in response to the live television coverage which had received very high viewing figures. And again when he was sent the front pages from the main Argentinian newspapers which featured headlines like 'Sir Kun', 'Super-héroe', 'Illustrious Citizen Agüero', 'Kun is now a legend', 'The era of Kun', 'King Kun', 'City of Agüero' and which spoke of the great season he had enjoyed in his first Premier League

campaign, with 30 goals and eight assists, now crowned by a Hollywood ending.

Any final missing pieces of the jigsaw were finally put into place 48 hours later, when, in the intimacy of his own home, he began to look back at the videos of the epic victory – something that everyone had quite rightly insisted he should do. Those images conveyed to him exactly what had happened both on and off the field, and enabled him to catch up on what he had not seen on the day.

With City's own carefully positioned cameras, he could see for himself the madness that ensued on the City bench after the goal, with Mancini first clinging on to his assistant Brian Kidd before sprinting off in a circle and ending up in the arms of David Platt and the rest of the coaching staff. And also a magnificent close-up of Joe Hart which showed that strange yet simultaneously beautiful solitude of the goalkeeper in his area, with no-one close by to celebrate with, but still taking huge joy from running and screaming with his arms outstretched, until he found Gael Clichy and they hugged each other without wanting to let go, both so full of emotion.

There were images of the crowd before and after the goal, with the transformation from despondency and anxiety to an explosion of tears of joy and excitement, and the resultant outpouring of emotion that created thousands of faces he felt mirrored his own. Then there was the shock and anguish of title rivals United, still out on the field of play after their final whistle, when they heard that City had scored the winning goal to bring them level in the league table on 89 points, but knowing that their goal difference – inferior by eight – meant they would be robbed of their status as champions by their 'noisy neigh-

bours', who right at that moment were noisier than ever.

He saw the best of the crazy celebrations on all the fan videos uploaded to YouTube and the various social media networks, as people reacted to the winning goal in pubs and at home.

Age did not matter as young and old alike did laps of honour around their front room or jumped on tables or bars as part of celebrations that would go on for many a long hour.

He saw television presenters and pundits who he did not recognise – powerless to keep a lid on the emotions that this amazing finale had stirred in them – in a frenzy live on camera, in a way that he had never seen before.

He listened to commentaries on the goal in different tongues from all around the world, each delivered with equal passion, confirming to him that although the languages were different, football itself transcends them all.

He browsed through the pictures taken by Manchester City's star photographer, Sharon Latham – she had skilfully taken a snapshot of events and emotions that happen only once in a lifetime.

In order to finally get back down to earth, he watched the highlights of the game and saw the effort put in by all his team-mates, and said to himself that they were indeed the worthy champions. He watched Dzeko scoring his fine goal to make it all square, and the way Balotelli fought for the ball until the final seconds in order to set up the winning goal. And he felt that it was about everyone, both those on and off the field. And right there, as he watched the goal again in slow motion, he felt – in every sense of the word – that something had been completed. Like one piece that fits perfectly into another, he understood that those seven wonderful seconds that the final move for

the goal had taken had happened not just by coincidence, but that they were the moment when all those years of living and breathing football finally, perfectly, came together.

He saw himself a few minutes earlier when he had said to himself that 'he would still get a chance, that he would play a one-two and get on the end of it', and he took strength from having been able to spontaneously trust in his own intuition and ability, in such an extreme situation, even when it could have all gone wrong.

He saw the commitment that he was able to show at that instant and he understood that the strength – "I don't know where I got it from" – actually came from his parents' example, from his family who had fought tooth and nail for him in the very worst of conditions.

He could not help but be amazed when he saw himself dropping deeper out of the area to look for the ball that De Jong was carrying forward, and he recalled the words of Tojo, his coach from the Argentinian national youth sides, who would tell him "once your midfielders have got hold of the ball you simply have to make a move to go looking for it. You have to look if anyone is coming with you to be able to receive the pass or, if not, just halt your run and then go again, and when you have two or three on you it's easier to take a touch and then look to play a one-two…"

And he saw himself playing that one-two with Balotelli, with the outside of his boot, controlling the ball just like he had learned to do back on the *potreros* where he lived, out of necessity, as the fruit from the eucalyptus trees scattered on the ground sometimes gave the ball a mind of its own.

He saw himself bursting into the box and he remembered

some of the other coaches from his youth team days, like Jorge Rodríguez who would always insist to anyone who would listen that "you have to keep Kun on the pitch for the entire 90 minutes as he is a player who can win you the game at any moment"; or like Cacho Barreiro, who instilled in him that chances on goal were there to be taken.

And he watched himself scoring, putting away the chance that he had carved out so well for himself.

Just then he paused the highlights and began to think back on his time at Independiente, his debut aged 15 in the Primera División, his five years at *Atléti* and the experience he had gained there.

He remembered his arrival at Manchester City and how he wanted to keep improving his game, insisting to himself on concentrating for the full 90 minutes, and running for the whole game, as demanded by such a competitive league like the Premier League.

So yes, he pressed play and continued watching. He saw himself swinging his shirt above his head. He was touched by the elation of his team-mates, the widespread delirium, everyone's tears and, more than ever, he felt like he was complete. Because of those seven unforgettable seconds which thoroughly summed up who he was and where he had come from, but which also drove him forwards towards the future.

He already knew that that final game was only a starting point. A platform for even greater challenges. To go all out for more. To continue feeding his own passion and that of everyone else. By using his greatest weapons, unique only to him, the ones he knows best. The ones that quite simply allow him to play football for his own enjoyment and excitement and to be able

to fill other people with those same emotions. The times ahead would prove this to be exactly the case.

The deadliest striker

'Over time we're going to gradually realise the importance of what we achieved. I think that breaking a run of 44 years without winning the league title is the beginning of a new era for City. I say it modestly but we can do it, because the nicest thing about winning it this time is feeling like we can aim to win more trophies and that this is just a beginning.'

It was a much calmer, but no less enthusiastic Sergio who addressed his supporters a few days later with these prophetic words. He sent them out via his Twitter account, which had grown substantially since his arrival at Manchester City.

To be precise, shortly after joining the Citizens he hit one million followers. One year down the line, and coinciding with the Premier League triumph, he managed to double that figure, becoming the first Argentine to attract more than two million followers on Twitter.

Kun's impact on the world of social media was a reflection of his permanent presence on the different networks, where he would communicate on an ongoing basis with the people who he was connected to, and send almost daily updates about his activities.

It was also thanks to his more global exposure as a result of the extended reach of Manchester City and the Premier League to the furthest corners of the world as well as, of course, his own growth and development as a footballer.

This trend was not about to be reversed. Quite the opposite, as his number of Twitter followers continued to climb until, in 2014, it surpassed the seven million mark, putting him on the podium for Premier League players with most followers alongside Wayne Rooney and Mesut Ozil, as well as featuring in the worldwide list of the top 10 footballers.

Similar was to happen on Facebook, where he would also pass the figure of eight million followers. He enjoys a wide popularity on Instagram as well, commanding one million subscribers in the photo-sharing network.

The significance of winning the league title and the key role he had played in that success really hit Sergio upon his return to Argentina, where his popularity had shot up. The footage of his goal against QPR was still getting a lot of airtime on television stations, and sports programmes repeatedly requested the chance to speak with him when he reported for international duty with national team coach Alejandro Sabella.

The latest round of qualifiers for Brazil 2014 was coming up and the *Albiceleste* had a tough fixture to play against Ecuador. Fate decreed that the game would be played on June 2nd, the day of Kun's 24th birthday. He could not have asked for a better birthday present. The national team won 4-0 with Sergio scoring one of the goals, as they moved a step closer in pursuit of their eagerly awaited qualification for the World Cup. A quiet celebration at his parents' home rounded off a period of festivities spent in his country and close to his loved-ones.

In spite of so much success, his hard-earned holidays would have to be put on hold once more. Kun was in the national team squad due to play against Brazil in a friendly in the United States. Neither side disappointed in a superb game that

Argentina won by the odd goal in seven, with Messi netting a hat-trick.

Before joining up with City for their pre-season training in Austria, Kun spent some time in Buenos Aires and was presented with a commemorative plaque prior to an Independiente home game, where he was given a big ovation by the crowd in a packed Libertadores de América stadium. He also managed to fulfil his wish to go back to the Villa Domínico training centre, where he started out as a young footballer with *El Rojo*, and pay a visit to the youngsters from the various youth teams there, who welcomed him like a living legend and listened attentively to his every word.

"It isn't easy to make it as a professional footballer. I know that you all dream about playing in the Primera División, just like I did when I was here. For that to happen you have to work really hard and make huge sacrifices. Do not give up your dreams, and work twice as hard to achieve them," advised Kun who, while receiving a warm round of applause from the kids who were staring at him in awe, spotted that there was a picture on the wall behind him of his friend, Emiliano Molina, who had died some years earlier in an accident.

In silence, he touched the image with his hand and then in turn kissed it, in a gesture of acknowledgement and remembrance. Reflecting on the tour of the training facility and those pitches where, not so long ago, he had given of his best. Being close to so many hopes and dreams, just like the ones he had enjoyed; spending a few hours in the place where his brothers Mauricio and Gastón were also trying to make a name for themselves in the world of football. It all led him to appreciate even more where he had got to in life, and to make an even

greater effort to keep striving for further successes.

Being back so close to his roots had fuelled him with renewed motivation and it was with that positive outlook that he began his pre-season with Manchester City in the town of Seefeld, in Austria, the location chosen for the squad to get back into shape. The town is nestled in an exceptional winter sports domain, and its three thousand or so residents offered up a special welcome to the Premier League champions and clearly enjoyed having them as guests. The same went for the players and coaching staff, who appreciated both the locals' displays of affection and the respect with which they were treated.

Sergio, along with a number of his team-mates, took advantage of such freedom by cycling on a daily basis from the hotel where they were staying to the training facility. Their two-week stay there featured gym work in the morning, as well as tactical work out on the pitch. Friendly games against Al Hilal, Dynamo Dresden, Besiktas, Arsenal and Malaysia rounded off the ideal preparations in July 2012 before facing up to the challenge of the new Premier League season and, firstly, the Community Shield against Chelsea.

Even though the arrival of any new signings had been put back to nearly the end of the transfer window, City – with Kun in the starting 11 – managed to beat Chelsea on August 12th by three goals to two, and in doing so picked up another trophy.

Before the Premier League 2012/13 season got underway, there was one more trip away with Argentina, this time to Germany for a friendly game in which they defeated the home side by three goals to one, leaving Kun in a very good place ahead of the season opener against Southampton at the Etihad.

With another statement of intent reflecting his desire to keep

on winning trophies, Sergio had made it quite clear, in an interview for his official website, that there was to be no resting on any laurels. That was how the crowd saw things too as they poured into the Etihad on August 19th for the first match of the season and greeted the champions with a reception befitting of their status. They welcomed Kun too on his return to the site of his unforgettable feat, achieved just a few months earlier, and he trembled at the ovation received in acknowledgement of it.

He felt 100 per cent both physically and mentally, to go for it all again, only this time to aim even higher. So it was with this mindset that he proudly strode out onto the field of play with his team, and with his little boy Benjamín holding his hand.

But just seven minutes into the game, as he turned with the ball in the middle of the park and ran powerfully towards the opposition goal, the unexpected happened. Sergio was caught sharply on his right knee after a tackle by Nathaniel Clyne which left him lying on the floor looking in some discomfort. The sight of Kun holding his knee with both hands indicated that the injury might be serious. He was nevertheless able to walk off the field by himself but then, as a precaution, he lay down on the sidelines and, after an initial assessment, was taken away on a stretcher for a more detailed examination. And, while on the field City turned around a 2-1 deficit to win the game 3-2. The news coming from the dressing room provided some respite but was disappointing nonetheless. Kun himself gave the update.

"The tests I've had have confirmed that the injury is not serious but simply a bad knock on the knee. Tomorrow the medical staff will take another look at it to see how long my rehab will take. I cannot thank everyone enough for all their concern and I'd say to you that all these good wishes will ensure

a speedy recovery. I also want to congratulate my team-mates for the fight they showed in turning the result around. Right now more than ever, COME ON CITY!!"

Further examinations confirmed the original diagnosis. It was not a serious injury but he would be out of action for at least a month. Although this period of absence was sizeable, given the initial fears it could only be good news. Roberto Mancini revealed: "We were very worried when the injury happened because we thought he could have been out for six months or even longer, which would have been very bad news. So this latest news that the injury is not serious is a relief for everyone."

Sergio began his rehab work immediately. Both at Carrington and at home, he followed the programme of exercises outlined by the physios in order to be able to return within the time stated and in the best possible shape.

At the end of August, City discovered their fate in the draw for the group stage of the Champions League. The Citizens were once again drawn in what the press christened the 'Group of Death', along with three other league winners from their respective countries: Real Madrid from Spain, Borussia Dortmund from Germany and Ajax from The Netherlands.

"Big opponents for a big tournament," said Sergio at the time, convinced that to keep growing as a team you needed to play against the best, although he recognised how tough it would be facing such difficult opposition. As a team still maturing, City's lack of experience in Europe would be key as that season's Champions League tournament unfolded.

Sergio's rehab was in full swing at the beginning of September 2012, the next FIFA date for international fixtures which saw Argentina facing Peru and Paraguay in the World Cup qualify-

ing tournament. A lightning visit to Buenos Aires, where he was checked over by the national team's doctors and consequently ruled out of those games (a 3-1 victory against Paraguay and a 1-1 draw against Peru), was the forerunner to his return to full training with the rest of the squad at Carrington.

He did not make the squad for the game against Stoke at the Britannia Stadium, which City drew 1-1 with a goal from debutant Javi García, one of that summer's new arrivals along with Jack Rodwell, Maicon and Matija Nastasic.

However, once fit, Roberto Mancini did call him into the squad for their first game in the 'Group of Death' against Real Madrid at the Santiago Bernabéu. Having not played since his injury, Sergio had to settle for watching from the bench as City did enough to warrant the headlines and the victory, but were in the end resigned to defeat as Madrid twice came back from behind to ultimately prevail by three goals to two.

That result in Madrid set the tone for the rest of City's campaign in Europe's premier competition. What was to follow (an agonising draw with Dortmund at the Etihad, a 3-1 defeat in Amsterdam against Ajax, a 2-2 draw against the Dutch side and another 1-1 draw with Madrid, both at home, and a 1-0 defeat in Dortmund) left the team wounded, having suffered the additional blow of finishing bottom of the group and not even qualifying for the Europa League.

Sergio could not hide his concern at the poor run of results, and in particular felt like he owed something to the supporters, who had invested much hope in the team.

"It hurt a lot, because we were hopeful of doing well, but once again we were drawn in a very difficult group. None other than the champions of Spain, Holland and Germany, and at

that level it is a fine line between winning and losing. It is no use thinking that we were very close to starting off with a great result in the Bernabéu and if this or that had happened it would have been a different story. Football is like that and it all counts as experience. The Champions League is unfinished business for us and I'm sure that in the future things will go better," was his analysis of the situation although, at the same time and looking beyond those results in isolation, he wanted to put City up where they deserved to be.

"Did we fall short of people's expectations? I think that everyone has the right to their own opinion. That's football and always will be. It's fine for people to expect more from us. But what I do think is that sometimes people do not give this team enough credit for everything it has done and continues to do. We are the current Premier League champions and we won the title fair and square. We did it because we never gave up, even when many people said that United were too far ahead to be caught. We were the best team throughout the entire season. It is the same when people devalue us by saying the club has bought success. As if the rest of the clubs would not have done the same.

"You only have to look at what happened in last summer's transfer window. Because as far as I am aware, Barcelona is one of the few teams that currently has a good number of players who have come through the youth set-up. No one else has. Everything needs to be put into context."

Sergio's line of thought was consistent with a typical need to respond to an observation, becoming more widespread among experts on the game, that City were content 'to wave the chequebook' without giving them the credit or recognition

they deserved and being unaware of their history in the English game and their loyal fan base.

One thing was for certain: even though the team had shown some inconsistent form in the second half of 2012, they still retained the ambition and desire to defend their title. And this was in spite of having sustained serious injuries to key players which had left them lagging behind in the domestic league table.

City ended the year with 12 league victories, six draws and two defeats, one of those a heartbreaking loss at the Etihad Stadium against Manchester United by three goals to two, City having temporarily clawed back a two-goal deficit before seeing Van Persie score an injury time winner.

That record saw them finish the year in second place, seven points behind their biggest rivals, who topped the Premier League at that point. That gap in the league table was not exactly what they had planned, and it meant that Kun was unable to savour, as he would have liked, finding out in November 2012 that he had become the top flight's deadliest striker in terms of goals scored per minutes on the pitch, ahead of legends such as Thierry Henry (third), Ruud Van Nistelrooy (fifth) and Alan Shearer (eighth place).

In fact Sergio headed up the All-Time Top Ten with 28 goals in 3,116 minutes at a rate of a goal every 111.3 minutes.

Of those still in action, he was ahead of Javier Hernández (second), Edin Dzeko (fourth), Robin Van Persie (sixth), Demba Ba (ninth) and Mario Balotelli (10th place), as well as his fellow countryman, the now retired Hernán Crespo (seventh place).

Nevertheless, having his goal against QPR chosen as one of FIFA's 12 'moments of the year' and receiving the accolades

while representing City alongside Vincent Kompany at the BBC Sports Personality Awards gala gave him reasons to be cheerful during a difficult end to his year. For he was also going through a painful period in his personal life as a result of his separation from Gianinna Maradona, which had been initiated during the previous six months.

Having always chosen to keep this matter strictly in the private domain, Sergio himself now explained his feelings on the subject in an interview with the Buenos Aires newspaper *Olé* in early 2013.

"In these last few months I have been trying to settle in to a new period in my life since my separation. It is not easy because Gianinna and I enjoyed some very intense years together with some profound experiences.

"During that time we grew as people and, above all, we had Ben, the fruit of our love and a true blessing. That is the tough part of it for me. Because Ben is in Buenos Aires and for obvious reasons I am in Manchester."

Sergio was quite categorical when asked if this situation was having an effect on any other aspects of his life.

"I'm trying for it not to, because you aim to be as professional as possible. I don't think it has affected my performances on the field, if that is what you are referring to. But being far away from your son is not easy. It is impossible not to miss Ben," Kun explained, making it clear that he preferred not to expand upon the subject ("out of the respect we have for each other and everything we experienced together, it has to remain private") and so avoid the over-exposure in the media that the separation had generated in Argentina.

The second season was always going to be a difficult one on

the pitch after the emotion of the previous campaign, not just for Sergio, but for all of his team-mates.

"I think we caught a lot of teams by surprise in our title-winning season because nobody was that aware of us or what we were capable of," explains Sergio. "We'd brought in three or four new players and it changed the way we played, so when teams came to the Etihad to attack, they usually went away having been comfortably beaten. This was a new City with a different way of playing and nobody expected us to score as many goals as we did.

"Towards the back end of 2011/12, we found the goals dried up a little at home because teams were coming to the Etihad, keeping things tight and making things difficult for us. That continued into the 2012/13 campaign when teams knew that probably the only way to get something – or avoid a heavy loss – was to defend in numbers and it could be frustrating at times. We'd maybe become a little too predictable in our ways, though I don't mean that in a negative way. It was like meeting old friends every week who knew your habits, strengths and weaknesses. By sitting back and waiting for us to come at them, it prevented us counter-attacking which had become a large part of how we played.

"On the road we were unpredictable and it seemed whenever we won, United won and whenever we dropped points, United still won. They were a model of consistency and were just doing enough, winning games by a goal or two and not really conceding many and our success had perhaps driven them on even more.

"Sometimes it's just difficult to follow a season like we'd had with the adrenaline rush on the final day and I maintain we had

a little bit of a mental hangover. We dropped too many points at the start of the season and I think that was what really cost us in the end and we just couldn't make up the deficit at the top.

"At least we still had a chance of winning some silverware because our form in the FA Cup had been good and we'd reached the semi-final where we played Chelsea. Wembley is such a beautiful stadium to play football in, especially against one of our biggest rivals. Things went well for us on the day and I was happy to score a rare headed goal in a 2-1 win – for a moment, I was Peter Crouch! So while we were resigned to being runners up in the league, we had the FA Cup final to look forward to and the possibility of another trophy.

"Everyone was making us the big favourites to win the game because Wigan Athletic were in danger of relegation, but we respected Wigan and, as I always say, in football anything can happen. We prepared well but they played really well and deserved their victory on the day.

"The thing that I most regret and sticks in the craw is that their goal came so late in the game – there was no time for us to respond and that's always the danger when the score is 0-0. Had they scored 15 minutes earlier or if we'd gone into extra time, I think we could have turned things around.

"There is a lot of talk that the players maybe suspected that Mancini would be replaced at the end of the season but I never heard anyone speaking about that happening. I always got on well with Mancini – that perhaps wasn't the case with everyone at the time, but I never had a problem with him. As far as I was concerned, he would still be our manager and I had no reason to think otherwise.

"Yes, we heard one or two things being chanted from the

stands but I didn't think too much about it. The surprise for me was that Mancini was sacked before the end of the season – not something that happens that often in English football.

"For me, I had been there before and managers changing during the season was nothing new to me – at Independiente I once had eight managers in one season! At Atletico there were three in one season so I understand what is possible.

"Every manager has their own way of working, tactics and style of play, and it's different every time. As a player, you do what the manager says and implement his ideas out on the field. There are misunderstandings along the way but that happens at every club and it happened at City but generally, everything was fine under Mancini.

"And so, with the manager gone, and after a brief post-season trip to New York, we went our various ways for the summer. I didn't think too much about who would be coming in because I know the sole focus of this club is to make it more successful and that they would only choose somebody who they believed could take us forward."

Pellegrini takes over

"I knew of Manuel Pellegrini because he'd managed teams in La Liga when I was with Atletico Madrid for a number of years.

"Villarreal were known as a team who annually fought against relegation and struggled in La Liga before Manuel took over. After that, they were always challenging near the top of the league, qualifying for the Champions League and always looking to finish in the top four. They earned a reputation for

playing quality football under his stewardship and I had heard only good things about him.

"He was a manager who instilled the confidence in his players to go out and play good, attacking football. He isn't interested in long-ball tactics. As I've got to know him, I've discovered he's a very good man-manager and he will never give up or allow his players to give up no matter what the situation is, and on a personal level, I get on very well with him. When you have everyone at the club pulling in the same direction, you become a powerful force on and off the pitch and I think that was evident during his first season in charge of City.

"We had begun the season well under Manuel apart from the set-backs at Cardiff and Aston Villa and we went into our first Champions League game against Bayern Munich looking to get off to a good start in the group stages.

"What it's worth remembering is that we were up against one of the best club sides in the world and the European champions no less. They played extremely well and gave us a bit of a runaround and we lost 3-1. I think we learned a lot that night against a side who are very experienced in the competition whereas we are relatively new to everything. We went to Bayern a few months later and it was a completely different game – yes they had already qualified, but we beat them 3-2 in the Allianz Arena – after being 2-0 down early on – and that was with one or two fringe players in our team that hadn't played so much – so I think we proved what we are capable of and perhaps silenced one or two of our critics.

"Back in the Premier League and the goals continued to flow. I'd forged a good partnership on the pitch with Alvaro Negredo and we sort of hit it off from the first few games of the season.

It helps that we both speak Spanish. Just one word during a game can make a difference and we complemented each other really well.

"As the season progressed, I also played a lot with Edin Dzeko and I enjoy partnering him up front as well. Unfortunately, a series of injuries that both myself and Alvaro suffered meant that we lost the rhythm we had and the excellent communication we'd built up earlier in the season was lost."

If it had continued to progress at the same rate, Kun's exceptional goalscoring form in this, his third season at City, suggested that a new record might have been on the cards. But on December 14th, 2013, there was a setback, as he felt some pain in his right calf and was forced to leave the field just as the second half of the game against Arsenal had got under way.

He had opened the scoring with a volley in the 13th minute – his 19th goal of the season in all competitions – with Negredo doubling the advantage on 39 minutes. It would become a high scoring rout which ended 6-3.

Kun's injury, was confirmed as a muscle tear. Sergio intensified the rehab work on his right calf while at the same time welcoming his family over especially to visit him during the festive period. His parents and brothers and sisters being around always provided that important affection and support to which he could now add that of his new partner, Karina Tejeda, a popular Argentinian singer, with whom he had formed a strong bond throughout the course of 2013.

Even though Karina was living in Buenos Aires, her trips over to Manchester managed to shorten the distance between them and consolidate the relationship. Surrounded by his nearest and dearest, Sergio stepped up his preparation for a return to

the side on schedule and in the form and same state of mind in which he had begun the season.

Evidence of that self-assurance could be seen as he made his first team comeback on January 15th against Blackburn Rovers in the FA Cup. He came on as a substitute and in less than 50 seconds, with only his first touch, he scored his team's fourth goal of the game, which they went on to win 5-0. The injury had kept him on the sidelines a little over a month but his goal-scoring instinct remained intact.

He confirmed this with an assist and his 21st goal of the season after coming off the bench in the 4-1 win over Cardiff, followed by goal number 22 in the 3-0 Capital One Cup semi-final victory over West Ham, helping City reach their first League Cup final in 38 years. The match would take place on March 2nd at Wembley.

Pellegrini's team underlined their continued good run of form in all competitions in an FA Cup tie against Watford, in which they had to call upon all their energies to overturn a surprising 2-0 half-time deficit.

A convincing second-half display was proof they had upped their game. It ended 4-2 with a hat-trick from Kun, his second since arriving at the club, and a strike from Kolarov. Sergio was showered with praise from all corners of the world.

However, fate would be about to deal him another unfortunate hand. On January 29th, against Tottenham, Sergio was once more showing just what a great moment of form he was in, scoring the first goal and generally making a real nuisance of himself for the goalkeeper Hugo Lloris, who had saved two certain goals, from two of his headers, until another muscle injury would once more force him out of action.

The image of Kun sitting in the middle of the field with a look of disbelief at what had happened once again after just pushing off to try and win back the ball, said it all. He hobbled off the field holding his right hamstring. The ovation he received from all four sides of the Etihad was of some comfort, but the frustration at this latest spell on the sidelines that he now faced was not easy to conceal.

It was alleviated in some part by City going to the top of the league that weekend following their defeat of Spurs by the final score of 5-1. But his annoyance was quite apparent. He wanted to withdraw into his own private world in order to lick his internal wounds. But in spite of that initial sensation, and true to his positive outlook on life, that very night, while still in physical pain and also hurting mentally, he vowed not to give in to this latest setback. So as soon as he received confirmation that this latest tear would keep him out for another month he threw everything into making the best recovery he could. And he did this on every possible level – emotional, spiritual and physical.

In each of these areas he searched for, and found, the support he needed to strengthen his muscles and lift his spirits. Lee Nobes, one of City's physiotherapists, accompanied him throughout all his rehab exercises, which gradually intensified as the days went by.

In search of a more comprehensive approach to his recovery programme, his work would include yoga sessions that Sergio would take at Carrington in the afternoons following his treatment throughout the morning, which would include massage, ever more demanding exercises and constant examinations.

On an emotional level, the arrival of Benjamín, just before

his fifth birthday, gave Sergio a great lift, his son providing the best companionship Kun could have wanted during his stay in Manchester. They braved the cold and went fishing on more than one occasion, and even though they did not get the result they wanted – the fish were playing hard-to-get – nothing could prevent those outings from providing a real psychological lift.

It was a similar story when they played golf together at a course very close to his house in Wilmslow, where he had started living that year. Both father and son, kitted out in their golf gear and each with their own clubs, strode out on to the course in high spirits without a care for the weather.

Sergio was enjoying himself, and of course he also felt proud to see Ben copying the way he hit the golf ball and picking up how to play a shot. For his age, Benjamín was already showing clear signs of an eye-catching ability to understand how best to strike the ball. He copied his father but also looked up for his glance of approval when he succeeded in getting one of his shots in the hole.

Although he had not played for some time, once again Kun found golf to be a good way to relax and enjoy his time off. He would watch the big tournaments on television and enjoyed seeing Tiger Woods, a player he particularly admired.

Against that background, and strangely for a footballer, it was quite common to see the 50-inch television screen in his spacious lounge almost permanently tuned to a golf channel. Unless of course there happened to be a big football match being shown and, if scheduling and the time difference with Argentina allowed it, maybe one featuring his beloved Independiente, who had been relegated and were now fighting for promotion.

For Sergio, fighting for fitness was the main goal and he was doing everything in his power to play a part in the title run-in.

In spite of all his efforts, it was through injury that Sergio had to miss the Champions League round of 16 tie against Barcelona. Playing at this stage of Europe's most important competition had been one of his biggest motivations all season. Therefore, not being involved was a source of much frustration, and even more so given the stature of the opposition and the opportunity to rekindle the healthy competition he shared with his good friend Leo Messi.

The night of February 18th, 2014, Sergio arrived at the Etihad just in time. He had been at Carrington working on his rehab and the heavy traffic had let him down. The huge interest generated by the game made it extremely difficult to get to the stadium.

In the end, he still had enough time to say hello to his teammates in the dressing room and even bumped into Messi in the players' tunnel, with whom he shared a short exchange of banter about who was going to win the game.

"Coming up against Barcelona was always going to be a huge challenge but, of course, it gave me the opportunity to face one of my closest friends. When the draw was made we texted each other – I sent one to Leo saying 'Why us?' and Leo said 'I know, of all the teams we could have drawn we end up playing each other.' We were happy in one respect but it meant one of our clubs would be going out," says Sergio.

"It felt a bit strange not sharing the same dressing room as him. Whether it's the training camp or playing for Argentina, I always sit between Leo Messi and Ángel Di María with Javier Mascherano and Ezequiel Lavezzi either side of them. We are

all around the same age except for Mascherano and Pablo who we call the old men of the team.

"I'm always at the side of Leo, and if I'm not, he'll ask, 'Why aren't you next to me?' and I'll usually say, 'I don't know, why are you not next to me?' I always room with Leo the night before an international game and have done since 2005. He tends to fall asleep quite quickly and the only thing that annoys him is that I like to watch TV with the sound down and when I fall asleep, he wakes up and comes looking for the remote.

"When he's asleep I have to tiptoe to the toilet and stop my phone from vibrating in case it wakes him up. Towards the end of the 2013/14 season, I didn't go on a couple of international trips because of injury and the last time I did go, Leo was injured – when that happens, they always put me on my own and it's the same when I'm not there, Leo is on his own.

"Last time he sent me a text saying, 'Who have they put you with?' so I text back saying, 'Don't worry about it, love – I'm alone!' he text back saying 'Don't be cheating on me!'

"There was a time not so long ago when the fitness coach who organises where everyone sleeps suggested single rooms for everyone and Leo said that was fine, but Sergio and me are staying together! But don't worry we're just friends, and we are always laughing and joking together. He is like a brother to me.

"We weren't at our best in the first leg at the Etihad. We had to be mindful of what Barca can do if you let them play so we had to adjust our thinking a little and try and get a result that would give us something to hold on to in the return leg.

"We prepared well but because we aren't used to playing teams like Bayern and Barca, maybe we asked too many questions in our heads during the game and weren't as sure of ourselves as

we should have been. If there was a 50/50 ball you might find yourself thinking, 'if I commit against a certain player, he could hurt us if I don't come out on top' and that uncertainty showed at times. I don't think that's how we would approach it next time because we've learned and grown as a team, but a little apprehension made our task more difficult and we just didn't play our normal game on the night.

"So Leo scored the only goal, we ended with 10 men and we had a mountain to climb in the return game at the Camp Nou which was always a difficult place to go and on a personal level, things didn't go well. I picked up an injury early on after a challenge with my room-mate Leo – my partner and buddy!

"It was maybe three minutes into the game and we were both chasing a ball near the halfway line and as I tried to kick on and accelerate away, I felt something go so for the rest of the half I was asking myself whether I had what I needed to make an impact and by half-time it was clear that my body wasn't responding to the questions I was asking of it and I had to come off.

"It was disappointing because obviously you want to play in games of that magnitude and be at your best, but it wasn't to be and we lost 2-1 and exited the competition for that season.

"While we closed the book on that trophy, in between our two games against Barcelona, we won our first piece of silverware for the season by beating Sunderland in the Capital One Cup final at Wembley.

"I had been out for a few weeks with another injury and had only trained for a week before the final. I felt okay to play, but it was borderline – what I really needed was game time out on the pitch and, in truth, I wasn't quite match fit but we won 3-1."

It was the first trophy of the season for City, the first for Manuel Pellegrini and one more for Sergio in just three seasons in England. Following the trophy presentation, players from both sides and their respective families could be found sharing a friendly post-match drink in the VIP lounge of the iconic London stadium.

Thrilled with this latest trophy, Sergio was embracing Oscar Ustari, the Sunderland goalkeeper and his former team-mate from his early days at Independiente. That night the celebrations took place in the Mandarin hotel in London where the City squad were honoured for their trophy win, and where many guests took the opportunity to greet the cup winners.

One of them was Noel Gallagher, who did not miss out on the chance to effusively introduce himself to Kun. "I love you man!" he said, affectionately gripping Sergio by the face as if he was about to land a full-on kiss on his lips. While Sergio was happy to share his joy, he was relieved it didn't go any further.

Back on the pitch the team soon found they couldn't take it to the next stage in the FA Cup.

"We had been going well but lost 2-1 to Wigan in the quarter-final – a game we had been expected to win comfortably – so our sole focus was now the Premier League," says Sergio.

"The 2013/14 campaign was proving to be the most difficult of my career so far in terms of injuries and it's something I've never experienced before. I was doing so well goals-wise and up to January felt I was on course for maybe 40 for the season so it was hugely disappointing.

"I can't put my finger on why because I wasn't doing things any differently and I won't be changing the way I train or play and will do what I've always done so maybe it's just one of

those seasons where things don't quite fall into place in terms of fitness.

"Leo Messi had a similar year at Barcelona last season whereby he picked up a number of niggling injuries so the best I can do is put that season behind me and try and stay fit next time around.

"I'd played only three of the previous 13 games as the title race started to reach the final few weeks. It was between ourselves, Liverpool and Chelsea and I was determined to help my team over the line. I trained or rested as needed and made the bench for the crucial game away to Liverpool. It wasn't a title decider, but whoever won would have a major advantage going into the final few games.

"We fell behind early in the game and started poorly, going 2-0 down with 26 minutes gone – it couldn't have begun any worse. I wasn't match fit enough to start so I had to watch from the bench as we struggled to find a way into the game but we made it to half-time without conceding any more goals.

"We had started to improve, so all was not lost, and when David Silva pulled a goal back on 57 minutes, we were right back in the game. Then Silva's shot deflected in off Glen Johnson to make it 2-2 five minutes later and we felt sure we would go on and win the game.

"I replaced Dzeko on 68 minutes but within the space of three minutes, the game and destiny of both clubs seemed to have been decided. I ran down the left, past one challenge and headed towards the penalty area where I saw Silva running through the centre. I played a low cross in and he stretched to make contact, just seeing his attempt go inches wide. Less than three minutes later, Liverpool scored what proved to be

the winning goal when Philippe Coutinho struck the ball past Joe Hart to send Anfield crazy.

"It was a bitter pill to swallow and it left us seven points behind Liverpool with only six games to play – though we had played two games less than they had. The title was no longer in our hands and we were relying on other teams doing favours for us, which was not ideal.

"Yet despite this, I still firmly believed we would become champions. I told Hernán, my representative, that I was convinced it would happen – and I maintained that belief even when we drew 2-2 with Sunderland in our next game, making the title even harder to win as we were still six points adrift with only one game in hand.

"I think it's safe to say that the whole country now believed the title belonged to Liverpool, but we refused to accept that and knew that we had been in this position before, when everyone had written off our chances but still triumphed. The thing is, when I say we will be champions, we will be champions! I said the same in 2012 and had the same belief and, in fact, it was even stronger this time.

"It is strange because I recall that interview I had with David Clayton in the final weeks of the 2011/12 season when I said 'we will fight to the end', because this has since become our mission statement – something that drives the players and supporters on. We never give up and we fight to the end. I will try and come up with a few more pronouncements that we can use in future seasons!

"That said, we had to win our final five games to have any chance of capitalising if Liverpool slipped up. We felt they would, sooner or later and, of course, they did.

"We beat West Brom 3-1, which we had to do and it was nice to score my first goal since January during a 3-1 win and I felt good – then came Liverpool's slip. We were preparing to play Crystal Palace so I didn't watch Liverpool's game against Chelsea because it was finishing a few minutes before we kicked off. Then came the news they had lost – our fans' reaction would have told us the result regardless of whether we tried to ignore what had happened at Anfield and though it was a massive result for us, we still had a very difficult game against Crystal Palace to play.

"If we didn't win, Liverpool's defeat would mean nothing, but we were solid and professional and we won 2-0. I watched Liverpool's game later in the evening and I didn't feel sorry for Steven Gerrard when he slipped and Demba Ba scored – I was only bothered about what was important to us and that was that they lost. That was all that was in my mind, not that I don't respect Gerrard, it was just his mistake helped Chelsea win which is what we needed to happen."

The magnitude of the incident wasn't lost on Goodison Park the following Saturday. The City fans started the ball rolling with their own adaptation of a familiar Kopite chant: 'Steve Gerr... ard, Gerr...ard. He slipped on his f***ing arse! He gave it to Demba Ba. Steve Gerrard, Gerrard'. All of a sudden, support- ers who found themselves in opposition were joined together as one harmonious choir – City fans wanting to 'thank' him for the mistake that had edged them closer to the league title, Ever- tonians not wanting to miss out on the opportunity to mock their eternal rivals and revelling in witnessing the title slipping away from them.

"With three games to go we went into that encounter with

Everton knowing that if we won our final matches, the title would almost certainly be ours. We had conceded an early goal so it was satisfying to score the equaliser on 22 minutes, but five minutes before I scored, I felt a strange sensation – not even an injury – but just a strange feeling in my groin and I felt I couldn't continue. It was more of a precaution than anything else and the fact I was able to play in the final game proved I was right," recalls Sergio.

Referee Lee Probert's final whistle was the signal for mass relief and euphoria among the City fans, who then streamed out of Goodison Park to begin their triumphant return to Manchester dreaming of the title victory, which to them had now become inevitable.

Similarly, down on the pitch the City players celebrated the victory with clenched fists, in the belief that the prize for which they had fought so hard was now within touching distance. Down among them, Kun embraced his team-mates in recognition of the shift they had all put in that afternoon, feeling confident that the league title would not escape them now.

He was more relaxed on a personal level too, after the requisite examination confirmed that the pain he had felt was nothing serious and that he would easily be ready in time to take part in the last game of the season.

'I came off just as a precaution. Fortunately I am fine and happy to have scored, happy that we won and happy our hopes are still alive,' Kun summed up in Twitter's 140 characters after the match. And as if to lay the ghost of any serious injury to rest, he turned up at Carrington bright and early the next day, not wasting any time in getting to work on the affected area of muscle.

He did the same the following day, Monday, when his initial positive feeling on the injury was once again confirmed. At any rate it was decided that he would have a fitness test before Wednesday, when they were to play their game in hand against Aston Villa, to then determine whether it was worth the risk for him to return for that match, especially following Chelsea's draw with Norwich, which left the Londoners even further adrift in the battle for the title. The picture would be complete after that weekend's remaining fixture, the Monday evening clash between Liverpool and Crystal Palace.

At home in Wilmslow, Sergio had finished talking to his son via Skype, something he did on a daily basis, before settling into his armchair in front of the TV where his agent Hernán Reguera and his colleague Rubén Domínguez had already started to watch the game.

For the last few days Hernán had been going on about how he was sure that Crystal Palace would be a difficult test for Brendan Rodgers' side.

"It's not an easy place to go, and there could be a surprise or two," he had insisted. His comments appeared to be rather misguided as Liverpool were 3-0 ahead with 11 minutes remaining, and were looking to score more goals in an attempt to make a dent in City's superior goal difference.

But Sergio, Hernán and Rubén's interest in the game perked up a little in the 79th minute, as Palace pulled a goal back with a shot from Delaney that deflected in off Glen Johnson. Not to mention two minutes later, when Dwight Gayle – having come on as a substitute a little earlier and coincidentally wearing the number 16 shirt – scored Palace's second. And Hernán was grinning like a Cheshire cat in the 88th minute, as his predic-

tion proved entirely accurate when Gayle slotted home once more to secure a 3-3 draw.

Sergio remained calm and showed no signs of elation as the final whistle was blown although, with that typical smile of his, he looked at Hernán and said to him: "I was convinced before, and I am even more so now: we are going to win the league."

So with all the results from that weekend's fixtures now complete, Liverpool were still top of the league with 81 points, with City just behind with 80 having played a game less, and then Chelsea on 79. They could put Chelsea out of the race by winning their game in hand against Aston Villa and then, simply by avoiding defeat in the last match of the season against West Ham, they would be crowned champions.

In other words, four out of the six available points would be enough to secure the eagerly-awaited title.

Guard of honour

As that final week of the season went by, Sergio felt a calmness that could only come with experience. Events at the end of the 2011/12 season served as a motivation to avoid having to go through anything similar again. For sure, a more predictable finale was preferable to more drama. This appeared to be the general feeling permeating throughout City, and nobody at the club wanted any surprises. It was therefore vital to win their game in hand against Aston Villa.

Sergio held onto the hope of being available for selection until the last moment. However, the medical team's opinion was that it would be better not to take the risk and that, with

a few more days' rest, he would be back in good shape for the match the following Sunday.

Once more he would have to follow the action from his box. In the welcome company of his girlfriend Karina, who had returned to Manchester to be at his side for the climax to the championship, Sergio watched the first 45 minutes somewhat nervously as City were unable to open the scoring. Villa's rigid defence had repelled all their attempts thus far. As the minutes ticked by, Sergio wondered whether he should have taken the risk and been on the field of play with his team-mates. He had full confidence in them getting the job done, but he was unable to shake off his anxiety at not being able to play a part at such a crucial stage.

Relief – as well as the return of his trademark smile – came after 64 minutes when Edin Dzeko opened the scoring, following an assist from Zabaleta. Another goal by the Bosnian forward and two more from Stevan Jovetic and Yaya Toure – the latter following a spectacular run – gave the final scoreline a convincing air (4-0) and sparked off scenes of joy all around an Etihad Stadium that already felt like it was on the eve of witnessing another championship triumph, for the second time in three seasons.

The celebrations – although measured, as the final hurdle was still yet to be cleared – could immediately be observed in the surrounding areas, where the presence of thousands of fans made it even more difficult for traffic to leave the stadium. After having greeted and congratulated his team-mates, Sergio had set off to drive home in his car and found the nearby roads already resembling a victory parade.

He enjoyed seeing the fans waving flags and honking their

horns, their windows down despite the low temperature, while they cheered on City and their players. These were exciting times, and being so close to the celebrations meant he could enjoy it all even more. And he was even able to become a part of that joy as he was recognised by various drivers in cars alongside his own, who started to bow down to him and make admiring gestures.

Sergio wound down his window too, so that he could say hello and sign autographs. This continued until one of the fans decided that everyone had to make way so that Kun could more easily get out beyond the congested road. And so, like an improvised traffic conductor, that fan – along with others who had also recognised Kun – started warning the other drivers who, creating a spontaneous 'guard of honour' for their hero, cleared the street so that he could get away more quickly and would not have to wait for the traffic to clear.

The unusual scene, greeted with an outpouring of applause and the sounding of horns from the other cars, made Kun feel extremely thankful. He wanted to explain to them that he had no problem with waiting. But he also knew that they were doing all of this out of the same gratitude that he felt towards them, and that rejecting that display of affection could have been mis-interpreted. And so, with one arm hanging out of the window, he greeted those who he came across.

The chant of 'Sergio, Sergio' accompanied him until he was back on the open road. Sergio, who felt people's affection on a daily basis and in many different ways, was touched by this new gesture of good will and by feeling so cared for. He looked then at Karina and his other companions and, after a sigh, only managed to say: "It's pretty awesome all of this, isn't it?"

The impression of feeling so at home had been with him since he arrived in Manchester in 2011, but he had thought that it would be difficult to surpass the respect and devotion that they had always shown him. However, on that day, the fans once again took him by surprise.

He would feel that same sensation of privilege for all that was happening to him again, this time during an interview for Manchester City's official website conducted by journalist David Clayton and published on May 9th, two days before the deciding fixture against West Ham.

David asked him how it felt to see that his phrase 'fight to the end' – that he had uttered in another feature in 2012 when City had slipped eight points behind Manchester United and all seemed lost – had been adopted by City and had become a slogan for the club and its fans, who had even made up a song using the phrase.

Sergio answered spontaneously: "I never thought it would become such an important message for City. But in football, anything is possible so that's why I say 'fight to the end and never give up' – I find it's a good way of staying positive. And the best thing is that I think that it's a motto that now belongs to all of us. To the club, to the team and to the fans."

Clayton also asked him about the final match against West Ham, and the inevitable comparison with the QPR game in 2012.

Sergio left no room for doubt: "I think it's going to be different, but that doesn't for one moment mean it's going to be easier."

And as to whether he would play the match due to the injury, he reassured everybody by confirming that he had already

recovered. "I'm not 100 per cent yet, but I should be by Sunday and even if I'm not, the emotion of the occasion and the desire of everyone will carry me through and I won't notice any pain."

Sergio's good frame of mind was boosted further with the arrival into Manchester on Friday, May 9th of father Leo and mother Adriana, who had come over especially to be with him as crunch time approached.

Adriana was there with all her eternal optimism, harbouring no doubts, just like in 2012, that City would win the title. And Leo too, unable to hide his delight to be with his son at such a special moment, just like he had been at all those other times, back when it was still impossible to envisage the future that destiny held for them.

The reunion at the house in Wilmslow after morning training found them making plans for dinner that Friday. They were all sure of one thing: that they must not change a winning formula and that, just as had been the case in 2012, Sergio would have to make the food.

On this occasion it was not meat and potatoes on the menu, but Kun's new speciality instead: pizzas, with the dough specially kneaded by him. He had picked up a knack for them turning out almost perfect. So much so that he prepared the dough 'by sight' without having to follow a recipe, in the style of the finest pizza chef.

Under the watchful eye of Adriana, who could only laugh at her son's kitchen skills, Kun firstly proceeded to form a good dough. He mixed yeast with water and flour and kneaded it by hand until he had the exact consistency required. After letting it prove, there were 10 balls ready to be made into pizzas. Those present were left surprised when, firstly with the rolling pin,

then with a finger, and finally using the palms of both hands, he managed to perfectly shape the dough.

He checked that the oven was at the exact temperature needed and started putting them in for an initial period of baking. He seemed happy and relaxed in his new role as a more refined chef. Pleased with his work, he applied the finishing touch by adding the ingredients for the final baking.

Proof of the success of his creation was clear for all to see during the dinner, as all of the pizzas were finished off by the guests. There were less than 48 hours to go until that decisive Sunday, and there was Sergio waiting for it to arrive: calm, relaxed, surrounded by his loved ones, confident, in the best of humour, and regaling those present with an endless stream of dinnertime anecdotes.

In the same spirits, Sergio headed off to the team base at the Hilton Hotel on Saturday.

"Our 2-0 win over West Ham was less dramatic than our win over QPR but nobody was complaining," says Sergio. "The support and emotion of the day helped carry me through because I wasn't fully fit and charging on all cylinders but I wouldn't have missed it for the world.

"You work so hard all season for that one moment and I couldn't wait for the game to begin, but as I say, this time it was more controlled and less frantic, but we still had a few psychological hurdles to overcome because we knew a draw would be enough to secure the championship, but we were never going to play it safe.

"I didn't score – it wasn't really my day in front of goal – but it was a privilege to be part of the occasion. Our second title in three years – it was very satisfying and I'm happy to have played

my part, even though I was forced to miss much of the second part of the season.

"Nothing is ever certain or guaranteed in football and until something is mathematically impossible, anything is possible and yet again, we have proved that this team never stops believing, never gives up and we will always fight to the end. It's an infectious attitude and one that has worked well for us and will continue to be our mantra for many years to come."

The party that ran on in the Etihad throughout the whole match reached its peak with referee Martin Atkinson's final whistle. And, as if wishing to establish a ritual which was alien to English customs, unexpectedly and just like in 2012 the crowd streamed onto the pitch.

It was impossible for the security officials to cope with this spontaneous reaction of the fans who, even without the excuse provided by the emotional release of that other victory, could not resist the temptation to continue their celebrations on the pitch with the players.

Sergio, like the rest of his team-mates, found himself immediately surrounded by fans, who started to shower him with affection in any way possible.

The second Premier League title in three years, won only moments earlier, was reason enough to let himself get carried away by the emotion of the fans, to let it become his own. And in this way, together as one, they could celebrate it as they deserved to.

In contrast to what had happened first time around, when the impact of an incredible finale had prevented him from truly taking in what he was experiencing, on that evening he was able to remain conscious of exactly what was happening to him.

And just as he was getting carried away by these feelings, some of the club's security men rescued him from the crowd, took him by the arms and, in order to cross the human sea, carried him in the air towards the changing rooms.

He paradoxically felt like his feet were more firmly on the ground than ever before while, at the same time, he was literally floating among all of those bodies around him. The natural and transparent smile drawn upon his face left his unbridled joy there for all to see. The same joy that he found among his teammates and coaching staff when, firstly in the changing room and then on that same pitch – by now cleared of fans – they celebrated the title with their respective families. The same joy that he recognised in one glance from Leo and Adriana as they were reunited on the turf.

They then saw each other again in the box, Kun taking advantage of a more private moment to honour Adriana who, coincidentally, was celebrating her birthday on that May 11th. And they remained there for an intimate toast to complete the celebrations, against the unique backdrop of an Etihad Stadium that was already almost empty in the fading light, another great achievement nevertheless still hanging in the air.

And there was Sergio, at the close of another triumphant season. Enjoying the present but always with an eye fixed on the future, ready to set new goals and aspirations. Essentially the same *pibe* who had left Los Eucaliptus, but one who had forged his own unique character as a result of a very personal journey.

Able to have complemented his natural charisma, as well as a talent reserved only for chosen ones, with the lessons learned from each of his mentors. In life, as well as in football. Through which he had ultimately shaped his own identity. One that

enchants, one that captivates, one that prevails thanks to hard work and an unbeatable charm.

Sergio, who never forgets where he came from. Sergio, who looks after his family. Who respects his elders. Who makes mistakes, but learns from them. Who is considered. Who can cry. Who can look back with pride. Who gives his all. Who approaches football, as he does life, for his own pleasure and to fill others with that pleasure; for his own excitement and to excite others. Who knows that he was born to play football. Who carries the sport in his bloodstream. And who, like the gladiator of his favourite film, is held in the highest esteem of others due to his dedication, his talent, his strength and, above all, his refusal to accept defeat and his determination to fight until the very last minute.